The
PETTICOAT
AFFAIR

Manners, Mutiny, and Sex

in Andrew Jackson's White House

JOHN F. MARSZALEK

LOUISIANA STATE UNIVERSITY PRESS

Baton Rouge

For

DAVID GORMAN

Louisiana Paperback Edition, 2000
09 08 07 06 05 04 03 02 01
5 4 3 2

Library of Congress Cataloging-in-Publication Data
Marszalek, John F., 1939–
    The petticoat affair : manners, mutiny, and sex in Andrew Jackson's White House /
John F. Marszalek.— Louisiana pbk. ed.
        p. cm.
    Originally published: New York : Free Press, c1997.
    Includes bibliographical references and index.
    ISBN 0-8071-2634-9 (alk. paper)
        1. Jackson, Andrew, 1767–1845—Friends and associates. 2. Eaton, Peggy, 1799?–1879.
3. Van Buren, Martin, 1782–1862. 4. Politicians—United States—Sexual
behavior—History—19th century—Case studies. 5. Women—United States—Sexual
behavior—History—19th century—Case studies. 6. Sex role—United States—History—19th
century—Case studies. I. Title.

E381 .M33 2000
973.5'6'092—dc21   00-044946

The paper in this book meets the guidelines for permanence and durability of the Committee on
Production Guidelines for Book Longevity of the Council on Library Resources. ♾

Contents

Prologue v

CHAPTER

1   "Great God! Do You Mention *Her* Sacred Name?" 1

2   "My Lord! What a Pretty Girl That Is!" 22

3   "There Are Great Objections Made to His Wife" 45

4   "She Is as Chaste as a Virgin!" 75

5   "Et Tu Brute" 106

6   "One of the Most Base and Wicked Conspiracies" 137

7   "A Want of Harmony" 157

8   "They Shall Not Drive Me From My Ground" 180

9   "An Influential Personage Now" 200

10 "They Are Now Her Neighbors" 228

Conclusion 237

Notes   241
Bibliography   270
Acknowledgments   285
Index   289

Prologue

History hardly furnishes an instance in
which the agency of woman, in maintaining the sacred rights,
the dignity and virtue of her sex, has produced so important a
change in a government, and at the same time exerted so decided
and powerful an influence in favor of public morals.

—*United States Telegraph,* August 17, 1831

The seventh president of the United States and his secretary of state
rode down Pennsylvania Avenue on horseback that spring of 1831, the
pencil-thin but ramrod-straight Andrew Jackson and the dapper Martin
Van Buren presenting a striking contrast in physical appearance. Their
genuine camaraderie was demonstrated to all who saw their animated
conversation. They had gone through a lot together since entering office
in March of 1829, and they had become good friends.

As they often did, they stopped at the residence of Secretary of War
John Henry Eaton and his wife, Margaret, looking forward to the
usually exuberant welcome from the vivacious woman of the house.
She was beautiful beyond measure, this daughter of a Washington
Scots-Irish-American innkeeper, and her magnetic personality had an
irresistible attraction. She could charm males with her looks no less
than with her conversation. When Andrew Jackson had earlier
boarded in her family's establishment, she had so completely charmed
him that he had developed an intense admiration for her. Martin
Van Buren liked her, too, but he liked all women and was famous for
his gallant attention to them.

As they dismounted in front of the Eaton house, the two men

wondered what Margaret Eaton would say today, considering all that had recently happened. Her husband and all the rest of the presidential cabinet had resigned their posts, and the word on the street and in the press held her responsible. The refusal of Floride Calhoun, wife of Vice President John C. Calhoun, and the cabinet wives to socialize with her had caused the great split, it was said.

Margaret Eaton was clearly distressed. She had no warm welcome for her visitors this time; she was too upset. She had lived through two years of rumor, disdain, and ostracism, her character and reputation the subject of the most damning gossip: she was an abjectly sinful woman who had given sexual favors to a multitude of men, betraying her first husband and causing him to kill himself in despair, the whispers were. Then she had married her most obvious lover, and when he became secretary of war, boldly and unabashedly, without even the faintest hint of shame, she presumed to claim a place of honor in polite society. Andrew Jackson had defended her fiercely, but even he had to bow to society's stubborn refusal to accept her. He still believed she was an unfairly wronged woman, but he had to right his administration by putting the controversy behind him. Margaret was crushed, and her face showed it. If Andrew Jackson no longer supported her, the fight was indeed lost. The sharp-tongued Washington women had won the battle over her place in society. She felt a deep disappointment at the loss of her champion, who saw no other way out.

Every historian of the Jacksonian period has discussed this so-called Eaton Affair, and countless novelists, playwrights, and satirists have dealt with it in imaginative prose.[1] Surprisingly, however, no modern scholar has studied the Eaton Affair systematically since Queena Pollack produced her well-researched but poorly written book over sixty-five years ago.[2] This matter is too important to be left unexplored, and, for this reason, I have undertaken the task.

Traditionally, the Eaton Affair is viewed as either a major political event or an inconsequential foolishness. Some historians have insisted that it influenced the choice of Jackson's successor, while others have ridiculed the notion. Almost without exception, however, historians have seen this affair as political intrigue. The nineteenth-century historian James Parton expressed this notion in one of the most famous double entendres in historical literature: "The political history

United States, for the last thirty years," he wrote in 1861, "dates from the moment when the soft hand of Mr. Van Buren touched Mrs. Eaton's knocker."[3]

In this book, I argue that the Eaton Affair cannot be fully understood outside the social context of the Jacksonian Age. The battle over whether or not Margaret Eaton was a worthy female began with, and was impelled by, the period's attitude toward women in general. "I don't like argumentative ladies," a future chief justice of the United States said in 1830. "They have no right to encroach upon our privileges. . . . The masculine is the more worthy gender and . . . we are entitled to an exclusive monopoly of all the wit [and] sensibilities in the world."[4] Women were to be properly submissive, and Margaret Eaton was both forthright and open with men and thus unwomanly. She was not what society demanded a genteel woman should be, so society had to exclude her.

This socially driven controversy did become a political issue, however, and it did influence the politics of the age. The president of the United States, after all, spent more time on this matter in his first two years in office than he did on any other question. His cabinet dissolved over it, and it became the underpinning for the worst split between a president and vice president in American history.

This is, therefore, a story of politics and etiquette, ambition and honor, personality and society. Major historical figures, irrational behavior, and devious intrigue intertwine to create a tale worth telling with historical accuracy. To say, as one writer insisted, "that the melancholy Dane could be more spared from the play that bears his name than could 'Peg' O'Neal[e] be dropped from the records of the period"[5] is exaggeration, of course. But if one wants to understand Andrew Jackson and the time in which he was president, the plight of the innkeeper's daughter is an excellent place to begin.

I have made several conscious decisions in writing this book. First, I never call Margaret Eaton "Peggy." She protested that her family never called her that, her mother at times calling her "Madge" but normally referring to her as "Margaret." Be that as it may, it struck me that calling her Peggy played into the preconceptions of the events of which she was a part. By referring to her as Margaret, I hope to give readers a chance to look at her from a fresh point of view so they can evaluate the information about her more objectively.

Margaret Eaton was not as "chaste as a virgin," as Andrew Jackson roared during the most amazing cabinet meeting in American history, but she was not a moral reprobate either. Her cardinal sin was thinking and acting in ways that the society of her day considered improper for a woman. Society viewed her as sexually loose, an unchaste and unfaithful woman before, after, and between her marriages. She was also perceived as a chronic violator of genteel convention, too forward and outgoing for proper society. Finally, Margaret Eaton simply rubbed people the wrong way, aside from any accusations of violating morality and gentility. She just did not fit in.

Clearly these are three separate issues, and different people reacted to her in these different ways. What actually took place, however, was a merging of these perceptions, a view that whether in one or in all three ways, Margaret Eaton was not a proper woman and should therefore properly be snubbed. She was a sexually loose, rude loudmouth who did not know how to behave and, therefore, for whatever specific reason, was unacceptable across the entire spectrum of proper womanhood.

In Margaret Eaton's story, readers will see, I believe, the struggle of women in all periods of history, including the late twentieth century, to escape from societal perceptions of the limited roles that society considers proper for them. Margaret Eaton posed a threat to the value system of that period, which established precise limits for women, and she had to pay the price for "unwomanly" activities, whatever they might be. Hardly a crusader for women's rights, she was, nevertheless, an aggressive proponent of her cause, the same cause of many others in later days: the right of women to go beyond the barriers that society has built to enclose them and vociferously uses to keep them in their place.

1

"Great God! Do You Mention *Her* Sacred Name?"

He stood tall and thin, six feet one inch, yet weighed only 140 pounds. His face was narrow, his nose pointed, his wide forehead melting into his frizzy hair, once a sandy red, but by the time he became president of the United States, a whitish gray. His eyes were blue, and when he became angry, they blazed fire, or so contemporaries imagined. Nearly sixty-two years of age when he took the oath of office on March 4, 1829, the ravages of time were evident in the creases on his face and the stiffness of his gait. Still, his appearance was impressive: erect in posture and exuding strength and power.[1]

Andrew Jackson was without doubt one of the most popular men ever elected president of the United States. Architect of the great victory over the British at New Orleans during the War of 1812, and the man who had crushed the Indians in the southeast, his execution of two British subjects in Spanish Florida only added to his appeal. Americans disliked the British and the Indians, two enemies they saw as barriers to the nation's progress. Because of Jackson's important victories over these groups, people began to refer to him as the "Old

Hero." A Floridian said he believed something a friend had told him, "as much as if General Jackson, or Jesus Christ, had said it."[2]

Despite his wide popularity, Jackson also became one of the nation's most reviled chief executives. To many Americans he appeared as the border ruffian from frontier Tennessee. He fought duels, he had a passion for horse racing and cockfighting, and his fiery temper seemed irrational and frightening. That the common people reacted to him so passionately provided even greater concern. He might be the "Old Hero" to some, but others saw him a dangerous demagogue, a threat to the very stability of the nation. A modern historian, though favorable to him, has written: "He was ill-educated, ill-tempered, opinionated, suspicious, unbending, dictatorial, . . . vindictive, and a fierce hater." A contemporary tried to find a middle ground: "If he was not as perfect and capable as his friends represented him to be, he was a better man than his enemies described him to be."[3]

His beginnings themselves are in question; North and South Carolina both claim him as a native son because the exact location of his nativity is unknown. Without debate, however, all contemporaries and historians agree that he came from Scots-Irish frontier ancestry.[4] His parents, Andrew and Elizabeth Jackson, had come to the British colonies from Ulster, Ireland, in 1765, eventually settling into the proverbial log cabin in the Carolinas. Andrew, the husband and father, died in March 1767, leaving behind a widow pregnant with the soon-to-be-born son. Upon the death of her mate, Elizabeth moved in with her sister and brother-in-law. She gave birth to Andrew, her third child, on March 15, 1767, and took over household duties for her sickly sister. Andrew Jackson, therefore, spent the first years of his life, carrying his father's name but fatherless and without a home of his own, the youngest of eleven children under his mother's care.

The boy went to school and quickly gained the reputation of being the most obstreperous of the horde of children in his adopted home. He pushed his mother's patience to the limit with his furious horseback riding, swearing, and fighting. She hoped that religion would save him, but the American Revolution proved to have the greater influence on his young life. The war forced him and his family to flee from the advancing British troops and their numerous Loyalist allies, people Andrew had known all his life. He and his two older brothers became soldiers, one brother soon becoming a war casualty.

In 1781, Andrew experienced a defining moment. The British captured him and his surviving brother, Robert, while wrecking their house. In the course of the pillaging, a British officer ordered Andrew to clean his boots. When the stubborn teenager boldly refused, the officer angrily swung his sword at the young boy, producing a deep cut and permanent scars on his head and on the fingers of his left hand, which he had thrown up to protect himself. Later, Andrew and Robert were thrown into prison in Camden, South Carolina, where they suffered from insufficient food and lack of medical attention. They would have died had it not been for their mother. Still nursing the sick and wounded as she had long been doing, she somehow convinced British authorities to include her sons in an exchange for some captive British soldiers.

Andrew's nightmare was hardly over, however. Robert died, and the debilitating fever of smallpox devastated his own body. His mother put him to bed at home. When he seemed out of danger, she hurried to Charleston to look after two nephews, both deathly ill on a prison ship in the harbor. Andrew never saw her again. In the fall of 1781, cholera struck her down as she nursed the sick.

His father, mother, and two brothers were all dead; his strong mother's departure was particularly devastating. A fearful, confused teenager, Andrew Jackson was forced to face the uncertain future alone. He grew angry and frustrated, no doubt developing his lifelong anger and dogged insistence on the unquestioning devotion of friends and relatives. All his life, Andrew Jackson wanted absolute assurance from those around him that they would always remain at his side. Having lost his family as a young man, he needed devoted permanent friends to take their place. He insisted on total loyalty, and he gave the same full measure.[5]

Several severe physical maladies added to the young Jackson's problems. He apparently suffered from something known as the "big itch," a rash that affected his entire body. Equally, if not more embarrassingly, he did not stop "slobbering" until after he became an adult. Any derogatory remarks about either ailment provoked him into a no-holds-barred fight, the skinny young man refusing to quit no matter how he fared in the scuffle. Andrew Jackson had "a morbid fear of being made ridiculous."[6]

Whether to test his perimeters or as a way of dealing with the losses and fears in his life, he became "the most roaring, rollicking, game-cocking, horse-racing, card-playing, mischievous fellow that ever lived in Salisbury" (North Carolina), where he settled after the war. Once, as a joke, he invited the town's well-known prostitutes to the Salisbury Christmas ball, feigning surprise when the respectable townspeople, particularly the women, had them escorted out. Early on, Andrew Jackson seemed unwilling or unable to understand society women and their protocol.[7]

Jackson had moved to Salisbury to become a lawyer, though clearly he did not keep his nose buried in the books. Still, he was admitted to the bar in 1787. He argued his first case in 1788 in Jonesborough (now Jonesboro), Tennessee, his sensitivity toward any perceived insult becoming sensationally evident. He challenged the opposing lawyer to a duel for what he interpreted to be a slander of him. Having already demonstrated that he would not stand silent before any perceived insult about his appearance, he disclosed now that his sensitivity to affronts included character as well as looks.

That spring of 1788, Jackson left the Carolinas and moved west to Tennessee, his home for the rest of his life. He eventually settled in the Nashville area and rose quickly, becoming a lawyer, jurist, politician, land speculator, plantation and slave owner, militia leader, Indian fighter, and husband and father. He made fast friends among other young men on the make, individuals like John Overton and John Coffee, who smoothed the way for him in those early days. He impressed William Blount, the new state's leading politician and wheeler-dealer. He served as Tennessee's congressman and then United States senator from 1796 to 1798. Then the state's power brokers named him judge of the Superior Court of Tennessee, a post he held for the next six years. In 1801, he helped found the Tennessee lodge of Freemasons. The following year he was elected major general of the Tennessee militia. By the age of thirty-five he had become one of the leading figures in the frontier state.

Despite his political successes, opponents in Tennessee came to view him as an adulterer and a murderer, the two accusations resulting from the same root cause: his controversial marriage to Rachel Donelson, the abiding love of his life. As a youth he had suffered from the painful loss of his mother; now another woman would bring him pain anew.[8]

Rachel Donelson was the daughter of one of the founders of Nashville, Colonel John Donelson. In 1780, Donelson had brought his family of eleven children from Virginia to the site he and others had already hacked out of the Tennessee wilderness. He had served in the Virginia House of Burgesses, so his move to Tennessee seemed less the result of desperation than the typical nineteenth-century American search for greater economic stature. Twelve years old at the time, Rachel still had not learned to read or write, skills she barely mastered in the next several years.

Not satisfied in Tennessee, Donelson decided to seek his fortune in another part of the frontier, in Mercer County, Kentucky. Here the pretty but untutored and flirtatious Rachel met a handsome, educated man named Lewis Robards. They fell in love and married in March 1785. Then disaster struck. Someone, Indian or white, killed Colonel Donelson during a trip between Kentucky and Tennessee. His widow took her unmarried children back to Tennessee, leaving Rachel and her husband behind in the home of Robards's mother. Among the other male boarders living there was John Overton, then studying the law in Kentucky and later to become one of Tennessee's leading justices and Andrew Jackson's closest friend.

It was obvious to anyone who spent any time at the Robards place that the young couple's marriage was a disaster. As family members watched, Lewis Robards proved "high-tempered, jealous hearted, . . . cruel [and] tyrannical."[9] He accused his wife, an outgoing fun-loving girl, of sexual promiscuity with the young male boarders there. Actually he was the one having the affairs, rumors persisting that he regularly slept with slave women. No matter. He continued to blame her and finally threw her out of the house, convinced that her forward openness with men was inappropriate for a married woman. Samuel Donelson came for his sister in 1788 and took her home to their mother. Robards's own mother, hoping to salvage the marriage, urged John Overton, since he was returning to Nashville, to bring the couple back together again.

When Overton returned to Tennessee, he took up lodging with the

Widow Donelson and soon brought up the possibility of the Robards's reconciliation. Rachel Robards agreed to try, and her husband moved to Tennessee and settled on land he owned in the area. Until the site was prepared, however, he and Rachel would live in her mother's house with the male boarders.

It was about this time, in 1789, that Andrew Jackson came to live on the Donelson property, sharing a small cabin with Overton. He had just arrived from North Carolina. He was immediately attracted to the vivacious Mrs. Robards. One of Andrew Jackson's enduring characteristics was his extreme gallantry toward women, manifested especially in his belief that they were innately weak and that men, as the stronger sex, were morally obligated to protect them. He no doubt displayed this solicitude toward Rachel Robards. Unfortunately, Jackson's attentions caused her husband to revert to the suspicious jealousy he had shown in Kentucky; he suspected Rachel and Andrew of having an affair. Jackson decided to move away to squelch any suspicions, but he confronted Robards first, insisting that the husband had no cause for jealousy. Robards exploded in fury, threatening to give Jackson a beating. Equally angry, Jackson suggested a duel instead. Both men backed off before matters became even more heated, and Jackson peacefully moved away. He was prepared, however, to give battle for his honor and for a woman he insisted was only a friend.

This near-violent encounter only exacerbated the Robards marriage problems. One day in May or June of 1789, Robards decided to go back to Kentucky, allegedly to bring back his furniture and other possessions. Yet sometime on the trip he told his travel mate that he had decided not to return at all. Rachel Robards remained married, but her husband, sure of her infidelity, had left her, without indicating just how permanent the separation might be.

In the fall of 1790, rumors filtered down to Nashville that Lewis Robards planned to force his wife to return to Kentucky with him. Taking the news seriously and unwilling to reconcile again, Rachel began making plans to escape to Natchez in Spanish Florida, where she could stay with friends until her husband's latest tirade subsided. She asked a Colonel Robert Stark, who was moving his family to that region, if she could travel with his party. Worried about the danger of Indian attack along the way, Stark looked around for another male escort. No

Donelson relative seemed willing or able to go, so the obviously smitten Andrew Jackson foolishly, but predictably, volunteered his services, agreeing to travel as Rachel Robards's protector on her dangerous trip through the wilderness.

If Lewis Robards had held any doubts about Jackson's intentions before, they vanished now. Jackson must have realized how suspicious this looked to a jealous husband and an increasingly skeptical community, but he plunged ahead anyway, perhaps hoping to spur the hot-tempered husband to divorce the wife he suspected of wrong-doing and make her available to him. Jackson's gallantry toward females in general and his increasing affection for this woman in particular caused him to ignore the obviously suspicious circumstances surrounding this trip. Rachel, for her part, went along without question, displaying the womanly subservience Jackson no doubt expected from her.

There is no way of knowing just what went on as the party traveled to Bayou Pierre, some thirty miles north of Natchez. They arrived on January 12, 1790, Rachel Robards remaining there for two years and Jackson apparently visiting her every chance he had. No one knows if the two lived together during his visits, but clearly their closeness became more than platonic and was obviously suspicious to anyone who cared to notice it. The bachelor lawyer and the separated wife had developed a relationship strong enough for Jackson to brave the hard trip from Nashville to Natchez more than once.

Meanwhile, Lewis Robards was busy himself. Since Kentucky was a district of Virginia, he asked his brother-in-law, a member of the Old Dominion's legislature, to file divorce papers for him. At the same time, in the fall of 1790, he published his divorce plans in the press, claiming his wife had eloped with another man. On December 20, 1790, the Virginia legislature gave him authority to sue for divorce in a Kentucky court. Before any judicial action could be taken, however, the legislative resolution said that Rachel Robards had to be ordered, in eight issues of the *Kentucky Gazette,* to appear before the court and respond to charges of adultery. Apparently only Lewis Robards knew all these conditions attached to his successful petition, leaving everyone else to think that the Virginia legislature had simply granted a divorce. Jackson, a lawyer, never bothered to investigate the matter himself.

Robards's behavior, after he learned of the enabling legislation, only added to the confusion. He did not publish the first mandated order in the Kentucky newspaper until an entire year had passed. Perhaps plotting to ensnare Andrew and Rachel further, he did not file for divorce in the Mercer County, Kentucky, Court of Quarters Sessions until 1793. The final decree did not get promulgated until September 27 of that same year. By this time, Andrew and Rachel had been married for more than two years, Jackson's preeminent biographer arguing that they had actually taken this step even before they had learned of the December 1790 Virginia legislature's enabling act/divorce.[10] They returned to Nashville in August of 1791 and lived openly as man and wife, they and their community ignoring the fact that Rachel Robards Jackson was clearly a bigamist.

Jackson did not learn of the recent Kentucky court divorce order until December 1793. John Overton, his close friend since their days together in the Donelson cabin, immediately counseled a legal remarriage. On January 24, 1794, a disturbed Rachel Robards Jackson and a stubbornly reluctant Andrew Jackson repeated their marriage vows; they became man and wife legally. The Nashville community ignored the complicated legality, and this confusing affair of the heart and courts had no impact on Jackson's solid political and economical standing in Tennessee.

Clearly, however, his marriage dispute bothered Jackson. He worried about its effect on his future. As an individual who would not tolerate criticism and who needed to feel secure in the permanence of his marriage, he reacted violently when two men threw it in his face. In 1803, John Sevier, Jackson's long-time political enemy, won election as governor of Tennessee. Still angry over some accusations Jackson had made against him in that campaign and during an earlier election for militia major general, Sevier accosted Jackson before a large crowd in front of the courthouse in Knoxville. "I know of no great service you have rendered the country except taking a trip to Natchez with another man's wife," Sevier yelled out. Jackson lunged at him, shouting: "Great God! Do you mention *her* sacred name?"[11] The crowd had to pull the irate husband off his accuser. Before they did so, however, Jackson challenged Sevier to a duel. No one was going to impugn his wife's integrity (and, of course, his own) without paying the price.

Jackson arrived at the dueling grounds at the scheduled time, only to have to cool his heels for two days because Sevier and his seconds were nowhere to be found. When he finally saw them approaching, he charged his horse forward, seeking to use his cane as a lance. Sevier, trying to dismount from his horse, fell off in his haste, and Jackson frustratingly rode around, hoping to find someone, anyone, to gore. The two men canceled the duel by mutual agreement, but Jackson never forgave Sevier for what he always considered a slanderous assault on the virtue of his beloved wife and on his own honor.[12]

In 1806, another aspersion on Rachel Jackson's purity brought forth the same violent response. Jackson and Charles Dickinson became embroiled in an argument over a horse race. In his anger and apparently while under the influence of alcohol, Dickinson ridiculed Rachel for her lack of morality, though he later apologized for his words. Jackson was not appeased, and the harsh dialogue between the two men continued for months. Finally there seemed to be no other way out: there had to be a duel.

As the sun rose above the horizon on the early morning of May 30, 1806, Jackson and Dickinson met on the field of honor in nearby Kentucky. John Overton had convinced his reluctant friend to wear a loose-fitting coat, apparently hoping to camouflage his thin frame in the expansive cloth. Dickinson, allegedly the best shot in the state, fired first, and Jackson's left hand reached for his chest, although he displayed no other sign of pain. Dickinson shrieked in fear, upset that he had not killed his opponent with the first shot. Jackson aimed his pistol, but it failed to fire. He then pulled the trigger a second time, and this time he drove Dickinson to the ground with a direct hit to the stomach. Jackson calmly walked away, blood flowing freely from a chest wound, but his stubborn will refused to give onlookers the satisfaction of acknowledging pain or injury. Dickinson died within the day.

Jackson never budged from his belief that he had only done what was right. He carried Dickinson's bullet where it lodged near his heart for the rest of his life, a constant reminder of his unbending resolve to protect his honor. The bullet also reminded him that his honor was inexorably intertwined with the virtue of the most important woman in his life, his wife Rachel. Any attack on her was an assault on him, too. Even in those days of the double standard for men and women, if his wife was a sexual sinner, so was he. The only difference was that he could defend himself and she could not. He had to do it for her even if it meant that he would have to dispute the appellation "murderer" for the rest of his days.

Jackson seemed convinced that martial exploits offered the best way to rehabilitate his reputation after the two duels. In 1805, he listened enthusiastically to Aaron Burr's nebulous scheme of military action against the Spanish Empire but then quickly became disenchanted with the whole idea. In 1812, just before the United States declared war on England, Jackson unsuccessfully tried to get Tennessee authorities to allow him to lead a military expedition against the Creek Indians. Thwarted and increasingly angered over apparent American impotence in the face of British assaults on land and sea and over his own inability to change it, he lashed out against an available target and once more defended a woman's honor.

In 1811, Silas Dinsmore, Indian agent in Mississippi's Choctaw region, tried to enforce a federal law requiring non-Indians passing through the territory to produce proper documentation. Slaveholders, for example, had to prove that slaves traveling with them were not fugitives. This administrative practice delayed the slaveholders on their travels to and from New Orleans, so they grew increasingly angry at the agent. When Jackson himself brought slaves from Louisiana to Tennessee, through Choctaw lands, he refused to obey Dinsmore's regulation and told anyone who would listen to him on his return to Nashville that his refusal had put a stop to further insults to lawful slaveholders.

Dinsmore had not backed down at all; indeed, he had only recently restrained a woman traveling with ten blacks through his territory. Angrily, Jackson wrote his congressman that the Indian agent had demonstrated *"lawless tyranny . . . over a helpless and unprotected female."*[13] He threatened to march into Mississippi and personally thrash the offending official unless the government took action first. It was not his wife or his mother who needed protection now, but rather a woman he did not even know. No matter, Andrew Jackson would not stand for an affront to any woman. Certainly Jackson's anger against Dinsmore concerned slavery and Indians more than it concerned this unknown female, but it is no accident that he expressed his frustrations by defending a seemingly wronged woman. To him, assault against any woman indicated the mark of unspeakable and unforgivable baseness and cowardice, and he would respond forcefully to thwart it.

Jackson found little satisfaction in his minispat with Dinsmore. His reputation still needed redemption, so he continued to feel frustrated at his lack of military action in the nation's recently declared war against England. He led a Tennessee militia to Natchez on his way to New Orleans to join the war, but he was shocked in February 1813 to receive a War Department order dismissing him and his men from the military service. Frustrated again, he refused to dismiss his soldiers, determined to force them to return to Tennessee as an organized unit. On the difficult return trip, his tough determination to drive his soldiers on, no matter the many obstacles, gained him the appellation "Old Hickory."

At this point, in September 1813, Jackson foolishly became embroiled in another bout of violence, this time with Thomas Hart Benton, later a prominent Missouri politician and supporter, and his brother, Jesse. Once again, Jackson believed it a matter of honor. He had acted as a second in a June duel between a member of his staff and Jesse Benton, and had become angry at Tom Benton's taunts over his role in the fiasco. Jackson physically attacked Tom at a Nashville hotel. Seeing his brother under assault, Jesse shot Jackson in the arm and shoulder. One bullet fractured a bone, and the other remained lodged in Jackson's left arm until it was removed years later during his presidency.

Although injured and in pain, Jackson was still determined to participate in the war that had broken out between the United States and England. In Alabama, the Creek Indians had begun a general uprising, and in August 1813 they overran Fort Mims, massacring many women and children. A horrified Jackson angrily led his Tennessee militia into Alabama to avenge the slaughter, and three months later he led a massacre at the village of Talluhatchee. After the killing, someone brought Jackson an Indian baby from the battlefield, and he tried to get some Creek women to adopt the child. They refused, telling Jackson to kill the boy since all his relatives were dead. Jackson, probably remembering his own orphanhood during the American Revolution, adopted the baby himself, and he and his wife gave the child a good home until the boy died of tuberculosis in 1828.[14]

After one more successful battle against the Indians, Jackson discovered he had an enemy in his own ranks. Malnourished from lack of food and reaching the end of their enlistments, some of his militia wanted to return home, an entire brigade rising in mutiny. Jackson stood down these defiant soldiers not once but several times, yet he still saw his force melt away. New recruits rushed to the colors, however, impressed by his determination to keep fighting. In March 1814, he slaughtered the Creeks, women and children included, at Horseshoe Bend, Alabama. This bloodbath broke the back of the Creek uprising, and later at the Treaty of Fort Jackson, the victorious Tennessean took most of the Indians' land. Promotion to brigadier general in the United States Army and command of the entire Gulf region quickly followed. Jackson's massacre of Indian women did not bother him; gallantry toward women extended only to white females and did not include Indians or blacks.

In late January 1815, Jackson led a motley collection of regular army men, militia, pirates, and free blacks to defeat an army of British regulars at New Orleans, a startling victory. He became the symbol of America's ability to stand up to the British, a hero whose stature equalled that of the leaders of the American Revolutionary generation. War gave him the status and the personal satisfaction for which he had been hungering. Importantly, too, it allowed him to rescue his dead mother from the shadow of the once conquering British, who had marched through their neighborhood and created the conditions that had resulted in her death and his orphanhood.

Andrew Jackson now became the nation's leading general. When he returned to Tennessee, it was clear that in his home state the Sevier and Dickinson duels were forgotten. Jackson was no longer a murderer, but a universally admired hero, the unusual circumstance of his marriage forgotten. Making sure this status stuck, John Henry Eaton, a little-known Nashville lawyer who had served with him in the army, completed a laudatory biography that only added to the Old Hero's fame. Meanwhile in Washington a young girl, later to be the biographer's wife and Jackson's maligned friend, survived the British sack of the capital and was growing into womanhood.

Jackson next negotiated several successful treaties with the southern Indians before the national government called on him to lead a campaign against recalcitrant Seminoles in Spanish Florida. These Indians were aiding runaway slaves from the United States, and Spanish authorities seemed powerless to stop them. Jackson's orders from President James Monroe and Secretary of War John C. Calhoun told him to pursue the Seminoles but not attack them if they took shelter in any Spanish fortification. Jackson quickly pushed into Spanish Florida, and just as quickly he went far beyond his instructions. In April and May 1818, he captured several Spanish towns, forced the Spanish governor to flee, and hanged two British subjects for allegedly aiding the Indians. Jackson's actions caused a major diplomatic flap and a serious disagreement in Monroe's cabinet. The majority of the president's inner circle, led by Calhoun, wanted to censure Jackson for going beyond his orders, and Speaker Henry Clay gave a scathing speech against Jackson on the House floor. The House itself refused to disapprove of Jackson's activities, however, and Secretary of State John Quincy Adams used this as a lever to force Spain to sell all of Florida to the United States. Adams's support in the cabinet kept any movement against Jackson from progressing very far. The Monroe administration knew their general had exceeded his authority, but it made good political sense just to let the matter drop. At that time and later, however, political opponents tried to use this so-called Seminole Affair against Jackson, and he took their partisan criticism personally, lashing out against it whenever it reared its head.

Andrew Jackson, the poor orphan boy of the American Revolution, had become one of the nation's most celebrated personalities as a result of the War of 1812 and his repeated successes against the Indians. Unfortunately, his activities in Florida revitalized the murder charges. His terrible health was another problem. His damaged left arm ached incessantly, and when he coughed, he often produced blood. The two bullets he carried in his body caused recurrent physical ailments, which would have killed most people, but Jackson's stubborn will kept driving him on. He continued to negotiate Indian removal pacts, he began building the Hermitage, and he spent an unhappy three months as governor of the Florida territory he had gained for the United States. He returned to Nashville in 1821, with public admiration for him growing. In July 1822, the Tennessee legislature nominated him for the presidency.[15]

By this time John Henry Eaton was Jackson's close friend and adviser. Born in North Carolina in 1790 the son of a wealthy landowner, John Henry Eaton had briefly attended the University of North Carolina, become a lawyer, and in 1808 moved to Franklin, Tennessee, near Nashville. Thanks to his father's wealth, his own enterprise, and his marriage to Myra Lewis, daughter of a large landowner who unfortunately died soon after the nuptials, Eaton lived a comfortable life complete with a suitable complement of slaves. He first met Andrew Jackson when he was his military aide with the rank of major. He then served in the Tennessee House of Representatives during 1815 and 1816. He completed the biography of Jackson in 1817, and Old Hickory gratefully described him as "a man of acquirements, a correct scholar, and a gentleman of great private worth." In 1818, he was appointed to an unexpired term in the United States Senate, then was elected and reelected in his own right in 1821 and 1827. He was to play a major role in the upcoming 1824 election.[16]

When the 1824 presidential campaign began, it proved to be a nasty one. Eaton penned *The Letters of Wyoming,* which appeared in the press in mid-1823 and later in 1824 as a pamphlet, extolling Jackson's virtue and the corruption of the opposition. At the same time Jesse Benton published *An Address on the Presidential Question* in which he discussed Jackson's less appealing interests in dueling, horse racing, cockfighting, foul language, and assorted other vices. Benton and others reinvigorated the old image of Jackson, the border ruffian, previously put to rest by the heroics at New Orleans. Even Jackson's valued military career was now being used against him: did the nation really want an undisciplined militarist as president of its rising democracy?[17]

In the November 1824 election, Jackson won the popular vote over John Quincy Adams, Henry Clay, and William H. Crawford by a wide margin. Since he did not gain a majority in the Electoral College, however, the election had to be resolved in the House of Representatives. Insisting that he was no politician, Jackson stood above the fray leading to the House vote. Others were not so altruistic and negotiated the best deal they could make for themselves and the candidates they supported. Henry Clay of Kentucky, like Jackson a candidate from the West and thus a major rival, threw his support to Adams. Clay could not stand Adams personally, but he found the New Englander's positions on public matters closer to his own than those of Andrew Jackson. On January 9, 1825, the House chose Adams to be the next president. Soon after, Adams chose Clay to be his secretary of state, the heir apparent to the presidency. Jackson roared in anger.

Throughout his life, whether it was the recurring matter of a woman's virtue, his own honor, or some public event, Jackson saw evil conspiracy and corruption in anything or anyone who stood in his way. In his own mind, his position, whatever it might be, was the correct one, the virtuous one; anyone who opposed him represented corruption. Just as Jackson was willing to duel whenever he believed someone called his honor as a gentleman into question, so he would fight to the finish whenever he believed he saw corruption. Consequently, the fact that he had won the popular vote for president, yet lost the election in the House, proved that he (and the people, his supporters) had been cheated. Adams and Clay had conspired together to thwart justice. A "corrupt bargain" had ensured that the people would not have the final say. "So you see," he shouted, "the *Judas* of the West has closed the contract and will receive the thirty pieces of silver . . . was there ever witnessed such a bare-faced corruption in any country before"?[18]

Andrew Jackson, hurt before by the British and by the bullets of those who challenged his honor and that of his wife, had never quit before, and he would not do so now. He would conquer his corrupt adversaries as he had conquered Charles Dickinson. There was no half way; he determined to defeat this evil before it defeated him and through him destroyed the people and the nation.

In 1825, the Tennessee legislature passed a resolution nominating him once again for the presidency, even though the next election was three years away. His supporters in Tennessee and throughout the nation began to organize into a loose coalition of state organizations that eventually came to call itself the Democratic party. They attacked Adams, Clay, and their supporters at every turn in the Congress and on the local level. Democrats shouted their determination to overthrow the "corrupt bargain."

But it would not be so easy. The 1828 election campaign was one of the dirtiest in American history.[19] Jackson's opponents combed through his past and attacked him viciously for his real and imagined transgressions. The so-called Coffin Hand Bill, the brainchild of John

Binns of the *Philadelphia Press,* purported to document Jackson's alleged murders of twelve men in duels, executions, and various other war and peacetime activities. Charles Hammond of the *Cincinnati Gazette* launched a similar attack. High among the accusations against Jackson stood his alleged propensity for cockfighting, gambling, and cursing. Henry Clay castigated him as being a "military chieftain," who threatened American liberties. As one modern historian has phrased it: Jackson was "pictured as a bloody-minded tyrant who executed militiamen without trial, a sensualist who lived in sin with a woman to whom he had never been married, an ignorant, unreligious desperado who could scarcely write his own name."[20]

On the most personal level, Jackson's opponents labeled his mother a British prostitute who had married a black man by whom she had given birth to Jackson, thus making him a black Englishman. Opponents dragged his own marriage through the mud, calling his wife a bigamist and an adulteress and accusing Jackson of being a wife stealer. "A vote for Jackson," an East Tennessee congressional candidate declared in an 1827 handbill, "meant a vote for a man who thinks that if he takes a fancy to his neighbor's pretty wife, he 'has nothing to do but to take a pistol in one hand and a horsewhip in another and . . . possess her.'" Shocked and angered at this attack, for political purposes, against his mother and beloved wife, Jackson wanted to lash out against his opposition, particularly Henry Clay, whom he thought especially responsible for such villainy. He told Duff Green, editor of the newly established Jacksonian newspaper in Washington, the *United States Telegraph,* to attack the opposition forthrightly but not unlimitedly. "Female character never should be introduced or touched by my friends," Jackson instructed, "unless a continuation of attack should continue to be made against Mrs. J. and then only, by way of *Just retribution* upon the *known guilty. . . . I never war against females,* and it is only the base and cowardly that do so."[21] But Jackson wished he could battle against those who dared attack his beloved Rachel, but he knew that, for once in his life, he had to remain silent.

As Jackson seethed, his supporters grew in numbers and became more unified. John Quincy Adams's vice president, John C. Calhoun of South Carolina, and New York political boss Martin Van Buren joined the Jacksonian bandwagon, as did Thomas Hart Benton, now a senator from Missouri. Journalists Amos Kendall and Francis P. Blair of Kentucky, Thomas Ritchie of Virginia, and Isaac Hill of New Hampshire were the leading figures from an increasing number of Jacksonian newspapermen. Closest to Jackson, and steadily growing in influence, were Tennesseeans Major John Henry Eaton and Major William B. Lewis, two longtime military colleagues.

Andrew Jackson's relationship with John Henry Eaton grew ever closer. Eaton regularly wrote Rachel Jackson about her husband, while simultaneously participating in the defense of their unusual marriage. When rumors spread that Henry Clay was helping gather information for more personal attacks, Eaton confronted "Harry of the West," as Clay was known, and forced him to back off. Jackson appreciated the concern Eaton regularly showed for his personal and political welfare and grew increasingly thankful. He came to consider Eaton "more than a son," and had, for some time, Eaton's portrait "in a tin case, *with my own.*"[22]

Jackson was instrumental in Eaton's 1826 reelection as senator in Tennessee, and Eaton played a major role in Jackson's presidential races in 1824 and 1828. He wrote letters on Jackson's behalf to political leaders like De Witt Clinton and Jackson's personal friends like John Coffee. He took a lukewarm position on the movement that led to the naming of John C. Calhoun as vice presidential candidate, but Jackson's acceptance of Calhoun did not lessen his affection for Eaton and his willingness to hear general advice on strategy and tactics from him. "I could wish therefore," Eaton said, "that the general should not in any way commit himself in opinion upon any subject, that when he comes in, he may be entirely free to shape his course accordingly as his views in reference [*sic*] to the best interest of the Country may dictate to him to be right." He especially tried to keep a lid on Jackson's volcanic temper. When Jackson's arch political rival Henry Clay made a particularly severe attack in early 1828 and rumors circulated that former president James Monroe was unfriendly, Eaton bluntly told Jackson to keep his mouth shut and not hurt his candidacy with an outburst. "Indeed the newspapers, happen what may, should be altogether avoided. Let your friends who are fully competent battle the affair; your course under any and all circumstances is *retirement and silence.*"[23]

While successfully keeping Jackson quiet, Eaton and other Jacksonians did not hesitate to attack his opponent, John Quincy Adams. The corrupt bargain charge continued to dominate, of course, but Adams was also accused of all sorts of alleged aristocratic transgressions such as using government funds to buy a billiard table for the White House and serving as a procurer of women for the Russian czar.

The closer it came to election time in November 1828, the more confident Jackson and his supporters became. Only Rachel Jackson seemed unhappy. The attacks on her reputation stung her, and her health appeared to worsen. In June, Lyncoya, the Indian boy her husband Andrew had rescued from an Alabama battlefield and adopted as his own, died at the age of sixteen. Rachel did all she could to save her son and, when she failed, she was devastated by his death.

She especially worried about becoming the president's wife and living in Washington, having to face the torments of public life. "I had rather be a doorkeeper in the house of God than to live in that palace at Washington," she lamented. No longer the attractive woman of her youth, she was, according to a contemporary description, "a coarse-looking, stout little old woman." She had a dark complexion at a time when the mark of beauty was to be pale. Yet she was "so good natured and motherly" that people felt "immediately . . . at ease with her." She was a plain but charming woman, "benevolent" being the word usually applied to her. Though worried about handling the duties of first lady, she determined to trudge ahead, to be the faithful, supportive wife that she had always been and that society expected of its women.[24]

Jackson's great desire and his wife's deeply felt dread came to fruition when he defeated John Quincy Adams to become the seventh president of the United States, winning a smashing victory in the Electoral College, 178 to 83. Eight hundred thousand more males voted in the election of 1828 than had participated in 1824. The "Old Hero" from frontier Tennessee defeated the incumbent president, son of a previous officeholder and representative of rock-ribbed New England and the elite tradition of the presidency. The elite were out, the people were in.

The nation had undergone a massive political change. The party of Thomas Jefferson, James Madison, and James Monroe, which, since the Federalist party demise after the War of 1812 was the only national political organization left, split in two. The Democrats of Andrew

Jackson harkened back to the states' rights position of the original Jeffersonians, while the National Republicans of John Quincy Adams and Henry Clay supported the federal government supremacy that Adams had attempted to establish during his term.

The two-party system was born with a vengeance. The National Republicans represented the traditional elites, while the Jacksonians advertised themselves as the representatives of the common people. To argue that this party development was philosophical, however, would misrepresent the issue. There were National Republicans who were common men, and there were Jacksonians who were members of the elite. Party efforts revolved around electing candidates more than implementing ideology. Consequently, the era saw the birth of the politics of personality. Politicians attacked one another more than they battled over specific issues. In fact, they consciously obfuscated differences to prevent alienating any block of voters. Attacking one's opponent, tarring him with the brush of corruption, produced electoral success. Earlier on, when politics was the avocation of gentlemen, such attacks against an opponent's character were considered inappropriate. This attitude changed dramatically in the 1820s.

As far as Andrew Jackson and his supporters were concerned, therefore, they had won a victory in 1828 over major corruption. The main point of dispute during the Adams administration, after all, had been the "corrupt bargain" of 1824. This issue represented to the Jacksonians what was wrong with American society and politics overall. Corrupt elitists used the government for their own betterment, Jacksonians insisted, and the people suffered as a result. Jackson, as the tribune of the people, smashed such corruption in the election of 1828, the argument ran, and he could be counted on to root out all its manifestations in the national government and its offices. The people would no longer be fleeced, as they had been under Adams. They would have honest government for the benefit of all—through the agency of Andrew Jackson, the people's representative and the agent of reform.

But not every Jacksonian viewed reality this way. John C. Calhoun, for example, was Andrew Jackson's running mate less because he wanted to reform the Adams administration (of which he was the vice president after all) than because he saw an excellent opportunity to become president when Andrew Jackson retired from office, or more probably when he died during his term. This was no treachery; it was simply reasonable, practical politics. Calhoun, the great nationalist of his early years in Congress, was moving toward becoming the philosopher of states' rights, so he felt more comfortable with Jackson's localism than he did with Adams's nationalism. He easily took his stand at Jackson's side. His native state of South Carolina was growing increasingly worried about threats to its slave system, so it viewed states' rights as a logical and effective defense against national encroachment on the institution.

Jacksonians, although they were hardly unified as a party, were pleased at the great victory of 1828. They were clearly in the ascendancy, and the future looked full of political promise. Only Rachel Jackson seemed withdrawn. She was pleased for her husband's sake, but concerned about her own future. She wondered whether she should even accompany her husband to Washington, only reluctantly accepting John Henry Eaton's advice that she not give in to those who had been attacking her. Women in Nashville began preparing a wardrobe for her, and the city scheduled a great day of celebration prior to the Jacksons' departure for the inauguration.

Feeling little enthusiasm and even less strength, Rachel Jackson bestirred herself to prepare for her travel to the nation's capital. She went to Nashville to do some shopping and there stumbled upon a pamphlet defending her virtue against opposition attacks. She had known before of the attacks against her and her husband, but had never realized the extent of their vehemence. She broke down, trying to hide her panic when she returned home, before finally telling Andrew Jackson of her discovery.

A few days later, she had a heart attack. She rallied briefly, but on December 22, 1828, to her husband's unbelieving horror, she suffered another massive attack and died. Jackson kept hoping that she would somehow still recover, but he was doomed to tearful disappointment. He stayed near her dead form all that night and through the next day, finally and reluctantly pulling himself away. His beloved Rachel was indeed dead, and there was nothing he could do about it. He could not fight for her any longer. After her funeral, he could only pray "that I may have the grace to enable me to forget or forgive any enemy who has ever maligned that blessed one who is now safe from all suffering and sorrow, whom they tried to put to shame for my sake!"[25] Convinced that his political enemies had killed his wife with their slanderous attacks in order to get him, by his lifelong code he had to vindicate her by punishing them. He may have prayed for grace to forgive, but in his heart he coveted revenge.

Jackson had an inscription placed over Rachel's final resting place in the Hermitage garden. It was a paean to his love for her and an expression of his belief in her goodness and worth. A key phrase stated that she was "a being so gentle and so virtuous, slander might wound but could not dishonor." Jackson did not write these words himself, though they expressed his sentiments completely. The author was his friend and close adviser, John Henry Eaton.[26]

The two men were never closer, their bond made stronger by Jackson's deep personal grief over the death of his wife. Within the year, their relationship would strengthen even more, and once again a woman, and a wife, would be responsible. The daughter of a Washington innkeeper would affect their relationship permanently. Andrew Jackson no longer had his wife to defend, but his sense of honor toward women and his determination to protect those whom he believed were unfairly wronged soon found a new beneficiary. Andrew Jackson, John Henry Eaton, and Margaret O'Neale Timberlake Eaton became bound together in the most famous debate over the meaning of womanhood in American history.

2

"My Lord! What a Pretty Girl That Is!"

Andrew Jackson's famous debate over womanhood began several years before his election to the presidency and the death of his wife. In 1822, when the Tennessee legislature had nominated him for the presidency, it had followed this anointing with an 1823 election to the United States Senate, joining Jackson with Eaton, the state's other senator since 1818. The two men traveled to Washington together triumphantly, greeted in Fredericksburg, Virginia, for example, with "drums & flags & cannon and an immense crowd." They arrived in the nation's capital on December 3, 1823, and took rooms at a boardinghouse where Eaton had lived since 1818. Eaton, Jackson, and Richard K. Call, Florida territorial delegate and another former Jackson military subordinate, were "the only occupants of one half the house of our worthy and amiable Hostes Mrs. O'Neall [sic] & her charming family." Here Jackson met Margaret O'Neale Timberlake, the married daughter of the establishment's proprietor William O'Neale, "a very good & worthy man."[1]

A bond quickly formed between Jackson and the twenty-three-year-old Margaret Timberlake. He liked the O'Neale family (father, "amiable pious wife and two daughters") and was pleased that they all took "every pain in there [*sic*] power to make us comfortable and agreeable [*sic*]." "I never saw a more agreeable and worthy family," Jackson said. But Margaret was his obvious favorite. He particularly enjoyed listening to her play the piano as, he said, "every Sunday evening [she] entertains her pious mother with sacred music to which we are invited." Jackson also attended the Methodist Church with the O'Neales. No letter to Rachel Jackson from Washington failed to mention them. This family, especially Margaret, became a permanent part of Andrew Jackson's life.[2]

December of 1824 saw Rachel Jackson accompany her husband to Washington, together with his niece and nephew, Emily and Andrew Jackson Donelson. They all stayed at the Franklin House, regularly seeing the O'Neale family living next door. Margaret made a particularly favorable impact on Rachel, although the Marquis de Lafayette made a bigger impression on Emily Donelson. Jackson was excited about having Rachel with him and even happier that she and Margaret got along so well.[3]

Unfortunately, Jackson's close friend Richard Call did not share his or Rachel's enthusiasm for the young Mrs. Timberlake. During visits to the barroom below the House chambers, Call heard stories about the young woman, rumors that implied that she had loose morals. He became more than intrigued since he already suspected (or was jealous) that his widower friend John Eaton had become very friendly with the boarding house owner's beautiful daughter. In later years, he remembered confronting Eaton about his suspicions, but Eaton had insisted that Call was completely wrong. Allegedly, Eaton told Call that if he was so suspicious of Margaret Timberlake, "Why do you not try her yourself?" Call told Eaton he would "if you will go to Baltimore for three days."

There is no way of knowing if this conversation ever took place, but there is no doubt about what did happen sometime later. Call found himself alone with Margaret Timberlake and tried to force himself on her. She fought him off with a pair of fireplace tongs and then went sobbing to Andrew Jackson. When Jackson later confronted Call, his old friend continued to insist that the young wife was an immoral woman, her rejection of his advances only being a transparent attempt to hide her true character. Jackson found that explanation unconvincing and became Margaret Timberlake's defender. He saw her as a wronged woman worthy of defense, like the many others he had defended during his lifetime.[4]

Even before she met Andrew Jackson in her parents' boardinghouse in the 1820s, however, Margaret O'Neale's life had been linked to an American president.[5] In her memoirs written many years later, she remembered that she had been born at the family establishment in Washington, D.C., on December 3, 1799. The only reason she knew her birthday, she said, was because her mother later told her that, exactly two weeks after giving birth to her, Rhoda O'Neale had sat up in bed and fixed her husband's hair so he could help perform the Masonic ritual at the funeral of George Washington the next day, on December 18, 1799.[6]

Margaret's parents, William and Rhoda O'Neale, were well known Washingtonians. Natives of New Jersey, where they married in Trenton in 1798, the two were of British Isles stock. William's ancestors came from Ulster County, Ireland, as had Andrew Jackson's father; Rhoda's forebears were from Wales. About the time Washington began to get its first permanent homes, O'Neale crossed the Potomac River from his home in Virginia and settled in the new nation's capital. "He was a tall, portly, handsome man," Margaret later remembered her father, "his hair drawn back and carefully made into a cue and tied with a black ribbon." In 1794, he purchased property for a house and established there a business building stoves, coopering barrels, and selling wood, coal, and feed. He also bought and sold buildings. Between 1817 and 1819, he had gained enough stature to serve on the city's Common Council.[7]

Of Protestant background, the O'Neales were raised as Methodists. Rhoda remained loyal to that denomination all her life, but William, for a time at least, attended the Baptist Church in Washington, much to the disgust of his New Jersey relatives. In reality, William was not a religious man. He had, as one observer noted, "some singular notions about the Scriptures and Christianity. He approves the New Test't but disbelieves many facts stated in the old."[8]

Rhoda was a Howell, and Margaret later identified her as a sister of Richard Howell, New Jersey's governor (1793–1801) and a forebear of the second Mrs. Jefferson Davis. Rhoda Howell O'Neale may have been the governor's sister, or her daughter's memory was faulty. Perhaps she was merely repeating a story her mother had told her, or she made the whole thing up as a way to gain stature. Existing records do not corroborate the kinship, and even if Richard Howell and Rhoda were related, they apparently had nothing to do with each other and the matter never came up at any other time in her life. In 1808, for example, when William O'Neale spent three months in New Jersey working to defeat a proposal to have the national capital moved from Washington to Philadelphia, he never mentioned any relationship to the deceased governor.[9]

Rhoda O'Neale was apparently the family's anchor. Unlike her husband, whom a later newsman remembered as "of ordinary intelligence . . . and cursed with inclinations that led downward instead of up," she "was cast in a larger and finer mould, a woman of good judgment, of pure instincts, of well-balanced intellect." She was "grave," almost "sedate," and provided the family with a balance that would otherwise have been missing without her presence.[10]

William O'Neale's participation in activities to save Washington as the nation's capital demonstrated the uncertain nature of the city's early existence. Congress did not stay in session the year round, so Washington was quiet most of the time. Congressmen and senators usually did not even bring their wives and families with them when the legislature was in session. They came, as Jackson and Eaton had, alone and lived in boardinghouses with other men, establishing a predominantly male world of easy camaraderie. William O'Neale ran one of these boardinghouses, and it became the source of his security and his fame. In 1796, he boarded only three or four congressmen in his three-story brick house at 2007 I Street. Located between Twentieth and Twenty-first Streets, about halfway between the Capitol and the village of Georgetown and only a short distance from the presidential mansion, the establishment had a steadily growing reputation. In 1805, he boarded up to twenty men, although he still sold coal and wood on the property. Two years later he advertised that he had room for only six or seven men with stable room for that many horses, but by 1813, he had expanded his facilities, adding another large building, fifty by forty feet in size, with twenty rooms and brand-new furniture. He now gave it a grand name, the Franklin House. In 1814, he opened a bar to add to his establishment's appeal.[11]

The Franklin House, therefore, was born over time and became one of the city's favorite boardinghouses, containing more than seventy rooms. The sign bearing Benjamin Franklin's image swung in the breeze above the front door and was a familiar sight to a generation of politicians. The city's omnibus, familiarly called Royal George, made regular stops there, providing rides for the congressmen to Capitol Hill, a mile and a half away.[12]

Washington in the early nineteenth century, when William O'Neale established his business, was an unimposing village that "lay in almost virgin nakedness." The population stood at only 3,210 people, and houses were few and far between. "Most of the area of the National Capital was then covered with bushes and undergrowth, which fell off here and there into pasture grounds and commons, or terminated in slashes and marshes." The Mall, of later fame, was a mosquito-infested swamp, and Pennsylvania Avenue was often muddy, though eventually it was covered with logs from nearby felled trees. Some wit referred to the city as a "mud hole almost equal to the great Serbonian bog." The Capitol building itself was impressive, however. One young South Carolinian, visiting the chamber of the House of Representatives in company with William O'Neale, boastingly asserted that there was "not in Europe a room equally superb." But in general, the city was sparse, less a reality than a hope. A visitor during these early days expressed this deficiency in rhyme:

> The famed metropolis, where fancy sees,
> Squares in morasses, obelisks in trees;
> Which traveling fools and gazetteers adorn
> With shrines unbuilt and heros yet unborn."[13]

As William and Rhoda established themselves and their boardinghouse in this nation's sparse capital, they also raised a family of six children: three sons and three daughters. William and Robert attended West Point, William being admitted in April 1815 as a fifteen-year-old and Robert entering in June of that year as a fourteen-year-old. Neither graduated, Robert resigning in November 1817 and William departing in April 1818. Both died within days of each other as young men, the victims of a fever Robert apparently caught in Havana while working on a sailing ship. Younger brother John fought in the Mexican War, and he, too, died from fever. The other female children consisted of Margaret's two sisters: Mary, whose husband later was Phillip G. Randolph, a War Department functionary, and Georgiana, who married the Reverend French S. Evans, a Washington minister and government employee.[14]

The O'Neale family lived in the boardinghouse itself until 1810, when they moved to a home across the street. Despite their move, the family maintained close ties to the boarders at the Franklin House. As the oldest and the most precocious of the six children, Margaret became a particular favorite of the lonely politicians. She spent many an hour on someone's knee, receiving the kind of attention the boarders wished they could be lavishing on their own absent children. When Margaret was not around, the boarders missed her. Elbridge Gerry, Jr., the son of the vice president of the United States, complained in 1813: "We live a while at O'Neale's [*sic*] tavern, and are disappointed, in looking around, to find no Peggy of immortal memory scampering in and out to sit on old gentlemen's laps and chuckle them under the chin." More often than not, however, Peggy was present, to joke and laugh with the men. William T. Barry, later postmaster general, wrote his absent wife in 1815 "of a charming little girl . . . who very frequently plays on the Piano, and entertains us with agreeable songs . . . that touch my heart."[15]

Not only were the boarders pleased with Margaret, but they also enjoyed the good food they received at the O'Neale boardinghouse and the good service that accompanied it. In December 1808, for example, breakfast consisted of "coffee, warm buckwheat cakes, chicken, corncakes, toast, broiled fresh pork &c." The 4 P.M. dinner was even more sumptuous. One day it might be "Ham, Turkey, chicken, roast beef, chicken pie, pudding, crackers and apples," at another time it might be "Goose, Fowl, Ham, Sausages and eggs &c. &c." An early evening supper completed the day's repast. Before the opening of the bar in 1814, no liquor—not even wine—was served with the meals. Spirits were only available to the boarders upon their request, as were cold cuts at any hour. Each boarder had a bell in his room which he used to call a servant whenever he wanted something to eat or drink.[16]

Literally hundreds of men stayed at the O'Neale Tavern/Franklin House from the late eighteenth century into the 1820s, including congressmen and senators from all over the nation. Perhaps the most famous boarder was George Clinton, seven times governor of New York and a leading figure in the American Revolution. Twice elected vice president of the United States, he was a fixture at the O'Neale's. In fact, one of the tragedies of young Margaret's life was Clinton's death from pneumonia on April 20, 1812. To witness Clinton's daughter Maria's anguish over her father's demise and share in her grief was not easy. When she had first learned of his illness, Maria had already exclaimed: "O my God it seems as if my poor Hart [*sic*] would burst[.] my Dear Father. O God thy will be done." Such grief—the somber ceremonies with cavalrymen escorting the body from the boarding house to the Capitol, and all the important people, including President James Madison, observing the prescribed rites of mourning—all this sorrow must have been difficult for Margaret and her family. Her father, after all, had lost an old friend and a steady boarder. Perhaps the gift of a breast pin containing a lock of Clinton's hair and a payment of over $700 for the cost of boarding helped assuage William O'Neale's grief.[17]

Another famous boarder was Thomas Sumter, the "Gamecock of the Revolution," so celebrated in South Carolina that he had the famous fort in Charleston harbor named after him. John Milledge of Georgia, another Revolutionary fighter, also lived at the O'Neales'. He served in the House and the Senate, eventually becoming governor of the state and one of the early patrons of its university. He was so revered in Georgia that the state capital was named after him: Milledgeville. Once, when William O'Neale was absent in Philadelphia on business, Milledge was concerned enough about him to ask a friend there to tell him that his family was all well back in Washington.[18]

John Wayles Eppes, a son-in-law of Thomas Jefferson, also boarded at the Franklin House, as did Felix Grundy, one of the War Hawks of 1812. On and on the list could go. Margaret O'Neale came to know and be known by the leading figures in the early American nation.[19]

One can only imagine how many conversations Margaret heard at the table or in the parlor, first as a youngster on someone's knee, then as a young woman more discreetly listening on the fringes of the group or more directly participating from a chair in the middle of it all. The boarders, after all, were among the nation's leaders, and the Franklin House was their home away from home, the O'Neales their surrogate family. Fortified with a good meal and a drink if they rang for it, and with a great deal of time to sit around and talk, these politicians no doubt let their inhibitions go and spoke freely. The curious and obviously intelligent young girl received a civics lesson every day. In 1808, for example, the boarders pointedly discussed their tax vote during John Adams's presidency and then debated whether or not Congress should employ chaplains.[20]

The politicians also reminisced a good deal, the older men telling the young girl and her brothers and sisters about the founding days of the nation, the important events leading to independence, and the great men who fought to make it happen. No doubt Margaret's father, whom many called Major because of his service in the American Revolution, joined in such conversations with relish and told about his acquaintance with George Washington. Political history surrounded Margaret O'Neale at the Franklin House.[21]

It must have been particularly interesting one day in 1809 when someone asked Matthew Lyon about his experiences during his first term in the House of Representatives. The Revolutionary War veteran, a longtime member of the House from both Vermont and his later home, Kentucky, was a fiery individual, and he no doubt relished telling his tale.

Lyon had been involved in the first physical confrontation on the House floor. As one of the original Jeffersonians elected from New England, he had immediately become the target of Federalist party attacks both in Congress and in the press. In January 1798, he angrily spat into the face of another congressman for what he considered to be an insult to his war record. Several weeks later this still outraged legislator returned the favor by attacking Lyon with his cane. Federalist opponents then went one step further and prosecuted Lyon under the Sedition Act. He was sentenced to four months in jail and fined one thousand dollars. He served his time, paid his fine, and his constituents then overwhelmingly reelected him to the House. He became a national hero.[22]

Margaret must have hung on every word of monologues like that. To think that one of her father's boarders, one of her congressmen, had been so persecuted! It must have opened her eyes to the perils of politics. Most of the time, of course, her father's boarders did not have such dramatic stories to tell, talking more of the prosaic ins and outs of getting a bill made into a law, rhetorically debating the opposition on the floor, and winning or losing political battles. No doubt, too, they spoke of the official ceremonies and the private parties they attended. As she learned history and contemporary politics, the young Margaret also gained insight into Washington social life. Few Americans of her time, man or woman, gained such an education.

Margaret also had the chance to see that these great men were hardly paragons of perfection. She saw them at their best, and she saw them at their worst. John Milledge, the Georgia statesman, for example, had incredibly boorish table manners. A South Carolina teacher, who briefly stayed at the Franklin House while visiting Washington, was aghast at what he witnessed. Milledge "took a piece of bread in his fingers, sopped in the gravy of the Roast Beef and ate it all at one mouthful though large enough for three. Afterwards there being a pretty large piece of quince on the plate of preserves and some sauce, he hauled the saucer near, took the quince in his thumb and finger and gormandized the whole at a bite." These national leaders were certainly fallible human beings, and this insight no doubt kept Margaret from feeling too much compunction about considering herself their equal.[23]

Margaret was, after all, an unusual child.[24] Demonstrating that her father must have been doing well financially and that he had influence beyond that of the ordinary innkeeper, she attended Mrs. Hayward's school, reputedly the best in the capital. She was exposed to a wide array of subjects, ranging from arithmetic, history, English and French grammar to drawing, needlework, music, and dance. She grew proficient at the piano and was so talented in dance that her father sent her, after school, to take further lessons from a Mr. Generes, a dance master in Alexandria, Virginia.

On March 16, 1812, Generes held a ball at Georgetown's Union Tavern, one of Washington's favorite gathering places. The young girls took their turns performing before the large crowd, including Dolley Madison, the president's wife. They danced the minuet and the gavotte, Margaret clearly standing out. Dolley Madison crowned her as the best of the ball. The twelve-year-old Margaret O'Neale had scored the first major triumph of her life. The city's gentility had to have been impressed. Or did they become jealous and angry that an innkeeper's child had bested their daughters?[25]

The death of her paternal grandfather in Montgomery County, Maryland, a week later, the sale of all his property, and the demise of George Clinton just two weeks after that dampened Margaret's triumph. About this same time, too, the nation, angry that the English displayed so little respect for American neutral rights and thus for American honor, declared war on Great Britain, Margaret returned to school, now clearly less interesting to her after the thrill of victory at the ball and the news of the recently declared war. Matters were also more exciting at home as the addition to the Franklin House moved toward completion. Perhaps in the hope that a change of scenery would revive Margaret's academic interest, O'Neale sent her to Mr. Kirke's school. She did not remain there long either. The war intruded on the capital and changed her life permanently.

Few in Washington wanted to believe it could happen, but on August 14, 1814, 4,500 British fighting men pushed past American troops twice their number at Bladensburg, Maryland, and poured into Washington, then a city of about 6,000 people. Government officials fled in panic, taking what they could with them and gaining the ridicule of the public. Dolley Madison became a heroine for saving artifacts from the Executive Mansion, but her husband, the president, and his cabinet were ridiculed in doggerel: "Fly, Monroe fly! Run Armstrong run! Were the last words of Madison."

Secretary of State James Monroe lived at 2017 I Street, just a short distance from the Franklin House at 2007, and he had long been urging the Madison administration to prepare for an invasion. No doubt he warned O'Neale, his family, and guests that the British were indeed coming. O'Neale stayed behind to try to defend his property, but he sent his wife and family packing with forty mostly female Washingtonians led by Adjutant General of the Army Daniel Parker. It was a hard trip, the wind blowing dust into their faces and causing many of the travelers to cry. They left before the British reached the city, carrying what they could with them. They could see the flames of the torched capital's public buildings from their exile in the countryside. Then a terrible wind and rain storm blew in, and as a British soldier phrased it: "The flashes of lightning seemed to vie in brilliancy, with the flames which burst from the roofs of burning houses." The beautiful chamber of the House of Representatives was destroyed, but fortunately, the British spared most private dwellings and the Franklin House, much to the family's relief when they returned. Still, for a long time Margaret O'Neale remembered, "the sight of a red-coat" caused them a shock.[26]

As soon as the city came back to normal, William O'Neale rented his building to the government, it remaining the home of the Treasury Department until early 1816. O'Neale moved the boardinghouse to the older smaller dwellings on his property and soon after opened a bar in a corner section of the Franklin House/Treasury Department building.[27]

The burned city was a depressing place. Later Postmaster General William T. Barry noted, for example, the awful change in its navy yard. Before the British invasion, he reported: "It was then cheerful and busy with workmen, large vessels in the harbor and handsome public buildings in the most flattering state of progressive improvement. Now it is a scene of ruins. Even the monument erected to the heroes of Tripoli has been defaced by the rude hand of the enemy." Once more there was talk of abandoning Washington, but fortunately for O'Neale and the other businessmen there, nothing came of this threat. Andrew Jackson's spectacular victory at New Orleans on January 8, 1815, less than five months after the British sack of Washington, reinvigorated citizens of the nation's capital as well as the nation as a whole.[28]

As she experienced these thrilling adventures, no doubt sharing in the excitement over Jackson's triumph and perhaps wondering what kind of man the military hero was, the young Margaret O'Neale grew up and became an alluring woman. Men who had once seen her as a cute child now began to look on her as a sensual woman, and several began bidding for her affections. When she was fourteen or fifteen years of age, a nephew of William Jones, the secretary of the navy, took poison in despair over her lack of interest, while simultaneously trying to fool her into taking mint drops laced with a deadly potion. She became, for a time, the "flame" of the son of Thomas Jefferson's secretary of the treasury, Albert Gallatin.[29] Adjutant General Parker, a much older man, was also smitten with her, perhaps during their escape from Washington. But Margaret had no interest in him either. She was taken with a younger man, Major Francis Smith Belton, an aide to General Winfield Scott.

After a whirlwind courtship, the two lovers, she a girl of only fifteen, decided to elope. Just below Margaret's bedroom window lay a shed to whose roof she could easily step. From there she could step down to a water pump and then be lifted to the ground. The assigned night and hour for elopement arrived, and Belton and two friends stationed themselves next to the pump to lift Margaret to the ground. A clergyman waited in a nearby carriage to perform the wedding ceremony. As she made ready to step from the window to the shed roof, however, Margaret inadvertently hit a flower pot on the window sill and sent it crashing to the bedroom floor. Her father came rushing in and dragged her back into the house.

If she was chastened, she did not show it. Sometime after the foiled elopement, Margaret accepted the invitation of another army man, Captain Richard R. Root, an aide to General Alexander Macomb, to take a carriage ride. Upon arriving at a greenhouse, Root romantically presented Margaret with a rosebush, while her chaperoning sister watched in appreciation. When they returned home, however, they found Belton pacing up and down the sidewalk. Soon, Belton and Root were threatening each other, but, fortunately, Margaret's father and Adjutant General Parker intervened to prevent any bloodshed.

All this turmoil over a teenage girl seemed hard to believe. Margaret found it exciting, but her father was concerned. Watching his young daughter pay more attention to suitors than to school caused him to worry about her future. Like most fathers, he wanted her to marry and settle down, but he thought she was too young for that just now. What might she do next? he wondered. What would Washingtonians think of her forward behavior? He decided to get her out of town for a fresh start. Soon after the near battle between Root and Belton in late 1814, William O'Neale put Margaret aboard a stagecoach for New York, where he enrolled her in Madame Nau's French finishing school at 17 Dey Street, placing her under the weekend care of De Witt Clinton.[30]

O'Neale had probably come to know Clinton through his uncle, who had died at the Franklin House. De Witt Clinton was an important individual in his own right, having just completed several terms as mayor of New York City. When Margaret arrived, he was out of office, busily planning and promoting the idea of a state canal from Albany to Buffalo, connecting the Atlantic Ocean with the Great Lakes. Clinton was the father of the Erie Canal. He was also the first president of the Free School Society in New York City and the author of *Introductory Discourse,* a well-respected analysis of the status of the nation's scientific learning. He served as president of the American Academy of Art and helped found the New-York Historical Society and the Literary and Philosophical Society of New York. One of the few in his generation who took such a stand, he also strongly supported higher education for women.[31]

An individual of massive proportions (over six feet tall) with the nickname "Magnus Apollo," Clinton was clearly a person of great industry and purpose. He regularly rose early and maintained a rigorous work schedule. He read widely and kept a notebook of insights he gained from his books. He held his social life to a minimum, seeing such activity as frivolous. His wife, the daughter of a New York Quaker merchant, was similarly industrious. A warm mother to their family of four sons and three daughters, she, too, had little interest in social life.[32]

As soon as her father introduced her to her new guardian, Margaret sensed that her own social life was in danger. Clinton lectured her about the necessity of education, disciplined study, and the useless frivolity of excessive partying—no doubt just what O'Neale hoped he would do. Margaret listened, was briefly cowed, but immediately began to plot behind Clinton's back. The very first day she attended school, for example, Margaret told the headmistress her story of foiled elopement. She convinced this woman to allow Captain Root, who had followed Margaret from Washington, to visit her each evening. Clinton found out about these repeated rendezvous and lectured Margaret even more strenuously. She listened to his admonitions and responded by planning another elopement with Root.

The plotting failed because the intriguers had a falling out. Margaret's infatuation with Root now turned to disdain. She decided that she would never marry him. She wrote her father complaining of homesickness, begging him to allow her to return. The letter read: "Dear Father: for the Lord's sake come and take me home; and if you will do so I will promise to be the best girl you ever saw, and I assure you that under no circumstances shall either Root or Branch take me away from you."[33] This play on the name of her jilted admirer impressed O'Neale and perhaps even the intellectual Clinton. O'Neale came to New York City and brought his daughter back to Washington. Clinton agreed that she might as well return home since her admirer had followed her to New York anyway.

Margaret apparently never returned to any school. She continued her education at the Franklin House, where the O'Neale family now not only provided living accommodations for congressmen and senators in the boardinghouse but also provided liquor to the general male population of Washington in the tavern. Margaret participated in this part of the business as much as she worked in the boarding house. To call her a mere barmaid would be erroneous, but there seems little doubt that she helped accommodate her father's thirsty patrons. Her beauty, outgoing vivaciousness, obvious interest in male conversation, and numerous romantic adventures were hardly a barrier to good business. Margaret was an asset to the tavern, and her father needed all the help he could get as he was undergoing financial difficulties severe enough to force him to advertise the rent or sale of the establishment.

William O'Neale weathered the financial storm; but, even with Margaret's help, it was never easy. At the least, though, he had his daughter home, and Root and Belton seemed to be bad memories. Margaret's attention was focused on the mass of Washington men in the tavern rather than on any special man with ideas of marriage. Or so the O'Neales might have thought.

It all changed quickly and by accident. One morning in 1816, the sixteen-year-old Margaret looked out the family parlor window just as two men were riding by. "Come here, mother," she cried out. "Here is my husband riding on horseback." Her mother went to the window and laughed, "Margaret, you are too ridiculous for anything," but then added: "He is a handsome fellow."

Riding by that day was John Bowie Timberlake, a purser in the United States Navy. He noticed Margaret looking at him and exclaimed to his companion, another navy purser, "My Lord! What a pretty girl that is!" They stopped their horses, seemingly to admire the bushes and trees in front of the Franklin House, but actually to wait for an opportunity to meet Margaret. Soon after, Timberlake's companion spied William O'Neale and introduced Timberlake to him. In the course of the conversation, O'Neale bragged about his daughter's musical talent; Timberlake told the beaming father that being interested in music himself, he would be honored to meet her and hear her play the piano. O'Neale agreed and took him inside.

Matters proceeded quickly. Timberlake took Margaret and her sister to an afternoon outing on the Potomac River, stayed for tea at Rhoda O'Neale's invitation, and listened to Margaret play the piano. By 11 P.M., he had asked for and received her hand in marriage. Within a month, thanks to a furlough from the secretary of the navy, who knew the O'Neales, the wedding took place, on July 18, 1816, a Presbyterian minister officiating and a large group of friends and relatives witnessing the event. The bride later remembered that Secretary of the Navy Samuel L. Southard and Dolley Madison were among the distinguished gathering, but the local newspaper mentioned only the principals in the ceremony. Timberlake must have been a smooth talker to have convinced the O'Neales to such a fast marriage. William O'Neale, who had opposed her earlier marriage plans when she was fifteen, agreed to allow her nuptials now that she was sixteen. Perhaps one year of age made a difference to him or he simply liked Timberlake more than he had liked her earlier suitors. The marriage took place, but its occurrence could not have helped Margaret's O'Neale's reputation.[34]

Timberlake took his new bride to visit his mother in Port Royal, Virginia, traveling there in a grand carriage William O'Neale had provided his daughter and son-in-law for the occasion. Margaret and her new in-laws hit it off immediately. Mrs. Timberlake showed the new bride a dress that her grandmother had worn many years before, and the two women decided, as a lark, that Margaret would wear it to a barbecue scheduled that day. The older woman also found some old shoes with very pointed heels for her new daughter-in-law to wear. Walking in these unfamiliar shoes, Margaret slid down the highly waxed stairs and landed on her bottom. Good-naturedly she found a crutch to take to the barbecue, hurriedly throwing it away when the music and dancing began. The visit was a success; the outgoing young woman was enthusiastically accepted into her new family.

Soon after the young couple returned to Washington, William O'Neale gave them a large brick two-story home right next to his residence across the street from the Franklin House complex.[35] The two houses were connected, so the two families could easily move between the buildings. Timberlake opened a store in this house after he and his wife decided he would begin a new life away from the sea.

Timberlake's previous naval career had been turbulent. He had joined the fleet in 1809 and had served during the War of 1812, first on the frigate *United States* and then on the *President*. As a navy purser, he handled the ship's money and purchased groceries and other sundries with his own money for sale to the officers and crew for profit. As the ship's finance officer and storekeeper, he sold the goods on credit, then subtracted the total owed him from the money he distributed to the sailors on pay day.

During the war, this system broke down for Timberlake, once because of an American victory and the other time because of a defeat. The frigate *United States,* under the command of Stephen Decatur, captured the British ship *Macedonian* on October 25, 1812, returning triumphantly to New York harbor bearing its prize. Excited citizens threw the American crew a congratulatory dinner, and a number of the sailors enjoyed their meals, then promptly deserted. Timberlake suffered a significant financial loss as a result. The deserters owed him money for goods he had sold them on credit during the cruise, which he was unable to recover once they were gone.

Later in the war, while Timberlake was serving on the frigate *President,* once again under Stephen Decatur, he had another streak of bad luck. A British squadron gave chase to the *President,* and in order to lighten his ship for the race, Decatur ordered nonessential items from the *President* thrown overboard. Timberlake's merchandise was among the material cast off. The British ships captured the *President* on January 15, 1814, anyway. Boarding the ship, the British officers confiscated Timberlake's ledgers containing records of his credit sales to officers and crew. When the ship returned to the United States, Decatur ordered Timberlake to proceed with payday. Since he had no record of crew purchases and the sailors knew it, many of them denied receiving more than a few sundries. Timberlake was stuck with a huge financial shortfall.[36]

He hoped to solve his financial problems in the store next to the Franklin House, but he only made them worse. He lost money on land as he had lost it at sea. On December 17, 1817, with John's mother in attendance, Margaret gave birth to a baby boy, whom she named William after her beloved father. The child died within six months. On November 24, 1819, she delivered Mary Virginia (Ginger), and on March 16, 1825, Margaret Rosa was born. Timberlake was now a married man with family obligations. He had to do something to try to restore his financial stability.[37]

William O'Neale could not help his struggling son-in-law because of financial problems of his own. Business partners had taken advantage of his generosity and reneged on loans he naively had guaranteed for them. In order to make ends meet in mid-1816, he had to put his seventy-room hotel up for sale. Somehow he managed to avoid losing his property. Four years later, however, he was still struggling with creditors. In 1823, he wrote future president James Buchanan commiserating over having to sell the boardinghouse, though insisting that "not for debt was my property sold, [but] it was misplaced confidence in . . . false friends." He hoped Buchanan would stay at the boardinghouse his wife was now running, reminding him that "he that gives to the poor lends to the Lord."[38]

In December 1818, O'Neale and his family met the man who would change their lives. John Henry Eaton's arrival at the Franklin House in Washington proved to be the beginning of a long friendship with William O'Neale. He became a mainstay at the boardinghouse, getting to know the entire O'Neale family and the newlyweds, John and Margaret Timberlake. Eaton and Timberlake became fast friends, their friendship cemented when, in the spring of 1820, Eaton introduced Timberlake's petition to the United States Senate for relief from his naval debts and when, at a later time, he acted as surety for some of Timberlake's bonds.[39]

In his Senate petition, Timberlake asked to be indemnified for the losses he had sustained as purser on the *United States* and the *President*. Eaton presented the plea, and it went to the Senate's Naval Affairs Committee, where it immediately ran into trouble. On April 11, 1820, Senator James Pleasants of Virginia, Timberlake's home state, and the committee chairman, reported out a negative recommendation. Since as a purser Timberlake could sell private goods for his own profit, the recommendation read, he assumed ultimate responsibility for the products associated with the business. "The Government certainly never meant to become insurers in these cases," the committee report stated. As for the capture of the ledgers, why had Timberlake not made copies of these books or why had he not made a greater effort to get the British to return the originals? The desertion of the men from the *United States* was beyond Timberlake's control, however, and the committee believed that, in that case, he should receive "an allowance."[40]

The entire Senate disagreed. Three times it voted down any relief for Timberlake. When the other senator from his home state reintroduced the claim in early 1821, it went to the Committee on Claims, then to the Naval Affairs Committee, but failed again. On February 28, 1821, that committee voted to dismiss it. There would be no congressional relief.

Timberlake now had no choice. With his Washington store a failure, and Congress refusing to grant him any relief from his naval finance problems, he had to go back to sea as a purser, this time on the *Shark,* commanded by Matthew C. Perry, the naval officer later famous for opening Japan. Senator John Henry Eaton must have expedited this appointment, for why else would the navy want to take back a purser with such a checkered financial history?[41] Fortunately, Timberlake seemed to find himself. He punctually sent William O'Neale money for his wife's board each month and spiced that contribution with occasional containers of Caribbean fruit.

Throughout their marriage, whether Timberlake was running the Washington store or selling groceries as a purser on board a naval vessel, his wife maintained a high profile at the Franklin House. No longer a young girl but a mature wife and mother, Margaret Timberlake played a large role in the operation of the boardinghouse and tavern, maintaining her open manner with the men who made the place their home away from home or simply came in for an evening drink. Her participation in the debates over politics and other male topics, as they were then assumed to be, became more frequent and more open. Year after year she listened to the politicians, read the newspapers, and formed opinions. She was not only attractive, but she was also bright and interesting. What a novelty for Washington men to be able to see and hear such statements coming from such a beautiful woman. It was all exciting, but was it proper for a woman to engage in such unfeminine activities? After all, a married woman was not supposed to act like a flirtatious girl. Societal norms insisted that she tone herself down appropriate to her wifely station. At least a few people began to wonder about her. There were innuendoes that "her methods had much to do with the presence of lonesome legislators in her father's establishment."[42]

John Henry Eaton became especially attentive to Margaret Timberlake. His friendship with John Timberlake gave him the opportunity to develop a close relationship with the purser's wife, particularly when the purser was away at sea for years at a time. On November 13, 1826, while in Gibraltar, Timberlake conferred on Eaton his power of attorney. A week later Margaret Timberlake and her father, no doubt on Eaton's advice, settled some debts owed to her husband, accepting bank stock in lieu of cash payment. Margaret insisted that she "had known . . . [John Eaton since she had met him in 1818] as a gentleman, as my father's friend, as my mother's friend, [and] as my husband's friend; . . . he was a pure, honest, and faithful gentleman." Timberlake trusted Eaton so much, his wife later insisted, that on one occasion he wrote her that, should he die or become incapacitated, "there is one man to whose hands I should be willing to entrust you, and that is John H. Eaton, the noblest work of God, an honest man."[43]

Apparently with Timberlake's knowledge and approval, Margaret Timberlake and John Henry Eaton socialized frequently, Eaton serving as Mrs. Timberlake's escort, and the two often talked together at the Franklin House. Such public activity only caused the whispering to increase. Margaret O'Neale Timberlake became the subject of harsh Washington gossip. She was, for all intents and purposes, a tavern keeper, a woman, it was said, who, since her teenaged days, had openly consorted with males in a confined place where alcohol was served, inhibitions were loosened, and all kinds of talk took place. She was not simply listening to such talk, unfit for a woman's ears, but she participated in it as well and seemed to be quite good at it. Her husband was a ne'er-do-well who had failed in his previous career in the navy, had failed in his mercantile business in Washington, drank too much, it was said, and had run off to sea to escape his financial and marital problems. It had to be hell to be married to someone like Margaret Timberlake, the rumor mills ground. No wonder John Timberlake was on board a ship in some godforsaken port; he could not stand to watch his wife's behavior. Now she was consorting with Eaton. Such totally improper behavior made Margaret O'Neale Timberlake a dissolute woman, one whom decent Washingtonians should shun.

Try as it might, however, social Washington could not avoid her, not when the Marquis de Lafayette, Revolutionary War hero from France, stayed at the Franklin House in mid-October while in Washington during his national tour. The grand banquet in his honor was also held there. By this time, William O'Neale had been forced to sell the establishment; but the new owner, John Gadsby, had not yet completed the changeover to the National Hotel. O'Neale, therefore, remained in charge during Lafayette's stay. The public ceremonies for the old patriot were as grand as official Washington could make them; twenty-five young women, for example, were specially dressed to represent the twenty-four states and the District of Columbia. Following ceremonies and banquet, Lafayette continued his American tour, with Washingtonians pleased and William O'Neale receiving widespread praise for his role. No doubt Margaret Timberlake had been visible in the preparations for, and the implementation of, the banquet, the centerpiece of the visit. She received no mention, however, all the attention centering on the Revolutionary War celebrity, not on the innkeeper's daughter with the bad reputation. It was long said, however, that her father gave her the silver service Congress presented him on the occasion of the Lafayette visit. It came to be known in the family as "Papa's Lafayette silver."[44]

While Margaret Timberlake's reputation became the focus of Washington gossip, John Timberlake seemed to be doing well at sea. He had become the purser on the *Constitution* beginning on June 28, 1824, and the letters and gifts home continued to arrive on a regular basis. When in 1823 John Henry Eaton had purchased the Franklin House from a foreclosing bank and then resold it the following year to John Gadsby under conditions he hoped would benefit William O'Neale, he had asked Timberlake for help with the process. The purser sent him his power of attorney and a bank draft for about $2,500. Later Eaton made Timberlake a loan of approximately $1,800 as short-term help with Timberlake's shipboard accounts.

There had long been rumors of Timberlake's drinking on land and at sea, and they circulated again. Margaret ignored such whisperings, more worried about her husband's asthma than about his drinking. She had seen what an asthma attack could do to him. In the middle of one night at home, she related, John had such a severe attack that she had taken first-aid action herself, according to the medical doctrine of the time. "I bound his arm tight with my garter," she remembered in later years, "opened a vein with a penknife, flung a wrapper around myself, rushed across the street, and brought our family physician, old Dr. Simms, who pronounced my hurried treatment as the salvation of the life of my husband under the circumstances." At sea, the asthma attacks continued. One of his commanders later said that, during some attacks, John Timberlake became "so tortured that he grew black in the face."[45]

In late March of 1828, Timberlake wrote his wife a warm letter telling her of his attendance at a ball and about picking grapes in a Mediterranean port. His ship was heading home, he said, and he urged her to meet him in Boston. He also told her that if anything happened to him, he wanted his friend John Henry Eaton to take care of her.

John Timberlake was clearly worried about his health; indeed, he had suffered a variety of physical and emotional ailments during this cruise. Several friends noted his recurrent anxiety and depression over his earlier financial difficulties and agreed that he suffered from "debility and consumption." To the day he died, however, his friends remembered his expressions of affection for his wife and family and his good friend, John Henry Eaton.[46]

As the ship sailed for Spain, its last stop before the return voyage across the Atlantic to Boston, Timberlake became gravely ill. On April 2, 1828, he died, the ship's log reporting only: "Wednesday, April 2, 1828. At 2 departed this life, John B. Timberlake, Esq., Purser." The official cause of death was pulmonary disease. When the ship arrived at Port Mahon, Balearic Islands, off Spain, Timberlake was buried with proper military ceremony, and a monument was placed before the grave. Then a special dinner, complete with food from his purser's stock, fed the hungry navy mourners.[47]

The commander of the Mediterranean Squadron sent news to the Navy Department in Washington of Timberlake's death, "after a long and painful illness." Eaton heard an earlier rumor and decided to break the news to the family immediately. At dinner that day, he told William and Rhoda O'Neale first. Margaret Timberlake was busy with a seamstress in another room and kept delaying her arrival to the table. Finally she noticed that something seemed wrong, so she stuck her head into the dining room and jokingly asked if there was a problem. Her mother dropped her head, her father put down his eating utensils, and Eaton looked sad. When she asked again, her father bolted from the table. Eaton gently led her into the parlor and broke the bad news. She refused to believe it, but three days later official word arrived from Secretary of the Navy Samuel Southard. She and her father immediately left for Boston to meet the ship and collect Timberlake's property: a few gold coins, a locket, and a wooden box addressed lovingly "For my bonnie moggie lauder" with the cryptic inscription, "Noli me tangere" (Do not touch me). Was this a warning to other sailors to stay out of his personal possessions or did Timberlake mean something deeper? No one ever said.

Margaret Timberlake eventually learned that her husband had died with his wedding ring tied around his waist, because his fingers had become so swollen that he could not wear it on his hand. Her picture was found near his heart, and a likeness of the children was in his hands. She also discovered that he had not died from pulmonary disease but at his own hand by cutting his throat. Shipmates insisted that he had not committed suicide, however, but that his death "was simply the mad act of a man in delirium."[48] Margaret always held that an asthma attack was the cause of the self-inflicted wound, but few believed her, particularly since John had almost killed himself in the same manner several months previously.

Word spread quickly in small-town Washington of the sensational death of the husband of the increasingly controversial innkeeper's daughter. It did not take long for the gossips to proclaim the asthma explanation for Timberlake's death ridiculous and Margaret's grief insufficient. Timberlake had committed suicide, the story spread, because, in a drunken and depressed stupor, he could no longer face his wife's infidelity with John Henry Eaton.

It was all very shocking, especially so to Andrew Jackson. He was in the middle of a presidential campaign in which his wife was being accused of bigamy and adultery; and now the young Margaret, his favorite O'Neale from the family that he so revered, faced similar charges of sexual impropriety. When his maligned wife, Rachel, died in late 1828 from what he considered a broken heart because of the vicious accusations against her, his feelings for Margaret Timberlake only increased. The other accused party in the gossip, John Henry Eaton, was his close adviser and friend, so Jackson felt that much more resolute in support. How could the woman who played religious music on a piano for her mother and the guests at the O'Neale boarding house be guilty of such grievous wrongs? How could a man of integrity like Eaton be the lover of a married woman and the cause of a shocked husband's suicide? The answer was simple. Jackson concluded that, like his wife, the young widow was the focus of unfair assaults, obviously hurled at her for ulterior motives. Margaret O'Neale Timberlake was a wronged woman and Andrew Jackson's friend; she deserved his support, and she would receive it. But the whole issue could not have come up at a more inappropriate time: Jackson was mourning his own loss and preparing to come to Washington to become president of the United States. Even for this man of stubborn strength, the demands he placed on himself to govern, grieve, and defend were incredibly difficult.

Margaret Timberlake was a new widow, the mother of two young children, and the daughter of a financially troubled father. Fortunately, she had John Eaton by her side, and his continued presence comforted her. Andrew Jackson, John Henry Eaton, and Margaret O'Neale Timberlake found themselves in 1828 in a triangle of despair—all the result of sudden death and unforgiving gossip. Jackson had to overcome the loss of his beloved wife so he could govern the nation; Mrs. Timberlake had to begin a new life without her husband. The president, his trusted friend, and the innkeeper's daughter were thrown together in sadness and in the complicated etiquette of Washington society. Their lives would never be the same again.

3

"There Are Great Objections
Made to His Wife"

That midwinter of 1828–1829 was the most difficult time in Andrew Jackson's hard life. The death of his beloved wife, Rachel, was a loss beyond his comprehension. "My heart is nearly broke," he grieved to a friend as he battled depression at his Tennessee home. "I try to summon up my usual fortitude but it is in vain." His spirits sank to the depths, and rumors began to spread that he looked near death, and finally that he had died. He still lived, of course, but he wondered how he would ever be able to face his duties as the soon-to-be-inaugurated president of the United States. Deep in his heart, he must have tried to keep down the guilt feelings he no doubt felt over his political ambitions, which had provided the occasion for the attacks on Rachel and which, he was convinced, had killed her. She frequently had made clear her wishes that he stop all such activity and settle down with her at the Hermitage. Now he wished he had listened to her.[1]

In his grief for Rachel, his thoughts must also have turned to his favorite young woman, Margaret O'Neale Timberlake. Like Jackson, she had recently lost her spouse, but her grief was not as deep or as enduring as his. She had not seen her seafaring husband for several years, and thus she had already become accustomed to life without him. She had her father, mother, and family; she remained busy at the small boardinghouse her mother still maintained; and she had John Henry Eaton. His solicitude had helped her get over her loss and brought them ever closer together. During the fall of 1828, Jackson and Eaton had spent extended periods of time at the Hermitage in Tennessee discussing the young widow back in Washington, and letters continued to pass between them when Eaton returned to Washington. Jackson's friend was in love with the controversial Mrs. Timberlake, and he wanted the president-elect's advice about the propriety of asking her to marry him. He worried how Jackson would respond in light of his painful grief over the attacks on his Rachel for alleged nuptial improprieties. Eaton told Jackson of his love for the widow and his desire, "at a proper time," to "tender to her the offer to share my life and prospects with her." To Eaton's relief, Jackson quickly supported the proposal, his encouragement providing additional determination to the love-struck Major Eaton to marry the Widow Timberlake.

Reenforced with Jackson's support, John proposed to Margaret in December 1828 and happily received her willingness to make a final decision after the adjournment of Congress the following March. When a letter from Andrew Jackson arrived at the O'Neale boardinghouse "suggesting the propriety of acting forthwith or changing my residence," John immediately decided to set an earlier date. Margaret was not sure she wanted to get married this quickly, concerned that twelve months had not passed since Timberlake's death. Eaton pressed his case. He did not want to allow "the whispers of those city gossipers, who attend to every body's reputation[,] character[,] & business to the neglect of their own" to determine their marriage plans. Besides, he continued, Timberlake had been away for four years, and his death at sea far from home only made that fact more obvious. Margaret listened closely and needed little persuasion. The couple made plans to marry on January 1, 1829, unhappy only that a distant Jackson would be unable to witness the ceremony.[2]

To think of marrying so quickly after the death of a husband violated one of the most serious proscriptions of genteel American society. A widow of gentility was to alter her life significantly for one to two years after her husband's death to indicate proper respect and acceptable grieving for him. She had to wear prescribed black, then white clothing, and she had to behave in an appropriate manner. During the first month, no grieving widow was to leave her house except to go to church or take care of essential business. She was certainly not to partake in any social events, especially festive events like weddings. She was not even to sew during this first month because being able to concentrate on such activity meant she was not sufficiently upset over the loss of her spouse. Society demanded a public expression of sorrow, and if a woman did not grieve according to the established rules, it revealed for all to see her lack of gentility and character. Margaret Eaton's plan to marry less than a year after her husband's death, therefore, defied convention and revealed once again her commonality, her lack of refinement.[3]

Tennessee politicians immediately saw the political danger in Eaton's nuptials. They caucused on the matter, and Congressman Robert Desha and Senator Hugh White discussed it again later. Someone, Desha insisted, had to dissuade Eaton from making this politically disastrous mistake. White refused to do it, citing his certitude that whoever talked to Eaton this way would gain an enemy for life. Desha decided to approach Eaton anyway, pulling him off the Senate floor one day to discuss the matter. He pointed out all the rumors about Margaret and hinted at Jackson's displeasure. Eaton would not listen. He knew Jackson approved of the forthcoming marriage. Secure in Jackson's blessing, Eaton refused to budge. But he had to worry about his future with the controversial Margaret Timberlake, complicated by his marrying her so soon after her first husband's death.[4]

The next several weeks must have been hectic at the O'Neale house as the family prepared for the remarriage of their widowed daughter to longtime boardinghouse resident and friend John Eaton. Margaret's two daughters must have been especially excited to think that their new stepfather would be the person they knew so well. In the excitement, no one seemed worried about violating the grieving ritual. The wedding took place on the evening of New Year's Day, 1829, in the living room of the O'Neale home. Methodist Minister William Ryland, longtime chaplain of the Senate and House, officiated at the candle-lit ceremony. The bride looked radiant, but then she always did. Now thirty years old and several times a mother, she had not lost her stunning attractiveness: "a well rounded, voluptuous figure, peach-pink complexion, . . . large, active dark eyes, . . . [and] full sensuous lips ready to break into an engaging smile." The groom was thirty-nine years old and "in the prime of life," a slender man of medium height with a pointed nose and face. Contemporaries called him "a handsome, graceful man," the famous newswoman Anne Royall finding "his figure noble and commanding."[5]

A large crowd of friends and neighbors attended the wedding, both the high and the lowly, but no accurate description or count has survived. Among those present, however, was John M. Berrien of Georgia, soon to become a member of Jackson's administration. The major Washington newspaper of that day, as was the custom, announced only the names of the bride and groom but gave no further details. A New York newspaper described the event as "a great show of fashion at Georgetown, and a western frolic," and then facetiously added: "What the peculiarities of a western frolic are, other than an exuberance of good cheer and warm feeling, we do not know." Still, the reporter believed, "General Jackson's Boswell is entitled to enjoy himself, now that his hero has been elevated. May his union be auspicious."[6]

Unfortunately, not everyone in the nation's capital proved as generous as this distant newspaper. Eaton and Jackson had hoped that this wedding would end the whisperings about their beloved Margaret, but it only caused the gossip to increase and become more vicious. Leading anti-Jackson newspaperman Charles Hammond of Cincinnati wrote, "J. H. Eaton has made an honest woman of his mistress," and Louis McLane, later a member of Jackson's second cabinet, said that Eaton had "just married his mistress—& the mistress of 11-doz. others!!"[7]

Margaret Bayard Smith, the Philadelphia-born daughter of a member of the Continental Congress and the wife of Samuel Harrison Smith, the founder of the *Washington National Intelligencer* and the president of the Washington branch of the Bank of the United States, reflected the city's disgust at the news of the nuptials. A leader of Washington society, Mrs. Smith bluntly called Margaret "a lady whose reputation, her previous connection with him [Eaton] both before and after her husband's death, has totally destroyed." Besides, based on her youthful indiscretions, "she has never been admitted to society," Mrs Smith sniffed. Yet unaware of Rachel Jackson's recent death in Tennessee, she concluded: "The General's personal and political friends are very much disturbed about it; his enemies laugh and divert themselves with the idea of what a suitable lady in waiting Mrs. Eaton will make to Mrs. Jackson and repeat the old adage, 'birds of a feather will flock together'."[8]

Several congressmen exceeded Mrs. Smith in tastelessness. New York congressman Churchill C. Cambreleng reported to his friend Martin Van Buren, the newly elected governor of New York: "Poor Eaton is to be married tonight—to Mrs T! There is a vulgar saying of some vulgar man, I believe Swift, on such unions—about using a certain household—and then putting it on one's head." A Virginia congressman facetiously complimented Eaton for marrying "a lady with whom it is said he has been on very familiar terms for several years past. She was the wife of a purser in the Navy, whose duties called him to foreign ports," the politician continued, "but the lady, notwithstanding her lonely condition, increased & multiplied surprisingly. She had several children, & though Major Eaton boarded in the house all the while, it would be great scandal to say that anything improper passed between them." But, of course, that was precisely what Washington was saying. Even Henry Clay, secretary of state in the outgoing John Quincy Adams administration, helped spread the gossip. Prince Hal, as Clay was known, derogatorily discussed the new Mrs. Eaton at a party that took place soon after the wedding.[9]

Rumor had it that Eaton was going to be Jackson's attorney general and that his wife would be "mistress of ceremony to Mrs. President Jackson." It particularly galled people that Margaret dared to think that the society women, who had been refusing to accept her "for all they hold their noses so high now, will be ready enough to wait upon her" once Jackson became president and she and her husband became part of his administration. "They tell pretty much the same story about her as they did about poor Mrs. Jackson," a woman wrote her husband after calling on the Jackson family. Rachel and Margaret became linked together in the public mind—because of sexual transgressions. Andrew Jackson had never allowed his wife's name to be slandered without fighting back, and he had always been a protector of all unfairly wronged womanhood. Since he, too, linked Rachel and Margaret, her accusers had to face a powerful enemy.[10]

Whether Margaret gave such attacks any credence or even heard them is unknown, but if she did, she did not allow them to spoil her honeymoon. Her adoring husband placed "a great basket of silver" next to their bed the day after the wedding, and later that morning the two happily departed on a honeymoon trip. Their coach broke down near Wilmington, Delaware, and when other passengers discovered she was a bride, she became the center of concerned attention. On board a ship during the next leg of the journey, Margaret overheard two women discussing "the brilliant wedding in Washington," the "handsome" and "rich" groom, and the "beauty" of the bride. "She was a widow with two children," one remarked. "Now why can't we two girls make such a match as that?" Fearing that one of the women might ruin the mood by saying something negative, Margaret quickly introduced herself to the two speakers, and one of the women became so excited that she came near fainting.[11]

In Philadelphia, the Eatons stayed at the Heiskell Hotel for several weeks. They were wined and dined, society being friendly there, according to the *United States Telegraph,* "much pleased with her intelligence and affability." Margaret, however, almost ruined it all through an act of unthinking impetuosity. The hostess at an elegant dinner party used snuff, as many women did during those days, and she offered Margaret a pinch. John tried to indicate unobtrusively to his bride that she should not sample any of this concoction; but Margaret, in what she later described as "an evil movement, [when] my feelings of politeness got the better of my judgment," placed a generous pinch of tobacco in her nostril. Then she suffered the agony of deciding whether she should expel it into her beautiful bridal handkerchief or the fancy table napkin. "I can never tell how much I suffered in disposing of that snuff; nor do I think anybody will discover what became of it."[12]

From Philadelphia, the couple traveled to the City Hotel in New York, then to Niagara Falls, and finally back to Washington. Other than a brief illness on Margaret's part in New York, the tour was a great success. Everywhere the couple went, they were received graciously. Either society people outside Washington had not heard the rumors about her or they did not care. John Eaton's position as confidante of the new president may have overcome any scruples. Whatever the reason, Margaret Eaton returned to Washington happy at her reception as the wife of the senator from Tennessee. Perhaps, she thought, Washington women would indeed come around, too. Most probably, she gave it little thought in the euphoria over her wedding and honeymoon.[13]

While the Eatons traveled in joyous celebration of the marriage he had encouraged, Andrew Jackson journeyed toward Washington for his March inauguration, still weighed down with grief over the end of his own marriage. He did not travel alone when he left Nashville in mid-January; a large group of relatives and friends accompanied him. John Overton was particularly welcome because he had known Rachel as long as Jackson and was his closest friend. The party also included Andrew Jackson, Jr., the new president's nineteen-year-old adopted son, and his devoted nephew and niece, Andrew Jackson and Emily Donelson, she to become presidential hostess. Trusted political confidante Major William B. Lewis and his wife and a number of other ladies and gentlemen completed the entourage.[14]

All along the way, average people struggled to get a glimpse of their new president, the man they identified with, the symbol of everything they believed was good and right about the nation. In his mourning for his wife, Jackson discouraged any shows of public exuberance, but there were still rifle companies, cannon firings, and huzzas all along the way. In Cincinnati, two steamboats escorted Jackson's boat into port, as cannon roared and people lining the shore shouted their approval. Little by little, Jackson seemed to force himself out of the gloom that had overwhelmed him. Perhaps the most touching, yet humorous, encounter occurred on an Ohio River boat going to Pittsburgh. A begrimed working man approached the president-elect, clearly worried about the rumors he had heard of Jackson's death. "General Jackson, I guess. . . . Why they told me you was dead," the man said. The president-elect replied: "No. Providence has hitherto preserved my life." "And is your wife alive too?" the man continued. Jackson slumped back at the mention of Rachel's name, no doubt suppressing a smile at what he heard next from his questioner. "Aye, I thought it was one or t'other of ye."[15]

The trip from Nashville to Washington was long and slow, and the presidential party did not reach the outskirts of the capital until February 11, 1829. Knowing that Jackson did not want to undergo the formal welcome local dignitaries had planned, John Henry Eaton sent a coach to meet the entourage and bring Jackson quietly into the capital. A young army officer watched what he called the "highly remarkable" entry into the city, one "possessing . . . a great degree of moral sublimity," so unlike "the entrance of European potentates into their capitols to take possession of their thrones. . . . There passed my window about half past 10 o'clock," he wrote his sister, "a plain carriage drawn by two horses followed by a single black servant, & preceded by perhaps 10 horsemen who had perhaps joined it by accident on the road." To the disgust of Washington society and the opposition press, however, Jackson refused to call on outgoing president John Quincy Adams, blaming him for the attacks on Rachel during the 1828 campaign. This newcomer was a frontier ruffian, the word spread. He did not possess the manners that a president should have.[16]

With less than a month to go before his inauguration, Jackson became very busy as all manner of office seekers accosted him in the National Hotel suite where he was staying. The people who looked to Jackson as their hero also looked to him for reward, perhaps a clerkship in a government office or a position in some backwoods post office. Every day hundreds of men descended on his suite, thrusting their résumés into his hands and expecting quick resolution to their demands for patronage. There were, Senator Daniel Webster cynically pointed out, "'a great multitude' [of office seekers], too many to be fed without a miracle." At the same time, incumbent government workers were "quaking with fear," as more and more deserving Jacksonians made ready to take their jobs in the new administration's openly proclaimed rotation system.[17] Jackson struggled with this onslaught, trying to find time to give necessary attention to the preparation of his inaugural address and the choice of his cabinet. No doubt, the happiest of these hectic days occurred when he first saw the newlyweds and reiterated to John and Margaret Eaton his blessing of their union.

Unfortunately, not everyone was this happy to see the Eatons. Jackson's vice president and his wife, John C. and Floride Calhoun, felt particularly confused over what to do about the controversial woman. Not only had she violated the grieving ritual, but she also seemed to threaten proper womanhood on a variety of other fronts. A woman's place was in the home. That was her "sphere," as society termed it, where she safeguarded societal morality while her husband and other males struggled in the harsh world of business, commerce, and government. She was to exemplify submissiveness, piety, purity, and domesticity, that is, she was to be the repository of goodness, thereby ensuring the survival of a moral society despite the male onslaughts against it. She was to remain physically within the home, although her influence extended far beyond its four walls. She provided moral guidance to her husband and other males; she ruled in the area of morality while he dominated business and politics. Her job was to stay out of the world, but at the same time ensure that this world remained properly moral in the face of all the assaults against it.

In order to know how to behave properly in her role as moral arbiter, a woman had to follow explicit rules. In response to this need for guidance, publishers in England and the United States printed advice and etiquette manuals providing women (and men, too) with direction in proper behavior. Violating societal mores was a cardinal sin and labeled a person as lacking in gentility. For example, a woman simply did not visit another woman without following a set procedure. In the United States of the mid-nineteenth century, in this land of uncertain democracy, there was a regularized ritual about who should be visited first, how the visit was to be returned, and so forth. Women had calling cards, and when they visited, whether or not the other woman was at home, they left one of their cards to demonstrate the fulfillment of their social obligation. To visit someone was a serious matter; it indicated acceptance of that individual into the genteel society of that community. Not to visit someone or not to return a visit was indication of improper manners or a statement that the person involved was not an acceptable member of society.[18]

Soon after their marriage, the Eatons paid an official call on John and Floride Calhoun, Washington's protocol requiring senators and their families to call on the vice president and his family first. Calhoun had been vice president under John Quincy Adams, and he was to continue with Andrew Jackson, having switched allegiance in the meantime. When the Eatons arrived, Calhoun was absent, but Floride received them politely. Even though she had not been in Washington since 1826, she must have known all about her visitor, if for no other reason than through her friendship with Margaret Bayard Smith. Mrs.

Calhoun was in Washington only for the inauguration, prepared to re-turn home immediately to her children, who had been left behind there, and to deliver another baby that August.

Thirty-seven-year-old Floride Calhoun was a small woman of Charlestonian aristocratic background with dark hair and eyes, no longer the striking individual she had once been, but still attractive. She was pleasant to the Eatons, no doubt carefully evaluating this well-discussed woman sitting in her parlor. John and Margaret stayed only briefly and departed to mutual well wishes. They had made their point. Margaret Eaton was fulfilling the obligations of society like any other genteel member.

Soon after the Eatons had departed, Calhoun came home to news of the visit. Husband and wife discussed Margaret and her place in Washington society in general terms and then moved on to other top-ics. The next morning, Floride made an important decision. She would not return Margaret's visit. She told her husband that "she con-sidered herself in the light of a stranger in the place; that she knew nothing of Mrs. Eaton, or the truth, or falsehood of the imputation on her character; and that she conceived it to be the duty of Mrs. Eaton, if innocent, to open her intercourse with the ladies who resided in the place, and who had the best means of forming a correct opinion of her conduct, and not with those, who, like herself, had no means of form-ing a correct judgment." Calhoun listened and "approved of her deci-sion," though he worried what political problems it might cause him with Eaton and the president. Floride Calhoun, the highest ranking woman related to the Jackson administration, had decided to snub Margaret Eaton. She saw it as a matter of honor and etiquette; and, be-sides, she would soon be returning to South Carolina and had no plans to spend much time in the capital city anyway. Let others worry about the matter; she certainly would not indicate her acceptance of Mar-garet Eaton, in the meantime.[19]

Other Washington women reacted equally negatively. The story circulated around the city that Margaret had left her cards at the homes of several leading society lights and, when ignored, demanded the return of the cards, "they having been left there by mistake." At a "very brilliant party" at the home of Sir Charles Vaughan, the British minister to the United States, Margaret served as the center of marked curiosity among "all the distinguished belles of the city," but was otherwise left to herself. The wife of a member of the opposition party gossiped about the whole matter but wanted her words kept silent— because they "might cause my husband a duel."[20]

Margaret always said that numerous society women left their cards in her basket while she was on her honeymoon, and particularly insisted that Floride Calhoun was one of these. As proof, she insisted that her sister's black maid, who had served Mrs. Calhoun previously, had rushed out to greet the visitor when she spied her carriage. It was at that time, Margaret said, that Floride left her card, telling the servant to be sure to present it to Mrs. Eaton. Similarly, William O'Neale was so excited about the vice president's wife calling on his daughter that Rhoda had to rebuke him for excessive pride.[21] The point was that if Floride Calhoun had visited her, Margaret Eaton was an accepted part of society, Mrs. Calhoun's present insistence to the contrary notwithstanding.

William O'Neale's pride in his daughter was soon deflated. While riding a stage from Washington to Baltimore, he heard other passengers discussing the recent Eaton marriage. In the process, they insisted that Margaret and John Eaton had been "intimate" before their marriage. O'Neale grew increasingly upset as a debate developed over his daughter's purity. He felt a bit better when one of his fellow travelers said that common sense proved that a man of Eaton's stature would never have married "a widow with two children if that woman had ever allowed him to take improper liberties with her person." Someone else disagreed, however, and the debate grew hot. O'Neale suffered in silence, afraid to speak up.[22]

Margaret Eaton had clearly become an openly controversial woman, the butt of gossip and condemnation. Some of the attacks against her were obvious: she had allegedly violated the central premise of true womanhood; she was impure. She had allowed men to take sexual liberties with her, before and after her marriage, the story went, and then her husband committed suicide out of shame at her brazen liaison with John Henry Eaton. She had been in such a hurry to marry Eaton that she did not even honor the normal mourning period as any decent woman should. Then she dared think society would ignore all these transgressions and admit her into its circle. How pretentious.

Consider, too, who she was: the daughter of an Irish boardinghouse keeper, at a time when to be an Irish servant girl meant being considered "unsettled, reckless, slovenly, dishonest, [and] intemperate."[23] Margaret Eaton was hardly a servant girl and she was Scots-Irish, not pure Irish in heritage. But she and her family had long waited on the politicians who stayed at their boardinghouse. It was easy, therefore, to equate her with the poor women who waited on and cleaned the houses of the genteel middle class. To imagine an uncultured servant girl as a lady was too difficult a task for Washington society.

Margaret also was a vivacious beauty who radiated sexuality in a manner that was deemed highly improper. The mark of feminine beauty and style during these years was to be "frail, pale, and willowy," just the opposite of how contemporaries described Margaret. A well-known newspaper reporter talked of "her dark hair, very abundant, clustered in curls about her broad, expressive forehead, ... finely curved mouth, with a firm round chin." She was "a profile of faultless outlines."[24] She was distractingly attractive, disturbingly so. Her very being seemed to be a threat to purity, to the very moral order that a woman was supposed to ensure.

Her public behavior only intensified that threat. She had served men in a boardinghouse and a tavern, and she seemed to enjoy that relationship too much. She did not know her place; she forthrightly spoke up about anything that came to her mind, even topics of which women were supposed to be ignorant. She thrust herself into the world in a manner inappropriate for a woman. She stood out, instead of remaining coyly in the background as a proper woman should. How was it possible for her to instruct males in proper virtue and morality, if she debated with them about politics and business and laughed and joked so uproariously?

This Margaret Eaton was clearly a shocking person. She seemed to be all that a genteel woman should not be. Yet she visited other proper women, individuals who knew their place and their tasks in society, and she expected them to welcome her as one of their own. That was simply impossible. Accept her, and society was in danger of disruption. Accept this uncouth, impure, forward, worldly woman, and the wall of virtue and morality would be breached and society would have no further defenses against the forces of frightening change. Margaret

Eaton was not that important in herself; it was what she represented that constituted the threat. Proper women had no choice; they had to prevent her acceptance into society as part of their defense of that society's morality.

Jackson seemed unaware of a rising tide of opposition to Margaret Eaton and, by extension, to her husband. The most important of his activities was the selection of his cabinet, the public speculation about its makeup growing intense. "He will have to appoint some of his friends and most probably convert them into enemies," one observer wryly noted. Jackson listened to anyone who had any advice to offer; but, as Virginia political leader William C. Rives correctly analyzed it, "I think the old General is determined to be his own master." At one point he allegedly even told a friend that he would appoint no cabinet at all, because as a general, he had never had a council of war. Such gossip was usual around Washington, so few people gave it much attention, and there remained enormous interest in whom Jackson would choose for his administration. South Carolina politicians became especially worried about not having sufficient influence in the process, and thus not being able to protect their state and region against the high protective tariff of 1828 that they had so opposed. Five of them paid Jackson a visit in mid-February to suggest cabinet appointments that, they said, would be satisfactory to the South. In an attempt to build further support, South Carolina Senator Robert Y. Hayne even sent the same list to Martin Van Buren, promising that the state would not be *"selfish."*[25]

Jackson listened carefully to the delegation and made it clear he would make his own choices. Since Vice President John C. Calhoun was a South Carolinian, Jackson's refusal to take advice from the Palmetto State was jarring. It began to appear to more than one politician that the choice of these cabinet members was becoming intertwined with the question of who would run for the presidency in 1832. Jackson had not even been inaugurated, and his supporters were already planning for the presidential election four years hence.[26]

Many observers also worried about Jackson's capacity to conduct affairs of state. Opponents saw him as "bigoted, arrogant, ambitious, irresponsible," a person who "needed the help of able men, experienced men, statesmen, who would steer him and restrain him."

Daniel Webster, one of the nation's leading senators, held this opinion: "Genl. J. has not character enough to conduct his measures by
his own strength. Somebody must and will lead him." Margaret Bayard Smith worried about the new administration's direction because
of Rachel's death, "a wife who could control the violence of his temper, soothe the exacerbations of feelings always keenly sensitive and
excessively irritable." She worried about "this restraining and benign
influence being withdrawn."[27]

Jackson displayed no such hesitation. He quickly decided on whom
he wanted to be his secretary of state, the first position in any presidential cabinet and very often in the past the road to the Executive
Mansion. He asked Martin Van Buren to take this post. Long a power
in New York politics as head of the so-called Albany Regency, Van
Buren had held various offices at the state level and, in 1821, he had
been elected to the United States Senate. A man of great political
shrewdness and social skills, he was a wizard to his friends and an unprincipled trickster to his political enemies. In 1824, he had supported
William H. Crawford for the presidency, but by 1828, he was firmly in
the Jackson camp—in fact, a leader in the formation of the Jacksonian
coalition. Recently elected governor of New York, he was still clearly
open to a cabinet offer from Jackson. The two men had first met in
1823 in the Senate where they had served together. Jackson had heard
about Van Buren's reputation for waffling, and he listened carefully
during the New Yorker's speech on a major issue. Van Buren made
such a strong statement that Jackson turned to his fellow senator John
Henry Eaton and asked, "Is there anything non-committal about
that?" No, Eaton agreed. This Van Buren was a man of substance,
Jackson thought.[28]

Jackson must also have noticed Van Buren's striking appearance.
Forty-seven years old, short and stocky with a light complexion, he
dressed to best advantage. During a campaign tour for Jackson in 1828,
for example, he arrived at the wealthiest church in a small New York
community and made an immediate impact. "On this occasion," an
observer noted with awe, "he wore an elegant snuff-colored broadcloth,
with velvet collar; his cravat was orange with modest lace tips; his vest
was of pearl hue; his trousers were white duck; his silk hose corresponded to the vest; his shoes were morocco; his nicely fitting gloves

were yellow kid; his long-furred beaver hat, with broad brim, was of Quaker color." Admirers were impressed with his appearance, but his opponents considered him a dandy. Davy Crockett said he "struts and swaggers like a crow in a gutter. He is laced up in corsets, such as women in a town wear, and, if possible, tighter than the best of them." A widower, he was especially appealing to women of all ages because of his manners and suave ability to charm. He liked women for them- selves, and "he did not curry favor for some ulterior motive."[29]

Van Buren did not wait long to respond to Jackson's invitation to join his cabinet. He readily accepted the offer, but he hoped Jackson would give him some time to take care of assorted gubernatorial duties before he tendered his resignation. Because of a delay in the mail reaching Washington, Jackson worried that Van Buren was hesitating, especially since a number of leading figures in the national party (ap- parently Calhoun supporters) were planning to recommend that he not accept. Van Buren's good friend James A. Hamilton, Alexander Hamilton's son, nervously wrote Van Buren twice in two days urging him to accept immediately. The arrival of Van Buren's acceptance made the general happy, and Van Buren was no doubt pleased that the mail delay had caused his stock to rise with the president-elect.[30]

Van Buren's acceptance was a major accomplishment for Jackson, though it left supporters of Vice President John C. Calhoun unhappy. They worried about Van Buren's favored position close to the presi- dent. Their opposition, however, was muted. They, like others, turned to the other cabinet offices that Jackson had to fill. Jackson considered geographical distribution, but he seemed less concerned with that or anything else than with his own desires and wishes. There seemed to be little rhyme or reason to Jackson's cabinet choices beyond his per- sonal preferences. He certainly did not consider any possible successor in making his choices.

For the Treasury Department, Jackson looked to reward Pennsylva- nia for its firm support. At first he settled on Henry Baldwin, a leader of the party there. Unfortunately, Baldwin headed the anti-Calhoun faction in the state, and the Pennsylvania pro-Calhoun party protested so vociferously that Jackson turned instead to Samuel Ingham. Already a successful paper manufacturer in Bucks County when he entered politics, Ingham was not among the top rank of politicians in the state,

Henry Clay considering him a "knave and fool." An individual "of medium height, with broad shoulders, . . . small light blue [eyes] . . . "grave and dignified [personality] . . . [but] warm-hearted and devoted to his friends," Ingham was only fifty years of age. His health was so bad, however, that, in 1828, his friends thought he was on the verge of death. When he accepted Jackson's offer of the Treasury secretaryship, he was still ill; in fact severe head pain caused him regularly to miss two or three days of work weekly well into the summer of 1829.[31]

Jackson offered the post of attorney general to John MacPherson Berrien of Georgia. Born in New Jersey of distinguished Revolutionary War stock, Berrien had come to Georgia at the age of two. He had studied the law in Savannah and from 1810 to 1821 served as a federal judge on the eastern circuit. After one term in the state senate, he came to Washington as a United States senator in 1824. A staunch supporter of Indian removal, he had battled John Quincy Adams on this and other issues, his anti-Indian and anti-Adams positions giving him appeal in Jackson's eyes. Like Ingham, however, he was not one of his state's leading political figures.

A widower of forty-eight years of age when he entered the cabinet, Berrien had a much more youthful appearance: "exceedingly compact in his frame, agile in all his movements, of a fresh and healthy complexion, neat and even elegant in his attire." His personality, however, was hardly appealing. "His cold, formal manner," a biographer has noted, "rendered effective communication with most people difficult, and he seldom attempted to unbend."[32]

For secretary of the navy, Jackson chose John Branch of North Carolina. A native of that state and holder of many political offices including governor, the forty-seven-year-old planter had a well-deserved reputation for the lavish entertainments he held both at his home in North Carolina and in Washington when he became a United States senator in the 1820s. A tall individual of "dark complexion" and "oval face," he was "very grey for his years." He exuded the "urbanity common to the southern gentleman," a feature which he demonstrated frequently in the social whirl where he excelled. In October 1830, his daughter entered the Jackson family when she married Daniel Donelson, the brother of Andrew Jackson Donelson. Branch was a longtime Jacksonian, and since Jackson refused to reward South Carolina with a cabinet post, he chose a supporter from North Carolina, "a plain un-ambitious state, which has thrust forward no claims to high offices although in merit she is not inferior to her more showy neighbors," that is, Virginia and South Carolina.[33]

For the office of postmaster general, Jackson reappointed the incumbent, John McLean, the man who had obtained that post from James Monroe and remained on John Quincy Adams's reappointment. Famed for his excellent administration of a difficult institution, he had also worked against the reelection of John Quincy Adams. These facts and his reputation for firing incompetent and corrupt postmasters caused Jackson to consider him an excellent choice for the job.

At this same time, a seat on the United States Supreme Court became vacant, and Jackson thought to appoint William Barry, but McLean let it be known that he would prefer that office to remaining in the post office. In the sort of switch that sounds impossible to modern ears, Jackson gave the court seat to McLean and made Barry, his original court choice, postmaster general.

Forty-four years of age, William T. Barry was a native of Virginia, but as a young man he had moved to Kentucky for the better life that the frontier promised. He became a lawyer and was elected to the state house of representatives at the age of twenty-one. After serving several terms, he spent a brief time in Washington as a U.S. senator (at which time he lived at O'Neale's boardinghouse) and four years as lieutenant governor, eventually becoming a leader of the so-called relief party, later known as the "New Court" party. This political faction tried to aid average Kentuckians caught in the grip of bank failures and consequent financial ruin during the Panic of 1819. An early supporter of Henry Clay, he switched to Jackson during the 1828 presidential election and carried the state for Old Hickory, though he himself narrowly lost the governorship. As a reward for these activities, Jackson planned to give him a Supreme Court seat, but then the switch with McLean took place, and Barry became postmaster general.[34]

The only other cabinet spot was that of secretary of war. Here, even more than in his selection of the other officers, Jackson thought only in terms of his personal desires. "Left as he was alone in the world," Jackson told a friend, "he desired to have near him a personal and confidential friend to whom he could unbosom himself on all subjects."

He knew, from the start, therefore, that his secretary of war would be either Hugh Lawson White or John Henry Eaton. Both men were already in Washington and along with Major William B. Lewis, Jackson's old army quartermaster and close adviser, were helping Jackson with his cabinet choices. There was, therefore, scant discussion within Jackson's inner circle about the War Department. Later on, a dispute developed over what actually happened, but the fact seems clear that Jackson was unwilling to make a choice between his two close friends and left the decision up to them.[35]

Both men wanted the post, but Eaton outmaneuvered White to get it. He wrote White that, sometime previously, Jackson had written him indicating his desire that one of them be secretary of war. More recently, Eaton continued, Jackson had "remarked that he had a full and free conversation with you; and at the close remarked that he desired to have me with him. I presumed, without inquiring, that he had probably talked with you on the subject, and that you had declined accepting any situation, as you before had told me would be your feelings." Of course, Eaton continued, he would not stand in White's way, but if White did not want to be secretary of war, Eaton would gladly take it. Under the strict gentlemanly code of those years, White could do nothing but accede to Eaton's wishes. The thirty-nine-year-old Tennessean, still celebrating his recent marriage to the beautiful Washington widow, now became, by Andrew Jackson's own definition of the situation, the most influential member of the cabinet. Hugh White said nothing, but this appointment marked the beginning of his later split with Jackson.[36]

Throughout the month of February, all this decision making allegedly took place in secret, but information on Jackson's choices filtered out. The rumors proved accurate. At first, there was frustration that Jackson was conducting all this business "perpetually surrounded [only] with a *coterie* of his personal friends, Genl. Eaton &c. . . . The efficient political heads of his party—the men of some pride and character get no access to him," leading anti-Jackson politician Edward Everett reported with feigned criticism. "The Virginians & South Carolinians are already disgusted," clearly because no one from either state was among those rumored to be tapped for office. Daniel Webster, like Everett an anti-Jacksonian, was even blunter. "A prodigious excitement has been produced by the new Cabinet List. It has set all Washington in a *buz*—friends rage, & *foes laugh*."[37]

Some Jacksonians were indeed upset. Maryland political leader Louis McLane was surprised that Jackson had not consulted more people. "I do not believe it [the cabinet] will be acceptable anywhere . . . it can make no appeal to the moral intelligence of the country." It just made no sense to him, and his subsequent conclusion indicated the beginning of a problem. Jackson could not possibly be responsible for this debacle, McLane said; Vice President John C. Calhoun had to be the villain. A friend of Martin Van Buren agreed. Calhoun "produced this" mess to hurt Van Buren, sabotage Jackson's administration, or control the cabinet himself. A Calhoun-Van Buren split was already evident even before the administration took office. At this point, however, anger was less the predominant emotion than was disappointment. South Carolinian James Hamilton, Jr., expressed the feelings of many Jacksonians: "I am perfectly cool—damn cool— never half so cool in my Life." It was bad enough that the cabinet was unrepresentative and lacking in talent, but it also exacerbated intraparty stress and included the husband of a woman with a bad reputation. It was weak and controversial at the same time.[38]

All the speculation and uncertainty, but not the criticism, was put to rest on February 26, when the Jackson paper in Washington, the *United States Telegraph,* published the official list of nominees. "The Cabinet is not strong enough to carry on a mere *party* administration," Daniel Webster chortled. Levi Woodbury, a leading New England Jacksonian, was more circumspect but still unhappy. "On the selection it is not befitting me to speak," he said; "we must hope for the best *even if we hope against hope.*" Poet-newsman William Cullen Bryant gave way to lament: "Where are the great men whom the General was to assemble around him—the powerful minds that were to make up for his deficiencies?"[39]

Most Jacksonians accepted the *fait accompli* and lined up behind their leader. C. C. Cambreleng insisted that "the short and the long of the matter is this—the democrats were all not only satisfied but gratified with the result." Richard M. Johnson, leading Kentucky Jacksonian, characterized the cabinet as a "strong, high minded, amiable & honorable Cabinet; a business Cabinet. . . . confidence . . . in your judgment, [has] produced perfect acquiescence," he exaggeratingly told Jackson.[40]

Such was hardly the case. Even what to Jackson was his most obvious choice, the most personal one he made and the one he most wanted, proved to be extremely controversial. Merely the rumors of the appointment of John Henry Eaton as secretary of war unleashed a torrent of criticism, both from friends and opponents. "Eaton having a department outrages," Edward Everett said, and James Gallatin wrote his father, Albert, Thomas Jefferson's secretary of the treasury, "The great objection to this gentleman is his wife whom, it is said, is *not* as *she* should be." Even later Jacksonian adviser Amos Kendall spread the gossip of what Everett called "concubinage" between John and Margaret. "Eaton boarded at her father's, and scandal says they slept together," Kendall said.[41]

Margaret Eaton learned of the uproar personally. At a party, Minnie Bankhead, the wife of the secretary of the British legation and a close friend, told Margaret that rumors were spreading that John Eaton was going to be named minister to France to hide the fact that his wife was illicitly pregnant. Margaret became furious and, soon after, told Andrew Jackson that there was no way she would ever leave the country for at least the next ten months. Jackson grew angry himself at such rumor mongering, but he told her to ignore it. Rachel had suffered even worse attacks. "I tell you, Margaret," he said, "I had rather have live vermin on my back than the tongue of one of these Washington women on my reputation."[42]

Jackson learned the extent of the opposition in a similar face-to-face meeting. The day the cabinet was announced, the army paymaster, Colonel Nathan Towson, hero of War of 1812 battles on the Niagara Frontier and a leading figure in Washington social circles, paid Jackson a visit at his National Hotel suite. The parlor was crowded as always with office seekers, so Towson asked Jackson if there was anywhere they might go for a few private words. Jackson invited him into his bedroom, but Towson drew back when he saw William B. Lewis writing at a desk inside. Jackson assured Towson that Lewis was his confidante. The colonel nodded, and the two men took chairs in front of the fireplace. Lewis kept writing, he later said, but he heard the whole conversation.

Was that an accurate listing of his proposed cabinet? Towson asked the president-elect. "Yes sir," Jackson responded. "Those gentlemen will compose my cabinet." Well, Towson said, "there is one of them your friends think it would be advisable to substitute with the name of some other person." Towson, of course, meant Eaton, and Jackson knew it. "Mr. Eaton is an old personal friend of mine," Jackson replied. "He is a man of talents and experience, and one in whom his State, as well as myself, have every confidence. I cannot see, therefore, why there should be any objection to him." "There is none, I believe, personally, to *him*," Towson said, "but there are great objections made to his wife."

At this statement, Jackson no doubt stirred in his chair and took an extra deep puff on the long-stemmed pipe he habitually smoked. Having become accustomed to holding his tongue during the long campaign, he might have hoped to maintain his composure, but the more he listened, the more agitated he became. "And pray, Colonel, what will his wife have to do with the duties of the War Department?" Jackson asked. "Not much, perhaps," Towson responded from the chair opposite the increasingly agitated president-elect, "but she is a person with whom the ladies of this city do not associate. She is not, and probably never will be, received into society here, and if Mr. Eaton shall be made a member of the Cabinet, it may become a source of annoyance to both you and him."

The smoke grew thicker, and the president's words became more measured and determined, his voice rising in anger. "Colonel, do you suppose that I have been sent here by the people to consult the ladies of Washington as to the proper persons to compose my Cabinet? In the selection of its members I shall consult my own judgment, looking to the great and paramount interests of the whole country, and not to the accommodation of society and drawing rooms of this or any other city. Mr Eaton will certainly be one of my constitutional advisers." There the conversation ended, and Towson was ushered out. Jackson was disgusted. "How fallen the military character," supposed to be "the protector of Female character—to become the circulator of slander against a female upon mere rumor," he complained.[43]

If Towson had been the only person to approach Jackson about dumping Eaton, Old Hickory might have shrugged the suggestion off as the meddling of a gossipy socialite. But Jackson received other visitors, among them a delegation of supporters from Tennessee who belonged to a Jacksonian faction there in competition with Eaton. Amos Kendall called them "malcontents," but Jackson said they were "some of my Tennessee friends who were made the dupes of my designing enemy." Jackson had decided that Henry Clay, his despised opponent from the "corrupt bargain" days of the 1824 election, was behind these attacks on Eaton. "I could not, nay I would not, abandon an old and tried friend," Jackson said. "I sustained him, and I have no doubt he will become the most popular of the heads of the Departments and the War office will be well directed." No matter the opposition, Jackson was determined to stand firm. "I was born for a storm and a calm does not suit me," he said with feeling.[44]

Jackson may well have believed that this strong stand would end his problems with the Eaton appointment and that he could go into his presidency without any further controversy. He honestly believed, after all, that his cabinet was "one of the strongest . . . that ever have been in the United States." But he was wrong on all counts. Vice President John C. Calhoun opposed Eaton's inclusion in the cabinet because the latter had tried to keep Calhoun off the 1828 ticket and because, Calhoun believed, Eaton was friendly to Van Buren. Society leader Margaret Bayard Smith supported the Tennessee delegation's failed mission and insisted that public opinion would "not allow of Genl. Eaton [*sic*] holding a place which would bring *his wife* into society (for this is the difficulty). Every one acknowledges Genl. Eaton's talents and virtues—but his late unfortunate connection is an obstacle to his receiving a place of honor, which it is apprehended even Genl. Jackson's firmness cannot resist." Mrs. Smith and Letitia Porter, the wife of Buffalo congressman and outgoing secretary of war Peter B. Porter and the social leader of the outgoing Adams administration, spent a rainy afternoon soon after, sitting before a fire, happily gossiping about Jackson's cabinet: "We tore it all to pieces," Mrs. Smith reported delightedly to a friend. It was "the most unintellectual cabinet we ever had," a disgruntled politician insisted; it was "the millennium of the minnows," a newspaperman said in giving this cabinet the name it would carry forward into history.[45]

As much excitement as existed over the announcement of Jackson's cabinet and the feared entry of Margaret Eaton into society, it did not match the hubbub surrounding the inauguration ceremonies on March 4, 1829. In many ways, the swearing-in of any American president is a national renewal, a chance for democracy to begin again.

Jackson's inauguration was particularly significant because it came at a time when the nation was beginning to experience an important transformation. According to the 1830 census, it had a population of just under 13 million people, primarily rural, with but few recent immigrants. It also had candle or whale-oil lamp lighting (friction matches were yet in little use); scythe and cradle farming; home spinning, weaving, and sewing; a minuscule 6,000-man regular army; poor public schools; overwhelming white adult illiteracy; and only the glimmerings of a genuine American literature and art. The beginnings of a factory system were evident, however, and worker cooperation (unionization) quickly followed in the wake of the increasing centralized mechanization. Americans were mobile, moving ever westward, bumping into the frontier wilderness and the Native American and conquering both to expand the nation. Cities were small and few in number, but their influence was growing. The Methodists, Baptists, and Presbyterians had replaced the Anglicans and Congregationalists as the nation's major religious sects, aided by the Second Great Awakening of the late eighteenth and early nineteenth centuries.[46] A transportation revolution of better roads, canals, steamboats, and railroads would soon connect the nation in a way that allowed the development of a national and even international market economy. Goods traveled to markets far from the source of production, making even small farmers dependent on economic forces they could hardly understand. People could now travel long distances at what seemed like breakneck speed on steam-propelled boats and trains, sometimes giving up their lives to the exploding engines of progress.

Property and other requirements for voting had also been essentially eliminated for white male voters, so the electorate grew broader than ever before. The gentlemen elite running for office now had to gain the votes of the common men, had to appeal to their sensibilities and express their undying affection for their wisdom. Common beginnings seemed more important than present stature, the "log cabin" becoming the symbol of this politics.

It was exciting but also frightening. The tried and true seemed under attack, and the future was uncertain. It was not all good or all bad to most people. But it was disconcerting. The earth was shifting beneath the traditional footing of society, and no one seemed sure where it would all end. The nation would have to see how Andrew Jackson fared as president before it made up its mind about the ultimate meaning of the direction of American society. Women's role as defenders of morality became, therefore, that much more important in this time of flux. If women failed in their task of preserving societal morality, there was little hope for the future, and change would bring disaster, not progress.

The capital city where Jackson was to take his oath of office represented the unfinished, uncertain status of the nation. With a population of about 39,000 people, slaves included, the District of Columbia had experienced steady growth since its founding in the late eighteenth century. Still, it remained an unimposing place. A British visitor found the capital "very commanding and beautiful," but was "tempted even in the heart of the city, [to ask] 'Where is Washington?'" The city, he decided, was "not like one village but like several little villages thrown together with a small space between them." It was, one modern historian concluded, "generally an oversized frontier town with an 'unkempt' appearance," another scholar noting the "hospitable taverns . . . [serving] endless draughts of gin slings, gin cocktails, sherry cobblers, mint juleps, snakeroot bitters, timber doodle and eggnog." Washington was not large or impressive, but one could easily get drunk there.[47]

The capital city was not even easy to reach, so the people who traveled to Andrew Jackson's inauguration that March of 1829 had enormous difficulties getting there.[48] But they came by the thousands anyway, anxious to watch their new president, their hope for the future, take over the reins of government and hoping they might gain a job in the process. They filled all the hotels and boardinghouses, and some ended up sleeping "on the floors in taprooms, and many in less choice places." More than a few slept under the stars, the warm weather proving to be a fortunate break from the miserably cold snowy and rainy days just before. The optimism was great, though hardly universal. A minister in Washington, expressing the anxiety of

the city's genteel society about the new order, preached a sermon entitled "When Christ drew near the city he wept over it."[49]

At dawn of Inauguration Day, March 4, 1829, the boom of a thir-
teen-gun salute reverberated through the city. Pennsylvania Avenue,
the main thoroughfare, became choked with people trying to get to
the Capitol for the ceremonies on the East Portico. Meanwhile at the
National Hotel, where Jackson was staying, a large crowd waited for
the president-elect to appear. At 11 A.M., the sixty-one-year-old man,
dressed all in black out of mourning for his recently deceased wife,
stepped out of the hotel, and a troop of American Revolutionary and
Battle of New Orleans veterans escorted him as he walked to his
swearing-in. Women in "hacks, gigs, sulkies, wood-carts and Dutch
wagons" rode alongside as the small parade proceeded along Pennsylvania Avenue.

When Jackson arrived at the Capitol, he went inside to the Senate
chamber to watch the swearing-in of Vice President John C. Calhoun.
Washington's political elite was present, with the exception of outgoing president John Quincy Adams, who boycotted all the ceremonies
because of his anger over Jackson's refusal to pay him the accustomed
personal call before he took his oath of office. Andrew Jackson had ignored a cardinal rule of etiquette, and proper society shuddered at the
new president's lack of gentility.

At noon, people from the vice presidential ceremony walked together outdoors to participate in Jackson's swearing-in at the East Portico, the first such outdoor inauguration in American history. The
decision to move the ceremony outdoors proved to be a wise one. A
crowd of 12,000 to 20,000 people was on hand, described by a young
Salmon P. Chase, later Civil War secretary of the treasury and chief justice of the United States, as "prodigious numbers."[50] People pressed
against a barrier placed at the base of the stairs leading to the Portico,
straining to get as close to the ceremony as they could. The marine
band and two artillery companies stood at attention. Women filled
their assigned places on the Portico to capacity.

When Jackson appeared outside, the crowd responded with a huge
cheer, while the band played "The President's March," and the artillery units boomed out a twenty-four-gun salute. Cannon at the navy
yard and arsenal answered in response. The ladies standing on the Por-

tico waved their handkerchiefs, Floride Calhoun and the wives of the cabinet members among them. Margaret Eaton was somewhere in the sea of color. The bright dresses of the women were in happy contrast to the dark suits of the males.[51] Jackson, wearing one pair of spectacles on his eyes and another resting on top of his head, gallantly bowed toward the assemblage.

As the crowd quieted but the distant cannons continued their roar, Jackson gave his inaugural address, doing so before he took his oath of office. Martin Van Buren had hoped that Jackson would "*not find it necessary to avow any opinion upon Constitutional questions at war with the doctrines of the Jefferson School,* and underlined these words to emphasize his point. "Whatever his views may be," Van Buren wrote to South Carolina political leader James Hamilton, Jr., "there can be no necessity of doing so in an inaugural address." Obviously Van Buren was unsure just where Jackson stood on all the issues and only prayed that his evident states' rights position, what Jacksonians identified with Thomas Jefferson, would hold true. Other politicians had called themselves Jeffersonians and then showed themselves to be nationalists, Presidents Monroe and even more so John Quincy Adams being two conspicuous examples. If Jackson did this, too, Van Buren worried that the recently formed loose Jacksonian coalition would not hold.[52]

Van Buren had no reason to worry; only those close to Jackson could even hear what the president-elect was saying. The crowd tried to listen, but "not a word reached their eager ears," an observer noted. Few seemed to care, however; people were just happy to be there. When he finished his address, Jackson heard another roar of approval. James Hamilton reported to Van Buren that Jackson's speech was "excellent chaste patriotic sententious & dignified[,] it says all that is necessary to say on such an occasion and exposed no weak flanks that it may be necessary [to] defend hereafter." Andrew Jackson had thankfully not produced any surprises.[53]

Chief Justice John Marshall swore in Jackson, and the new president's response electrified the onlookers. He kissed the Bible, and, after shaking hands with the chief justice, he made a grand bow to the crowd. Once more there was an eruption of approval, and the barrier at the base of the steps leading to the Portico gave way before the press of the crowd wanting to reach the Old Hero. Hundreds rushed up to shake the new president's hand. "In his whole bearing," an observer said, "there was an exhibition of that self-reliance which the possessor derives from the inward consciousness of strength, but which, at the same time, is neither presumptuous nor distasteful."[54]

If there had been a person particularly critical of Jackson's coming to the presidency, that individual was Washington socialite Margaret Bayard Smith. Even she, however, was enormously impressed with what she saw. When Jackson kissed the Bible and bowed to the people, "Yes, to the people in all their majesty," she saw in the gesture a "majesty, rising to sublimity, and far surpassing the majesty of Kings and Princes." She described Jackson as "the Servant in presence of his Sovereign, the People. . . . It is beautiful, it is sublime!" she concluded, in agreement with attorney Francis Scott Key, in whose company she witnessed the events. In early January, the very thought of Jackson becoming president had caused her to predict: "I should cry all day long on the 4th of March." When that day came, however, she was taken in by the excitement of the occasion, but more, she was swept off her feet by the majesty of Jackson's action and bearing. She shed no tears because this supposedly uncouth western military chieftain displayed a dignified bearing worthy of his new position.[55]

The swearing-in completed, Jackson had to fight his way through the congratulatory crowd to get to his horse so he could ride to the Executive Mansion for the afternoon reception. Mounting his animal, he rode down Pennsylvania Avenue, accompanied by two members of the inauguration committee: U.S. Marshall Tench Ringgold and Army Paymaster Colonel Nathan Towson. With great exuberance, the crowd followed the trio along the street: "country men, farmers, gentlemen, mounted and dismounted, boys, women and children, black and white. Carriages, wagons and carts all pursuing him to the President's house." At least one Jackson supporter noted that "bright sunshine was resting on the president's house where he was going . . . [while] the smoke of the city was borne by southerly winds in the direction of Porter's house where Mr. Adams had taken refuge, and almost concealed it from view."[56] Perhaps in all the bedlam, Margaret

Eaton's name came up between Jackson and Towson. Now that the president had been inaugurated, she was officially a cabinet wife, and the validity of Towson's early warning would be tested.

The Executive Mansion was a scene of complete chaos. The residence and the grounds around it were alive with people. Antoine Giusta, John Quincy Adams's steward, had remained in service to Jackson and set out three long tables of food in the unfurnished East Room. He had also prepared whiskey-spiked lemonade and orange punch to help the revelers wash down the chicken, cakes, pies, breads, and ice cream. Everyone wanted to get close to the president and to share in this repast, so they pushed and shoved to get into the building. Jackson soon found himself pinned against a wall in the Oval Room, while dishes of food and drink could be heard crashing under the human pressure. Even the building's floor began to shake from the weight and movement of so many people. Several of Jackson's associates had to lock arms and become a human shield to extricate him from the clutches of his enthusiastic supporters so he could escape to his suite in the National Hotel. When Mrs. Smith arrived on the scene about 3 P.M., she was appalled at what she found: "The *Majesty of the People* had disappeared, and [there was now] a rabble, a mob, of boys, negroes [*sic*], women, children, scrambling, fighting, romping. What a pity what a pity!" she moaned.[57] The good feeling of the swearing-in was gone, and Mrs. Smith's worries about an uncouth administration had returned.

Despite Jackson's departure from the building, which many never realized, people continued to pour in. "Ladies fainted, men were seen with bloody noses and such a scene of confusion," Mrs. Smith said, was "impossible to describe." Servants threw open the windows, and Giusta put large tubs filled with punch on the lawn, hoping to lessen pressure on the building. Slowly the chaos lessened. Mrs. Smith and Washington's gentility were disgusted. "Ladies and gentlemen only had been expected at this Levee, not the people en masse," she sniffed. "But it was the People's day, and the People's president and the People would rule. . . . [But] of all tyrants," she warned, "they are the most ferocious, cruel and despotic. The noisy and disorderly rabble in the President's House," she decided, "brought to my mind descriptions I had read, of the mobs in the Tuileries and at Versailles." To Washington society, the barbarians were not merely at the gates, but they were already inside beginning their inevitable destruction. Margaret Eaton was only the most obvious of the frightening invaders. It was all very unsettling and frightening for the future of the nation. Change bore the face of barbarity and the loss of society's proper gentility.

The grand inauguration ball held at Carusi's Assembly Rooms that night was much more genteel. Twelve hundred people paid five dollars each for tickets, which were available only by invitation, the price and the screening thus eliminating everyone but proper society. Andrew Jackson did not attend out of respect for his deceased wife and, no doubt, because the afternoon experience had exhausted him. Vice President John C. Calhoun and his wife, Floride, were the honored guests. Cabinet members and those wives who were in town attended, too. According to Mrs. Smith, it was all "elegant, splendid, and in perfect order." The new administration regained some standing with the gentility. Even the *Washington National Intelligencer* concluded that, while the "Sovereign People were a little uproarious" during the White House reception, generally speaking, "the whole day and night of the Inauguration passed off without the slightest interruption of the public peace and order."[58]

But such was not really the case. During the swearing-in, the White House reception, and the grand ball, whether Andrew Jackson noticed it or not, Margaret Eaton was completely ignored—snubbed. No woman spoke to her or made any attempt to talk to her. Even at the evening supper table, everyone avoided her.[59] Washington society, aided and abetted by the Vice President's wife, the wives of cabinet and other political officials, and even Emily Donelson, soon-to-become mistress of the White House in her Aunt Rachel's place, had declared war on Margaret Eaton. They let her know in the most conspicuous way that she would be ignored, her husband's cabinet rank producing no change in society's long-standing rejection of her for her unwomanly ways. The president's closest friend in the cabinet and his favorite woman from his boardinghouse days were social pariahs even among his family and supporters. Andrew Jackson saw it all as the work of Henry Clay and his minions, but, as he was soon to see, the rejection of Margaret Eaton was primarily the work of the women of Washington's society and his own incoming administration. The snubbing of Margaret Eaton was society's determined counterattack against the frightening changes abroad in the land and in reaction to the allegedly ungentlemanly administration of the frightening military man from wilderness Tennessee.

4

"She Is as Chaste as a Virgin!"

The excitement of the inauguration quickly faded, and Washington began adjusting to the strange new administration. Congress was not scheduled to meet until December, so after the swearing-in ceremonies and after consenting to Jackson's nominees to office during a special session of the Senate, representatives and senators returned home. Even Vice President John C. Calhoun and his wife, Floride, went back to South Carolina on March 18 to remain home for Floride to have her baby and for John to read, ruminate, and run his plantation. The president and his family stayed in the capital, but Andrew Jackson remained in mourning for Rachel and tried to stay out of the public eye. Cabinet officers took over their offices, although not all their wives stayed with them. Mrs. Samuel Ingham, for example, went back to Pennsylvania, with no plans to return until the fall. Deposed officeholders in the outgoing Adams administration similarly departed, and those who stayed were "trembling for fear of losing offices." Only uncertainty and concern alleviated the dullness of the times. The permanent residents of Washington, the arbiters of society, were unsure what the future would bring and unhappy about most prospects they considered. Everyone wondered if the new administration would sweep all longtime government employees out of office.[1]

People in Washington also continued to buzz over Margaret Eaton's future. She was, after all, no longer just the daughter of a boarding-house and tavern proprietor, or simply the wife of a senator from far-away Tennessee; she was now a cabinet wife. She had attended all the festivities accompanying the inauguration; and even before that, she had made formal calls on Washington's leading citizens, leaving her card as appropriate and thus indicating her expectation of receiving a visit in return. That only a few women had reciprocated drove home the point made on Inauguration Day when Mrs. Eaton was so roundly snubbed: she could not expect her new marital status to redeem her reputation or elevate her place in Washington society. She was a loose, brazen woman, the ladies of the capital insisted, and no decent female would have anything to do with her. Rising Washington politician Amos Kendall wrestled with the issue in his correspondence with Francis Preston Blair, a Kentucky Jacksonian newsman. He defended Margaret as being guilty of no sin except being "too forward in her manners." The *New York Herald* discussed her negatively in one of its columns, but the *New York Enquirer* hastened to her rescue. Mrs. Eaton, the latter paper said, had "probably made enemies from the free manner in which she has ever advocated the election of General Jackson at all times and on all occasions. . . . There are those who cannot admire what they cannot imitate; and talent when combined with spirit and winning manners in a female cannot always escape ill-natured calumny or envious feelings."[2]

Like the New York newspaper, Andrew Jackson viewed Margaret Eaton's poor treatment as part of a political campaign to force her husband out of the cabinet and thus hurt the new administration. The president was lonely, and he struggled with depression as he worked on launching his government. Political enemies hoped to gain advantage, happily noting that "discontent pervades the Jackson ranks" over the Eatons' presence in the cabinet. Word had it that Jackson would solve the problem by sending John Eaton to an overseas diplomatic post. Margaret later remembered that Jackson had indeed told her husband that if Hugh White became secretary of war, he could have either the British or the French assignment. In fact, Jackson never had any such plans, although rumors that he had refused to die. He was determined to keep John Eaton close by, and no snubbing women or opposition politicians were going to change his mind, not when he thought of earlier attacks on his beloved Rachel. Andrew Jackson was not going to stop defending wronged women, not now that he had reached the very pinnacle of power. As if to make the point as unmistakable as possible, in late March 1829, he appointed Margaret's father, innkeeper William O'Neale, one of the five inspectors of the national penitentiary established in Washington.[3]

Although he was upset at the attacks from political opponents, these were at least anticipated, but Jackson never expected opposition from his own friends. The Reverend Ezra Stiles Ely had been a fervent supporter of Jackson; indeed, some had already said that he had been too fervent for Jackson's good. A graduate of Yale University, he served as pastor of the Third Presbyterian Church (also known as the Old Pine Street church) in Philadelphia; and from 1825 to 1836 he acted as stated clerk of the General Assembly of the Presbyterian Church of the United States and in 1828 as moderator of the same denomination. In 1813, Ely had gained national fame with the publication of the two-volume *Visits of Mercy*, the story of his chaplaincy among prostitutes in the New York City Hospital and Almshouse. In May 1827, in his role as Presbyterian stated clerk, Ely published a report on the state of religion in America, publicizing recent progress, but condemning the "prevalence of immorality." He opposed the breaking of the Sabbath through the operation of the post office, nonemergency travel, and the driving of wagons, stagecoaches, and steam and canal boats. He also lamented intemperance and lotteries. Then he preached a Fourth of July sermon, which was published in 1828 and drew widespread national attention. Entitled *The Duty of Christian Freemen to Elect Christian Rulers,* it called for "a Christian party in politics," which would ensure the election of only orthodox Christians to office and keep out those of more liberal tendencies. In the election of 1828, this position put him squarely in the camp of Andrew Jackson, a Presbyterian, and in opposition to John Quincy Adams, whose deeply held religious views were Unitarian and thus liberal and nonorthodox. Ely's views seemingly called for a union of church and state, though the minister vociferously denied any such aim. A firestorm of national protest developed. Before the 1828 election, Andrew Jackson even wished that the outspoken minister had stayed out of politics; but after his victory, which he credited to "the interposition of divine providence," Jackson thanked Ely for his longtime support.[4]

Ely did not wait long to take advantage of his acquaintance with the new president to push his religious agenda. As Jackson prepared to begin his trip to Washington for the inauguration, Ely cautioned him against traveling on the Sabbath, "both from your sense of duty & your desire to gratify a numerous class of your firm supporters. . . . If ascending a river in a boat, you would of course, and with propriety, proceed in it," Ely preached to Jackson with Pharisaic precision, "but when on land, if the stage of Monday would carry you in season to the place of destination, I feel confident that you would set an example of resting on the day previous."

John Quincy Adams had only recently angered clerical leaders by unnecessarily traveling on Sunday, Ely said, so he wanted to make sure that Jackson did not repeat that mistake. Apparently happy with the way Jackson conducted himself on his trip to Washington, Ely did not bring the matter up again. Instead, he tried to use his influence with the president to obtain a chaplaincy in the U.S. Navy for a pro-Jackson acquaintance. He also decided to provide Jackson with even more detailed moral instruction. Two weeks after attending the inauguration, and after several conversations with Richard K. Call and a minister friend in Washington, Ely wrote the new president a long letter of advice urging him to fire John Henry Eaton because of his wife's purported immorality.[5] He presented his case as a matter of religious morality, but he placed it in a political context. In effect, he asked Jackson how he could preside over a Christian nation if his administration included such a sinful woman?

Ely attacked Jackson's most tender spot to try to carry his point. He cited the main reason for his letter as concern for Rachel Jackson's memory. Margaret Eaton was being compared to Rachel, Ely said, and people were saying that Jackson could not very well keep her out of his cabinet, considering his own wife's transgressions. "This rouses my indignation," Ely wrote with all the persuasion he could muster, "and I cannot endure it that Mrs. Eaton should be named in connexion [*sic*] with your ever to be honored and lamented wife," especially since, he said, Rachel had refused to return a visit to Mrs. Eaton, then the wife of John Timberlake. "She was too pure to countenance such a character as Mrs. E then sustained."

Ely also insisted that he was speaking up because everyone else in Washington—except for the minister who had married the Eatons and a solitary individual who had once lived at the O'Neale boarding-house—"all said that she was a woman of ill fame before Major Eaton knew her and had lived with him in illicit intercourse." A leading Jacksonian had told him in Baltimore, Ely said, "that on account of Mrs. Eaton the most influential Jackson men could not lift up their heads." This same supporter reported, however, that he and everyone else believed that Jackson was unaware of Mrs. Eaton's sins. For all these reasons, Ely said, he had to write Jackson. All he asked was that the president not force Emily Donelson or Mary Eastin, the two nieces living with him, "to return the civilities of Mrs. Eaton," thus, of course, providing her entry into society. After all, he reminded Jackson, Rachel had not done so. "Whether with truth or not, Mrs. E is generally spoken of in Washington and Baltimore as having been a lewd woman, excluded from society, before her *first* and *second* marriage." Washington women had not and would not "be on visiting terms" with her, and their husbands supported their stand.

Ely next presented a catalog of Margaret Eaton's alleged sins. At the National Hotel, where Jackson himself had stayed, a man told four others, Ely reported, that "Mrs. E brushed by me last night and pretended not to know me. She has forgotten the time when I slept with her." Another individual said he had heard Margaret tell a servant not to call her children Timberlake because John Henry Eaton was really their father. This same man said that Timberlake had told him he would never return home again because of "Eaton's seduction of his wife." A Washington clergyman told Ely that Margaret had undergone a miscarriage at a time when Timberlake had been away at sea for over a year, while some congressmen indicated that Margaret and John Eaton had stayed at a hotel as husband and wife before they were actually married. At a New York boardinghouse, moreover, Eaton had removed the lock from the door between their supposedly separate rooms, while the management of another establishment "refused to receive them a second time because their intimacy disgraced their house." During one session of

Congress, Ely continued, some friends of Eaton had convinced him to live at another Washington boardinghouse, other than the O'Neales,' to get him "free from Mrs. Timberlake."

"Dear General," Ely beseeched in conclusion, "I have seen enough of Mrs. Eaton to confirm these reports in my own mind. . . . She will do more to injure your peace and your administration than one hundred Henry Clays." And to make sure Jackson did not hesitate taking action after this anti-Clay appeal, Ely called on Rachel's memory one more time. He told Jackson how Mrs. Ely had "triumphantly vindicated Mrs. Jackson's honor" during the Elys' trip by ship between Washington and Philadelphia. In answer to Mrs. Ely's defense of Mrs. Jackson, however, another woman on board the ship responded, "And pray, Madam, do you also defend Mrs. Eaton?" Ely concluded: "As a minister of God, as a man, and a christian [*sic*] I would forgive Mr. and Mrs. E and do them all the kindness in my power; but, forgiveness does not imply that a woman of lewd character for years should on marriage be received, at once, into chaste society." Send John Henry Eaton to France, Ely advised, so that "he might live away from Washington long enough for his wife to prove her reformation."[6] Ely could not countenance Margaret's entry into society, not in the depths of his Christian heart and his political soul.

The letter left Jackson "astonished and mortified." Ely had previously supported the nomination of John Eaton for a cabinet post, and while in Washington for the inauguration, he had told Jackson of his plans to take his wife for a visit to the Eatons before returning to Philadelphia. Therefore, such a letter, full of accusations against a couple Ely had previously praised, was startling. Jackson wrote a long letter in response, blaming everything on "the great exertions made by Clay and his partisans, here and elsewhere, to destroy the character of Mrs. Eaton, by the foulest and basest means, so that a deep and lasting wrong might be inflicted on her husband." A friend had told him, the president reported, that Mr. and Mrs. Clay themselves had lambasted Mrs. Eaton, and when asked for the basis of the accusations, Clay had responded *"rumor, mere rumor."* Then, demonstrating that he had not forgotten his long-unused attorney skills, Jackson lectured Ely against making unsubstantiated charges of such a magnitude. He insisted that he knew countless individuals who had lived at the O'Neale boardinghouse prior to Eaton's arrival in Washington, who denied that Margaret had ever had a bad reputation. He also had letters from individuals all over the nation supporting John Eaton's nomination to his cabinet post.

Then Jackson turned to Ely's use of Rachel's name. He wanted to know the names of those who had been critical of his wife. When writing those lines, he perhaps felt a twinge from the bullet still in his body from an earlier defense of her reputation. "Men who can be base enough to speak thus of the dead," Jackson said, "are not too good *secretly* to slander the living; and they deserve, and no doubt will receive, the scorn of all good men." The truth of the matter was that Rachel Jackson had never snubbed Margaret Eaton, and "to the last moment of her life, believed Mrs. Eaton to be an innocent and much injured woman." He himself had known John Eaton for twenty years, Jackson continued, and were the lies of a few Washington slanderers now to change his high opinion of his friend? Eaton was a Mason and so were O'Neale and Timberlake. No Mason would ever "have criminal intercourse with another Mason's wife, without being one of the most abandoned of men." Eaton was a man of honor; therefore, he never committed such a foul deed.

Jackson pointed out that he had long known the O'Neale family. He had lodged in their boardinghouse and had been present when John Timberlake went off to sea. He remembered the navy purser parting with his wife most affectionately and making his farewells with John Eaton in the friendliest manner possible. Jackson said his room in the boardinghouse had been so situated that, if anything untoward had been going on between Margaret and John, he would have known about it. Jackson remembered that rumors had begun even then, and upon investigation he had found that all were traceable to a woman "against whom there was as much said as is now said against Mrs. Eaton." Rachel had heard these tales, too, and she had never believed them either. Neither had Timberlake, if indeed he had heard them at all. As he wrote this letter, Jackson reported, there lay on his mantle a Turkish pipe that Timberlake had sent him just three weeks before his death at sea. He had sent it through his friend, John Eaton.

John proclaimed the other accusations equally false and slanderous. The person who talked of sleeping with Margaret "would not hesitate to slander the most virtuous female in the country, nay, even the Saviour, were He on earth," Jackson insisted, appealing to Ely's often-proclaimed Christianity. Continuing on this tack, he questioned the unnamed clergyman's story. "It seems to me to be so inconsistent with the charities of the Christian religion, and so opposed to the character of an ambassador of Christ, that it gives me pain to read it," he said. Furthermore, John Eaton never changed his lodgings; and, as far as Jackson knew, he and Margaret never traveled together except once when Timberlake was along. Even if they had traveled together and some unknowing clerk had mistakenly registered them as Mr. and Mrs. Eaton, that proved nothing. Mrs. Eaton was presently planning a trip to Philadelphia to buy some furniture and would probably be traveling with William B. Lewis. Jackson wondered if this innocent fact would soon cause further gossip about her.

He had not seen Mrs. Eaton since Inauguration Day, Jackson reported; but when he did, he planned to treat her as he always had and as he treated others. The only rule he would lay down for his nieces was that they treat everyone kindly. They were not required to visit anyone they did not wish to see.

Jackson then lectured his "dear and highly esteemed friend" on rumor mongering and the protection of women. "Female virtue is like a tender and delicate flower," he rhapsodized; "let but the breath of suspicion rest upon it, and it withers and perhaps perishes forever. When it shall be assailed by envy and malice, the good and the pious will maintain its purity and innocence, until guilt is made manifest— not by *rumors* and *suspicions,* but by facts and proofs brought forth and sustained by respectable and fearless witnesses in the face of day. . . . The Psalmist says, 'The liar's tongue we ever hate, and banish from our sight.' "[7] Jackson threw Ely's religiosity back in his face.

Ely immediately put the best interpretation on Jackson's letter. He was happy, he said, that the president would not force his nieces to socialize with Margaret Eaton and "rejoice that you intend Dear General, to let Time and the Ladies work the right issue." He did not plan to pursue the matter any further because he worried that Eaton might try to duel half of Washington in response and end up killing someone or getting killed himself. It was a fact, however, that a "gallant man," friendly to both Jackson and Eaton, had earlier told them both about the rumors and had expressed his belief in their validity. "Except in this matter of temptation," Ely wrote, "I think Genl. E a very amiable, capable, clever fellow; and in this matter I consider *him* tempted as Joseph, without the religious principle of Joseph to make resistance. My heart's desire is that he may be a true penitent, confess *to God,* become happy and find salvation. The same blessing I implore for his wife," the Presbyterian minister prayed.[8]

This prayer's influence on God is unknown, but it hardly impressed Jackson. "I must remark, that I have always thought *repentance* presupposed the existence of *crime,* and should have been gratified had you pointed to the proof of Mrs. Eaton's criminality before you recommended repentance." Then he was off again, dissecting the accusations and insisting that they had no foundation in truth. As for the "gallant man," whom Jackson identified as Richard K. Call, the president said Call had no justification, except rumors, to make any accusations. He also forwarded to Ely some letters supporting the Eatons that he had gathered, and a power of attorney Timberlake had given his friend. He cited these as a proof that the two men had been close. Jackson tried to overwhelm Ely's charges of religious immorality with a mountain of secular data claiming just the opposite.[9]

Ely backed down almost completely. The letters of support from Timberlake's shipmates and the power of attorney convinced him, he said, that Eaton and Timberlake had indeed been friendly. Then he astonishingly admitted that all his accusations against Margaret Eaton came from a single government clerk whom he had only barely met. This man was either wrong or a liar, Ely now admitted. As for the miscarriage tale, which a clergyman friend had learned from "the reported declarations of a dead physician," this, too, he knew, could not stand the test of proof. "I hope to convince the clergyman *who told me what the physician told him,* that he ought to do everything in his power to repair the injury done Mrs. Eaton." The New York boardinghouse stories were similarly "untrue," Ely admitted. "Nothing more than imprudent familiarity could be asserted against them [the Eatons]; and that, perhaps by a lady who may have been fastidious." Ely admitted his earlier accusations simply had no factual basis and were pure rumor.[10]

Clearly, Jackson won his debate with the gossipy preacher, but it had taken a concerted effort. He had gathered information from individuals in New York, from U.S. Navy officers who had served with Timberlake, and from anyone else with anything to say about the matter. The President of the United States in the first months of his initial term was spending a major amount of his valued time tracking down information on the purity or licentiousness of the controversial wife of his secretary of war. This matter had the highest priority during his early months in office.[11]

Jackson was hardly free of other controversy during this same period, however. He pushed forward his plan to replace entrenched government bureaucrats with deserving Democrats, especially targeting incumbents whom he believed were guilty of financial or political corruption. He never removed as many officeholders as his opponents charged, but the perception of wholesale removal frightened entrenched Washingtonians and only increased their view of Margaret Eaton as a symbol of what was wrong with the new administration. The Eaton Affair and the removal of officers—this was the face of Jackson's administration that Washington saw during his first year in office.

True to her driving personality, Margaret Eaton did not remain a passive victim in the escalating controversy about her. She kept informed about the latest rumors sweeping Washington. According to the most recent tale, she was already with child and would soon deliver, although she had been married only a few months previously. When John Eaton told her that Jackson was gathering information to prove her innocence, she rushed off to the Executive Mansion to confront Old Hickory and tell him that his well-meaning efforts were "absolutely insulting." She did "not want endorsements [of virtue] any more than any other lady in the land." She stomped out and went to her husband's office to cry and protest further, but finally John convinced her that Jackson was doing the right thing. She went back and apologized to the president, who saw her fire as proof of her innocence and only increased his efforts on her behalf.[12]

Unfortunately, all this controversy began to take its toll on the new president. The editor of the *New York Evening Post* said he had just learned from a visitor to Washington that Andrew Jackson was proving to be a complete incompetent, citing his handling of the Eaton matter as the best example of his failings. Margaret Eaton had told Jackson of her ill treatment at the hands of "the high-spirited dames of Washington," the newspaper reported, and had extracted from him a pledge that he would "teach the females of that place that they should bend in low submission to one whose rights he would protect and defend, 'by the eternal God.'" Based on this information, James A. Hamilton lamented to his friend, Secretary of State Martin Van Buren: "For God knows we did not make him president . . . to work the miracle of making Mrs. E an honest woman."[13]

Such gossip circulated everywhere. In his Washington home, former president John Quincy Adams called John Eaton "a man of indecently licentious life." A Connecticut woman erroneously identified Margaret Eaton as "the head of the President's establishment at Washington," and the daughter of a Connecticut river pilot. "Her character is as *low* as his family," she said. Virgil Maxcy, a leading Virginia politician, told Vice President John C. Calhoun in South Carolina that Duff Green, the editor of the Jacksonian *United States Telegraph,* had told him of his worries about Margaret Eaton's "furious passions . . . operating on [John] Eaton who controls Jackson's secretary-adviser, William B. Lewis. . . . It has come to this," Maxcy lamented, "that all our glowing anticipations for our country from the integrity, sagacity & firmness of Gen[era]l J[ackson] must be extinguished and we must submit to the melancholy conviction, that the U.S. are governed by the Pres[iden]t—the Pres[iden]t by the Sec[retar]y of War—& the latter by his W[ife]." Calhoun must have shaken his head in disbelief at this news, but he made no move to return to Washington to see for himself. He remained in South Carolina, continuing to distance himself from his president and the problems in Washington.[14]

If John and Margaret Eaton were really as powerful in the Executive Mansion as rumor had it, they were certainly unaware of it. Indeed, they were outraged that they received the same rebuffs there that they were experiencing in Washington as a whole. Andrew Jackson Donelson and his wife, Emily, refused to have anything to do with the notorious Mrs. Eaton, even though their uncle, the president, was carrying on a determined battle to defend her.

Andrew Donelson had long been Jackson's favorite ward, the son of Rachel's brother. When his father died, he had come to live at the Hermitage. Jackson treated him like a son, sent him to West Point, and upon graduation, made him his aide-de-camp during the Florida campaign. Resigning from the army, Donelson became a Tennessee lawyer in 1823, and in 1824 he married his cousin, Emily. When Jackson be-

came president, the twenty-nine-year-old man became his private secretary, bringing his wife of twenty-one with him to live in the Executive Mansion. Emily Donelson had studied at the Nashville Female
Academy, where she had learned the proper behavior and etiquette of
the day. "Of medium height, with dark auburn hair, dark brown eyes,
fair complexion, a slender symmetrical figure, and hands and feet tiny
as a child's," she made a striking appearance because she also knew
how to dress to best advantage. With the death of her Aunt Rachel, she
became the mistress of the president's home and, thereby, an important arbiter of Washington society. On August 31, 1829, she also gave
birth to a baby girl in the Executive Mansion, much to the president's
delight.[15]

At first, the Donelsons met the Eatons socially, Emily frequently visiting Margaret at the Eaton home. As she gained friends in Washington
society, however, Emily began to change her behavior. Margaret, noticing the increasing coolness, confronted her that April. Emily may have
heard that her new friends had been friendly to Rachel Jackson, Margaret said, but actually Rachel had little regard for them. They had tried
to convince Rachel that "a certain woman was not a proper character
for her to associate with," Margaret said, but Rachel calmly replied: "I
did not come here to listen to little slanders and to decide upon people's
characters." Following her aunt's example, therefore, Emily should have
nothing to do with such slanderers. Emily found the lecture insulting
and began to pull away from Margaret. Andrew personally let Washington women know that he and his wife planned to "leave the matter
[of Margaret Eaton's character] with the society which had originated it
and that our associations should be independent of it." In other words,
Emily Donelson would no longer have anything to do with Margaret
Eaton because she was so outspoken and because she tried to choose
Emily's friends for her. There was no mention, at this point, of Margaret's reputation for licentiousness.[16]

Emily let others know her feelings, too. One day that spring, she
asked Martin Van Buren why he never talked about Margaret Eaton.
Personally, she found the woman "possessing a bad temper and a med-
dlesome disposition. . . . The latter had been so much increased by her
husband's elevation as to make her society too disagreeable to be en-
dured." Van Buren disagreed. Even if Margaret was disagreeable,

Emily should not continue to "decline her society to the extent" she had, considering her role as Jackson's hostess. Similarly, she should not be "controlled in her course" by other, "unduly influenced" people. At these words, Mary Eastin, Emily's cousin, who was listening to the conversation, began to cry, and Emily became agitated. Van Buren had touched a sensitive spot, but the two women continued to refuse to have anything to do with societal outcast Margaret Eaton, despite their uncle's firm defense of her reputation.[17]

John Eaton then decided to confront Emily himself. He became convinced that she was developing into a leader in the snubbing of his wife. He wrote her a patronizing letter, advising her, as Van Buren had, to stop taking advice from slanderous Washington women. "You are young and uninformed of the ways and of the malice and insincerity of the world," he remonstrated, "and therefore do I speak to you." Those who were making inflammatory statements about his wife would soon be slandering her, he warned; that was their normal behavior.

Emily immediately responded, and her husband attached a note of further explanation. She very formally disagreed with Eaton's statements and, in a manner that was impossible to misunderstand, indicated that her reputation protected her from the unfair assaults that Eaton had warned her about. Her husband added the statement that there was no one more willing "to pay to yourself and to Mrs. Eaton every proper mark of respect, and by my example, to recommend the sentiment which justifies it to my family. But beyond this[,] my regard for them, and my duty to society does not require me to go." When he sent the letter, however, he crossed out that last sentence.

Donelson repeatedly denied any wrongdoing in the treatment of Margaret Eaton. He told others that the only problem the administration had was "unhappy prejudice which from some cause or other prevailed against Mrs. Eaton previous to her marriage. We have nothing to do with it," he disingenuously said, "but to leave it to its natural course." In short, he and Emily neither believed it nor denied it, but they accepted society's ostracism of Margaret Eaton and would abide by it—whether it was based on the truth or not.[18]

The relationship between the two families remained tense, and in July 1829, it reached a breaking point. During a steamboat ride from Washington to Fortress Monroe and Norfolk, with Andrew Jackson, his family, and several other public officials and their wives aboard ship, Emily Donelson suddenly felt faint. She was, after all, in her seventh month. Seeing Emily's distress, Margaret offered her a fan and a cologne bottle. Rather than accept the concerned offer of help from the woman she had been snubbing, Emily preferred to faint. Margaret grew livid. She told Andrew Donelson she felt "pity" for him. Andrew Jackson had promised her that he would send the Donelsons back to Tennessee if they did not start behaving differently. Jackson had said nothing to his nephew himself, so Andrew was shocked at Margaret's threat. Apparently, the president was not confronting an obvious problem in his own household.[19]

The incident on the boat remained a painful example of the snubbing Margaret continually faced everywhere she went. Such ostracism was clearly a cause for continual frustration. John Eaton remained so testy, indeed, that when city assessors attempted to determine the value of his household goods as required by law, he refused their numerous requests for entry and upbraided the two officials who appeared at his door.[20]

He was boiling with anger. He confronted two men in Washington over their society wives' behavior and feverishly investigated the source of a rumor circulating among congressmen. "If Eaton can trace it to a source worthy of notice," Jackson warned, "they will feel the chastisement that such base conduct and secret slander merits." Later, Eaton sent a second letter to leading Washingtonian George Graham, warning him that if he did not "make his Wife hold her tongue, he [would] hold him responsible." A supporter of Henry Clay even intimated that Eaton sent an anonymous letter to the wife of an army officer, no doubt Colonel Towson, threatening to give her husband "a severe Chastisement" for her recent unfriendliness to Mrs. Eaton. John Eaton appeared to be on the verge of violence.[21]

Not all was so negative, however. The Eatons lived in an excellent neighborhood across the street from the residence of the British minister, Sir Charles Vaughan. Andrew Jackson visited them frequently and carefully noted their other visitors, pointing out, for example, that Mrs. Louis McLane, the wife of the Delaware politician, had paid Margaret a visit during her recent stay in Washington. So had a Virginia politician's wife, Mrs. William C. Rives. Mrs. Richard Rush, the wife of a diplomat, and her sister, the wife of an army general, had also exchanged visits with Margaret. Postmaster General William Barry, his wife, and family lived with the Eatons while their own house was being prepared for occupancy. Barry was an outspoken supporter, calling Margaret "an artless, sincere and friendly woman. She may have been imprudent," he said, "as most of the ladies here are, but I cannot believe she was ever criminal." All the accusations against her, Barry believed, were the result of her being the innkeeper's daughter who had moved up into society. "This has touched the pride of the self-constituted great, awakened the jealousy of the malignant and envious, and led to the basest calumny," he insisted. It was not impurity; it was snobbery, Barry held.[22]

When one of the Barry children, a baby named Leonard, became seriously ill in June 1829, Margaret's solicitude caused the family's estimation of her to soar. She declined an invitation to dinner at the British ministry one evening so she could stay home and tend the child. She kept "Leonard in her arms day and night without sleeping, nursing him as tenderly as [if he was] her own child." Despite her care, Andrew Jackson's personal concern, and the ministrations of several doctors, the child died. As the family grieved, they spoke thankfully of Margaret's efforts. "Mrs. Eaton has been very kind and attentive to our family," an older son reported to a distant sister. "She has devoted herself to Leonard during the whole of his sickness, and has hardly taken any repose from her labors."[23]

Most people knew nothing similarly good about Margaret. All they heard about her were the alleged scandals. They never learned of her concern for the sick baby or any other positive activities. A Virginia politician named David Campbell was curious to see the infamous Mrs. Eaton for himself because he believed "that the stories about her are not true; but that she is a bold forward woman and has caused them by her levity." Margaret Eaton was too pushy and outgoing; these attributes, not impurity, were the cause of her ostracism. Eaton's good work at the War Department was winning over military officers, however, and this was helping their cause, Campbell said. But he still wanted to meet her to see for himself.[24]

He got his chance a few days later when he attended a gathering at the Eaton home. Some twenty to thirty people were in attendance that evening from all over the nation. Campbell had met John Eaton before but remembered little about the acquaintance. He was disappointed in what he saw now. He found Eaton "clownish and stiff." He was "very friendly—but with as little grace as you can conceive." He discovered, upon meeting Mrs. Eaton, that "she seemed to be very much at ease." She immediately joined "into conversation[,] talked *away* about anything and everything—jumbling great and small things together in a kind of *hodge podge*—and on some subjects seemed to be smart enough. . . . She loves admiration and bedaubs [*sic*] every one almost with flattery who notices her." There was only "one unfavorable mark in her conduct," said Campbell, "and that was this: she seemed to go out of the road to make us believe she was extremely fond of her husband." A longtime Washington resident told Campbell that for at least the past ten years Margaret Eaton "had often been pointed out to him as a woman of easy virtue," though "he had [never] heard her charged with any particular impropriety," and "he did not know any thing of his own knowledge." Margaret Eaton was infamous for no particular transgression, but everyone heard the rumors that she was an immoral person and that was enough to stigmatize her.[25]

The following Monday the inquisitive visitor returned to the Eaton home, this time to dine. He left with further mixed feelings. "Her ladyship knows how to cook," he said, "but she is decidedly the greatest fool, I ever saw in any genteel situation." He thought she was "a woman of good heart, but has no sense of propriety." Eaton would be hard pressed "to get along with such a woman," Campbell concluded, though giving no details to clarify his jumbled evaluation. It was clear, however, that Campbell found Margaret Eaton's behavior jarring because it was so unwomanly.[26] She was too talkative, too forward, and too foolish.

This same individual met Andrew Jackson at the Presbyterian Church on the following Sunday. He walked back to the Executive Mansion with the president and spent three hours there while Old Hickory "conversed openly and freely upon every subject—men and measures—and in his old open and candid manner." No doubt Jackson gave Campbell an earful on the Eatons and their snubbing by Washington society, because he seemed to be expressing his aggravation every chance he had. "I am happy to say to you," Jackson told a friend "that every charge that calumny has set on foot against Mrs. Eaton has vanished on enquiry. . . . The cloud is blowing over," Jackson believed. "The world was mistaken in me. The attempt was made to induce me to abandon my friend, *it failed.* I would sink with honor to my grave, before I would abandon my friend Eaton."[27] Andrew Jackson would never abandon a friend, and he was sure his stout stand had defeated the gossipers.

Once again, Jackson was wrong to think his problems were over. The rumors and the snubbing continued both in his home and among the cabinet wives. Only Mrs. William Barry was consistently friendly to Margaret Eaton. Jackson, meanwhile, watched as his problems increased daily. He continued grieving his wife's death. In Tennessee, his old friend, Governor Sam Houston, suddenly left his wife and went to live among the Indians in Arkansas, causing a scandal of the first magnitude. Jackson's determination to reform the national government by ridding it of corruption had led to the sensational embezzlement case of Tobias Watkins, a well-known Washington figure during the Adams presidency. "My days have been days of labour, and my nights have been nights of sorrow," Jackson lamented. When a woman asked for his autograph, he sent her a poem that demonstrated his depressed but determined feelings:

Now to my tent, O God, repair,
and make my servant wise;
I'll suffer nothing near me there,
that shall offend thine eyes.
The man that doth his neighbour wrong,
by falsehood, or by force,
The scornful eye, the slanderous tongue,
I'll banish from my doors.
I'll seek the faithful, and the just
and will their help enjoy,
These are the friendships I shall trust,
The servants, I'll employ.[28]

Despite these concerns and duties, Jackson did not slack in his efforts on Margaret Eaton's behalf. He no longer boarded horses at

O'Neale's establishment as he had at first done, but he no doubt kept Margaret's father informed on the latest twists and turns in the Eaton matter. He frequently visited John and Margaret at their home, and here they carried on long and frank conversations. A congressman who saw Jackson arrive one August evening in 1829 was greatly surprised at how warmly the president greeted Mrs. Eaton and Mrs. Barry, "as a parent does his affectional children." Margaret also visited him at his home. One time she was so upset about some rumored accusation against her that she demanded Jackson tell her all he knew about it. He cut her off, telling her that this was not her concern or her responsibility. He and her husband would take care of everything. "Margaret Eaton, go home and cook your bacon and greens and eat your dinner in peace," Jackson cajoled in true nineteenth century advice to a woman. She refused to accept her domestic role, and he did not settle her down until he told her: "If I had not believed that you had been a perfectly true and faithful daughter and wife and mother, having known you in all these relations, I never would have recommended you as wife to Maj. Eaton—one of the truest and best men I ever knew." Jackson's blessing of proper womanhood touched and soothed Margaret, but her calmness did not last long. Later that month, she finally discovered what Jackson and her husband were trying to keep from her: the Ely accusations.[29]

Learning about Ely, she quickly rejected the submissive role Jackson had recommended to her and society expected of proper women. She decided to confront the minister at his Philadelphia home, violating societal rules which insisted that men protect their women against abuse and women remain silent and patient in the background. Certainly not every woman followed such proscriptions, but even among those who did not, Margaret's bluntness was shocking. Traveling with her mother to the Pennsylvania city, she sought out Samuel Bradford, publisher of Ely's *Visits of Mercy,* a member of Ely's church, and the investigator of the boardinghouse charges. He agreed to accompany Margaret to Ely's house and introduce her to him. Ely expressed happiness at meeting her when Bradford made the introduction, extending his hand. Margaret made no movement and then responded forcefully. "What, sir? Offer to me the hand that would filch from me the highest treasure a woman can possess and transmit to her children?"

Ely stammered as he tried to respond to these blunt unfeminine words, but Margaret only poured on the shot even more. "You have turned aside from your high calling," she ridiculed Ely, "to clap this slander on my back. . . . I do not intend to leave these premises, sir, until I drag the whole of this thing out of you. . . . Every brick here [in this house] shall crumble into dust before Margaret Eaton will leave[,] until she gets the whole of this thing out of you."

Ely's wife now joined them briefly, and they had "a long and excited conversation" for the next six hours. Ely kept trying to end the confrontation, but Margaret insisted on knowing the name of the minister who had made the miscarriage charge. Ely tried to get Bradford to leave him alone with Margaret, but, wanting a witness to verify the conversation, she insisted that the publisher stay. Finally, after more arguing back and forth, Ely named John N. Campbell, his former student and the pastor of the Second Presbyterian Church, Margaret's own congregation in Washington, the church of Andrew Jackson, John Quincy Adams, Margaret Bayard Smith, and many others of Washington's gentility. Margaret refused to believe Ely's revelation, thinking that he was only lying to protect himself. After all, Mrs. Campbell had paid her a friendly visit only recently.

Margaret Eaton fearlessly continued to interrogate the minister in a manner displaying none of the feminine virtues women were supposed to display. She was aggressive and pressed her accuser in a manner society reserved for the dominant male. Women were not to conduct themselves this way; that was the job of their fathers, husbands, and brothers. Margaret did not care. She peppered the minister with questions. Where had John N. Campbell obtained the information about the miscarriage? From a physician, now deceased, who had told him about it, Ely replied. Who was the physician? Margaret demanded. "I ask you not to press me on that subject. I will see Maj. Eaton and give him the information," Ely pleaded, in the hope of a return to gender normality. Margaret continued to demand an answer, however, and finally Ely named Dr. Elijah Craven, a physician Margaret remembered from her neighborhood.

Continuing her pressure, Margaret forced Ely to tell her what Campbell had allegedly learned from Craven. The physician had told the minister, Ely said, that the O'Neales' had called him to treat Margaret for the effects of a carriage accident. Entering her room, Craven said, he had found her hurt and an old lady sitting near her bed, whom he guessed was her mother. Margaret had begun laughing loudly. "You ought to have been here a little sooner and you would have seen a little John H. Eaton," she allegedly had said, obviously referring to the miscarriage she had just suffered. The old lady then laughed loudly. "Yes, Dr. Craven; you lost a good fee; for Maj. Eaton would have paid you well."

Margaret was outraged at this tale of alleged callousness during such a crisis. "I sprang to my feet and approached Dr. Ely in a menacing attitude; for it was no time then to remember proprieties." She hurled the words at the stunned preacher: "State to me, sir, in the depth of your black heart[,] can you cherish the idea for a moment that any decent mother would sit by and make a joke of the infamy of her daughter?— but no; the whole thing is a lie." Ely was clearly rattled at this threat of mayhem and happily saw his female antagonist depart without inflicting the unfeminine punishment she seemed to be threatening.[30]

Margaret left Philadelphia to return to Washington, and Ely, realizing the trouble he was in, tried to distance himself from his fellow minister and former student. He advised Campbell that if he had any doubts about the validity of the miscarriage story, he "ought to say so" right away because the Eatons deserved justice, and the nation, the church, and Campbell's honor required it, too. Campbell was no fool; he realized that the president of the United States, a member of his church, would be furious once he learned what had happened, so he hurried over to see Andrew Jackson Donelson. He explained to him as a "relative and intimate friend" of the president that, during the inauguration he had told Ely the miscarriage story so that Jackson might better be able to make an important decision about his cabinet. Campbell, when he had first arrived in Washington in 1822, had learned of the then Mrs. Timberlake's bad reputation and had gone to Dr. Elijah Craven, a much respected Washingtonian, to discover the reasons for it. Craven told him about the miscarriage, which story he had indeed related to Ely. He asked Donelson to inform Jackson and then make an appointment so Campbell might see the president himself. Donelson refused to speak to Jackson, but he agreed to make the appointment for September 1.[31]

John N. Campbell was a complex individual. Married to a woman from a wealthy background and thus "accustomed in the circle of his wife's family, to gay and fashionable society," the genteel order of proper womanly behavior, his reputation as a pastor was "kind and Christian . . . so full of love." He was a "perfect master of Rhetoric," parishioner Salmon P. Chase believed, with "a mild and subdued expression which insensibly prepossesses the hearer in his favor." Yet he was also a stern religious taskmaster. According to John Quincy Adams, another of his flock, Campbell felt strongly that "unbelief [w]as the great sin of the impenitent" and that "the great delusion, almost universal, of sinners, [was] that they cannot control their own belief." Campbell was obviously firm in matters of right and wrong. When he appeared at the door of the Executive Mansion on September 1, he came as a person of set moral attitudes, social and religious. In Andrew Jackson he confronted an equally unbending individual.[32]

Either because Donelson forgot to make the appointment or Campbell missed his appointed time, he did not arrive until late that evening. When the doorman announced his arrival, the president hurried to his office. Campbell mistakenly thought Donelson had forewarned Jackson, but he had not. When Campbell explained himself to Jackson, the president "was much astonished at this avowal," expressing disbelief that Campbell was the source of *"this vile tale"* of Margaret Eaton's supposed miscarriage at a time when her husband, John Timberlake, had been away from the country for more than a year.

Campbell repeated Craven's story in detail and Jackson immediately pointed out its "absurdity." Did he not understand, Jackson asked, that the law prohibited physicians from providing information about their patients? Campbell said Craven was not the primary physician but had only stumbled onto the situation, thus apparently having no obligation to silence. But it made no sense, Jackson retorted, for a married woman, with her husband allegedly distant for a long time, to "so wantonly publish her own disgrace and infamy to the world." Campbell, a man of the Christian cloth, should have known better than to broadcast such ridiculous slurs.

Jackson then pointedly asked Campbell for the date of this supposed miscarriage. Campbell replied that it was 1821. What if Timberlake had been in the country that year? the president asked. No, Campbell responded, Dr. Craven thought he had been absent. Well, if that were not the case, Jackson pressed, "as a Christian and preacher of the Gospel," would Campbell not be duty-bound "to repair the injury he had done female character." Campbell did not respond and cringed when the president brought up Campbell's friendly relationship with Margaret before he heard this story and his refusal to meet her socially afterward. Jackson wondered why Campbell had never discussed the matter with her himself. "This would have given her an opportunity of showing her innocence, or, if she failed, then, with a clear conscience, . . . [you and your family] could have withdrawn from her society." Jackson echoed society's belief that if a woman could not prove her innocence of sexual transgression, she could properly be snubbed even though he contradictorily argued just the opposite in the case of his own wife, Rachel, and his friend Margaret because he did not believe them guilty of such sin.

At this point, the meeting ended inconclusively and Campbell left. Jackson told William B. Lewis to find out whether Timberlake had been in Washington in 1821. Jackson was sure, in his own mind, that Timberlake had come to Washington immediately after the War of 1812 and had not gone off to sea until 1824, but he wanted definite proof.[33]

Lewis took on the task with relish. A massive figure over six feet tall, brother-in-law to John Eaton through Eaton's first marriage, and efficient quartermaster to Jackson's army during the battle of New Orleans, Lewis was Jackson's close admirer, so close, in fact, that he lived in the Executive Mansion. During the presidential campaign, he, along with Eaton, had been the leading defenders of the Jackson marriage. He was always there whenever Jackson needed him for personal or political advice of the most practical kind. Friends and enemies both suspected him and frequently lamented the sinister power he was thought to have over Jackson. The president liked having him around, however, because he got things done.[34]

Lewis came through again. The next evening, he reported to the president that Timberlake had indeed been minding his Washington store in 1821; Margaret Eaton had the establishment's books. Jackson immediately went to the Eaton house, only to find on his arrival that John Eaton was nursing an ill wife. He invited Jackson into the room, and, from her bed, Margaret told him that she had her first husband's books, and Jackson was free to look at any of them. Upon examination, Jackson found that Timberlake had indeed been in Washington in 1821. Some other records, those of William O'Neale and the O'Neale family doctor, corroborated the same point. Jackson could hardly wait to present this evidence to Campbell. Upon returning home, he told Donelson to have the minister appear the next evening to discuss the matter further.[35]

The afternoon of the Campbell-Jackson meeting, Margaret had been busy herself. Upon returning home from her encounter with Ely in Philadelphia, she had told her husband what had happened, and he had grown angry. "He declared I ought not to have done it; that it was his business to defend me," she said. She dissented, once again challenging contemporary standards of behavior for women, which insisted that they were to let their men defend them. "Maj. Eaton, I am the one charged; you are not. Everybody says that you are an upright, high-minded gentleman. . . . I am the solitary sinner, and I am going to right it myself." She said she was going to see Campbell, and though John Eaton agreed to go with her, it seemed clear that she was going to do most of the talking herself.

When the couple entered the Reverend Campbell's study, Margaret Eaton let both males quickly know that she was no submissive woman. "I am glad to see you," Campbell said. Margaret replied: "But I am not glad to see you." And when John Eaton began to say something, she cut him off, too. "Now, my husband, be still. For your life do not put your hands on Mr. Campbell, for that is what he wants." Turning toward Campbell again, she began explaining her visit to Ely, at which point Campbell requested that Colonel Nathan Towson be asked to join them as a witness; Margaret agreed immediately. "If you told Dr. Ely what he says you told him, you are capable of any deception, any falsehood," she said to Campbell. "If you lied then, you will lie now."

When Towson arrived and, not surprisingly, agreed with Campbell that the date of the supposed incident was in 1821, Margaret immediately sent a servant over to the nearby Navy Department and obtained information showing that Timberlake had not been at sea that year. She knew this fact already from the store records she had at home, but she did not tell her two antagonists that. Towson replied that there had to be some error, to which comment Margaret grew so upset that she felt dizzy and nearly fainted, striking her head against the corner of the sofa. Seeing his wife bleeding, Eaton sprang after Campbell, but Margaret had enough of her senses left to get in his way. Eaton took her home and put her to bed, where she was recuperating when Jackson came to inspect the books the next night.[36]

The following morning, September 3, 1829, Campbell returned to Jackson's office for another conversation; this time Donelson and Towson were also present. The president told Campbell that he had incontrovertible proof that Timberlake had been in the country in 1821. Campbell responded that Jackson "must have misunderstood him as to the date." That was impossible, Jackson replied incredulously. They had discussed the matter in great detail during their previous interview. If 1821 was not the correct date, then what was? Jackson asked in exasperation. Campbell refused to answer. After shuffling some papers, he said that Timberlake had been absent in the fall of 1822. He still refused to settle on any specific date for the miscarriage, however. Jackson was appalled and grew even angrier when Campbell told him that he had retained Francis Scott Key as his attorney, and Towson would corroborate the miscarriage evidence based on an interview with Craven's wife and mother.

Campbell also reported a recent Eaton visit to the Cravens, where Margaret had allegedly threatened the younger of the two women with violence or a lawsuit. Despite such threats, Campbell said, the mother still insisted that Timberlake had frequently unburdened himself to her son about Margaret's infidelity and his desire to go off to sea to escape her. Towson then reminded Jackson of their conversation at the National Hotel before the inauguration, to which Jackson reminded Towson that he had then replied. "I have not come here by the people's will to make a Cabinet for the fashionable ladies, but for the benefit of my country" and that he had known Eaton for twenty years and "there was not a speck upon his moral character." He saw no reason to change his mind now. The meeting ended there. Immediately after, Jackson sent Ely a full report. He told him to come to Washington immediately—and stay at the Executive Mansion. Jackson still looked upon Ely as an ally, his earlier retraction convincing the president that he could provide help in defeating Campbell, his fellow minister and former student.[37]

Both sides began a flurry of interviews, questioning anyone who might support their positions. This was, after all, an important issue. The very relationship between men and women was on trial. If Margaret was guilty of the wrongs attributed to her, then for the sake of society's welfare, she, a tainted woman, had to be forced out and punished to keep others from following her lead. If she was really the innocent target of vicious gossip, then she had to be defended, so that no other woman would have to suffer such unfair stigma.

Campbell and his friend Salmon P. Chase called on a longtime neighbor of the O'Neales, an old woman who said that Rhoda O'Neale had once told her that Margaret had delivered twins while Timberlake was at sea. Others provided similar information—more than enough, Chase told his diary—to support Campbell's every allegation. Not to be outdone, William B. Lewis, who was coordinating Jackson's effort, had the same woman interviewed. She had nothing but good to say about Margaret, although she did know of the miscarriage because Rhoda O'Neale had told her about it. But she also knew that it had occurred when Timberlake was present or soon after he left. Chase's brother also warned him about publishing anything connected with the case, and his mentor, the leading politician William Wirt, told him to tell Campbell to be careful. "An indictment for a libel would be a most painful proceeding to a clergyman."[38] Campbell's cause was growing increasingly perilous.

Meanwhile, all sorts of affidavits supporting Jackson's position poured into the Executive Mansion. Jacksonian newsman and Baptist preacher, the Reverend O. B. Brown, accompanied by Margaret Eaton, called on the wife and mother of the now famous Dr. Craven. These women said they had never heard the physician tell the miscarriage story. Craven and Brown had been good friends, it turned out, and Craven had discussed many personal matters with his fellow minister yet he had never told Brown this story and never said anything critical about Margaret Timberlake, the minister insisted. Dr. Craven had died on December 4, 1823, but Timberlake had never left Washington until after that date. A former boarder at O'Neale's boardinghouse called Margaret a "virtuous woman" in his written statement, while an individual Ely had named as a source of negative comment denied it and said he believed the rumors were all false. A neighbor of many years defended Margaret's honor and insisted: "It is the duty of the old and genuine friends of General Jackson to stay by Major Eaton, and sustain him against the wicked, envious, and unfounded calumnies of his enemies."[39] Defending Margaret of course meant supporting Andrew Jackson; the social issue was actually a political one.

The Reverend William Ryland, who had married the Eatons, chimed in with his unwavering support for the couple and denied that there had ever been "any improper familiarity between them" before their wedding. A man alleged to have a letter from Margaret Eaton that proved her immorality denied that the letter had any such meaning. Margaret had threatened to sue him once, but this financial dispute certainly did not prove any lack of womanly virtue. A former senator and judge who had boarded at the O'Neales' also vouched for Margaret's reputation. He had never even heard "her use an expression incompatible with the delicacy becoming a lady." Eaton, meanwhile, traced John E. Hyde, the New York merchant who allegedly had made the statement about sleeping with Margaret, to England. Hyde denied ever making the remark, in fact denied ever knowing her.[40]

Although all these defenses thoroughly discounted the truth of the charges about Margaret's impropriety, some of the statements contained the germs of information that helped explain the source of the original gossip. Clearly, Margaret Eaton was a controversial figure, even to those who defended her. A man who had watched Margaret grow up in the boardinghouse blamed all the accusations on the late J. H. Henshaw, whom he characterized as "a disappointed mad lover of the lady he so wantonly traduced." He called Margaret "gay, animated, and volatile, generous, kind . . . and sometimes imprudent in her remarks and conversations; and so much so as to subject herself to ill natured comments from those but partially acquainted with her independent character." Only those who knew her well knew that "her good qualities more than made amends for any unguarded expressions."[41]

Another individual related investigating the New York boardinghouse charge and found it completely false. He also told of living at the O'Neale boardinghouse under "the amiable and pious Mrs. O'Neal[e]" and her husband, "and a better conducted one, I have seldom, if ever, seen." The then Mrs. Timberlake and John Eaton had never exhibited "any improper familiarity," though Margaret was "gay and some times volatile," he admitted. "She is a lady who as the French say 'porte la coeur dans la main' (carries her heart in her hand) thereby in unguarded moments, laying herself open to the envious remarks of those who cannot attain her naivete or sprightliness and charm of conversation." In short, Margaret did not know her place as a woman. She was bold and aggressive in manners and speech and thus suffered the consequences.[42]

It was another former boarder who demonstrated how accusations of impropriety against Margaret had become the conversational wisdom. At first, he had lived at the O'Neale boardinghouse by himself but later returned with his new bride. He and his wife developed a close relationship with the entire O'Neale family, including Mr. and Mrs. Timberlake. As this boarder and his wife moved into wider Washington society, however, they noted Margaret's absence and began to ask why. They learned that "she was not generally visited." Because this boarder held "but an humble situation under the government it was not for me to attempt to give tone to society, by dictating who should, and who should not be visited. It was our duty to either fall in with the current and float along on the surface, or seek the eddy and remain in obscurity. We gradually wound up our intimacy with the family, and eventually all intercourse between us ceased." When the young couple heard "the slanderous reports in circulation respecting Mrs. T . . . they were regarded by us as idle gossip, conceived in envy and propagated in malice." This husband and wife did not believe the stories about Margaret, but they snubbed her anyway because society and their future ambitions required it. A pattern was clear. Those who snubbed Margaret Eaton did so not because of any personal knowledge of her wrongdoing but because of unverified rumors of numerous alleged transgressions and society's consequent condemnation. Proper societal procedure required the snubbing of Margaret Eaton or there would be similar treatment for those who did not comply. It was automatic; no questions need be asked.[43]

On the evening of September 10, 1829, the president of the United States decided to settle the matter once and for all. He summoned the Reverends John N. Campbell and Ezra Stiles Ely, secretaries Andrew Jackson Donelson and William B. Lewis, and the entire cabinet save John Eaton. The only agenda was a discussion of the character of Margaret O'Neale Timberlake Eaton and the propriety of her ostracism. Vice President John C. Calhoun was still absent at his home in South Carolina, so he played no role in this meeting or the previous disputes.

On the surface, such a meeting seems incredible, but, in reality, what more important matter could the nation's leaders discuss than an alleged assault on the very bedrock of society—the special position of women as examples and defenders of the nation's values. Besides, Andrew Jackson was determined to meet the issue head-on, which he certainly did by calling such a cabinet meeting.

Jackson's methodical presentation of his evidence quickly demonstrated to the assembled group that the president was deadly determined. They were aware of his volcanic temper and that all that spring and summer his "whole [physical] system seemed out of sorts": his legs and feet had swelled, he had chest pains and shortness of breath, terrible headaches, and vision and stomach problems. According to a later physician, he was suffering from severe kidney problems, complicated by his chronic pulmonary infection, malaria, dyspepsia, osteomyelitis, bronchiectasis, totally decayed teeth, an impacted bullet, and his regimen of lead and calomel. It had been a tremendous effort to put in all the time he had obviously spent defending Margaret Eaton while he felt so awful.[44] The cabinet sat in uneasy silence, unsure of what to expect from him or what to do, but afraid to say anything that might disturb the ailing but stubbornly determined chief executive.

Jackson began the meeting by having Donelson read the correspondence that had passed between president and Washington minister and a series of affidavits Jackson, Eaton, and Lewis had received from individuals defending Mrs. Eaton. Jackson followed this reading with an eloquent defense of the Eatons. Ely then described his role, explicitly denying the validity of the New York boardinghouse story. He said that he was unaware of anything to impugn John Eaton's integrity. "Nor Mrs. Eaton, either," Jackson added. Given the chance to retract his accusation against Margaret Eaton, Ely refused. "On that point" he replied to Jackson, "I would rather not give an opinion." Jackson roared in anger: "She is as chaste as a virgin!"

As a stunned cabinet shuffled in its seats in the aftermath of that blast, Campbell began to try to validate his position. Jackson broke in sharply. Campbell was there to present the facts, not discuss them, the president said. The shaken minister responded that he was obviously present under false pretenses, then. "I have therefore only to say, that I stand ready to prove, in a court of justice, all I have said, and more than I have said, or would have dared to say three days ago." He bowed and walked out, later angrily telling former president John Quincy Adams that all he had wanted was the chance to present his side of the story. As it was, however, "Mr, Ingham, Mr. Branch, and Mr Berrien were all satisfied of the perfect correctness of his statements." Clearly, Jackson had not converted the recalcitrant in his cabinet with the meeting—an ominous sign.[45] Those opposed to Margaret Eaton remained adamant and gave no indication that they would ever accept Jackson's assertion of her innocence.

Thus, Jackson's meeting with his cabinet, instead of extinguishing the fire, only further fed the flames of the controversy. Two days later, Eaton told Campbell to retract the statements that even Ely had walked away from or they would have to fight a duel. This challenge should not have come as a surprise to Campbell. According to Salmon P. Chase, Margaret, after fainting and bleeding from the cut on her head, had told Campbell that his blood would have to "be spilt for his audacity." Andrew Jackson had similarly warned Ely that he did not know John Eaton's plans about this slander, "but I have often heard him say, that my Christian mother's advice was a good one, never to sue a man or indict him for slander." The only thing left was satisfaction on the field of honor.

Eaton sent his formal note of challenge to Campbell by way of Dr. P. G. Randolph, his brother-in-law. Campbell sent a reply through his friend Chase. The men were working through seconds, a dangerous development, but Campbell refused to say anything until he could have his day in court. The angry husband wanted no part of any court action and threatened to insult the minister to his face about being "brave enough to circulate a slander, and too much of a coward to repair it." Thus, minister or not, Campbell would have to respond in defense of his honor. Campbell refused again, once more insisting that court action, not a duel, was the answer.[46]

Not getting anywhere through seconds, Campbell and Eaton met face to face to try to settle their dispute. The meeting turned out to be a miserable failure. Eaton gave Campbell a list of questions that he hoped the minister's "sense of justice would enable him, promptly to reply to." Campbell refused to accept these interrogatories but said he would be willing to consider them if Eaton sent them in the mails. Eaton said he opposed further written communication, and Campbell continued to refuse to discuss the matter orally. Frustrated and unable to obtain what he called "satisfaction which strict justice would accord him," Eaton told Campbell he would "seek it now in my own way or in another way."[47]

Eaton turned to Duff Green, the editor of the *United States Telegraph,* whom he sent to see Campbell. The minister told the newsman he would say nothing further unless he was forced to protect himself or a friend. He denied slandering Margaret Eaton, insisting that what he had told Ely was meant to be confidential. Green approved of Campbell's desire to end the matter, and consoled him that he really should not worry about a duel or a trial. His clerical collar protected him from the former, and Eaton, as "a man of honorable feeling, never would permit a jury to pass sentence upon the character of his wife." He told Campbell that Eaton would continue to investigate the accusations and would take revenge against those whom he implicated. Eaton would, Green thought, "hold Col. Towson personally responsible if he could identify him with you." In order to prevent the bloodshed that a duel between Eaton and Towson would cause, Green told Campbell to give Eaton all the information he wanted.[48]

Campbell stood by Towson. He wrote Andrew Jackson of the threats against the army paymaster and expressed a willingness to remain silent if Eaton reciprocated, so "that I at least might be forever set free from a concern most uncongenial both to my taste & my pursuits." When Jackson received the letter, he took one look at the signature and ordered it returned to Campbell. The president considered the minister a liar and wanted to have nothing further to do with him. To make his disdain public, he left Campbell's church and joined another. The stress on Jackson remained enormous. His health continued to suffer under the pressure, and close friends in Tennessee became concerned enough to send a representative to Washington to check up on him. It was only his "trust in a kind Providence" that kept him going, Jackson said.

Campbell was also suffering from the stress of the encounter, so upset over the threat of a duel that "it wholly unfitted him for everything else" for an entire week. In late January 1830, finally, through the aid of a New York congressman, he gained relief from the problems of Washington. He received a call to a church in Albany, where he remained for the next twenty years. Rumors spread that Jackson was going to send Eaton to a diplomatic post in Mexico, but, once again, these predictions proved completely inaccurate.[49]

Despite all the anger and shouting, nothing had been solved. Margaret Eaton remained the center of controversy, her reputation now elevated into a major social and political issue. The president viewed the assaults against her and her husband as shafts aimed at him and his administration. He believed that John Eaton came "forth like double refined gold, and Mrs. Eaton without a single speck upon her virtue." Yet, in his own house, his nephew and niece continued among the leading detractors of the Eatons. While Jackson battled Ely's and Campbell's accusations against the Eatons, his secretary/nephew expressed, with obvious satisfaction, the opinion that John Eaton should never have been brought into the cabinet in the first place. "The disinterested and sincere friends of the General in this district, at least the great part of them," Donelson said, "will never consent to meet his [Eaton's] wife in society, and as she is a very indiscreet woman you can well imagine how unhappy is the effect." A political opponent was even more blunt. "Jackson showed himself stupid above all things in dabbling in such waters & running his head into a quarrel with the church."[50] No man could debate religious figures on moral codes and expect to be successful. Andrew Jackson had simply blundered, this political enemy believed, in placing himself in such a position. There was no way he could win.

Clearly, Jackson thought he had won the first battle in the conflict over Margaret Eaton. The war was far from over, however. Throughout the past months, he had tried to ignore the behavior of members of his own household. The Donelsons increasingly snubbed the Eatons, and because they were relatives, their actions were that much more bothersome. Jackson could not look the other way much longer, not if he hoped to ensure Margaret Eaton's acceptance into Washington society.

5

"Et Tu Brute"

Convinced he had defeated the two Christian zealots, Andrew Jackson still found himself battling for Margaret Eaton's acceptance into society. She had actively joined in the fight to vindicate her reputation, and her husband had even threatened to duel for her honor. Nothing seemed to work. Margaret and John Eaton, under the generalship of the president of the United States, seemed to be losing the war against society.

The political opposition gleefully watched Margaret wrestle with the problem. Associates of the absent Henry Clay kept him fully informed, concluding by the fall of 1829 that Jackson's cabinet was hopelessly split over the wife of the secretary of war. And, they optimistically insisted, the split was between those who supported Secretary of State Martin Van Buren for the presidency and those who backed Vice President John C. Calhoun. Eaton, William Barry, Martin Van Buren, and the president stood on one side of the chasm, while the vice president and everyone else in the cabinet allegedly stood on the other. Rumor had it that Postmaster General Barry, whose family lived with the Eatons, had become so angry at the behavior of Treasury Secretary John Branch that he had verbally accosted him in Jackson's presence.

Calhoun, who remained in South Carolina, seemed uncertain about what to do, whereas Martin Van Buren was in complete control. "With some adroitness, and a great deal of *meanness*," one correspondent told Clay, Van Buren "has availed himself of many advantages, growing out of *that affair*." What these were remained unsaid. The intensity of the controversy over Margaret Eaton, another Clay supporter reported, had surpassed the highly charged debate over a high versus a low tariff.[1]

At first these disagreements remained private, but there was no way of keeping them from reaching the public. During all presidential administrations, there are social functions at which public officials have to come together publicly. The refusal of society women to visit Margaret Eaton was a private matter and could be kept discreet, but the refusal to acknowledge her presence at receptions, dinners, and parties became public and impossible to hide. When administration women, including Emily Donelson and those from Washington society as a whole, snubbed Margaret at the inauguration ceremonies, anyone paying attention could not mistake what was happening.

A definite protocol to party-giving existed in early nineteenth-century Washington. The president first held a dinner for his cabinet and their wives, and then beginning with the secretary of state and following in order of precedence, the other cabinet members held their own social functions. Normally the president scheduled his dinner early in his administration, but Andrew Jackson delayed as long as he could. His grief for Rachel certainly affected his delay, but it seems clear that he procrastinated out of fear that cabinet wives would snub the wife of his secretary of war as they had during the inauguration. A friend of Martin Van Buren predicted with great foresight that Margaret Eaton was destined "to be the turning point of parties this winter!"[2]

There were, of course, other less formal social functions that were held in the Executive Mansion. For example, Jackson held the customary levee (or reception) on the Fourth of July. An hour past noon, White House doors were flung open, and Washington paid its respects to the president. The rainy weather kept the crowds down, but the "very little disposition among the old and settled population of the city to mix in the present political circles," as one newspaper phrased it, was a factor, too. Jackson's levees drew a variety of people: "a motley crowd," as one Washingtonian described it, from the leading politicians "to an intoxicated laborer in a dirty red plaid cloak." It was "a striking picture of democracy," a social-climbing army officer complained, adding, "it strikes me with disgust." Society found it "painful that their wives and daughters should thus be compelled to mingle with the very lowest of the people." Jackson "broke down the barriers of careful respect . . . [and] a disorder and rudeness characterized those receptions hitherto unknown, and which no private gentleman in the country would have tolerated in his own home."[3]

At the Fourth of July levee, the president and his family greeted this variety of people, and Margaret and John Eaton must certainly have been in attendance. Nothing untoward happened to create a stir, however; after all, what contemporary historian George Bancroft called "all the refuse that Washington could turn forth from its workshops and stables" made Margaret's presence less controversial. She was hardly the person especially to avoid in such a democratic gathering.[4]

Despite the success of this and other levees, Andrew Jackson delayed scheduling his dinner party. It remained on his mind, however, and he brought it up as he and Secretary of State Martin Van Buren conversed during one of their almost daily horseback rides in the fall of 1829. "Long-limbed and thin . . . [and] born to the saddle," Jackson told the "small, dapper, and round" Van Buren, whose "riding was the product of art rather than instinct," that he had delayed this first gathering hoping that the animosity toward Margaret Eaton might lessen. With Congress about to come into session in December, however, he thought he could delay no longer. He must go ahead and host his dinner party.[5]

The presidential dinner was finally set for November 26, 1829, in the recently refurbished East Room. Proper invitations were sent, and, to Jackson's relief, all members of his cabinet and the foreign service attended with their wives. Only the Calhouns, still at their home in South Carolina, were absent. The diplomats and military officers were decked out in their colorful sashes and medals, while civilian males "disported themselves in pumps, silk stockings, ruffled cravats, and two or even three waistcoats of different colors."

Women appeared in a variety of dresses of the latest styles, though at an earlier levee, Margaret Eaton, Emily Donelson, and several other women had appeared in plain western calico to express the simplicity of the new administration. Whatever the material, "their tight dresses [and] confounded splits, are murder outright," a male observer noted. Jackson escorted the wife of Secretary of the Treasury Samuel Ingham to the table, and widower Martin Van Buren escorted Emily Donelson. Margaret Eaton, Mrs. John Branch, the daughters of John Berrien, and Mrs. William Barry followed after. No menu has survived, but judging from the accounts of other dinners in the Jackson Mansion, this one was no doubt similarly sumptuous, the wine flowing copiously. At another such event there was a massive horseshoe table "covered with every good and glittering thing that French skill could devise, and at either end a monster salmon in waves of meat jelly." According to Van Buren, there were "no very marked exhibitions of bad feeling in any quarter"; and William T. Barry said it was "the most splendid entertainment I have ever been at in Washington."

Still, the evening was a failure. A cold stiffness existed that even the affable president could not defrost; the participants consumed rather than enjoyed the meal and left as quickly as they could escape. Jackson, whose health continued to be bad, now suffered even more "from mortification at what was passing before his eyes." Van Buren, and no doubt other observers, felt sorry for the Old Hero. He must have missed Rachel as he watched Margaret Eaton suffer rejection.[6]

At the least, however, there had been no scenes to publicize the cabinet rift over Margaret Eaton. Perhaps if the administration could continue to function with a modicum of civility, even though with no warmth, the situation would improve over time. Perhaps. But Martin Van Buren was certain that such a rapprochement would be exceedingly difficult. As secretary of state, he was next in line to give a dinner party, and he knew full well that the danger of a social catastrophe remained. He planned his dinner with trepidation. John C. Calhoun was expected back with the reconvening of Congress, but his wife planned to stay home with her new baby and the rest of the children. Calhoun would be hosting no entertainment this social season.

According to protocol, Van Buren would escort Mrs. Ingham, wife of the secretary of the treasury, to the table, she being the highest ranking woman present. Thus, she would preside over the dinner. It would hardly do to have one of the leading snubbers of Margaret Eaton sitting in such a seat of prominence. Besides, Van Buren wanted to do everything else he could to make the gathering so irresistible that no one would want to stay away. So, skilled as he was in social matters, he invited Martha Jefferson Randolph, the widowed daughter of Thomas Jefferson, to be the guest of honor and, therefore, the prominent person at the dinner. He also invited several military officers and their wives but bypassed Commanding General and Mrs. Alexander Macomb because she, too, was a leader of the opposition to Margaret Eaton. He sent out the invitations and anxiously awaited the R.S.V.P.s.

The responses were not long in coming. Every cabinet member accepted for himself, but made an excuse for the women in his family. John Branch, for example, said his wife and daughters could not attend because "circumstances unnecessary to detail will deprive them of the pleasure." Even Margaret Eaton and Mrs. William Barry refused to come, unwilling to place themselves in an untoward situation. The second cabinet dinner of the season, therefore, took place with no cabinet wives present. Those women who came had a good time, as there was no concern about any repercussions growing from the presence of Mrs. Secretary of War.[7]

Van Buren enjoyed social events, so he organized another party, even larger than the first one. This time he displayed less trepidation than he had shown before. Cabinet wives and daughters once more sent their regrets, except for Margaret Eaton and Mrs. Barry. The event received marked publicity when a letter signed "Tarquin" appeared in the *Washington Daily Journal* accusing Van Buren and British minister Sir Charles Vaughan of trying to force Margaret upon Washington society. In retaliation, the letter insisted, no one should attend Van Buren's party. Needless to say, this publicity only guaranteed a large gathering, including Mrs. General Alexander Macomb. John C. Calhoun came, but since his wife had remained in South Carolina, he attended alone and remained in the background.

Feeling the stress of the evening since Margaret Eaton was present this time, Van Buren waited until the dancing had begun and slipped away to rest on a sofa on the floor below. A short time later, a friend came down to tell him, in a joking voice, that he should not be lying down but should be upstairs trying "to prevent a fight." Mrs. Eaton and Mrs. Macomb had inadvertently bumped into each other on the dance floor, with resulting words and a scene. Van Buren thought it was all a joke but, unfortunately, it was not. A leader of Washington society and the infamous Margaret Eaton had come close to blows over an innocent bump in a crowd. Van Buren's party had produced the public scene that could only exacerbate an already difficult social and political situation and put him squarely into the dispute—on Mrs. Eaton's side.[8]

Later in life, Van Buren reminisced that in 1829, "for reasons not now necessary to assign," he had made up his mind to treat every cabinet member and family equally and not to get "mixed up in such a quarrel." As a widower with no daughters, he did not have to explain his behavior to any women in his family, and he quickly came to see, from the closest perspective, how emotionally involved Andrew Jackson had become in defending the Eatons. During their long horseback rides when they discussed policy and people, he frequently heard the president's laments about the snubbing of Margaret Eaton and how Jackson saw it as a manifestation of opposition to him. Van Buren genuinely liked and admired Old Hickory, seeing him as a friend he was happy to help. At the same time, the political advantages of being pleasant to Margaret Eaton were not lost on him. Van Buren's opponents quickly concluded that he was using this controversy to position himself to replace Calhoun as Jackson's successor. "He has availed himself of the Case of the Lady to Commit himself with Eaton & Barry & through them to obtain the confidence of the President," a supporter told Henry Clay. "This is the Nucleus of the Van Buren party[,] & Calhoun is forever extinguished."[9]

Van Buren's activities can, indeed, best be understood from both a personal and a political vantage point, the two not mutually exclusive. If he could force Margaret's acceptance, Van Buren would gain Jackson's gratitude and his political support. If he failed, Jackson would still give him credit for trying and would blame others for their intransigence and anti-Jackson political motivation. So, no matter what happened to Margaret Eaton, Martin Van Buren would benefit from trying to help her. Besides, he liked the woman. He embarked on the task with more than his usual high energy.

Foreign diplomats regularly gave parties in Washington, but they generally followed society's rules of etiquette, the violation of which would make their work in the nation's capital impossible. They particularly had to be on the best of terms with the secretary of state. If that official wanted something they could provide, it made sense to accommodate him. Since Sir Charles Vaughan and the Baron Paul de Krudener, the British and Russian ministers, like Van Buren, had no wives and frequently held parties, it was easy for them to put the controversial Margaret Eaton on their invitation list. She was, after all, a cabinet wife and snubbing the secretary of war could prove harmful. Moreover, the Eatons lived near the British minister and he knew them well, making it only natural for him to invite them. Van Buren may have hinted his desire for their social cooperation, but the bachelor diplomats needed little encouragement.

Vaughan and Krudener both held grand balls soon after Van Buren's second party. Once again cabinet wives refused the invitations, but Margaret Eaton came and so did most of Washington society. At Vaughan's great ball, therefore, every cotillion in which Margaret appeared "instantly dissolved into its original elements," an observer noticed. When Vaughan escorted her to her proper seat at the table, the women nearby utilized "that instinctive power of inattention to whatever it seems improper to notice," and ignored her completely.

It was even worse at the baron's. According to a story attributed to Madam Huygens, the wife of the Dutch minister to the United States, Chevalier A. de Bangeman Huygens, Martin Van Buren orchestrated Krudener's party. He went to see the minister's wife and told her that Washington society had decided to accept Mrs. Eaton at the baron's festivities. That was fine with her, Mrs. Huygens replied, because her relationship with Mrs. Eaton was based only on following the lead of the Washington ladies. That the sophisticated secretary of state would be clumsy in this matter is difficult to believe, but the story's circulation made gullible listeners willing to accept its veracity.

The night of the ball, Mrs. Huygens found that Van Buren had not been truthful. Since the secretary of state had no spouse and almost all the cabinet wives were absent, Krudener escorted the wife of the highest ranking cabinet member present to dinner. He grandly gave his arm to the wife of the secretary of war—Margaret Eaton. That was bad enough, Mrs. Huygens allegedly said, but then Van Buren did not even escort her to dinner as he should have, she being the only diplomat's wife there. Van Buren kept playing cards and, to her horror, she found that John Henry Eaton had been assigned as her escort. She was furious, refused to walk with him, then reluctantly did, only to find that she was supposed to sit next to Margaret. She and her husband quickly departed, letting it be known that she would retaliate for what she allegedly believed were Van Buren's machinations by refusing to invite Margaret Eaton to her forthcoming party. An anonymous letter to the local press satirized the whole incident to Margaret's disadvantage, forcing John Eaton to demand a retraction. Meanwhile, Mrs. Huygens held a party to which she did not invite Margaret. Now, the diplomatic corps had joined Washington society in snubbing Margaret Eaton. And if Margaret complained to the baron for this slight during his party, she probably received little immediate satisfaction. Krudener was "deaf as a post."10

When Andrew Jackson heard the story about Mrs. Huygens's threat and then learned about her party and several cabinet gatherings from which Margaret Eaton had been excluded, he summoned Martin Van Buren to his office early one morning. The secretary of state found the president looking as though he had not slept all night. Jackson told Van Buren to go see the Chevalier and Mrs. Huygens and find out the truth of the rumors he had heard. Van Buren, who was close to the Huygenses, their mutual Dutch heritage being a major factor in their friendship, told Jackson that he found the whole story difficult to believe. But if it were true that Mrs. Huygens and members of the Jackson cabinet had conspired against Margaret Eaton, thereby insulting the president, Jackson would be perfectly correct to send the diplomat home and fire the cabinet members.

Van Buren hurried to the home of the Dutch minister. He assured the Huygenses that the president did not want to interfere in any way with their social lives, and Mrs. Huygens denied what had been attributed to her. Although it was clear, however, that she had consciously not invited Margaret to her recent unofficial party, Van Buren indicated that the administration believed in freedom of association. The Chevalier supported his wife, and Van Buren reported to the president his satisfaction with the interview. Jackson accepted the Huygenses' explanation, but he remained angry at the Berriens, the Branches, and the Inghams, the three cabinet members who had not invited the Eatons to their parties. Jackson and the Barrys continued to be friendly with the Eatons, so the social split remained. Daniel Webster, among others, recognized its ever increasing political implications. "It is odd enough," he said, "but too evident to be doubted, that the consequences of this dispute in the social and fashionable world is producing great political effects, and may very probably determine who shall be successor to the present chief magistrate."[11] The social war was reaching the highest levels of office in the nation's capital.

While this social war raged on the party circuit, it did not disappear from the mails or the rumor mills. Nicholas Biddle, president of the Bank of the United States (the financial institution Andrew Jackson was preparing to attack), dined at the Eatons during a visit to Washington. Learning of this fact, an opponent whispered that the banker was using Margaret as a way of influencing the president, this belief no doubt aided by the continuing conventional wisdom that Margaret held the old man in her control. As one person phrased it, she "flatters up the old General in great stile and it runs down even to the hem of his garment like oil."[12]

As a result of all this controversy, the issue grew increasingly heated. Susan Decatur, wife of the deceased commodore, received an anonymous letter warning her to stop associating with Margaret Eaton if she ever hoped to have her financial claim against the government validated. She passed the note on to Jackson, who told her to ignore "such base, corrupt, and unprincipled villains." He continued to support her claim as he remained assured that Margaret Eaton was "a moral, virtuous, and correct woman." Sarah Polk, the wife of Tennessee supporter and future president James K. Polk, joined in the ostracism, but old friend Hugh White made a special effort to greet Margaret Eaton after church one Sunday. White made sure that everyone noticed him helping her and Mrs. Barry into their carriage. Eliza Johnston, the wife of one of Henry Clay's close friends, even began to feel sympathy for Margaret, but insisted that as long as society snubbed the war secretary's wife, she would have to go along. No one was willing to take the chance of being forced to join Margaret Eaton on the outside, no matter the truth or falsity of the accusations against her.[13]

Once more John Eaton became involved in a series of threats and counterthreats. Several months earlier, he had challenged Colonel Nathan Towson to a duel but had never received an answer. During the intervening period, Mrs. Towson became the target of accusations like those against Margaret, and Towson clearly blamed John Eaton. He demanded to know the names of his wife's slanderers. Towson's friend handed the letter of inquiry to Eaton's brother-in-law and second, but Dr. Randolph threw it to the ground, refusing communication except concerning the original argument. Whole batches of letters then flew back and forth between Eaton, Towson, and their seconds, but fortunately cooler heads prevailed, and there was no duel, but there was no end to the hard feelings.[14]

If threatening Towson was not enough, Eaton also became involved in an extended argument with fellow cabinet member John Branch. At first, the two men simply did not speak to one another. Then Eaton demanded to know if Branch had told a disappointed office seeker that he should blame Eaton for his failure to obtain a government post. The relationship became so tense that Jackson had to arrange for the two men to meet with Van Buren and Barry to try to work out their differences. When they met, they firmly restated their positions. Branch said he could not force his family to meet with Eaton's wife, though he had no opposition to their doing so. Eaton agreed that no one should be forced to visit anyone if he or she did not wish to. The two men shook hands at parting, but the problem of the treatment of Margaret Eaton had not been resolved.[15]

It was, after all, Margaret who suffered the stings of the continuing ostracism. When Andrew Jackson attempted to make up for these slights at his receptions, critics derogatorily called her the "unofficial first lady." After one dinner, an observer described the gathering as consisting of "fifty guests, one hundred candles and lamps, silver plate of every description, and for a queen, Peggy O'Neale, led in by Mr. Vaughan (the British minister) as head of the Diplomatic Corps, and sitting down between him and the President." Jackson's solicitude for his friend caused people like former president John Quincy Adams to call his behavior "an over-display of notice."[16]

Adams savored all the gossip, enjoying the spectacle of turmoil in his successor's administration. One day he reported in his diary that after Margaret saw Emily Donelson visiting the wife of a physician living next door, she immediately forced her husband to evict the couple. She then allegedly told her milliner that "if it had not been for that d——d old granny," nothing like the persistent snubbing she was suffering "would have happened" to her. Adams admitted that he could not vouch for the veracity of this story, but "it is her style of conversation." Many people had previously reported many such "examples of her ordinary discourse." The caustic, judgmental Adams was only too ready to believe rumors against the wife of the secretary of war without bothering to verify their validity.[17]

Andrew Jackson grew tired of watching his cabinet splinter in gossip and rumor. In January 1830, he decided to confront the three men whom he believed were at the very center of the controversy: Secretary of the Navy John Branch, Attorney General John M. Berrien, and Secretary of the Treasury Samuel D. Ingham. He sent an emissary to see them, an individual friendly to them all. Colonel Richard M. Johnson was a strange choice to settle a problem of proper societal behavior, considering his own controversial personal life. A longtime member of the House and Senate from Kentucky, he had achieved notoriety because of his claim to have killed the great Shawnee Indian leader Tecumseh during the War of 1812. Later vice president of the United States under Martin Van Buren, Johnson had cohabited with a black woman, and later had tried unsuccessfully to introduce one of his mixed-race daughters to society. He had brought her to a Fourth of July barbecue in Kentucky, but the crowd forced her to sit in the carriage while he gave his speech. A Kentucky newspaper then compared his attempt to force his mulatto daughter on Kentucky society to Margaret Eaton's attempt to force herself on Washington society. Johnson hardly seemed like a promising mediator for a controversial social problem.[18]

Johnson first approached Samuel D. Ingham in the Treasury Department, and the Kentuckian's social problems did not enter into the discussion. He told the worried and frequently sick Ingham that the president was upset at the lack of harmony in the cabinet, obvious in the fact that three families refused to have any social discourse with Margaret Eaton. Jackson had asked him, Johnson said, as a friend to all three men, to see if there was anything that could be done. The president wanted the wives and daughters of his cabinet members to include Mrs. Eaton when they held a large party and to pay her a formal visit by leaving a card, as etiquette required. Unless this was done, Johnson said, Jackson would ask them to resign.

Ingham was taken aback at this news, but quickly recovered. He expressed a willingness to deal harmoniously with everyone and promised he would never do anything to make Mrs. Eaton's difficult situation any worse. He had been fair to her, he believed, having thus fulfilled all that the president could expect of him. Etiquette did not allow anyone to force another into society, and since Mrs. Eaton had never been accepted, there was nothing he or the president could do about it. He denied Jackson any authority to force him or his family to do anything in the matter of "social intercourse," and he would accept any consequences that might result from this stand. He was willing to suffer political penalties to maintain social proprieties. Left unsaid, but at issue, was the accepted etiquette that it was the right and duty of Mrs. Ingham to make this decision and her husband's duty to support it. It was none of Andrew Jackson's business.

Now it was Colonel Johnson's turn to be taken aback. He had planned to speak to Berrien and Branch, too, but after hearing what Ingham had just said, he wondered if such a conversation made any sense. Jackson was so upset, Johnson said, that he was "like a roaring lion" and was even considering sending home a foreign minister and his wife. He suggested that the two of them meet with Berrien and Branch that evening to discuss the matter further.

When Johnson met Ingham to go together to Branch's house for the meeting, he told him that the president was planning to issue personally the warning Johnson had already transmitted. When the two men met with the cold unbending Berrien and the outgoing sociable Branch, Johnson repeated his warning. The two other secretaries supported Ingham. When the three of them later attended a party at Colonel Towson's house (with Margaret Eaton definitely not in attendance), they were shocked to find that rumors of their removal were already rampant.

The next morning Johnson returned to see Ingham and once more threatened removal unless he and the other secretaries agreed to treat Mrs. Eaton more graciously. Once again, Ingham refused. Johnson left but returned during the evening to say that the president had spoken to a number of friends and had calmed himself down. He no longer insisted on his cabinet members visiting Mrs. Eaton. All he wanted the secretaries to do was help him protect her from her slanderers. When Ingham saw the president the next day, Jackson forthrightly defended Margaret Eaton and threatened to send Mrs. Huygens home. All he wanted from his cabinet, he said, was help against the slanders. Even Andrew Jackson knew he could not force any woman to accept his view of social propriety because this was in women's sphere. Still, as head of his cabinet, there had to be something he could do.[19]

Jackson prepared to send the three secretaries a memorandum. Instead, Martin Van Buren suggested, Jackson should read the statement to all three men at the same time and make it clear that he was not trying to control their social lives. Jackson agreed. He called the men to his office for a face-to-face conversation. He read from the memorandum which he held before him. "I do not claim the right to interfere in any manner in the domestic relations or personal intercourse of any member of my Cabinet," he said, clearly following Van Buren's advice, "nor have I ever in any manner attempted it." But he would not tolerate any of them encouraging attacks on Margaret Eaton, thereby hurting John Eaton and the whole administration. This he considered "a wanton disregard of my feelings and reproof of my official conduct." He had personally called Eaton into his Cabinet, so he was "responsible to the community for this alleged indignity to public morals. I will not part with Major Eaton from my Cabinet," he said, "and those of my Cabinet who cannot harmonize with him had better withdraw for harmony I must and will have."

The three secretaries unanimously denied there was any conspiracy against Margaret Eaton, but they insisted they "could not undertake to control their families." Jackson said he wanted to believe them "and hereafter it would be well . . . [to] conduct [themselves so] as not to give room to the world so to construe your conduct." He repeated his determination to keep Eaton in his administration and to have harmony in it. "Any attempt to degrade him I viewed," Jackson reiterated, "and should continue to view, as an indignity to myself." The three secretaries replied that they would do "nothing on their part . . . to destroy the harmony of the cabinet."[20]

On the surface, then, the rift seemed healed. Branch and Eaton had held an amicable meeting, and Andrew Jackson had put three cabinet members on notice. "Harmony prevails at present, personally as well as politically," Postmaster General Barry happily noted. At a February 23, 1830, White House cabinet dinner, everyone was present except for Berrien, who was ill. Emily Donelson and the cabinet wives were unenthusiastically civil to Margaret Eaton, and the evening went off well. At the home of the British minister to the United States, Sir Charles Vaughan, Margaret Eaton was later escorted to dinner by the ministry's popular secretary. Out in Frankfurt, Kentucky, newsman Francis Preston Blair breathed a sigh of relief. "On all accounts," he said, "I think it is fortunate that this affair has ended in explanation and peace, instead of invective and war."21

Once more, Jackson had not really put an end to the social and political war. The controversy was hardly solved. Even Barry, who noted the rebirth of civility, noticed that "a few impudent men and women of our own party . . . still are busy with Mrs. Eaton's character." John Quincy Adams saw the same thing. Meanwhile, Margaret Eaton won over the diplomatic corps because they felt sorry for her and because Jackson insisted on their cooperation. Many congressmen and their families also got into line. "Her circle of acquaintance is large and respectable," Barry said, but, he added with resignation, "Society is [still] unhappily divided about her." An opposition politician even predicted that Martin Van Buren would sacrifice John Eaton to further his own cause and that Eaton "himself is ready to *yield to the storm.*" The controversy raged on; it was hardly over.22

Adding to John Eaton's difficulties was the simultaneous Navy Department's investigation of John Timberlake's handling of money during his last tour as navy purser. An anonymous accusation appeared in the Washington press implicating the embattled secretary of war in the investigation. Allegedly, Eaton improperly used some of Timberlake's money—therefore government funds—to help save William O'Neale's boardinghouse and property for him; later, Timberlake received a loan from Eaton to help defray his purser expenses. Eaton responded firmly. Any charge that he took money from Timberlake, caused his default, or was now in any way responsible to the government for the shortfall was simply ridiculous, Eaton said. Illegally obtained government money had not paid for William O'Neale's property.23

On February 17, 1830, the Senate of the United States, seeing a chance to embarrass the president, demanded to see the results of the Navy Department investigation. It was at this point that Amos Kendall, the fourth auditor of the treasury, began to draw increasingly closer to Jackson. Born in Massachusetts with a frail constitution, he had grown up performing hard labor on his father's farm. Graduating from Dartmouth College, he later became a lawyer and moved to Kentucky in 1814, where he spent his first year as a tutor to the children of Henry Clay. In 1816, he took over a Lexington newspaper, the *Argus of Western America,* and at first was a strong supporter of Clay. By 1826, however, he had become a devotee of Andrew Jackson. When Jackson carried Kentucky in the presidential election of 1828, Kendall was rewarded with the position of fourth auditor of the treasury, a job he held for the next six years. When he handled the investigation of allegations against John Quincy Adams's officeholders in a manner that Jacksonians found appropriate, his stock rose even more. His similarly good service in this John Timberlake investigation advanced him still further. He was destined to become a major figure in the Jackson administration, one of the president's key advisers.

His appearance belied the fierce ability within. "He was lank, almost ungainly, slight of figure, ashen-faced." He had a high-pitched voice that irritated his listeners, and a head full of prematurely white hair. His health was terrible; he so frequently experienced chills and fevers that, even on the hottest day, he would appear on the streets of Washington wearing an overcoat buttoned to his neck. Still, "he had a way of impressing, in one fashion or another, all those with whom he came into contact."[24]

Kendall sent a report of the Timberlake matter to Secretary of the Navy Branch. He indicated that his investigation centered on Navy Lieutenant Robert B. Randolph, the purser who took over Timberlake's books upon his death at sea. Kendall also included the text of an anonymous letter threatening retribution against Eaton. This letter convinced Kendall that there was a conspiracy behind all the accusations. Unsaid but obvious, John Henry Eaton's inclusion in the case was the result of the controversy over his wife. A friend told Andrew Jackson in mid-March that he had concluded that "Mrs. Eaton is a persecuted woman and that for political effect." Her husband was a similar victim.[25]

DREADFUL FRACAS ATWEEN THE GINERAL AND THE BENTONS AT NASHVIL

Andrew Jackson's early life was filled with violence. No matter how large or small the disagreement, he fought rather than compromised. *(Library of Congress)*

Jackson was especially determined to protect the honor of his beloved wife, RACHEL DONELSON JACKSON, whom he married under unusual circumstances. When she died, just before his inauguration, he believed that slander had killed her, and he never got over his anger. *(Library of Congress)*

(Above) This was the way most Americans pictured ANDREW JACKSON: the military hero who defeated the Indians and secured national honor with his glorious victory over the British in New Orleans during the War of 1812. *(Library of Congress)*

(Left) Jackson's hero status resulted in a political career, and HENRY CLAY became his chief rival. In 1824, when Jackson lost the presidential election, he never forgave Clay for the "corrupt bargain" he believed stole the election from him. *(Library of Congress)*

JOHN QUINCY ADAMS was the beneficiary of the "corrupt bargain" with Henry Clay, becoming president of the United States in 1824. Jackson defeated Adams in 1828, declaring the victory a triumph of morality over evil, the people over the elite. *(Library of Congress)*

ackson's long-time confidante JOHN HENRY EATON narried Margaret O'Neale Timberlake a few months efore he joined the president's cabinet as secretary of ar. Their suspicious courtship provided the wives nd families of other cabinet members and Vashington society in general the justification to nub her. *(Library of Congress)*

Leading the moral brigade against Margaret Eaton was EZRA STILES ELY, a Presbyterian minister who earlier had demanded the election of Andrew Jackson to insure a "Christian nation." *(Presbyterian Historical Society, Philadelphia)*

MARGARET O'NEALE TIMBERLAKE was a favorite of Andrew Jackson from the days when he lived in her family's boarding house. Since photography was a later invention, this photograph is only an early twentieth century guess at her appearance. It expresses, however, the sensual beauty contemporaries suspected was an indication of her immorality. *(Alfred Henry Lewis,* Peggy O'Neal*)*

The March 1829 INAUGURATION of Andrew Jackson produced an outpouring of emotion for the "people's" president. *(Library of Congress)*

The president named John Henry Eaton territorial governor of Florida, and Margaret Eaton became a popular figure during her brief stay in the frontier capital, TALLAHASSEE. *(Library of Congress)*

Vice President JOHN C. CALHOUN reflected contemporary attitudes that women regulated morality and he supported his wife in her decision to snub Margaret Eaton. Andrew Jackson came to view Calhoun's actions as an attempt to wreck his administration by destroying an innocent woman. *(Library of Congress)*

When Margaret Eaton paid the required social call on Mrs. Vice President FLORIDE CALHOUN, this South Carolinian aristocrat refused to return the visit. *(Library of Congress)*

Nephew and presidential private secretary, ANDREW JACKSON DONELSON, like Calhoun, supported his wife's and society's stand against Margaret Eaton—to Jackson's chagrin and anger. *(Library of Congress)*

Official Executive Mansion hostess EMILY DONELSON, Jackson's niece, upset Jackson terribly when she joined Washington society in refusing to accept Margaret Eaton. *(Library of Congress)*

(Above) Secretary of State MARTIN VAN BUREN, a dapper widower, gained Jackson's affection by treating Margaret Eaton with civility. He replaced Calhoun as the heir apparent to the presidency. *(Library of Congress)*

(Right) Representative of the rising class of American newsmen, DUFF GREEN edited the Jacksonian paper, the *Washington Telegraph*. He became so anti-Eaton and pro-Calhoun that Jackson replaced him with Francis Preston Blair's *Washington Globe. (Library of Congress)*

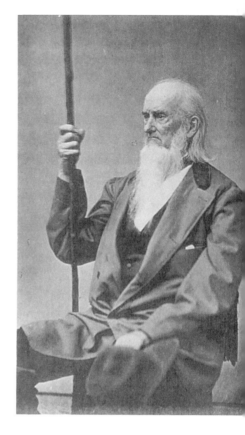

Secretary of the Treasury SAMUEL D. INGHAM and Secretary of the Navy JOHN BRANCH refused to coerce their wives and families into associating with Margaret Eaton, so Andrew Jackson fired them—and the rest of his cabinet. They did not leave quietly. *(Library of Congress)*

The dissolution of Andrew Jackson's cabinet in 1831, the only such event in American history, inspired this famous cartoon, which appeared in various forms. Note how Jackson is attempting to prevent the Van Buren rat from getting away. *(Library of Congress)*

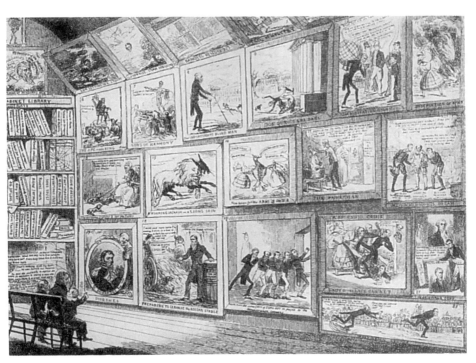

This cartoon left no doubt that, no matter Andrew Jackson's denials, Margaret Eaton was the cause of his cabinet's split. Notice the titles of the books to the left, for example, *Slave of Passion* and the panel at bottom right where Jackson is shown tripping over a petticoat in an ice skating race with Clay. *(American Antiquarian Society)*

This is the earliest known photograph of MARGARET EATON, taken some years after her turbulent time as a snubbed cabinet wife. *(Library of Congress)*

After her residence in Florida and several years in Spain as wife of the United States minister, MARGARET EATON became a widow again, married a twenty year old Italian dance master who fleeced her, and died in poverty. This is her appearance in her final years. *(Library of Congress)*

The Senate hearing found Timberlake (and by extension, Eaton) blameless; Purser Randolph was the culprit. The navy lieutenant demanded a military court of inquiry, which also found him guilty, and Andrew Jackson finally ordered his removal from the service in April 1833. He became so enraged that on May 6, 1833, he assaulted Jackson, the first physical attack on a president in American history. Randolph twisted Jackson's nose so violently that he caused it to bleed uncontrollably. This bizarre event only further validated the investigative exoneration of Timberlake and Eaton; but, perhaps more important, it once again associated Margaret Eaton's name with untoward behavior. Andrew Jackson never had any doubts about what was going on. He saw this investigation and every such attack as part of a "secrete & wicked combination to destroy Eaton for political affect."[26]

It was this political effect that increasingly dominated the heretofore social discussion. Those who agreed with Jackson that Margaret Eaton was without blemish and those who viewed her as a scarlet woman refused to budge as the months wore on. Jackson had long insisted that the attacks were really assaults on John Eaton and attempts to subvert the Jackson administration. The villains were Henry Clay and his supporters, the architects of the 1825 corrupt bargain that gained the presidency for John Quincy Adams and the authors of the vicious attacks on Rachel. Unfortunately for Jackson, this interpretation could not stand the test of facts. Too many Jacksonians were against Margaret Eaton for the president plausibly to believe it was all a Clay conspiracy. Over time, he shifted the blame for the Eaton Affair from Henry Clay to Vice President John C. Calhoun.

Jackson and Calhoun had never been particularly close, although they had both opposed the nationalist direction of John Quincy Adams's administration and, even more, the union of Adams and Henry Clay in the "corrupt bargain." Jackson and Calhoun reached out to one another politically, and Martin Van Buren supported the fusion. Calhoun's political strength in South Carolina helped Jackson, and Jackson's poor health seemed to be a guarantee of Calhoun's ascendancy to the presidency no later than 1832. As Jackson's biographer phrased it, the union of Andrew Jackson and John C. Calhoun was "a logical step." Still, once the election was over, Calhoun had played no direct role in the selection of the cabinet, and he maintained little contact with the president, remaining in South Carolina for the better part of the administration's first year.[27]

Even before Jackson and Calhoun took office, members of the Jacksonian coalition had begun planning for the president's successor. Smart money supported Calhoun, seeing only one man strong enough to block the South Carolinian's way to the Executive Mansion, that man being Martin Van Buren. The two men were friendly and politically close, so there was no innate animosity between them; however, divisions quickly formed over competition for the top spot. It was no surprise, therefore, that the social controversy over Margaret Eaton soon developed into a political conflict. Even in the Washington of this early day, politics and society were difficult to separate. Calhoun's wife had snubbed Margaret during the inauguration ceremonies and refused to return her visit during her brief time in Washington. As a result, she and her husband unfairly came to be seen as the leaders of society's opposition to Margaret, even though they had been in South Carolina for most of the year and had played no role in Washington events during that period. Van Buren, conversely, made valiant attempts to get society to accept Margaret, and he commiserated almost daily with the president about this and other matters, as the two men rode their horses around Washington. As John Quincy Adams facetiously analyzed it, "Calhoun heads the moral party, Van Buren that of the frail sisterhood."[28] The ever-present secretary of state not only surpassed the absent vice president in the president's personal estimation, but he also gained enormous political advantage when Jackson began to equate the social attacks on Margaret with the political ambitions of the vice president.

Calhoun was the kind of man whom the public admired but found difficult to like. He could be affable in private, but he was usually serious. "Tall, thin, straight, wiry . . . with sharp angular features; hair, originally black, but turned quite grey before he died," his very physique expressed his purposefulness. When he spoke in public, for example, an observer described him as "standing with every feature and muscle tense with emotion, his hair on end, and large drops of sweat on his forehead." A close friend, who admired him enormously, still found him "too intellectual, too industrious, too intent in the struggle of politics. . . . There is no recreation in him," the friend complained. "I never heard him utter a jest," a woman wrote at the time of his death, and though this was no doubt an exaggeration, Calhoun never cared much about society. He particularly found disputes among women to be a waste of time, "admit[ting] of neither inquiry nor explanation." Since Van Buren was a master of socializing, he had an enormous advantage over Calhoun in this social dispute. John Quincy Adams noticed that Calhoun increasingly "appeared to be exceedingly at a loss [as to] what to do" about the Eaton Affair. Van Buren seemed to have no such problem.[29]

By the end of 1829, the vice president's friends were clearly worried about Van Buren stealing a march on their champion. Eaton was the president's "alpha & omega," and "Van sees the ready avenue to the old man's ear." "If something is not done," feared a supporter, "the game is up [and] Calhoun is a dead man." A Clay supporter thought Van Buren was actually overplaying his hand, but he admitted that Margaret Eaton was the central issue. "You may think this Very strange that the admission of a certain Female into respectable Society at Washington should be made the basis of political orthodoxy by one branch of the reigning party, and her rejection Equally So by the other, but strange as it may appear, it is no less Strange than true." The false rumor that Floride Calhoun stayed away from Washington rather than have to associate with Margaret Eaton certainly added to Calhoun's problems, as did his lionizing by genteel Washington women at social gatherings to which Margaret had not been invited.[30]

Andrew Jackson, as did others, noted ever more frequently that he and his vice president were in disagreement on a variety of contemporary issues. Both men believed in states' rights, but Calhoun espoused South Carolina nullification, the right of a state to nullify a federal law such as the hated tariff. Jackson saw nullification as a dangerous threat to the survival of the Union. Jackson feared the growing power of the Bank of the United States, while Calhoun identified the tariff as the nation's major problem. The two men also differed on the national debt, redistribution of the federal surplus, and who should or should not be appointed to federal offices. That his message to Congress had received good press notice everywhere except in one district of South Carolina did not surprise Jackson. "I had hints that some of my old friends had changed," he said, and were using the Eaton Affair as an opportunity to hurt the administration.

Amos Kendall, ever on the watch for the latest political wind, began to hear rumors linking Calhoun to the Eaton problems, but he could not ascertain the truth of these stories. If they were true, he thought, Calhoun had to be "a madman . . . and he is not a wise man if he does not put an end to it." John Quincy Adams even linked the Timberlake investigation to the Van Buren-Calhoun split, arguing that if Van Buren won the intramural battle, the truth about Timberlake (and, of course, John Henry Eaton) would never be known. Francis Preston Blair expressed the feelings of many Jacksonians; he liked both Van Buren and Calhoun and did not want to have to choose between them. William T. Barry agreed: "I like Mr. C. as I do Mr. Van B., but I like General Jackson better than either."[31]

Something had to be done to calm the increasingly stormy political waters. A group of disgruntled Tennessee politicians held a secret meeting in mid-March 1830 to see how they could eliminate Eaton from the cabinet and still the continued turmoil. What actually happened remains a mystery, but one individual later claimed to have heard about one hundred congressmen, about half the House of Representatives, threatening to break away from Jackson if something was not done. He immediately alerted William Barry. The postmaster general said he had already told the president, so when this man discussed it with Jackson, the president "instantly raised himself to the full height of his noble stature & with his eyes lighted up with feeling & determination . . . [said] 'Let them come on—let the whole hundred come on—I would resign the Presidency or lose my life sooner than I would desert my friend Eaton.'" The secret meeting amounted to nothing, and Andrew Jackson continued to refuse to face up to the true political ramifications of the Eaton controversy. His opponents alone were at fault for it all, he continued to believe. His position was pure; his opponents were base and hypocritical. Jackson was determined to destroy his opponents politically—the equivalent of shooting an antagonist during a duel—or lose his life in the effort.[32]

To ensure greater stability, enhance the political fortunes of Martin Van Buren, and undercut John C. Calhoun's plans for 1832, Major William B. Lewis wrote a letter to the political establishment in Pennsylvania letting it be known that if the Keystone State quickly nominated Jackson, he would agree to run again in 1832. Jackson had originally planned to serve only one term—if his health allowed him to complete even those four years. Lewis wanted the Pennsylvania state legislature to nominate Jackson in such a way that Calhoun's plans would be thwarted. Pennsylvanians rose to the challenge and nominated Jackson, sixty-eight men signing the statement of support, Ingham and his supporters conspicuously not among the signers. New York politicians, worried about being left behind, jumped on the Jackson bandwagon, too. Lewis had achieved a marvelous coup. The renomination of Jackson was secure, and what Amos Kendall called the ambitions of a "too impatient" yet "noble" John C. Calhoun were dashed for another four years. After Jackson, the major winner was Martin Van Buren. Word spread that Van Buren would run for president in 1836, when Jackson retired. His vice presidential running mate then, the story continued, would be John Henry Eaton.[33]

Van Buren's victory and Calhoun's loss were hardly definitive, however. Calhoun and Jackson had not broken with each other, and, as vice president, Calhoun had an excellent platform from which to fashion a rapprochement. Instead, matters grew worse. In January 1830 on the floor of the Senate, Robert Y. Hayne of South Carolina, a Calhoun associate, defended individual state nullification of a federal law as the best safeguard for his home state and the South against national encroachment. These views clashed directly with the president's opposition to state sovereignty, and nullification thus became the major controversial expression of states' rights. In the Senate, Daniel Webster of Massachusetts spoke in defense of the Union, rhetorically painting a frightening picture of a rent nation if nullification gained ascendancy. All the listeners knew that Webster was not simply contesting Hayne but contradicting the philosophy associated with the man presiding over the debate, the vice president of the United States, John C. Calhoun.

The president and vice president, therefore, disagreed on the very core meaning of the government, and their difference soon became dramatically apparent for all to see. On April 13, 1830, the annual Jefferson Day dinner took place in Washington, and all the leading politicians in the Jacksonian coalition, including the president, were there. Jackson was so worried that the occasion might be used to trumpet the nullification doctrine that he carefully prepared his toast beforehand. As a hundred participants ate and drank, they heard twenty planned and eighty volunteer toasts. John Henry Eaton, for example, drank to "Public men: The people will regard with warmest affection those who shall be found to act from principle." A friend of Eaton's father-in-law considered this statement "a *home thrust to some men*," obviously the supporters of John C. Calhoun. Robert Y. Hayne, fresh from his debate with Webster, lifted his glass to "the *Union* of the States, and the *Sovereignty* of the States." Nullification was well represented.

Finally it was Jackson's turn. Getting out of his chair, and, as some later said, looking directly at Calhoun, who was sitting near him, Jackson exclaimed: "Our Union; *it must be preserved*." Indicating publicly his difference with Jackson, Calhoun followed with: "The Union. Next to our liberty, the most dear." The president and vice president had disagreed in public on the very nature of the nation's government. Once again, Jackson was appalled at what he had heard, now convinced more than ever that Calhoun and his supporters were involved in a conspiracy against his administration, that their attacks on the Eatons were designed to replace John Eaton with what contemporaries called a "nullie."[34]

Even before the Webster-Hayne Debate and the Jefferson birthday battle of the toasts, word had begun to circulate about another Jackson-Calhoun disagreement. Rumor had it that Jackson and Calhoun were about to split over a personal issue dating back twelve years. In 1818, Andrew Jackson had led an invasion of Florida in pursuit of the Seminole Indians. He had seized that Spanish territory and executed two British subjects without government authorization. In James Monroe's cabinet, only Secretary of State John Quincy Adams had defended Jackson's actions, though Jackson had always thought that Secretary of War Calhoun had been his main defender, and Calhoun had never contested this belief. Jackson had always held Secretary of the Treasury William H. Crawford responsible for the attacks on him. In reality, Calhoun had supported punitive action against the overzealous general. Congress had investigated the matter, and in the Senate John Henry Eaton had been Jackson's staunch defender. In later years Jackson heard rumors against Calhoun, but he ignored them because he and Calhoun were working together to defeat John Quincy Adams. The controversy seemed a dead issue as Jackson and Calhoun took office in March 1829.[35]

It came to life in November. Jackson held a large dinner for visiting former president James Monroe. A close friend of Monroe's, Tench Ringgold, the marshall of the District of Columbia, sat between Eaton and William B. Lewis. He commented on how pleased he was to see the two presidents enjoying each other's company, adding that Monroe had been Jackson's sole strong defender in the Seminole controversy. The entire cabinet, even Calhoun, had opposed Jackson? Lewis asked. All the cabinet, Ringgold replied. What about the letter Adams wrote in support of Jackson? Lewis probed. Oh, Monroe made him do it, Ringgold responded.

Later that evening, Lewis and Eaton were alone with the president. He seemed to be lost in his thoughts as he puffed on his pipe, and Lewis began discussing the earlier table talk. Jackson perked up when he heard what was being said but refused to believe the assertion against Calhoun. Lewis now sprang his obvious trap. He told Jackson about a letter from Governor John Forsyth of Georgia to James A. Hamilton in which Crawford was quoted as making the same accusation against the vice president. Jackson immediately ordered Lewis to go to New York to retrieve the letter.

When Lewis saw Hamilton, the New Yorker thought it only proper to get Forsyth's permission first. The Georgian then thought it made more sense to get a direct statement from Crawford, and this was immediately arranged. All this took time, of course, and it was not until the spring of 1830 that Jackson possessed all the documentation. Though he had long known the rumors about Calhoun's cabinet activities, Jackson now expressed anger at his discovery. "I have evidence to unfold to you," he told his good friend John Coffee, "the base hypocracy [*sic*] of the great secret agent as it respected myself as early as 1818, under the most positive assurance of his friendship."[36]

Jackson wasted little time in confronting Calhoun. On May 13, 1830, he sent his vice president a copy of the letter in which William H. Crawford accused Calhoun of opposing Jackson during the Seminole incident deliberations in Monroe's cabinet. Jackson asked Calhoun if Crawford's accusations were correct. Calhoun must have been completely shocked, delaying a reply until his "leisure may permit." He expressed pleasure that the persistent political attempts "to injure my character are at length brought to light."[37]

Jackson immediately demonstrated an anger toward Calhoun that clearly went beyond the simple rediscovery of this stale incident. Obviously reacting to the combination of differences he had developed with Calhoun, particularly his belief that Calhoun was behind the attacks on Margaret Eaton, Jackson used language that expressed calculated gloating and revenge rather than fierce anger over perceived disappointment. "He will either have to deny the truth of his statement, in Mr. Crawford's letter, or be in a delicate situation, if he admits the fact," Jackson said. When he received Calhoun's long and detailed explanation, he found it did not deny the accusation but blamed its appearance now on a political combination organized against him. Calhoun wanted no break with Jackson, but the president refused to give him any leeway. He told Calhoun that the vice president had missed the point of his letter. It had nothing to do with "either your conduct or your motives," Jackson said. It was a matter of Calhoun's "deception." He had heard accusations made against Calhoun before, but he considered the vice president so honorable he had refused to believe them. "I had a right to believe that you were my sincere friend, and, until now, never expected to have occasion to say to you, in the language of Caesar, *Et tu Brute*." Knowing what he knew now, Jackson said, "no further communication with you on this subject is necessary."[38]

Calhoun refused to capitulate, and the mails grew full of letters between the two men and the other participants in the 1818 controversy. No one convinced anyone, and Jackson's rhetoric escalated the more he thought about the whole matter. By the fall of 1830, he was calling his vice president "the most profound hypocrite he had ever known." He felt total animosity toward him. The family and friends of one member of Jackson's cabinet, who remained unidentified, "cherished an absolute conviction that the divulgence of Calhoun's opinion was purposely made by the friends of General Eaton to avenge Mrs. Eaton's wrongs."[39]

Andrew Jackson grew sick of this social and political mess and decided to escape to Tennessee, to the grave in the garden behind the Hermitage. He needed to go back home; he needed to get away from all these frustrations. But there was also business on hand. Jackson had continued pressuring the Indians east of the Mississippi to move to new lands across the river. The Chickasaws wanted to meet with him to discuss their future, so he agreed to a meeting. Secretary of War John Henry Eaton and old friend John Coffee were the government negotiators, so the Eatons would go to Tennessee, too.[40]

Jackson traveled with the Donelsons, leaving Washington on June 17, 1830, and proceeding along the National Road by stage and then on the inland rivers by steamboat. He received an enthusiastic welcome everywhere he passed, some 60,000 people cheering him in Cincinnati alone. Andrew Donelson remarked that it seemed that Jackson's popularity had not "waned at all." He and the Donelsons arrived in Nashville on July 5, Donelson hopeful that Jackson's old friends John Overton, John McLemore, and John Coffee would be able to talk some sense into the Old Hero about the Eaton controversy, "that subject," Donelson said, "which the master of the blue devils can alone fathom."[41]

John and Margaret Eaton moved west by a more roundabout route. John had decided to visit West Point first. He and Margaret left Washington three days before Jackson did, moving north toward New York City and arriving there on June 18, 1830. The plan was for the two parties to reunite in Wheeling, Virginia, a circumstance that Andrew Jackson Donelson dreaded. The Eaton Affair was moving west.[42]

The two-day West Point visit proved very successful. Though the cadets of the United States Military Academy must have peeked at the notorious Margaret Eaton from beneath their high hats every chance they had, she remained in the background. Superintendent Sylvanus Thayer and the faculty were determined to make a good impression on the secretary of war of an administration that viewed the academy as an elitist haven worthy of disbandment. Thayer and the staff went out of their way to make both Eatons feel completely welcome. Henry Clay's son, then a cadet, noted what a determined effort the academy made. Officers and cadets named their summer encampment "Camp Eaton" in the visiting secretary's honor. The Board of Visitors complimented him on his tenure as secretary and made sure that word of their praise got back to the president. The Eatons were clearly impressed, and John Eaton expressed support for the institution. He authorized Thayer to hire the music teacher the superintendent had requested and ordered extra compensation for officers commanding cadet companies.[43]

The Eatons next stopped at Newburgh, New York, for a public dinner and a ball. Traveling by steamboat to Albany, capital of New York and Martin Van Buren's seat of power, they received a cannon salute upon arrival. The wife of Charles E. Dudley, Van Buren's successor in the Senate, had already paid a visit on Harriet Butler, the wife of leading New York politician Benjamin Butler, soliciting her help in welcoming Margaret Eaton to the city. Mrs. Dudley had been in Washington with her husband and had been friendly to Margaret there. She wanted to make sure that Albany society treated the visitor well when she stayed with the Dudleys during her stay. Mrs. Dudley, with exaggeration, told Mrs. Butler that it was because of Margaret that Van Buren had gained his cabinet seat, and therefore his friends should, for his sake if for no other reason, be polite to Margaret. Mrs. Butler was not so sure, but the more she listened the more she was convinced that Margaret Eaton was indeed a wronged woman. "I cannot reflect upon this matter and think her an innocent and injured being without getting in rage," she said. "I will call on her if she comes to Albany," she told her husband. "I think I will."

Senator and Mrs. Dudley, assisted by Albany's mayor, also escorted the Eatons to the arsenal in the neighboring town of Watervliet. John Eaton conducted a three-hour inspection of the establishment and expressed himself well pleased with all he saw. A delegation from nearby Troy offered a public dinner, but the Eatons declined the offer due to the press of time. John and Margaret moved west toward Utica, a large delegation of Albany society following in their wake.[44]

Andrew Jackson viewed the Albany visit with great satisfaction, and he would have been happy to learn of the further invitations the Eatons had received. A Virginia politician mistakenly thought they were traveling that way and asked them to stop by, while one of the organizers of Fourth of July ceremonies in Buffalo, New York, did the same. These and no doubt other social events delayed the Eatons' progress, and they did not catch up with the Jackson party at Wheeling as planned. Indeed, they did not reach Nashville until July 18, almost two weeks after Jackson's arrival. All this time, Old Hickory worried like a parent awaiting a tardy child. He was disappointed not to find the Eatons at Wheeling and watched for them at every river port his boat reached. He had heard that Margaret was feeling ill at the beginning of the trip, and he was concerned about her. He was also upset when he learned that the

Donelsons had decided not to stay with him at the Hermitage but were residing with Emily's mother instead.[45]

Shortly before everyone had departed from Washington, another example of the Eaton problem had surfaced and predicted problems in Tennessee. Jackson had invited the Eatons to dinner one evening, and Margaret declined the invitation, not because of him, she said, but because she "could not be happy at your house for this would be to expect a different course of treatment from part of your family," a more pleasant reception, than "it has been my good fortune [yet] to meet." Even so, she continued, "I have spoken of your family in no other manner than a respectful one."

When Andrew Jackson Donelson saw this letter, he exploded with self-righteous indignation. He denied that his family had ever done anything *"unkind"* toward Margaret except for "their refusal to acknowledge her right to interfere with their social relations." This letter, he continued, was "abundant evidence of the indelicacy which distinguishes her character, and is disgraceful to her husband." "Childish importunities," "poison," "wretched expedients," and "vain desire"— the words poured from Donelson's angry pen. The Eatons and the Donelsons were clearly at open war.[46]

Still ignoring the Donelsons, Jackson concentrated on ensuring that Margaret and John Eaton received a warm reception from the people of Tennessee. He had the couple spend time with his old friend John Overton, one of Nashville's most respected figures. Then he made sure that there would be public dinners and receptions so that a variety of people could welcome the visitors. He invited them to the Hermitage, and he visited them at their home in nearby Franklin. He orchestrated it all through his friends and political allies, even though not all of them agreed with his position. John C. McLemore was deeply concerned that "the most rascally combination of scoundrels" was duping Old Hickory, and unless his good friends told him honestly what was happening, he would suffer a major loss. No woman except for the sister of a female who had traveled to Nashville with the Eatons planned to visit Margaret. Since no one seemed willing to stand up to Jackson, McLemore lamented, his friends would have to convince Eaton to withdraw, perhaps become a minister to a foreign land and leave the country.[47]

If anyone confronted Jackson as McLemore suggested, it did not show in the president's actions. He was no more willing to stop supporting the Eatons in Nashville than he had been in Washington. The first thing he told John Eaton on his arrival in Tennessee, in fact, was of his continued determination to break up his cabinet if its members remained in disharmony and especially if they plotted with "a foreign lady," (i.e., Mrs. Huygens). He insisted, all facts to the contrary, that he had never demanded, and never would demand, that any cabinet family associate with the Eatons. That was strictly a private matter, Jackson said, continuing to insist that politics and social relations could and should be kept separate.

He now also turned his attention to his relatives, the Donelsons. He told his friend John Coffee that "my duty is, that my household should bestow equal comity to all; the nation expects me to control my household to this rule." Had he been able to achieve this, "happiness would have been mine, and peace in the administration." In short, Jackson now blamed his niece and nephew for the whole Washington mess. It was the "combination of the most heterogeneous mass of base enemies and boosom [sic] and dear friends" that was at the bottom of it all. If the Donelsons had only stood firm with him, this Calhoun-led combination would have failed.[48]

When Jackson noticed the coolness developing in Nashville toward socializing with the Eatons, he immediately blamed the Donelsons' all-too-willing cooperation with Calhoun. "That my Nephew and Nece [sic] should permit themselves to be held up as the instruments, and *tools*, of such wickedness, is truly mortifying to me." Jackson was so angry that, as had been rumored in Washington at least since March, he contemplated firing Donelson as his secretary and actually was already beginning to look for a replacement. "I know I can live as well without them, as they can without me," he said in obvious reference to the Donelsons' absence from the Hermitage, "and I will govern my Household, or I will have *none*." When he later received an anonymous letter warning of a plot against him, that unnamed individual's assertion rang true to him because he had come to the same conclusion: "Your worse enemies are those of your own house."[49]

Since Nashville seemed determined to snub the Eatons, Jackson angrily wrote the city off. Riding to pay a visit to the Eatons at their Franklin home in late July, Jackson was ecstatic when he found three to five hundred people honoring them. He learned further that the town's women "had received Mrs. Eaton in the most friendly manner." They had extended that polite attention due to her. "This is as it should be," he said, "and is a severe comment on the combination at Nashville, and will lead to its prostration." He invited the Eatons to the Hermitage where he promised they would "receive that heartfelt welcome that you were ever wont" to receive, when Rachel was alive. "The presence of her old and sincere friend," he said to Eaton, "will cheer me amidst the melancholy gloom with which I am surrounded." His old friend John Coffee had arranged "a visible, and sensible change in my connections," he reported, "and they will all be here to receive you and your Lady. . . . I trust you are aware that I will never abandon you or separate from you, so long as you continue to practice those virtues that have always accompanied you." Jackson was literally changing friends in support of the Eatons.[50]

What happened during that Hermitage visit only brought Jackson closer to the Eatons and convinced him even more that he was correct in Margaret's defense. During the sumptuous meal consisting of barbecued pig and all the trimmings, Jackson was his usual charming self, personally passing out the bread to make all his guests feel welcome. As the diners left the table, however, he suddenly disappeared. John Eaton told his wife to see if she could find him in the garden, suspecting where he was. She discovered him lying prostrate on his wife's grave. "Come, General," Margaret softly said, "you must not do this. Please recollect what a company you have in the house. You must not come out here to grieve." Jackson stirred and responded equally softly: "Margaret Eaton, the woman that lies here has shed a thousand tears for my reputation and her own; and won't you allow me the privilege of shedding a few tears over her grave?" But, then, wiping his eyes and dusting himself off, he sadly walked arm in arm from the grave of his lamented wife with the person he saw as a new wronged woman. Jackson's dedication to Margaret Eaton was sealed at his wife's grave.[51]

John Overton followed the Hermitage dinner with one of his own, and the people in Franklin and the surrounding territories responded enthusiastically. Some forty women came, "the bone and sinew of the country," Jackson called them. The party was a rousing success. When the women were alone after dinner, Mrs. Overton and the other ladies convinced Margaret that if she was to be considered one of them, she would have to chew one end of an althea tree twig, then dip it in some snuff, and rub it vigorously on her teeth. Margaret agreed to the initiation ritual, and the next thing she knew she had thrown up all over her dress. The eagerly observing women laughed uproariously and seemed pleased when Margaret took the grossness as a good joke.[52] One can hardly imagine Mrs. Smith or Mrs. Calhoun thinking such behavior was funny, but the Nashville ladies did and so did Margaret. Washington society would only have chalked up another transgression against Andrew Jackson and Margaret Eaton had they known of this unfortunate occurrence.

The high point of the Eatons' time in the Nashville area may very well have come at the theater. John Eaton had helped found the institution in 1817 and had performed in several plays himself. He asked an old theater friend to arrange a performance of a play called *The Honeymoon*. As he and Margaret enjoyed the comedy several nights later, the audience roared with applause at a line that seemed particularly appropriate for the occasion: "The man that lays his hand upon a woman, save in the way of kindness, is a wretch whom it were gross flattery to call a coward." Since melodramas emphasized the necessity of female purity, making no allowance for even suspected transgression, John Eaton chose his play wisely. The night at the theater was a social and a political hit.[53]

Even the official duty went well. On August 17, 1830, Jackson traveled to Franklin to meet with Eaton, Coffee, and the Chickasaw Indian chiefs for an extended gathering, which resulted in a treaty leading to that tribe's move across the Mississippi River. Legend has it that the gathering took place near the Eaton home in Franklin, and that Margaret had her piano moved to the porch to entertain the delegates with her playing and singing. The one hundred Indians were not sure what it all meant, but they listened with great interest anyway. One wonders if Andrew Jackson enjoyed Margaret Eaton's music as much as he had in the 1820s as a boarder in her father's establishment. Unlike her hymn playing on those occasions, Margaret Eaton had here demonstrated her willingness to become involved in an explicitly male activity. She violated societal mores, which required a woman to stay in the background when men were conducting the business of their male world. It was the kind of inappropriate behavior that Margaret had practiced all her life and was a major cause of her social problems. She was simply too forward.[54]

Later in the year, though at first she protested the idea of entertaining "dirty old tobacco-smoking Indians" in her house, she made several tubs of lemonade to welcome a delegation. When they arrived and made her a gift of a silver set, she was won over and even took the peace pipe and smoked it with them. Society must have been shocked yet again at such unwomanly behavior.[55]

As the summer of 1830 turned to fall, Jackson, the Donelsons, and the Eatons had to begin making plans to return to the nation's capital. It was obvious that their respite in Nashville had solved nothing; indeed, it had only made matters worse. The Eatons and the Donelsons were further apart than ever before, and Jackson's anger against his niece and nephew was growing steadily. His Tennessee friends were afraid to tell him what they really thought, but through their quiet coolness toward Margaret Eaton they severed their friendships with him. The controversy over the wife of the secretary of war, up to this time a Washington spectacle, had now been played out in Tennessee, too. It was steadily becoming a national issue.

Someone, perhaps Jackson himself, decided that the best way to solve the problem was to convince Margaret Eaton and Emily Donelson to stay behind in Tennessee. They should not return to Washington until matters had settled down. Jackson grew convinced that if Margaret stayed in Franklin until midwinter, not coincidentally until after the social season was nearly over, "she would obtain a complete triumph every where." She might at least wait until the waters on the rivers rose, then bring her aged mother-in-law back with her more safely. John Eaton thought this was a good idea, too, but Margaret had no desire to allow her husband to return alone to Washington. She refused to be the submissive wife and accept her husband's decision.[56]

Jackson had less of a problem with Emily Donelson. For a time it seemed as though she would remain in Tennessee "with her widowed mother," and Andrew Jackson Donelson would remain there also. When word reached Washington that both Margaret and Emily would not be returning to Washington until some later undefined time, Duff Green, editor of the *United States Telegraph* and increasingly a Calhoun supporter, saw it all as a plot. Margaret Eaton was conniving to win in Tennessee what she could not accomplish in Washington: social acceptance.[57]

Andrew Jackson and his nephew returned to Washington at the end of September, while Emily Donelson remained in Tennessee with her mother. The Eatons stayed at their Franklin home for another month, the secretary of war receiving criticism from opposition newspapers for being absent so long from his Washington post. Rumor had it that Eaton was unhappy with "his reception in the west." Meanwhile, Donelson told his wife to hold her ground: "You cannot visit the madam—Mrs. Eaton," he said. "I have informed Uncle that you will treat her politely and socially . . . in his house, but that out of it I will make no pledges of such a character."[58]

Although Andrew Jackson was a lonely man in Washington, he was equally stubborn and not about to give in to his relatives. He wrote to Mary Eastin, making it clear that, lonely though he might be, he was not about to budge. He was blunt as ever. "I have long known the hypocrite who was at the bottom of this, secretly wielding his pulpits, afraid to act in open day. His hand is seen in the letters from Washington, as well as those from Nashville, but he will fail in this, as he has before when he attempted to stab me in the dark, when to my face and to the public, crying out he was my friend and would support me." The treacherous John C. Calhoun—this was the man that the Donelsons were supporting. Emily had better not come back to Washington "until such arrangements are made here, to secure harmony for the future. Better to put up with the separation for a short time than to come on and introduce again those scenes here that has cost me so much pain, which first and last has almost destroyed me, and this too produced by my dearest friends, uniting with and pursuing the advice of my worst enemies."[59]

At the offices of the *United States Telegraph*, Duff Green had a totally different perspective. "Van Buren has acted through Major Eaton upon the President." If he knew about this comment, the accused secretary of state had no reason to respond. He was feeling so secure in his relationship with the president that he could joke with Andrew Jackson: "Tell Mrs. Eaton if she does not write me I will give her up as a bad girl."[60]

6

"One of the Most Base and
Wicked Conspiracies"

As the Tennessee travelers returned to Washington in the fall of 1830 and the opening of Congress increased the pace of life in the nation's capital, it did not take observers long to realize that nothing had changed. The controversy over nullification remained unsolved and destined for a crisis, the tariff issue still particularly in dispute. Indian removal and the fierce debate over its justification and methods continued. Federal land policy was still in question, as was the government's role in the building of new roads and internal improvements in general. Andrew Jackson had stiffened his position against the Bank of the United States, and in foreign policy, his attitude toward England and France remained similarly determined. The president and his administration had a great deal on their minds, but, once again, the case of Margaret Eaton took center stage.

A congressman surveying the late 1830 scene in Washington noted that "the petty intrigues of this place have commenced and we shall have the same scenes acted over again this winter that were acting during the last. . . . Mrs. Ingham gave a splendid party last night," this individual noted, "& left out Mrs. Eaton." Secretary of the Navy John Branch hosted "a great wedding party" another night, as did one of Washington's leading socialites, a Mrs. Pleasanton. John and Margaret Eaton were "left out of both." Gossip had it that Jackson was so fed up with the mess that he was planning to jettison Margaret Eaton or Mrs. Ingham or both.[1]

Andrew Jackson's own family increasingly became his major problem. During the summer, one of his Nashville supporters, after spending a day with Andrew Donelson, was confident that he and Emily were ready to return to Washington on their uncle's terms. "Harmony . . . as well as system" would be restored to the Executive Mansion. The cabinet could quickly be brought into line. Then, all of Jackson's friends could "endeavor to rivet the public attention on the great measures of the admin. and not on petty rascally scandals."[2]

Harmony remained elusive, however. Emily Donelson did not return to Washington, and John C. Calhoun and Andrew Jackson had not resolved the Seminole Affair. To make matters worse, these problems became the fodder for one of early America's angry newspaper disputes. In Tennessee, meanwhile, a local political contest that fall had become wrapped up in the virtue of the wife of the secretary of war in Washington. Matters were not improving. They kept getting worse and worse for Andrew Jackson and his administration.

Through it all, Margaret Eaton remained unbowed. In December 1830, she held a large dinner party. One attender, who identified himself as "a backwards Missouri judge," but was actually a circuit court magistrate visiting Washington, was thrilled at his invitation from "the distinguished, fashionable and beautiful lady of the American Minister of War." He was so excited about his experience that he did not want to talk about it in his letter home, promising to tell "of wonders" when he returned.[3]

Official Washington was not nearly as impressed, of course, and nodded knowingly when Eaton's opponents unfairly ridiculed his annual War Department report, insisting that the editor of the *United States Telegraph* had actually composed it. These critics also charged Eaton with improprieties in his handling of Indian legislation, while a disgruntled patronage seeker accused him of accepting a bid for provisioning the emigrating Indians that was higher than the one he had rejected from him. When in March 1831 Jackson reappointed Margaret Eaton's father, William O'Neale, to another term as an inspector for the Washington Penitentiary, opponents carped about this, too. No doubt, they agreed with John Floyd, the governor of Virginia, who considered O'Neale nothing but "a roguish, impudent Irishman, without any principles, but a good tavern-keeper." As O'Neale's daughter and as his son-in-law, Margaret and John Eaton could obviously not be much better.[4]

Andrew Jackson decided that he would never get to the bottom of these problems if he did not first solve his difficulties at home. The Donelsons had to take his advice, turn their backs on the women snubbing Margaret Eaton, and treat her with social civility. Then, the conspiracy would quickly collapse. Since Emily remained in Tennessee, away from her husband in Washington yet encouraged by him to hold her ground, Jackson's family conflict was not even close to resolution.

Jackson and his nephew must have had extended discussions concerning their disagreement on their long return trip to Washington from Nashville. They traveled about thirty miles a day, normally beginning with "coffee by candle light, and breakfast at 10 or 11 after about 12 miles ride."[5] What other topic could have been more important to the two men than the missing Emily and the reason for her absence? Jackson may very well have so nagged his nephew that Donelson grew weary of the topic. Perhaps, too, Jackson used his vaunted temper on the young man and tried to intimidate him into changing his position. Whatever happened, it had no effect. When the two men settled into the close confines of the Executive Mansion in Washington, they remained miles apart on the most important issue in their relationship.

The problem was complicated by the fact that Andrew Donelson was an insecure individual. He wanted to please his uncle, his uncle's political opponents, and society's gentility all at the same time. That he worshiped his uncle was clear, but he did not think Jackson understood society and was politically naive besides. He worried that if he accepted his uncle's view of Washington, he and his wife would find themselves suffering the same ostracism they supported against Margaret Eaton. He was Andrew Jackson's son in that way. He stubbornly held to his view as a matter of honor, even if that meant opposing the very man who had taught him about honor in the first place.

Soon after Jackson and Donelson had settled into their own rooms at the Executive Mansion, uncle and nephew literally stopped talking to each other. One morning after what must have been yet another discussion of the matter, and a particularly intense one perhaps, Donelson "thought it best" to present Jackson with his "views in writing as the least painful mode of communicating them." Correspondence replaced conversation as the medium for Donelson and Jackson to wrestle over the problem separating them and affecting the nation.[6]

Donelson insisted, disingenuously to say the least, that when he and Emily had first arrived in Washington in 1829 they had "commenced an intercourse with the family of Majr Eaton ... [which] placed them upon the same footing that other respectable members of society occupied." Despite such generosity, Donelson said, John Eaton still sent a letter to Emily "in which he descends to the insinuation that she has placed herself under the guardianship of slanderers." Emily's friends were not slandering individuals, they were Washington women who had been friends of Aunt Rachel, he said. Later, when Emily did not react to Margaret's liking during a fainting spell on the boat ride to Norfolk, Margaret had threatened them both with a return to Tennessee. Therefore, Donelson said, he could not allow Emily to meet with Margaret Eaton except in Jackson's home—"if you think [it] proper to invite her return." He hoped Uncle would understand that his motives were upright, but he was upset at seeing "this petticoat affair employed in prejudicing old friends and in creating new ones." All he wanted now was a guarantee that, if Emily returned, she would not have to visit Margaret Eaton or "hold an intercourse with her" out of the Executive Mansion.[7]

Jackson was shocked that Donelson had turned to writing notes instead of having face-to-face conversations, since the two of them were living in the same house. Dejectedly, he promised an immediate reply anyway. Once again he defended Margaret Eaton's reputation and wondered how Donelson could repeat such slander against her without having read any of the testimony Jackson had gathered in her defense. Of course, "all people have a right to select their society, every head of a family have [*sic*] the right to govern their House hold," but it bothered him that Donelson, in his youthful inexperience, was acting on mere rumor. Thinking about it further, Jackson asked for "a free, friendly, and full conversation" on the whole matter. Donelson ignored that proposal and began to consider a return to Tennessee himself rather than force Emily into a social relationship with Margaret Eaton. Jackson, increasingly upset, could only ask for more talk and less writing.[8]

The two men put their pens down for a couple of days and then immediately reached for them again. Donelson continued to insist that it was John Eaton's attack on several good women of Washington, Emily's friends, that had created the original problem. Eaton's use of beloved Aunt Rachel to attack these women was also a major irritant, Donelson said. Still, he admitted, Mrs. Eaton deserved the same treatment in the Executive Mansion that any other cabinet wife received, but outside of that place any visitations would be degrading. "You did not when a prisoner in the revolutionary war obey the order of the enemy who had you in his power to clean his boots. Yet you find fault with my determination merely to keep out of the way of insult." As for Jackson's frequent complaint about them not staying at the Hermitage last summer, Donelson said Jackson should know that they had no choice. When Mrs. Eaton had refused to come to dinner because, she said, he and Emily did not treat her properly, Jackson had taken her side. "Were we not bound from respect even to your feelings not to put ourselves in the way of the honors you intended to pay to Mr. and Mrs. Eaton at the Hermitage?" Besides, Emily had not seen her mother for a long time and did not deserve Jackson's censure for wanting to stay with her.[9]

Then the discussion degenerated into nitpicking. Donelson had used the phrase "as your guest" so that it seemed to refer to himself rather than to Margaret Eaton as he had intended. Jackson expressed disbelief that his nephew would ever consider himself a guest in his home. "You were my family, my chosen family," not guests. It was "unjust," "humiliating to us all, and all the world must condemn it," Jackson lamented. Besides, all he wanted from him and Emily was to treat everyone who came to their home with "the same comity." Donelson replied that, of course, he considered himself a member of Jackson's family. He had miswritten the sentence. But even as Jackson's family, there was a limit to the social obligations he and Emily had to Mrs. Eaton. All right, Jackson responded, it was clear to him that Donelson was not willing to give in, that he viewed "the requirements requested by me, as a sacrifice." Jackson would, therefore, live in Washington without any women, and Donelson was free to go back to Tennessee whenever he wished, taking with him Jackson's love and prayers.[10]

Donelson made no move to leave, but he began to tire of the letters because he was getting nowhere with them. He reopened conversation, challenging Jackson's central belief that a refusal to meet with Mrs. Eaton on a social basis was proof of political animosity. The president responded with his conviction that political conspiracies, evident everywhere, were behind the social problem. He would never stop supporting Eaton, he said, and if the members of his cabinet did not change their attitudes he would simply get rid of them all. Forty members of Congress had asked him last winter if he was really in charge of his own administration, and he was going to prove that he was. Back and forth the debate flowed, day after day, neither man budging and Jackson expressing deeper and deeper hurt and frustration. Emily had replaced Rachel, he said, so she had a duty to act as Rachel would have acted in this circumstance. Since she declined to do so, her decision to stay in Tennessee was correct.[11]

As the two stubborn men unsuccessfully tried to find some agreement in Washington, Emily Donelson sought resolution in Tennessee. Her cousin, Mary Eastin, had shown her the heartfelt letter Andrew Jackson had sent several months previously, and Emily searched for just the right words to answer it. Her husband kept her informed of goings-on in Washington, and she tried to be supportive, even expressing a willingness to go back to their farm in Tennessee if they could not solve the problem. She repeatedly urged him not to do anything he would later regret or that would help Jackson's enemies. She urged him to stay through the winter for Uncle's sake. Her love for Uncle was undiminished, and she was willing to sacrifice her own happiness for his welfare. But she could not bring herself to socialize with Margaret Eaton, whatever Andrew Jackson wanted.[12]

Emily consulted Jackson's friend John C. McLemore on an appropriate response to Jackson's letter to Mary Eastin. She expressed her

love for Uncle, but stood her ground, reflecting well both her husband's and McLemore's advice. McLemore planned to follow up her
letter with one of his own in which he defended Donelson and put all
the blame for the controversy on William B. Lewis, whose presence in
the Executive Mansion the Donelsons had long resented. Eaton was a
fine person, McLemore said, but Jackson should send him to an overseas mission. Emily was willing to come to Washington and "treat
Mrs. E in a way to strengthen Mr. E so that it will aid him in getting
him through the Senate etc" on the diplomatic appointment. In the
meantime, Donelson must not leave Washington; Jackson needed him
too much. Unfortunately, the Tennessee solution sounded like more
of the same and boded ill for any final conclusion.[13]

Andrew Jackson carefully read the Nashville letters, and another
from Mary Eastin, then visiting family in Alabama. The young
woman expressed concern that Jackson was "so much aggravated by
the idea that your connections have deserted you." Neither this nor
anything else he read impressed Jackson very much. All he saw were
new conspiracies in Nashville that convinced him of the correctness of
his analysis and toughened his determination to stay his course. "My
dr Emily," he concluded, "I never *desert a friend, without cause; I never
will, a friend in distress,* and particularly one who has displayed his acts
in so many ways as Eaton has to me, and mine."[14]

In his sixteen-page letter to McLemore, written on Christmas Day
1830, Jackson reiterated all the arguments he had used since he had appointed Eaton to his cabinet in February 1829. He praised the friends
who had stuck by him, and he attacked Calhoun. He summarized the
whole controversy as "a combination unheard of before in any christian country . . . by which the most innocent female can be destroyed
by *rumour* which can be set on foot by a *hired slave* and propagated by
hired gossips . . . [and which] justice & truth combined with charity
must blush at & condemn." He reminded Mary Eastin that "a House
divided against itself cannot stand" and that "Friendship is a precious
jewel."[15]

As Jackson refused to give in, so did Andrew and Emily Donelson.
Mrs. Ingham praised Emily's stand and promised not to waiver herself.
Andrew also praised Emily's steadfastness and thought the whole mat-
ter would come to a head in a week or so. "If it be the wish of Uncle

not to have us in his household unless we can visit Mrs. E, there will be no reluctance on my part to give room to those who will gratify him in this respect." Absolutely not, McLemore admonished from Nashville, practically shouting the words across the miles: *"You must not leave the Genl not on any cost until I shall visit the city."* [16]

Unexpectedly, all these written and spoken words finally vented the mutual anger and frustration. In early January 1831, about the time when Jackson and Calhoun seemed on the verge of reconciliation over the Seminole Affair, Donelson noted that Jackson was not talking about the Eaton matter any more and seemed to be his old self again. Indeed, Jackson seemed suddenly to have caved in. When he and Donelson talked about the problem, Jackson told Andrew to decide when Emily should return. And, Andrew noticed, Jackson made this comment "without alluding to the influence which produced your stay in Tennessee; and with his former tenderness of feeling has disclaimed any wish to control in any way our own views of propriety touching it." Jackson expressed this attitude to Emily himself. In answer to her description of her visit to Aunt Rachel's grave at the Hermitage, he gave her a short lecture on how Margaret Eaton might "have her imprudencies, [and] if she has, let them be so considered and treated as improprieties, but not treated as [a] lady without virtue." Jackson understood Margaret's forwardness, but he insisted that it was no proof of her impurity. Emily and the other critical women were not making an essential distinction, he believed, and, instead, were unfairly linking the two separate matters against her.

It was all a plot, and she would some day understand it, Jackson wrote. "But enough of this my Dr. Emily," and he concluded with obvious resignation, "you have given me assurances, sufficient to satisfy me, that your course will be that of propriety *to all.*" Even John Henry Eaton let it be known that he held no grudges against Andrew Donelson, though Margaret's feelings at this time were left unsaid. Donelson had dinner with Martin Van Buren who, as was his habit, sent his best to Emily. He also had dinner with Secretary of the Treasury Samuel D. Ingham, demonstrating that he felt secure enough in his reconciliation with Jackson to socialize with one of the individuals Jackson particularly blamed for the Eaton problems. Perhaps he was following John

Coffee's advice to agree with Jackson on everything, disagreeing only when his "sacred honor" was involved.[17]

John Coffee's activities and those of John McLemore seemed to have borne fruit. Once again, the problem seemed solved to everyone's satisfaction. Andrew Donelson, however, wanted to make sure that the solution did not include any compromise on his or Emily's part. He was willing to have his family treat Mrs. Eaton as they treated everyone else during public ceremonies in Jackson's home, but he continued to refuse to accept any obligation to socialize with her as a prerequisite for being part of the president's Washington family. In short, Donelson had not moved an inch from the position he had taken in the very first letter he had written to Jackson on the subject. Apparently, though, Jackson was willing to let the matter slide—or, more logically, Coffee had convinced Jackson that his niece and nephew had moderated their position and, if Jackson just did not pressure them, everything would be fine. Since he remained busy debating Calhoun over the Seminole Affair, Jackson was happy to be finished with family arguments. As Andrew Donelson departed for Tennessee on March 8, 1831, to gather his family and bring them back to Washington, Jackson was excited as he anticipated their return.[18]

The very day Donelson began his long trip back to Tennessee, the tenuous agreement began to unravel. John Eaton was seriously ill and at risk of dying, yet Donelson made no effort to see him before he left town. Eaton lamented this omission, amazed that Donelson had departed without paying his respects, knowing that he might never see Eaton alive again. Jackson was appalled, too, upset that Donelson missed the opportunity that might have "produce[d] harmony and a restoration of friendship between those that ought to be so." He continued to see no difference between public politeness that Donelson seemed willing to promote and private intimacy that he refused to give.[19]

Within two weeks, the earlier good feelings had completely evaporated. Jackson was forthrightly espousing his original position, the stand he had never really given up but had decided not to push. He now pushed it very hard, no doubt also angry that the apparent agreement with Calhoun had fallen through. "But o my Dear Andrew, un-

less you can come . . . to harmonise and unite in council with me and
my friends, instead of associating with my hidden and secrete enemies,
better not come." In case there was any question about his meaning,
Jackson described a recent White House dinner in which his cabinet
displayed its "usual stiffness," but everyone else, especially the diplomats' wives, were "courteous and familiar." The guest of honor "was
particularly attentive to Mrs. Eaton." Reading these words, the Donelsons decided to stay in Tennessee until the new storm blew over.
Whereas Coffee had apparently established a fragile agreement, Calhoun's renewed animosity had helped destroy it. Andrew Jackson and
his niece and nephew remained estranged. And now even Andrew
Donelson was away from Washington. Jackson had no family of any
kind with him in the huge Executive Mansion.[20]

The storm around the administration that had been brewing
throughout the fall had, therefore, grown worse, but it was still some
time from reaching the peak of its ferocity. In Washington, the Seminole controversy with John C. Calhoun continued unabated; and in
Tennessee, a political race that previous November convinced Jackson,
if he needed any further convincing, that the attacks on Margaret
Eaton were indeed part of a giant conspiracy against him.

Two friends of Andrew Jackson's were opponents in a congressional
race in Tennessee during the fall of 1830. Robert M. Burton and ex-
Governor William Hall were both part of the Jacksonian movement
there, one that was clearly pulling apart. Robert Desha, the sitting
congressman, had decided not to run again and threw his support to
Hall. He was close enough to Jackson to have approached him as part
of a Tennessee delegation in February 1829 to advise him against including John Eaton in the cabinet. Jackson had, of course, been unhappy with that advice, but it had not ruptured their relationship.
Now, however, Desha was going around the congressional district
telling the voters that Jackson was hostile toward him because of his
stand on the Eaton nomination. In Gallatin, a small town in the heart
of the district near Nashville, Desha told the gathered citizens that he
had said to Jackson that "Mrs. Eaton was an abandoned woman and
that she had not been received into genteel society for five years before
Major Eaton had married her." At the same time, Desha reported,

Burton and his wife had visited Mrs. Eaton. Burton had supported a fallen woman, as did the president. Neither man deserved their vote.

Burton took up the defense of Mrs. Eaton, calling her "a persecuted and injured female." "The indignation of the crowd," Burton reported to Jackson, "seemed to be aroused to an unusual height." He easily overwhelmed Desha in the debate, he said. Later, however, he learned that Stokely Donelson, Emily's brother, was telling lies about him and Mrs. Eaton.[21]

Jackson was shocked at Desha's behavior, particularly since the congressman had only recently visited him at the Hermitage and had been silent about the controversy. He did not interfere in local races, Jackson said, and, besides, Desha's 1829 advice concerning Eaton had not affected Jackson's attitude toward him. He and Desha had a long discussion about the matter at that time, and it was clear to Jackson that Desha knew nothing about Margaret Eaton "of his own knowledge." Desha's speech, therefore, was simply not true, and he hoped Burton would counteract it with this letter.[22]

Jackson immediately concluded that Desha's behavior, when linked with the animosity some Nashville leaders had shown Margaret Eaton during her visit there, was another example of the Calhoun conspiracy against him. "The double dealing of J.C.C. is perfectly unmasked," he insisted, and Desha's "imprudence" simply let the world see it more clearly than ever before. It was, he lectured Emily Donelson, "one of the most base and wicked conspiracies" imaginable, and the fact that her brother was participating in it made it even worse. "A House divided cannot stand," he warned. Meanwhile, Burton and Desha got into a brawl at a county courthouse after a joint speech in which they had argued once again about Margaret Eaton's virtue. Burton tried to shoot Desha, but his pistol misfired so he threw it at him instead. Desha then broke a cane to pieces on Burton. As a barely literate observer—who offered himself and his friends as defenders of Mrs. Eaton—described the melee to Jackson: "Desha giumpt on him and gauged both his eyes badley so the fight ended—Desha was fined $37.20."[23] Eventually, however, William Hall won the election.

The Donelsons, to their misfortune, were closely connected to Desha. In March of 1831, when he wanted to let Emily know that he was coming home to get her, Andrew sent word through Desha. And in his first letter to Donelson in Tennessee when Jackson once more reapplied conditions for the Donelsons' return to Washington, the president was full of anger against John C. Calhoun. He continued to see his vice president as the mastermind of the giant conspiracy of which Desha, Stockley Donelson, and, he again feared, the Donelsons were all a part.[24]

What made this alleged Tennessee connection with Calhoun especially irritating to Jackson was the heating up of the Seminole Affair. Jackson had believed that once he confronted Calhoun, the vice president would be destroyed, his lies about supporting him on Florida finally having been unmasked. But this did not happen. Calhoun was just as stubborn as Jackson and just as convinced about a giant conspiracy. Jackson saw Calhoun as the key conspirator, while Calhoun put the blame on Martin Van Buren, the recently silent secretary of state. Calhoun was sure Van Buren was still angling to replace him as Jackson's successor. With Henry Clay waiting in the wings, Jacksonians continued to hope that the animosity between their president and vice president could be ended. Calhoun had a chance to offer an olive branch by attending Jackson's New Year's Day 1831 levee, but the vice president was conspicuous by his absence, even in the huge crowd of two thousand people who were there.[25]

Early into the new year of 1831, as Jackson fought his feud with the Donelsons, he and Calhoun continued their efforts to dig up dirt on each other. Gideon Welles, the future navy secretary in Abraham Lincoln's cabinet but presently a Hartford newsman, let Martin Van Buren know that a person close to Calhoun had tried to recruit him to the Carolinian's side and that "attempts" were being made "to create prejudice" against Van Buren. Meanwhile, the president wrote to John Rhea, the former Tennessee congressman who, he insisted, knew of his 1818 letter to Monroe soliciting permission to invade Florida. Calhoun similarly appealed to former Monroe cabinet members, Samuel Southard and William Wirt, about their remembrances and reached out to John Quincy Adams. The former president did not reach back. Ever since the inauguration, Adams said, Calhoun had practiced "icy-hearted dereliction of all the decencies of social intercourse with me, solely from the terror of Jackson." Adams grew concerned enough about being pulled into this dispute, however, that he had his wife copy sections of his 1818 diary concerning the cabinet discussions about Jackson's activities in Florida.[26]

Calhoun's supporters grew increasingly worried that Van Buren was outmaneuvering their man and began talking about publishing all the correspondence related to the dispute. A Washington newspaper reported this possibility, quoting an Albany paper, which asserted that John Quincy Adams had given Van Buren "minutes" of the Monroe cabinet discussions. Adams denied this, while Tennessee Senator Felix Grundy lamented the increasing lack of unity in the Jacksonian administration itself. At the end of January 1831, there was even a rumor of a near duel between Calhoun and Van Buren, and a nasty press battle was developing in the nation's capital reflecting and exacerbating the administration split. Andrew Jackson had major problems both in Tennessee and in Washington, and they were only getting bigger.[27]

The city's newspapers played an increasingly important role in the administration's conflicts. When Andrew Jackson had taken office in 1829, he had quickly let it be known that his newspaper would not be the staid *National Intelligencer.* Edited and published by Gales and Seaton, it was clearly the establishment newspaper, dryly presenting verbatim accounts of congressional debates and brief and gentlemanly support for the party of James Monroe and John Quincy Adams. As the 1824 and 1828 presidential elections split that party, however, it became clear that the *National Intelligencer* had outlived its usefulness. Each faction wanted a newspaper espousing its specific position, and a variety of papers emerged to fill that need. The *United States Telegraph,* edited by Duff Green, became the Jackson paper.[28]

Born in Kentucky, Green quickly became a major voice on the American scene. He had been a soldier in the War of 1812 under William Henry Harrison and had moved to Missouri after the war's end, where he developed several successful businesses, including the first trans-Mississippi River stagecoach line. He also became a successful lawyer, and when he entered the political arena, he made a prophetic toast that forewarned of his later political alliance. Sounding like John C. Calhoun at the 1830 Jefferson Day dinner, Green toasted in 1820: "The Union—it is dear to us but liberty is dearer." In 1823 he acquired a St. Louis newspaper, and a year later he purchased the

United States Telegraph in Washington. By leading the charge against the so-called corrupt bargain of the 1824 presidential election, he endeared himself to Jackson. He gained the contract as printer to Congress and settled in as editor of the administration's organ.[29]

Green was a fiery individual who spoke his mind and was more often than not disagreeing with someone. He had a rocky relationship with his employees, with his first partner at the *Telegraph,* and with Amos Kendall, whom at first he asked to join his newspaper but later fought a no-holds-barred political battle against. One of the major investors in the *Telegraph* was John Henry Eaton, and it was his persistence in the Senate that helped Green gain the congressional printing contract that was absolutely essential for the newspaper's survival.[30]

But by June of 1830, Andrew Jackson was ready to jettison Duff Green and the *United States Telegraph,* and Amos Kendall, increasingly a close adviser, agreed that this was a good idea. Both men were upset at Green, who, obviously holding out for Calhoun, had opposed the early renomination of Jackson for the presidency. Green also showed little enthusiasm for Jackson's growing animosity toward the Bank of the United States. More ominously, Green was increasingly turning against John and Margaret Eaton. In a long letter of justification to an obviously sympathetic Andrew Donelson, he insisted that his main opposition to Margaret was because of the damage she was causing Jackson. It was ridiculous, Green said, for anyone to equate Margaret Eaton with Rachel Jackson. Even Rachel's worst "enemies all admitted that she had been an exemplary wife for *thirty* years," and that opponents had unfairly attacked her for political reasons. Not so Margaret Eaton. "She is not content with the triumph which she has achieved in the person of her husband, she wishes to mark distinctly *her* influence—or in other words she wishes it to be understood that her influence predominates." Opponents were increasingly insisting that Jackson was "the mere creature" of John Eaton and Martin Van Buren, and Margaret Eaton's continuing influence only gave credence to such beliefs. Duff Green was obviously on the wrong side of the issue that his president saw as the key factor in the political attacks on his administration.[31]

Jackson, who sniffed out anti-Eaton comments with the determination of a good hunting dog, had to be fully aware of Green's attitude.

He could, for one thing, read some of Green's concerns in his newspaper, and the president's supporters were only too happy to point out anything else he might have missed. Being the impulsive person that Green was, he also no doubt bluntly expressed, in conversation, the same feelings he put into his letter to Donelson. Jackson could not tolerate such opposition; Green had to go. The question was, Who would replace the fiery newsman as the administration's editor?

Amos Kendall made the first substantive move to fill the position. Throughout his early tenure in the Jackson administration, Kendall had continued his correspondence with Francis Preston Blair, a Kentucky newsman on the *Argus of Western America.* In late August 1830, he told Blair to get ready to come to Washington with the incoming Congress. Francis Preston Blair agreed to come, having already paved the way by sending to Andrew Jackson the latest political news from his state, the first time he had ever written the president. It was obvious that he wanted the job, and Kendall wanted him to have it. Jackson agreed.[32]

The son of a former Kentucky attorney general of twenty years' standing, Blair graduated from Transylvania University with both undergraduate and law degrees but never practiced law because of his poor health. As a determined battler in the bank wars in Kentucky, he had come out of these debtor relief law fights much admired for his ability to frame political arguments in the most effective partisan perspective. He had worked with Kendall on the *Argus,* and when Kendall went to Washington he took it over. A staunch defender of Jacksonian positions, he had attacked a Henry Clay newspaper for conducting "vile insidious warfare" against Margaret Eaton. He seemed just the person Jackson wanted in Washington.[33]

Blair's reputation had preceded him, so when he arrived at Jackson's office, he shocked everyone with his unimpressive appearance. "Mousy looking, hardly weighing more than a hundred pounds," "a walking cadaver," a Jackson biographer later described him, looking even worse because of a cut on the side of his head from a recent accident. It made no difference. He and Jackson hit it off immediately, and on December 7, 1830, the *Washington Globe* began publication.[34]

At first, supporters of Blair's *Globe* insisted that it was being published only as a supplement to Green's *Telegraph.* Kendall encouraged

Blair to be sure and talk to Duff Green before he visited anyone else in Washington. Blair not only followed Kendall's advice but, with his friend's help, also flooded Green with letters from politicians professing support for the new press arrangement. Blair and Kendall were not completely truthful. For example, Kendall wrote to Virgil Maxcy, the solicitor of the treasury. He asked for his aid in making sure that the inevitable new paper that everyone was talking about (but that he did not identify) worked in "perfect concert on all material points" with the *Telegraph*. Blair and Kendall did not want to anger Green before they had their own newspaper to answer any attacks word for word.[35]

The Seminole controversy continued its ferocity into 1831, however, and the two newspapers split over its meaning. The *Telegraph* defended Calhoun; the *Globe* clearly supported Jackson, Van Buren, and Eaton. The Washington battle now received wide publicity. Other newspapers throughout the country followed the conflict, taking sides for or against the main protagonists. There had always been anti- and pro-Jackson newspapers; now there were Jacksonian newspapers that were battling among themselves, some supporting Jackson, others behind Calhoun.

The first major shot in the press battle proved to be Calhoun's long defense of his role in the Seminole Affair, which the *Telegraph* published in its February 17, 1831, issue and later republished as a pamphlet. Addressed "To the people of the United States," it was, according to the vice president, "strictly defensive in nature" and only meant "to vindicate my character, impeached as it has been." All the major letters were there, beginning with the writings of Crawford and Forsyth that had started the whole controversy. Calhoun defended his actions during those days of deliberation in the Monroe cabinet, as well as during the recent debate with Jackson. The only reason the matter was causing so many problems now, Calhoun insisted, was because it was being used to destroy him in Jackson's and the nation's eyes so that the way would be opened for another person to take his place. The night before his statement was published, Calhoun, again without mentioning Martin Van Buren by name, wrote a private letter in which he cited "a certain prominent individual" who was the "contriver of this profligate intrigue." Van Buren and his supporters certainly knew who Calhoun was talking about and so did anyone else familiar with the Washington scene.[36]

The *Telegraph* and the *Globe* published diametrically opposed reactions to Calhoun's publication and demonstrated how split they and the coalition actually were. Feeling "a deep regret at this difference" between two leaders of the party and "indignation against all who have been the plotters and movers in reviving this almost forgotten subject," the *Telegraph* said, "the many erroneous and distorted representations of the affair" made Calhoun's publication absolutely necessary. Almost every day, the newspaper defended the vice president ever more openly until its pro-Calhoun position could not have been any more obvious. The *Globe,* on the other hand, believed that Calhoun's publication "was wholly uncalled for. It is a firebrand wantonly thrown into the republican party," Blair wrote. Jackson had never demanded to know why Calhoun had acted the way he had in Monroe's cabinet; he had just wanted to know if Calhoun had indeed spoken against him. Calhoun could have provided that answer in a few lines; instead, he filled six columns in the *Telegraph*. Calhoun's publication, making a private matter public, was no more and no less than a direct attack on Andrew Jackson himself.[37]

That was the way the president saw it. In this case and in almost every other instance, Blair accurately reflected Jackson's attitude. To outline his position even more fully, however, Jackson wrote a long unpublished memorandum, defending his role in the invasion of Florida and then attacking Calhoun. He had trusted Calhoun completely when he began his administration, Jackson said, but he should have known better. The attacks on John and Margaret Eaton, begun even before the administration had taken office, were the inventions of "satalites [sic] of Mr. Calhoun." They "approached me with *slanderous rumours* about Mrs. Eaton," Jackson wrote, though they admitted that "they knew nothing of themselves derogatory to her character." When problems later developed in the cabinet, Jackson continued, he learned that Mrs. Calhoun and Mrs. Ingham were the individuals behind the women's opposition to Margaret Eaton. And when he asked "a certain Divine [whom Jackson did not name], who professed great friendship for Major Eaton" why Margaret Eaton had been slandered, that individual responded "with great earnestness" that it was because Eaton was "politically opposed to Mr. Calhoun." Then he knew, Jackson said, that there was indeed a "connection" between the politics and the slanders, and Calhoun was at the bottom of it all. The Seminole Affair was merely an extension of the attacks against Margaret Eaton. Calhoun only nailed shut his own coffin by continuing to undercut him, the president said. And to argue, as Duff Green did in his newspaper, that Jackson had approved this publication, why "a more palpable falsehood was never uttered," the president roared.[38]

The Eatons were deeply involved in this publication dispute. Felix Grundy, a Tennessee senator and friend of both Jackson and Calhoun, had tried to broker the problem in late January at the same time Jackson and Donelson were trying to reconcile their personal difference over Margaret Eaton. Grundy had gone to Jackson and Calhoun and urged them to compromise so the party would not be damaged. He especially hoped that there would be no publication of any kind by either man. Calhoun had remained intransigent in his resolve to publish his material, so Grundy had decided he would try to limit the damage. He and Richard M. Johnson spoke to Francis Blair, asking him to publish Calhoun's material with a prefatory statement that it was not an anti-Jackson publication. Blair refused. Grundy then approached Eaton with the bad news and asked him for his help in managing the publication in such a way that Jackson would not be angered. Grundy believed that if Jackson reacted mildly or not all to Calhoun's publication, the problem would quickly go away. Eaton had remained noncommittal but had agreed to meet Grundy at his house the next night, at which time the Tennessee senator would have Calhoun's text to show him.

Eaton arrived shortly after dark, and a servant told him that Grundy was at Ingham's house. When Grundy returned, he and Eaton went into the bedroom, where Grundy read the pamphlet aloud. Eaton listened and offered suggestions whenever he heard anything he "thought calculated to excite, or which by possibility might have that effect, or be misconceived."

After completing their work, Grundy asked Eaton if he thought Jackson would feel it necessary to respond to the document if Calhoun accepted the alterations. Eaton did not think so, but he could not guarantee the direction the press might take on the matter. "Will you see General Jackson and explain to him what has taken place?" Grundy asked. "I will see Mr. Calhoun, and if the course we have taken be approved, you shall be informed."

The two men parted, apparently having made an agreement. Eaton never discussed the matter with Jackson, however, because "upon reflection, I thought it improper to do so," he said later. Grundy sent a note "stating that all was right," Eaton remembered, "which I understood to mean that the suggestions offered had been adopted." The night before the *Telegraph* published the manuscript, on February 17, 1831, Duff Green sent Eaton two copies and went on to insist that, although some people thought otherwise, he was not Jackson's enemy. He wanted to do all he could "to relieve the President from all the imputations which his enemies will endeavor to cast upon him." Green had asked Eaton to give Jackson a copy, but the major had refused to do so. John Eaton, the angry husband, had punished, in the most public way, the tormentor of his wife. One can picture Andrew Jackson puffing away on his pipe and nodding with satisfaction, while lambasting Calhoun for going public without getting his approval first. Margaret Eaton said nothing, but she must have enjoyed seeing her opponents so publicly shamed. She obviously remained at the heart of this political struggle and had to be pleased to see it go her way so decisively, at least this once.[39]

The nation's press had a field day with this controversy. Every paper, no matter its political persuasion, no matter its location, kept a close watch on the battle and reprinted material from the Washington newspapers. In Baltimore, *Niles' Register* printed its usual collection of clippings from around the country, and James Watson Webb of the *New York Enquirer* kept several men busy for a week collecting and preparing "extracts from nearly 200 Democratic papers denouncing the course pursued by Mr. Calhoun & his dear friend Duff." Green, meanwhile, exhorted all of Calhoun's friends to "unite in opposition to Clay & Van Buren. Let them give it distinctly to be understood that their support of Genl Jackson is independent of any support of Van Buren and let them be prepared to prevent any persecution of Calhoun by such." The president looked with disdain on both Calhoun and Green. His popularity seemed untouched by it all. In Pennsylvania, a Jackson supporter told future president James Buchanan, then a congressman, that "in politics as in every other matter I, therefore (to use an expression of the 'dirty shirts'), 'go the whole hog' for Jackson."[40]

Duff Green filled the mails with letters to newsmen and others all over the country trying as best he could to put the right spin on what was happening to his idol, John C. Calhoun. He particularly worried about the rumors sweeping the nation that Jackson was going to get rid of Secretary of the Treasury Samuel D. Ingham, usually considered Calhoun's closest supporter in the cabinet. Van Buren, Lewis, and Eaton were spearheading the drive to eliminate Ingham and thus wound Calhoun even more, Green suspected. The reason: Ingham's refusal to have anything to do with Margaret Eaton. "The truth is," Green concluded, "that all our difficulties are easily traced to that unfortunate circumstance." Martin Van Buren agreed. "But for the Eaton *imbroglio,* all the problems with Calhoun "would, in all probability, have [not] ever arisen." Margaret Eaton was at the bottom of both the social and political events tearing at the Jackson administration.[41]

7

"A Want of Harmony"

Andrew Jackson had been fighting for Margaret Eaton since February 1829, a month before his inauguration. In the process, he had discovered to his dismay that his personal and his political families were among those causing him the greatest problem. Both the Donelsons and members of his cabinet refused to accept Margaret, yet he could not imagine anyone being opposed to accepting the wife of his secretary of war, unless they were part of a giant conspiracy against her, and thus against him. At first he had blamed his longtime enemy of "corrupt bargain" memory, Henry Clay, but then he realized that his own supporters were at fault. John C. Calhoun was the ultimate villain, he decided, the mastermind of the devious plan to destroy him. He thought he had eliminated Calhoun's influence during the Seminole Affair and when he told his niece and nephew to stay home in Tennessee. The cabinet had remained near him, however, full of animosity, thwarting his every attempt to win them over. He had threatened the most militantly contrary secretaries with dismissal early in 1830, but they promised cooperation and then returned to their old ways. There was no harmony in the cabinet. He had to take action against them or risk ignominious defeat. As he always did, Andrew Jackson made any problem he faced as deeply personal and menacing as was possible.

John C. Calhoun had taken a public beating over his recent Seminole publication, so Martin Van Buren, the vice president's chief rival, should have been content. The suave and charming secretary of state, after all, continued his daily horseback rides with the president, and the two men discussed all manner of issues fully and frankly. They remained good friends and political allies, even though they did not agree on everything, and Jackson remained master of his own destiny.[1] Jackson increasingly turned to Van Buren when Calhoun convinced him of his unfaithfulness. The urbane New Yorker had moved past Calhoun to become heir apparent to the presidential chair. Van Buren had judiciously maintained a low profile throughout the controversies sweeping around Jackson, but Calhoun and his press pointed to him and to his allegedly secret influence, anyway. Meanwhile, Henry Clay remained a factor, still very popular throughout the nation. What good would it be if Van Buren gained the presidential nomination over Calhoun and then lost the election to Clay?

Van Buren knew that Jackson was boiling with anger at his cabinet and that, repeatedly over the last year, he had threatened its dissolution if its members did not treat Margaret Eaton more civilly. His threats had proved to be empty, however, and the cabinet remained intact and unrepentant. What if he, was able to accomplish the dissolution of the cabinet? Van Buren thought he would gain Jackson's increased affection, and if he did it the right way, he might gain political favor with the voting public as well. He decided to resign his own post and thereby force the resignation of all the other cabinet members. The administration's problem would then be solved, Jackson would be grateful, and the public would be impressed at his self-sacrifice.

Before he could do anything, however, he had to get Andrew Jackson's approval. He made several attempts to discuss the matter with the president during early April 1831, but each time he failed to do so, and his son joked about his lack of nerve. One day, for example, when he and Jackson were out horseback riding, a storm forced them to take shelter in a tavern. This was a good opportunity for Van Buren to speak frankly, but he could not bring himself to broach the subject with Jackson. The president was depressed over his disagreement with the Donelsons, and the battles with Calhoun and the cabinet had exhausted him. He was in a terrible mood. After the storm cleared and the two men remounted for the ride back, Jackson's horse slipped and nearly threw the president. Van Buren helped steady the animal, and Jackson thanked him. "You have possibly saved my life, Sir!" he said, though he said he was not sure life was worth living. Van Buren simply could not discuss his resignation when the president was feeling this low.

A few days later when the men were out again and the weather was pleasant, Van Buren got up his nerve. Jackson was musing that he would feel better when the Donelsons returned to the Executive Mansion, and Van Buren quickly disagreed. "No!" he blurted out, "General, there is but one thing can give you peace." What was that, Jackson asked. "My resignation," Van Buren replied to Jackson's absolute shock. "Never, Sir!" Jackson said. "Even you know little of Andrew Jackson if you suppose him capable of consenting to such a humiliation of his friend by his enemies."

For the next four hours Van Buren plied Jackson with every argument he could muster. At one point, Jackson asked him what he planned to do if he left government. When Van Buren said he would go back to his law practice, Jackson said that would only provide their opponents with the appearance of a victory. Perhaps Van Buren could become minister to England; that would make more sense. Finally, Jackson said he would think the whole thing over. He asked Van Buren to come to his office the next day.

What Van Buren saw and heard the next morning shocked him. A somber president addressed his apprehensive secretary of state with little display of emotion. "Mr. Van Buren," Jackson stated in measured tones, "I have made it a rule thro' life never to throw obstacles in the way of any man who, for reasons satisfactory to himself, desires to leave me, and I shall not make your case an exception." "Oh no," Van Buren nearly shouted as he jumped from his chair. He would stay as long as Jackson wanted him. If the president could see into his heart, he would realize that he wanted to resign for Jackson, not for selfish reasons. Jackson broke down in tears, seizing Van Buren's hand, and asking for forgiveness. They would ride in the afternoon and discuss the matter further. That night Jackson met with Eaton, Lewis, and Barry, his closest associates, and they agreed to Van Buren's offer.

Later that same evening, Van Buren invited the four men to his house for a celebratory dinner. On the way there, Eaton suddenly stopped and blurted out that Van Buren was the best man in a cabinet that "required all of the General's force of character to carry it along," and here they were "consenting that he should leave it." Looking at Van Buren, he said: "Why should you resign? I am the man about whom all the trouble has been made and therefore the one who ought to resign." What about Margaret, someone asked, would she agree? He thought so, Eaton said, but he would have to ask her first. The others remained silent, wondering what was going to happen next, wondering where Margaret Eaton's streak of forthrightness would lead her.[2]

Unfortunately, there is no record of the discussion between John and Margaret Eaton over the resignation, though it must have been a heated one. Margaret must have argued against John's leaving the cabinet, seeing it, as Jackson first saw Van Buren's equivalent offer, as a victory for the opposition. Margaret must have thought of all those snubbing women thinking they had driven her out. How could she withdraw now, just as she seemed to be on the verge of victory? The clergymen had been defeated, the Donelsons were gone, and she was beginning to experience civility in the Executive Mansion. Why throw all this success away? Finally, however, after what must have been much shouting and tears, she gave in. She accepted Eaton's decision to resign, but she was not happy about it.

When she saw William Barry, the only cabinet member whose family supported her, she lashed out at the postmaster general, insisting that he was gaining prominence at her husband's expense. Realizing what she had said "in the paroxisms [*sic*] of her grief," she quickly apologized to Barry. Sometime later, when Jackson and Van Buren made an unannounced visit, as they were wont to do, she was still upset. She greeted them coldly, telling them in no uncertain terms that she was upset with Jackson over her husband's planned resignation. As he and Jackson left, Van Buren noted her harshness and wondered what it all meant. "It is strange," Jackson replied and kept walking. Deep down, however, he must have understood. Margaret felt that her friend had betrayed her. Jackson felt the same way about John C. Calhoun, Andrew Donelson, and a host of others who did not agree with him, so Margaret's attitude could not have shocked him. Only a few days later, two events provided a prophetic sign for anyone who noticed. The steamship *Bellona,* carrying the same name that some opponents called Margaret, was refused permission to land at a river port, and the *Andrew Jackson* suffered a wreck.[3]

Margaret's reluctance notwithstanding, Eaton submitted his official resignation on April 7, 1831. He did it, he said in a letter to Jackson, not because of any disagreement with the president, but because he had never wanted to join the cabinet in the first place. He had decided from the start "to avail myself of the first favorable moment, after your administration should be in successful operation, to retire. It occurs to me, that the time is now at hand." Jackson said that he was sorry to see him go, and agreed that Eaton had joined the cabinet in the first place only out of "my pressing solicitations. An acquaintance with you of twenty years standing assured me," Jackson concluded, "that in your honesty, prudence, capacity, and judgment, I could safely confide." That was it, not even a hint of the snubbing Washington women or cabinet wives. Eaton was simply leaving, he said, because he had never wanted to be there in the first place.[4]

The nation's press remained unaware of the Eaton-Van Buren plan, and, instead, argued over the rumor that Jackson had fired Ingham. If he had, one newspaper asked, was it because of the secretary's friendship with Calhoun? The *United States Telegraph* blamed Lewis, Eaton, Kendall, and Van Buren by name for all the administration's problems and described in derogatory detail Margaret Eaton's role. Duff Green hoped Jackson would "open his eyes to the intrigues which have produced the present unhappy state" in his administration. From now on, he said, he planned to speak out bluntly in order to "save" Jackson. The *Globe* ridiculed the whole idea.[5]

While the press debated Ingham's future, Van Buren resigned on April 11, four days after Eaton, and still only in private. His letter was much longer than Eaton's and his reason for departing was completely different. He was leaving, he said, because conditions out of his control had propelled him into consideration as Jackson's successor, and he thought that no one in that position should remain in the cabinet and cause the inevitable controversy. "Such being my impressions," he said, "the path of duty is plain: and I not only submit with cheerfulness to whatever personal sacrifices may be involved in the surrender of the station I occupy, but I make it my ambition to set an example," which he hoped would "prove essentially and permanently beneficial." In short, Van Buren was resigning for the good of his president and the good of the nation. It was a "sacrifice," an "example" for others to follow, the exact point he wanted the public to believe.[6]

When he left the country for London as the new American minister, the nation's perception of his altruism seemed secure. This time, Jackson's response was more revealing. He was sorry to accept Van Buren's resignation and, in discussing it, used a favorite term: "the harmony of my cabinet." His cabinet members had heard him talk about harmony before, notably when he had earlier threatened to fire them if they continued their animosity toward Margaret Eaton. All of them must have understood what was going on. The threatened cabinet dissolution of 1830 was taking place in 1831, not by presidential fiat as threatened, but apparently by voluntary resignation.[7]

Jackson called in Ingham and Branch (Berrien was out of town) and presented them with the facts of life. The socially outgoing Branch caught on immediately, but the duller Ingham had to have a second meeting to understand what was expected of him. Even then, it was not simple. When Branch tendered his resignation, he credited it to Jackson's "wish." The president insisted right back that he had never said that Branch should resign. He simply had told him that he "felt it to be indispensable to reorganize" the cabinet because having begun duty "harmoniously and as a unit, and as a part was about to leave me ... a reorganization was necessary to guard against misrepresentation." Branch stood corrected, he replied. Ingham also resigned now, emphasizing that Jackson had expressed satisfaction with his service.[8]

In a flash, four cabinet members were gone. Jackson intended to keep William Barry because, he told Branch, the postmaster general was not really a member of the cabinet and because his administration of the post office was under investigation and he deserved a chance to clear himself. Ingham told Berrien, still in Georgia, that he too was to be "reorganized," but he knew nothing about the details. Berrien expressed total confusion. He implored Ingham to keep him informed, deciding to do nothing further until he could discover what was going on.[9]

So far, all this activity had taken place in private. No official announcement was made about any of the resignations until April 20,

1831, when the *Globe* published the news. "From this," editor Francis Preston Blair surmised, "it is inferred that a new organization of the Cabinet is to take place." The *Telegraph* reprinted the same material and even provided an accurate list of the entire cabinet's replacements.[10]

This news caused tremendous disbelief in the capital and the nation. In Washington, people stood "gaping about the streets as if uncertain what to believe, but all greedily drinking in the news," one observer noted. The shock spread across the country and then across the ocean. Sir Charles Vaughan told Lord Palmerston, the British foreign minister, that the secretaries' refusal to meet with Margaret Eaton had split the American cabinet. Every newspaper editor either commented on the occurrence or at least reprinted the official letters. Several newspapers noted that similar cabinet changes were occurring in England and France at this same time. Such activity was normal for these countries, newspapers pointed out, but the dissolution of Jackson's cabinet was an uncomfortable event for the United States, what a later biographer called "a constitutional crisis of major proportion." Did this unbelievable event signal only the crash of Jackson's presidency or was it more fatal, the end of the American system of government? The Senate had the authority to confirm cabinet officers; did the secretaries' sudden departure mean the end of the Senate's constitutional role and the establishment of the all-powerful president? No one knew for sure, and the shock and uncertainty was unsettling.[11]

The press searched for an explanation to the unexpected event, and their answers varied enormously. Simply stating them, however, seemed to lessen—though it did not remove—the fears of constitutional collapse. To the *Washington National Journal*, it sounded like "the reign of Louis XV when Ministers were appointed and dismissed at a woman's nod, and the interests of the nation were tied to her apron string." An anti-Van Buren newspaper in New York characterized his resignation as being like all "the other trickeries of his inglorious career—*all alike false and hypocritical.*" Another paper accused him of sorcery: "He had only to raise his wand and the whole cabinet vanished." A Rhode Island newspaper commented that Eaton had retired "in consequence of the mortifications he has been subjected to by his ignorance, and specially by his domestic relations." It all happened, a

Boston paper said, because Jackson, having long searched for a pretext to get rid of those members of his cabinet who supported an opposing faction, used the opportunity of Van Buren's resignation to accomplish his aim.[12]

Newspapers also tried to outdo one another in making fun of the dissolution. One paper laughed at Jackson's description of his cabinet as a "unit." "This we think is correct," the paper said, "as it was the smallest figure ever known in political arithmetic." Another said that it "came upon us like a clap of thunder in a cloudless day," and now the country had "to explore our way through the mist which enveloped the whole subject." Still another editor likened the people of the United States to a fox caught in brambles, that begged a swallow not to drive away the swarm of flies bothering him because an even hungrier swarm might take their place. Jackson, unlike the bird, had driven off the flies, and now the poor country could expect a "more greedy . . . swarm of hungry office buzzers" to take their place. And to make sure that Van Buren was not left unridiculed, a New England paper likened him to a drunken horseman who having trouble staying atop his animal slid off to the ground. When asked by a young boy why he had gotten off his horse, the tipsy horseman replied: "'O, I only got off to get on better!'"[13]

Perhaps the most famous and most effective response to the dissolution of the cabinet was artist Edward Williams Clay's lithograph. Hurriedly published in Philadelphia in reaction to the news of the split, the cartoon shows a confused-looking Andrew Jackson collapsed in a broken presidential chair, while four rats scamper away. The rats have human heads clearly representing John Eaton, John Branch, Martin Van Buren, and Samuel D. Ingham. Three out of the four rats seem safely gone, but Jackson has his foot on the tail of the fourth—Martin Van Buren—preventing his escape. The cartoon was immensely popular, John Quincy Adams learning that two thousand copies had been sold in Philadelphia in one day, and ten thousand more were being printed. The illustration gave an unflattering picture of Washington activities, a Baltimore paper said. "No one can look at it without a good hearty laugh," but when the viewer pondered it longer, it caused "deep concern for the ultimate fate of our country when its affairs are thus evidently found in such weak and incompetent hands."

Clay later redid this cartoon to add John C. Calhoun as a terrier trying to keep a Van Buren rat from climbing the "Ladder of Political
Preferment." Another artist, David Claypoole Johnston, composed a
print full of direct references to Margaret Eaton, entitling it "Exhibition of Cabinet Pictures." Here, in a series of cartoons, he satirized the
cabinet split and made it clear that he blamed the Eaton Affair for the
breakup of the cabinet. In his suggested design for the U.S. coat of
arms, for example, he included corsets and petticoats. In another panel
he showed Jackson trying to wash a petticoat clean, and in another,
Jackson trips over a petticoat during an ice skating race with Henry
Clay. A caricature of Margaret Eaton was also shown carrying a book
about prostitutes. The print is full of ingenious satire, with Margaret
Eaton and Andrew Jackson receiving the brunt of the ridicule.[14]

As artists drew and newsmen searched for the cleverest ways to describe the cabinet split, Jackson busily defended his actions and those of
his retired secretaries of war and state. "This act of disinterested patriotism of Van Buren and Eaton," he told John Coffee, "must be long remembered by a grateful country." How different from the activities of
John C. Calhoun, "one of the greatest intriguers on earth and the fullest
of duplicity and deceit." How different, too, from "the unprincipled
course" of Duff Green. "There is a debt due to my faithful Eaton from
the state & myself," he wrote another Tennessee supporter. He wanted
Eaton back in the Senate; after all, his friend had left that body to join
the cabinet. As for Green and Calhoun, "poor Duff has politically cut
his throat & Calhoun is prostrate never to rise again."[15]

The individual who believed he had the most to gain from this cabinet breakup watched events with unalloyed glee. Henry Clay believed
that "our cause can not fail to be benefitted. . . . It [the cabinet split] is
a broad confession of the incompetency of the President's chosen advisers, no matter from what cause, to carry on the business of the Government. It is a full admission of that unfitness of those advisers for
their respective stations, which the whole country felt when they were
first selected." Calhoun might now "take bolder and firmer ground
against the President," and thus hurt Jackson's cause. Calhoun might
not run for the presidency himself, Clay surmised, but he might support someone else. No doubt, Clay hoped that the someone was he. As
for Van Buren, his letter of resignation was "perfectly characteristic of

the man—a labored attempt to conceal the true motives, and to assign assumed ones, for his resignation, under the evident hope of profiting by the latter." In sum, Clay believed there was "a certain progress towards the final eviction of the administration." As for Margaret Eaton, Clay told an appreciative gathering at a party, "Age can not wither nor time stale her infinite virginity."[16]

Other leading political figures provided their own analysis. John Floyd, the governor of Virginia, for example, believed the disruption of the cabinet was the result of only one fact: three cabinet officers "not permit [ing] their wives to associate with Mrs. Eaton . . . notoriously a woman destitute of virtue and of morals." George Watterston, the former librarian of Congress, a man who had lost his post to a worthy Jacksonian, had the same interpretation, which he wrote with even more enthusiasm. The split had occurred, he reported, due "to the influence of the wife of the Secy of War," a second Helen of Troy. "Her conduct at all counts was not such as to meet with the approbation of those who had a high sense of the obligations of the marriage tie or of the purity of female virtue." No matter her innocence or guilt, Watterston said, she was responsible for even greater evil. She "exercised an unbounded influence" over her husband and "the wretched fatuity of the Prest [president] who foolishly blended the private squabbles of his ministers with the affairs of state & seemed to regard . . . [her] as a public functionary."[17]

Even the son of William Barry, Margaret Eaton's sole defender in the cabinet, was happy to see her go as a result of her husband's resignation. "I pity her," he said, "but am sincerely glad she is no longer in the Capitol for to tell the truth she did possess too much influence on the Secty. Everything will now go on smoothly," he predicted, with Margaret Eaton no longer dominating the War Department as no woman should.[18]

Unfortunately, peace and harmony did not arrive as planned. The resigned secretaries began protesting their departures vociferously, aided by an energized partisan press. Andrew Jackson grew increasingly angry, particularly at the man he continued to consider their leader, John C. Calhoun. At the same time, Andrew and Emily Donelson's return to Washington remained uncertain, and Margaret Eaton's name was vilified even more, her husband's efforts to defend her growing more desperate as a result. Her position at the center of the great Washington controversy only grew greater and more public.

The immediate problem for Jackson was not Margaret Eaton, nor even John C. Calhoun. It was John M. Berrien. He was still home in Savannah trying to discover what was going on, anxiously reading the newspapers and his correspondence with cabinet friend Samuel D. Ingham. He clearly did not want to join his colleagues on the sidelines, because he had been consistently telling his Georgia constituents how important it was to their interests for him to be in the cabinet. He somehow had to convince them now that it was not his fault if Jackson forced him out and that his departure would not hurt their interests in any event. Consequently, he tried to remain silent on the resignations. He went out of his way at a public dinner to praise Jackson and Eaton for their excellent work on Indian removal. That, of course, reminded Georgians how the Jackson administration, of which he was a part, had looked out for their welfare. It also did not hurt his relations with Eaton and Jackson. Berrien seemed to be following Ingham's advice to sit tight and take no precipitous action.[19]

The attorney general maintained this low profile in Savannah for the next month, but finally he had to return to his department in Washington. At a public dinner prior to his departure in mid-June, 1831, he once more said nothing about the split, concentrating his remarks on Indian affairs, loyalty to and preservation of the Union within the context of state sovereignty, and Georgia's economic development. Having buttressed his home base without alienating Washington, Berrien hoped he had saved his cabinet post. As he traveled north with Maryland lawyer and composer of "The Star-Spangled Banner," Francis Scott Key, he pumped Key about Jackson's possible future actions. Key said no one was sure, but Roger B. Taney (who would ultimately replace Berrien) hoped the president would retain him. Key also told Berrien that Duff Green was insisting that Margaret Eaton was the core cause of the cabinet's destruction. If Berrien stayed on, Key said, he would have to deal with that interpretation. The shaky attorney general was not calmed. He still did not know what to expect.

When the men arrived in Washington, Key found a message from the president and hurried to see him. He learned that Jackson had no intention of retaining Berrien and so informed his traveling partner.

Without delay, Berrien tendered his resignation on June 15, indicating clearly that he did not like having to do it. "I perform this act simply in obedience to your will," he wrote. "I have not the slightest disposition to discuss the question of its propriety."[20]

John Branch, having received his marching orders from Jackson on his daughter's wedding day, was more than willing to discuss Jackson "and his vile parasites." "I have been driven to the wall and must vindicate my humble name from unmerited opprobrium," he wrote to Andrew Donelson with a passion that was most uncharacteristic of him. It was clear, he said, that "the President must and will have E and Mrs. E with him and about him." He would depart, therefore, and consider the offer of North Carolina friends that he run for Congress.[21]

On May 11, 1831, just before leaving the Navy Department, Branch published in the leading North Carolina newspaper a stinging letter justifying his cabinet career and attacking those who had driven him out. He stopped just short of naming names. This letter was widely republished, and even his friends were taken aback at his sharp words. Ingham had tried to edit out the more aggressive sections, but Branch restored them in the fit of his anger. A pro-Jackson newspaper characterized the publication as "puerile," while John M. Berrien was sympathetic but critical, and Andrew Donelson wished it had never been published. Andrew Jackson was "truly astonished & mortified" at Branch's words and his "sudden exit from here." "This conduct," he said, "gives to the world evidence of his weakness, if not of his depravity."[22]

John Eaton was specially angry at what he read. In return, he had Francis Blair ridicule Branch in the *Globe* for not having the courage to attack him by name. If he had, the paper said, Eaton would respond on the field of honor, and the matter could be settled quickly. Branch knew immediately that Eaton was behind the *Globe*'s words. He wrote Donelson asking for his advice, indicating that he was leaning toward publishing a response. Donelson told him he had already gone too far, and he should remain quiet and let some trusted North Carolina newspaper print a short anonymous rebuttal. His problem was with Jackson, not with Eaton, although everyone understood that when he used the term "malign influence" in his strong letter, he was referring to "the influence of Eaton[,] Lewis[,] & co" on Jackson. Eaton continued to press his case, newspapers commented on it, and Donelson continued advising Branch not to react. "The character of his wife has nothing to do with the question involved in your removal," Donelson said. "Regard any challenge from Eaton as 'mere bluster.'"[23]

Meanwhile, the former secretary of the treasury, Samuel D. Ingham, was attempting to protect his own reputation. He had always been more controversial than either Berrien or Branch because Jackson and Eaton perceived his wife to be a leader in Margaret Eaton's snubbing. In private correspondence, Ingham blamed the cabinet split on Jackson's desire to have around him only those who were "decidedly for V. B. & Mrs. E. and expressly hostile to Mr. Calhoun." Then, in a public letter, he directly contradicted Jackson and insisted that there had been no problems of harmony in the cabinet. "The official intercourse" among the secretaries had never been disrupted, he said.[24]

Meanwhile, the nation's newspapers continued digging into the controversy, searching for partisan advantage. In early June 1831, the *New York Journal of Commerce,* a newspaper closely linked to Duff Green, published an extended sketch of Margaret Eaton's life, blaming the cabinet split on the attempts to force her, a fallen woman, into virtuous Washington society. Green probably planted the story himself, and he took the opportunity of its publication to embellish it in his newspaper as a way to embarrass the opposition. In response, the *Globe* defended Mrs. Eaton and scolded Green for attacking her, particularly since his own wife had once been sociable to her. It was only when Green thought he could gain political advantage, Francis Blair wrote, that he turned on those who had financially supported his newspaper and began "support [ing] those who seem to look for elevation by calumniating female innocence."

Green shot back that, while it was true that Eaton had supported the *Telegraph* financially, that loan was now paid back. Between his family and the Eatons there had been "mere *formal* interchange of civilities," which were hardly the "*habits* of kind and friendly intercourse" that Blair tried to make them out to be. In any case, it all came down to several facts: "Will the *Globe* deny that Mr. Ingham, Gov. Branch, and Mr. Berrien were dismissed because they refused to compel their families to associate with that of Major Eaton?" And, did Martin Van Buren then not take advantage of the situation with the help of the "malign influence."[25]

This was the most extended publication yet of the panoply of charges against Margaret Eaton, previously only passed around in whispers by word of mouth, but now in print for everyone to read. John Henry Eaton became "much flurried," as another Washingtonian phrased it, and spouted "vengeance and destruction." He had long been angry at the whispers about his wife's role in the cabinet controversy, but to see them in print was too much. A sentence about Margaret in the June 17, 1831, *Telegraph* pushed him over the edge: "It is proved that the families of the Secretaries of the Treasury, and of the Navy, and of the Attorney-General refused to associate with her." Eaton scrawled out identical letters to the three men demanding to know—since this statement appeared in a newspaper professing to be "friendly" to them—whether they "sanction[ed], or will disavow it."[26]

Branch took Donelson's advice and ignored Eaton. Berrien responded that he did not owe Eaton an explanation. He would answer, however, for the public good. Upon his arrival in Washington, he knew nothing about Margaret Timberlake, so he attended her wedding. When he heard the rumors about her, he concluded that it was not "necessary, to decide upon the truth or falsehood of the statements which were made. It was sufficient to ascertain the general sense of the community . . . and having done so, to conform to it." When, in 1830, Richard M. Johnson had confronted him, Ingham, and Branch about inviting Mrs. Eaton to large parties, he said he had maintained his rights to govern his own social life. That was the whole story, Berrien said. John Eaton read this letter and "felt indisposed to believe that these attacks of Gen. Green could be authorized by you, or were made under your sanction." Berrien should have been pleased at Eaton's absolution, but he responded with a hair-splitting elaboration, which must have made him feel better but changed nothing. The matter died there in late June.[27]

Eaton was quick to let Berrien off the hook because he was deeply involved in a no-holds-barred argument with Ingham. Unlike Branch or Berrien, Ingham responded to Eaton's demand of June 17 with sharp words the very next day: "You must be deranged to imagine that any blustering of yours could induce me to disavow what all the inhabitants of this city know, and perhaps half the people of the United States believe to be true." Eaton was enraged at such an "impudent &

insolent" response, particularly since it was so out of character for the usually subdued Ingham. "I demand of you *satisfaction* for the wrong and injury you have done me. Your answer must determine whether you are so far entitled to the name and character of a gentleman, as to be able to act like one."[28]

Instead of trying to dampen the flame of emotion, Ingham continued to add additional fuel to the fire. He accused Eaton's brother-in-law, Dr. P. G. Randolph, now acting as Eaton's second, of barging into his room "with a threat of personal violence. . . . I am not to be intimidated by threats, or provoked by abuse," he said, "to any act inconsistent with the pity and contempt which your condition and conduct inspire." Eaton escalated the debate further, calling Ingham a coward and threw back his pity at him. He told Ingham he should "have pity of yourself, for your wife has not escaped them [accusations], and you must know it." No more letters, Eaton insisted, nothing "short of an acceptance of my demand." Ingham, apparently realizing that matters were getting out of hand, wrote Jackson on June 20 telling him that he was leaving his department immediately.[29]

The former secretary was preparing his exit for good reason. Eaton was serious about an immediate confrontation. According to Margaret Eaton's later recollection, he went to Andrew Jackson for advice, but never told her what he was doing. The president promised to study the correspondence and provide a quick response. One evening, she remembered, John was more affectionate than usual. She sensed that something was wrong and finally got him to tell her about his disagreement with Ingham.

After John and Margaret were already in bed, William B. Lewis's servant arrived, returning the letters John had given Jackson. John went outside to speak to the messenger, and Margaret tried to eavesdrop from inside the house. The only thing she heard was the servant saying, "Gen. Jackson says if he won't fight, you must kill him." When John returned, Margaret confronted him immediately: "Now look here, darling, you can't fool me. There is something serious on hand and I must know what it is." He told her that he had challenged Ingham and then showed her the entire correspondence.

"Now, darling, what can I do under such circumstances," John pleaded to his wife. "How can I endure this? I must make the man fight." "Husband," Margaret replied with equal feeling, "load your pistol well. Go after him. Make him give you satisfaction or shoot him; and let me go along with you to sustain you in what you do. I have always been afraid of a pistol until now, but give me the pistol and I will load it." In effect, Margaret was offering to serve as her husband's second in his duel with Ingham. She wanted to do what women never did: participate on the field of honor.

The next day, Lewis and Randolph accompanied Eaton as he went looking for the secretary of the treasury. Margaret kissed her husband good-bye, wondering if she would ever see him alive again but feeling "that we had all better be dead than in this misery." According to Ingham and his supporters, Eaton brought with him not only Lewis and Randolph but also John Campbell, the treasurer of the United States, and Major Thomas L. Smith, the register of the Treasury. They allegedly were "lying in wait," Ingham complained to Jackson, in the Treasury offices and in a nearby grocery store, "as I have reason to believe for the purpose of assassination."

Ingham armed his son and had someone search out Colonel Nathan Towson, the army paymaster, so he could safely get back and forth between his office and his home. That evening, however, having recruited additional manpower, Eaton's group "paraded until a late hour on the streets near my lodgings heavily armed, threatening an assault on the dwelling I reside in," Ingham said. He did not want protection, Ingham told Jackson. He just wanted the president to know what was going on since his duties included "maintaining good order" in Washington and "protecting the officers of the Government." Whether he thought about it then or not, Ingham came to believe that this activity against him "was planned in the Palace and with his, the Gen's assent & approbation." Meanwhile, the *Telegraph* published the letters that had been flying between the two men and reported about the threat Ingham had received the previous day. The *Globe* defended Eaton's behavior as perfectly proper.[30]

By this time, Ingham and an armed escort of six men had left town, amid rumors that Eaton chased them almost to Baltimore. Andrew Jackson, with no lack of satisfaction, pointed out that Ingham had departed even before his letter of complaint had reached the Executive Mansion. He later called Ingham's escape a "disgraceful flight," which reminded him of the scriptural passage, "'The wicked flee, when no one pursueth.'" Still, Jackson wrote to the four men Ingham had accused, expressing his confidence in them but wanting to know what had happened. Not surprisingly, all four denied every one of Ingham's accusations, providing detailed alibis for their whereabouts that day. All of them denied having been armed, or having been together as a group. Eaton denied any assassination plans of any kind, but he did admit that he had warned Ingham that if the treasury secretary did not respond to his challenge, "he might expect such treatment as I thought his conduct deserved." He did, however, want to apologize for his slur against Mrs. Ingham. He had included it inappropriately in the heat of the moment.[31]

Jackson did not let the matter die there. He sent the replies of the four accused men to Ingham, twitting the former treasury secretary that he would have preferred discussing the matter with him in person but was sorry that he had left the city at 4 A.M. He later wrote Ingham that his investigation had found that Ingham's accusations did "not appear to be founded in fact; and . . . [that he could not] but ascribe them to a reliance on false statements or vague surmises, or to the workings of an over-excited imagination." When he explained the conflict to Martin Van Buren, he called it a "ridiculous and cowardly farce." He especially enjoyed informing Andrew Donelson of "the infamous and cowardly conduct of Ingham," which only proved his belief that "a base man is always a coward."

When the *United States Telegraph* later tried to implicate Amos Kendall in this plot to assault Ingham, Kendall admitted that "several times [he] passed Mr. Ingham's dwelling with my wife on my arm," but he was only looking for a rental house. But, Kendall said, "I had no hostile design against Mr. Ingham, nor do I believe my wife had." Ingham briefly considered legal action, demanding a guarantee of immunity from job loss for anyone who testified, but Jackson ignored this request, and Ingham never pressed it. He worried that Jackson was in cahoots with Eaton.[32]

Ingham went home to Bucks County, Pennsylvania, and was immediately honored with a public dinner at the Bear Tavern. After he made a long noncommittal statement, the organizer of the dinner specifically asked about the "attempt to assassinate him before he left

Washington." Ingham described the threats from Eaton and indicated how he had stood his ground and refused "to disavow the fact that my family had refused to visit his." But the "guilt or innocence of his wife never was in controversy" between them, Ingham insisted. Others had excluded her from society, Ingham said, "and the attempt was to compel me and my family to associate with a woman whom the respectable society of that city had deemed unworthy of such countenance. *I resisted this attempt,* and this is the complaint of Mr. Eaton, for which, he sought my life."[33]

Public reactions to this sensational confrontation between Ingham and Eaton varied enormously. The Jackson press ridiculed the "Midnight Ride of S. D. Ingham," and the *Telegraph* criticized Eaton for attacking Mrs. Ingham while simultaneously insisting that others should never attack a female. It all came down to the contention that "Mrs. Eaton's influence has dissolved the cabinet," Duff Green said. She was "Bellona." A Philadelphia newspaper mocked Eaton's grammar and wondered why he went after Ingham when Colonel Towson had earlier made similar comments against Margaret. The reason was simple, the paper surmised. "As a military man, Towson might react to the challenge. . . . 'Blustering' . . . was intended, and not *fighting.*" A Rhode Island paper took the threats more seriously. It said the armed standoff "would disgrace the Hottentots or the inhabitants of the Barbary states."

Political figures were equally critical. An associate reported to Henry Clay that "Poor Eaton is crazed, Ingham is not much better. He is mad with rage." Presbyterian minister Ezra Stiles Ely told Ingham he supported him, indicating at the same time that his earlier attitude toward Margaret Eaton had not changed and his earlier letters of remorse to Jackson had been hypocritical. "I hope you will be the means of wiping away from our country the national scandal under which we have been suffering for two years past," Ely said. "At the proper time, and in a suitable way I design to lend you my public aid in supporting the cause of truth, republicanism and public morals." Even William B. Lewis wished the Eatons would go back to Tennessee, so that "the papers would cease to abuse them, and things here and elsewhere would become comparatively quiet."[34]

Eaton continued to be frustrated. He had silenced Berrien and

Branch, and he had driven Ingham out of town, made him, in fact, a "laughing stock." Yet no matter what victories he won, there always seemed to be more battles to fight. If he and Margaret tried to go home to Tennessee, word had it that they would experience a repeat of the coolness they had met in Nashville during the summer of 1830. Several rumors circulated again that Jackson planned to send Eaton to a diplomatic mission, as minister to Russia. "Peggy the Czarina of America" refused to go, however, so the Eatons would instead be sent to Michigan. Or perhaps, Jackson would just reappoint Eaton to the War Department.[35]

Criticism of the Eatons combined both racial and sexual morality. The story circulated around Washington that a "colored female servant" of theirs had become pregnant. In order to avoid the obvious scandal, Eaton had allegedly brought a male married slave from Tennessee to marry him off to the pregnant woman. The Reverend French Evans, the Eatons' brother-in-law, supposedly officiated and Jackson witnessed the ceremony, the story continued. The groom protested vociferously, but no one listened. "This outrage was spoken of openly throughout the city," the dismissed librarian of Congress said, offering as the only proof of the story's validity that "no one ever denied it." How typical of the Eatons, the point was, but more correctly, how typical of the rumor mills of Washington.[36]

Andrew Jackson remained loyal to the Eatons during this time of controversy, insisting that when John Eaton's "traducers are buried in forgetfulness, his name will be hailed by the good and great as one of the best and most virtuous patriots of his day." But he showed the stress of spending so much time and energy on this matter while trying to govern the nation at the same time through the nullification crisis, the Indian removal, and a host of other matters. His health continued bad, made worse by the movement to the surface of the bullet he had taken in his arm during the fight with Thomas Hart Benton in 1813. This bullet had to be surgically removed in early 1832. When he and Van Buren attended the wedding of John Branch's daughter, the same day Branch had to resign from the cabinet, the two men "resembled funeral guests rather than wedding guests." At a dinner several weeks later, Jackson was "napping constantly & finally sinking his eyes on his plate for an hour." These were not happy times at the Executive Mansion. Still, Jackson kept plowing forward. Francis Blair, in June 1831, said the president was "nothing daunted with all the plots & conspiracies & intrigues of which some hope he is to be [the] victim."[37]

Yet there was something Jackson wanted very much to resolve that kept eluding a solution. The Donelsons were still in exile in Tennessee. Jackson kept his nephew informed about the cabinet shake-up and early in the controversy said with obvious hope: "I have great need of your aid." John Coffee reported, however, that the Donelsons did not want to return to Washington out of fear that, beyond being respectful to Margaret Eaton, Jackson still wanted Emily to "become the intimate and social friendly visitor of Mrs. Eaton, which they think under all past circumstances would be degrading to them." Still, Coffee reported, Andrew Donelson wished that there was some way consistent with his honor that he could help Jackson, and Jackson needed all the help he could get at this time. In early May of 1831, Andrew Donelson decided to go east himself to see if he and Emily might not now be able to come back permanently.[38]

No sooner had Donelson begun his trip to Washington than Jackson mailed off a series of harsh messages. He supported Eaton, attacked Calhoun and the three former cabinet members, and strongly defended William B. Lewis, Donelson's bête noir inside the Executive Mansion. "I have nothing to regret on my part," Jackson said. "I will, and must, regret the course, you and your dear family have pursued as it respects myself and friends, but still, my friendship or solicitude for your welfare will not be withdrawn—you have made your election; I repeat, I sincerely regret the one you have made." As if to bar the door to return even more completely, he also told Andrew that he was going to get someone else, Nicholas P. Trist, to be his aide. And he told Mary Eastin that "if my family had adhered to me, what a brilliant & peaceful administration I would have had, and how much delight with them. But it is different. Be it so. . . . The only thing to be regretted, is, I am thrown upon strangers."[39]

When Donelson arrived in Washington, he found no evidence of the ill feeling Jackson had expressed in these letters. The president was in good spirits and happy to see him. He inquired about Emily and the children, but said nothing about Margaret Eaton nor her role in breaking up the cabinet. Donelson planned to sit down with Jackson the first chance he had and discuss the whole matter in detail. He also planned to visit Duff Green.[40]

Donelson got nowhere with Jackson. The president stubbornly held to his position, and Donelson could not imagine how his "refusal to make terms with Mrs. Eaton . . . [could be] treated as a state affair which nothing short of banishment from the White House can atone for." Jackson also remained angry at the role the Donelsons and their extended family were playing in the Desha Affair in Tennessee, another example of their opposition to Margaret Eaton. He continued to call for a united home, but Donelson persisted in his friendly disagreement. Jackson only "hope[d] his eyes are beginning to be opened that old friends never ought to be abandoned for new ones."[41]

If Donelson had learned anything about his uncle's demand for absolute loyalty, he did not show it. In addition to visiting the Inghams and Duff Green, he was exchanging letters with John Branch, now related to him through marriage. In this mail, and no doubt in person, he castigated Eaton and Van Buren as "those who expect the public voice to signify their victory by monuments to their *patriotism* and *disinterestedness.*" With these words, which Jackson fortunately did not see, he ridiculed the president's interpretation of the resignations. As for the "woman business," Donelson said, "I can only say that I can never yield the point . . . and if Uncle still makes it a *sine qua non* I must also be dismissed." And while Jackson was criticizing Branch, Donelson was assuring the former navy secretary "of my unalterable regard."[42]

Donelson and Jackson sat down one more time to discuss Emily's plans for the fall. As always, Jackson expressed his affection for his niece, but he was "still embarrassed by the delicate and painful apprehension that the circumstance of your not visiting Mrs. Eaton may have a tendency to confirm the prejudice against him and thus serve indirectly to injure him and cast a shade upon the character of his friend." This time, no doubt to Jackson's relief, Donelson agreed. His conscience seemed to have gotten the best of him. He saw that Jackson needed his help, and he remembered all that the man had done for him in the past. So, as he prepared to come home to get her, he told Emily that he had changed his mind, but it was not clear what he meant. Was he really willing for Emily to socialize with Margaret Eaton and would she accede to such wishes, or was there another fine distinction in the works?

Past history did not provide reason for optimism, and Donelson's behavior was not encouraging. He wrote an affectionate letter to Jackson as he left town, expressing his willingness to admit his mistake, but he also wrote John Branch promising a visit and, in direct opposition to his uncle's views, arguing that there was "no issue between you & Eaton. The character of his wife has nothing to do with the question involved in your removal."[43]

Meanwhile, the three former secretaries remained unhappy. As they corresponded back and forth, they decided that they had to place the blame for the cabinet dissolution on Jackson. They had to be seen as principled victims battling an unfair dictator. It did not take them long to realize that they had just such proof to make that point: the series of meetings they had held with Richard M. Johnson and Andrew Jackson in January 1830. Johnson, acting as an agent for Jackson, had warned them that if they refused to socialize with Margaret Eaton, the president would fire them all. Their 1831 firings, therefore, were the result of the 1830 meetings. Margaret Eaton, and nothing else, caused their forced resignations.

The debate over this matter began in late June 1831 and continued into August. The former cabinet members, Richard Johnson, the press, and, of course, Andrew Jackson each had something to say. Johnson repeatedly denied threatening them for the president, but the three secretaries insisted he had. It eventually came down to a battle of words between John M. Berrien and Francis P. Blair. Blair produced a copy of the memorandum that Jackson insisted he had read to the three ex-secretaries in which he denied any desire to control their social relationships. Berrien, with Ingham's and Branch's published support, explicitly denied ever having seen Jackson read from a paper and said that the president had made it clear that he expected socialization. Duff Green continued to blame Margaret Eaton, while the *Globe* defended her.

Back and forth the argument went, each newspaper demanding that the other prove its contention, while refusing to believe anything the other side alleged. Someone who signed himself "Young Hickory" blasted the three secretaries for saying that Jackson insulted them by demanding that their families meet with Margaret Eaton. Yet, the letter's author said, "they tamely submitted to the insult . . . [and joined the cabinet], an admission that they loved office more than they prized their honor." John Eaton continued angry at what he read in the newspapers and, once more to no avail, he demanded a duel, this time with John M. Berrien. There was no easy answer to it all, but the nation came to see that Margaret Eaton was somehow responsible for all the troubles leading to the disruption of the cabinet. The *Telegraph* expressed that belief clearly. "The only cause of complaint, the only cause of a want of harmony . . . [was] a refusal to visit Mrs. E"[44]

The dissolution of Jackson's cabinet, the only such event in American history, demonstrated the depth of the president's determination to have his way in the matter of Margaret Eaton. Focusing on her defense, he equated opposition to her as a political conspiracy against him. Even his relatives' refusal to have a social relationship with her only convinced him how huge a conspiracy John C. Calhoun had established. Andrew Jackson believed that there was no proof against Margaret Eaton violating social mores and those insisting there was were hypocrites of the first order. He insisted, despite the reality of life in Washington, that politics and society had to be kept separate. Ironically, in taking this stand he actually allowed it to become the political crisis it became. Andrew Jackson could never understand it, but it was he, not John C. Calhoun, who made the snubbing of Margaret Eaton into the political cataclysm it became.

8

"They Shall Not Drive Me
From My Ground"

The mass resignations were supposed to restore harmony to Jackson's cabinet and to his administration. Instead, they only brought on a widespread public debate over the issue that had created the cabinet disharmony in the first place: Washington's acceptance or nonacceptance of a cabinet wife. The debate had been going on for more than two years, and on numerous occasions, Jackson thought he had won it. Once again, he had to face failure. He had not resolved the issue by firing his cabinet; he had only exacerbated it. It was all so exasperating that he began yearning for a place next to Rachel in the garden behind the Hermitage. "I only wish if it pleased the will of providence, that I was by her side, free from all the deception and depravity of this wicked world. Then my mind would not be corroded [*sic*] by the treachery of false friends, or the slanders of professed ones."[1]

The controversy over the cabinet dissolution now centered on whether Margaret Eaton would willingly leave Washington and go to Tennessee with her husband. Regularly during the summer of 1831, someone wondered aloud just when the Eatons would leave. "I believe she resists all attempts to send her into banishment," Duff Green wrote with exasperation. Then the press announced that the Eatons would actually be departing on July 20. A week later, however, another paper announced that they would remain as long as "the kennel corps, Tray, Blanch and Sweetheard, growl[ed] and bark[ed] so fiercely." Eaton himself told a friend that he "had hoped to have been in Tennessee ere now; but cannot consent to depart while I am dogged as I have been. They shall not drive me from my ground."[2]

Since John was regularly challenging people over their publications in newspapers, most of his and Margaret's time must have been taken up keeping abreast of all the continued wrangling. No doubt they regularly conferred with the *Globe*'s Blair. They continued to be frequent visitors at the White House, though John's influence was weaker now that he was no longer a member of the cabinet. Lewis Cass, the territorial governor of Michigan, took over as secretary of war during the summer, and Eaton no doubt helped him adjust to his new office. Some Washingtonians wanted to hold a public dinner for him, but he thought it would make more sense to let matters calm down before accepting such an honor.[3]

Margaret was also busy on her own. She got away from Washington for a short visit to Philadelphia in August with her sister and brother-in-law, the Randolphs. The trip was insignificant, but reporting it provided a New England newspaper with the opportunity to anoint her with some new names. Adding to Peg, Peggy, Helen of Troy, Czarina of Russia, and Bellona, this newspaper called her "the late commander in chief of fashionable society at Washington . . . [the] chemical power which dissolved the late Unit, [and] the reservoir or conduit of Presidential favor." No doubt, she much preferred hearing what Andrew Jackson told her about the comments of Willie Blunt, the governor of Virginia. To Jackson's pleasure, he called her "an amiable, virtuous, intelligent & fine woman," someone he had long admired and continued to respect.[4]

Unfortunately, most of what Margaret read in the press involved the allegations that she was immoral and that she dominated the Jackson administration. Every time a newspaper criticized Jackson's actions toward his cabinet, it aimed the bulk of its criticism at her. For example, the focus of the debate between Richard M. Johnson and the three secretaries was about forcing or not forcing people to visit her or invite her to a party. When her husband reacted to something he read in the newspaper and challenged someone to a duel, it was in defense of her. It remained necessary for her supporters to defend her honor continually, as the *Globe* did in almost every article it published that summer. When, for example, the *Telegraph* reached into the past and threatened to call on the Reverends Campbell and Ely to demonstrate Margaret's lack of morality, the *Globe* protested against the "dark insinuation and secret slander, propagated through *confidential* whisperings."[5]

Society women had not moderated their animosity either. Margaret Bayard Smith, as she had throughout the controversy, continued to reflect the attitude of the capital's gentility when she characterized Margaret Eaton as "one of the most ambitious, violent, malignant, yet silly women you ever heard of." Jackson, she said, was "completely under the government of Mrs. Eaton." Everyone thought, Mrs. Smith continued, that when John Eaton had resigned his office, she would leave the city, content in her victory. "But she will not [leave]—she hopes for a complete triumph & is not satisfied with having the cabinet broken up & a virtuous & intelligent minister recalled & many of our best citizens forced upon by the President. Our society is in a sad state. Intriguers & Parasites in favor, Division and animosity existing." And who was at fault? Margaret Eaton. She was not even that important in herself, Mrs. Smith said. The real issue was "the principle whether vice shall be countenanced." Margaret Eaton symbolized the ultimate threat to the morality and the order of the nation.[6] Andrew Jackson might see political conspiracy behind the snubbing of his friend, but Washington women saw it as their legitimate enforcement of societal standards against a genuine threat to contemporary morality.

Anyone showing any friendship toward the despised Margaret Eaton risked ostracism herself, Mrs. Smith pointed out, even if she was an outstanding person in her own right. If Mrs. Louis McLane, wife of the next secretary of the treasury, continued in her apparent determination to be on good social terms with Mrs. Eaton, Margaret Smith warned, "she will doubtless gain great influence with . . . [the president], but will lose proportionately in society." It was all such "painful anxiety," this society life, Mrs. Smith lamented. "Domestic Life! there alone is happiness." A woman's best place was clearly in the home.[7]

At the Executive Mansion, although there were no females to snub Margaret Eaton, there was also no one to provide the domestic atmosphere that nineteenth-century people believed was the family norm. Jackson missed those quiet evenings in his sitting room with the logs blazing in the fireplace, the Donelson children scampering about, visitors informally coming in and out, and a peace prevailing over all. A Tennessee friend bluntly told Jackson that he badly needed "a presiding Lady," and that meant, of course, Emily Donelson. Andrew Donelson had shown his willingness to accept Jackson's terms so that he, Emily, and the children might all be able to return to Washington. Hope ran high in Tennessee that the Donelsons would soon be back in the capital city.[8]

This optimism did not last long. In early July, some lower-level officials dismissed in the cabinet shake-up held a dinner in Georgetown, and the tone of the gathering was anti-Jackson, anti-Margaret Eaton, and pro-Calhoun. The obligatory toasts after the meal, for example, included many direct attacks on Margaret Eaton ("The serpent beguiled the woman—the woman beguiled the Cabinet"). The assemblage also rose to celebrate several women by name: Mrs. Calhoun, Mrs. Ingham, and Mrs. Branch. There was even a toast directly honoring Jackson's niece: "Mrs. Donelson! Her example and unyielding propriety. Marble is too fragile to inscribe them on!" Upon learning of this salute, Andrew Jackson exploded. Once again, he found his niece linked to opponents of Margaret Eaton, and he knew in his heart, therefore, in opposition to him. He damned "blackguard toasts," which he said demonstrated "the combination which I at first suspected, and endeavored to keep my family clear of." Calhoun remained behind it all.[9]

The more Jackson thought about the dinner, the angrier he became. Once again he lectured his nephew on the plot against the Eatons, which was really against him, he said, and how he and Emily had been drawn into it. "The toast has arrayed Mrs. Calhoun, Mrs. Ingham, and your dear Emily, against those who associated with major Eaton and his family. . . . No greater indignity can be offered a lady than to be toasted for political effect, or for any other cause, than her own intrinsic virtues." Those who accused Margaret Eaton of violating the standard of gentility were violating these norms themselves. Women were not to be part of the political process, and these hypocrites were using them for political purposes in these toasts. Had it been Rachel, Jackson said, he would have protested profusely "that I felt the indignity offered to my wife by the toast" and "that I viewed the villain who could secretly pirate on female character worse than the pirate at sea, who is considered the enemy of man, and ought to be treated accordingly." And, in case Donelson still did not realize who the head pirate was, Jackson told him in a postscript to the letter. "I knew that Calhoun would destroy all those who sailed in his wake." So as much as Jackson would like to have the Donelsons with him, he told them, "you will at once see, how improper it would be, under present circumstances [for you to come]."[10]

The disagreement between uncle and nephew had reached a truly confused state. Jackson told the Donelsons not to come back, while Andrew Donelson continued planning to return and live once again with his family in Jackson's house. To try to avoid what seemed like an inevitable collision, Donelson met with John McLemore, an old friend of Jackson's; John Bell, longtime Tennessee politician; and Alfred Balch, Jackson's neighbor. Reading between the lines of a series of letters they had received from the president, the four men decided that the Donelsons and Mary Eastin should go to Washington. The Jackson family should be reunited. After all, "Maj. and Mrs. Eaton will have left the city before their [the Donelsons'] arrival and no difficulty can arise on this score. I now hope," McLemore reported to John Coffee, that "by prudence on the part of Andrew & Emily all things will work out after a while." To make sure that Jackson was not taken by surprise, McLemore and Bell let him know the Donelsons were coming, and if this action was "contrary to your wishes, we and *not him are to blame*." At the same time, Coffee lectured Donelson on how to avoid future difficulties. "I would make it a point," he said, "not to mingle or associate with anyone, whom the Genl believes was either personally or politically unfriendly to him, although he may have unfounded jealousies against individuals on that subject." And to restore Donelson to his former post as aide and secretary, Alfred Balch told Nicholas P. Trist, the person then holding that position, to step aside.[11]

With all the obstacles out of the way, the Donelsons arrived at the Executive Mansion on September 5, 1831, to find Jackson in the middle of a letter to Martin Van Buren, at the United States ministry in England. Jackson was extremely pleased to see his family, but he remained apprehensive. He hoped they came "with all those feelings which ought at first to have accompanied them hither. They know my *course,* and my wishes," he said with the tone of warning, "and I hope, they come to comply with them." Jackson's friends in Tennessee were ecstatic that the problem seemed now solved, that Jackson's family, particularly the women, were with him. After all, "a man long accustomed to a family of females cannot do without them. He can not work always and they are at least the best comforters amidst the troubles & aspirates [asperities] of political employment & strife," McLemore believed. This was woman's role, to reinvigorate her man from the stress of work. Jackson lacked this comfort and it showed.[12] Besides, since it was a woman who was responsible for much of that stress, the problem of Margaret Eaton was ever more ironic.

All went well with Jackson and his relatives. Andrew Donelson heeded all the advice he had received, admitting that his uncle had been correct in firing his original cabinet and establishing a new one. The change had proven beneficial "to the private comfort and happiness of Uncle . . . [and] to the strength and utility of his Presidency." Donelson's only concern now was that he still stood "in danger of being misrepresented" for some of his past positions (i.e., concerning Margaret Eaton). But the future looked secure.[13]

But the troubles were hardly over. Throughout the summer, before the Donelsons' return to Washington, the capital and national newspapers gave detailed coverage of the disputes among the former cabinet members, Richard M. Johnson, Francis P. Blair, Duff Green, and anyone else who had a pen handy and a desire to become involved. In the back of his head, Eaton began planning his own statement. He talked it over with Amos Kendall and, no doubt, Andrew Jackson and Francis Blair. Margaret Eaton must also have been involved in the planning, since it concerned her so directly and she had so much to say about it. With Kendall's help, Eaton began collecting information, and he let it be known that he would soon be putting something into print. A number of friends urged him not to do it, the new Secretary of the Treasury Louis McLane arguing that a statement now would only "keep alive a disgusting subject which was fast disappearing before the indignation of the whole community." According to Andrew Jackson, however, "the continued virulence of his persecutors" gave Eaton no choice but to publish a defense.[14]

Eaton, a frustrated and angry man, had planned to go home to Tennessee early in the summer, he said, but the attacks of Berrien, Branch, and Ingham had forced him to "remain here, to meet them, & arrest them in their foul course." So he stayed in Washington and completed a fifty-page pamphlet, which he was confident would convince all fairminded people of the correctness of his case and the baseness of the opposition. He realized that "a rough road" lay ahead, for "attacks more virulent than ever, will be dragged down on me." He planned to stay in Washington for a few days after the initial publication of his statement in the *Globe,* and then he hoped to return to Tennessee where he wanted to become "a plain, & I hope, a happy farmer."[15]

Excitement increased as the public awaited this publication. One newspaper disdainfully said that Eaton's comments were being exaggeratedly awaited as "the most tremendous *blunderbuss* that civilization has ever known." More confidentially, Amos Kendall worried that Eaton's extended comments were not as well written as they should have been, but that they would still suit the purpose. As soon as he received his advance copies, Jackson sent one to John Overton asking for his evaluation.[16]

On September 15, 1831, the *Globe* filled all but three of its issue's columns with "MR. EATON'S REPLY," which also quickly appeared as a pamphlet with the subtitle: "Candid Appeal to the American Public." Here, finally, was Eaton's response to all the attacks and accusations against him and his wife. Here, finally, John and Margaret were going to have their say.[17]

Eaton pulled no punches. "In civilized society, a man's house is his castle, and the circle of his family a sanctuary never to be violated. He who drags before the public its helpless inmates, and subjects them to rude assaults, deserves to be considered worse than a barbarian." He recognized that this was "a subject purely of personal character," but it had been used against the president and would probably be so used again. It was his urgent duty to speak up. He had hoped that once he retired from office, the attacks would stop, but they had not. "What before was whispered in dark corners, now glared in the columns of newspapers." Berrien, Branch, and Ingham were "filling the country with erroneous and discolored statements, and substituting falsehood for truth."

Did the attackers forget, he asked, "that she whom relentlessly they pursue, and who in nothing ever wronged them, has two innocent little children, whose father lies buried on a foreign shore." He had to write "in defence of the slandered wife of my bosom, and her helpless unprotected children," two daughters who were now teenagers and carefully shielded from their mother's and stepfather's turmoil. A man could protect his own honor, a woman had no such power or ability, Eaton wrote. "The innocent and the guilty [woman] alike, the envenomed tongue of slander may reach and destroy. It is a withering blast, which can blight the sweetest rose, as well as the most noisome weed."

Having justified his publication, Eaton got down to the facts. He asserted that he had never desired a cabinet post (conveniently forgetting the way he had maneuvered himself into that position at Hugh White's expense). Once he accepted it, however, he never expected anything but a good working relationship with his colleagues. He came from the same county in North Carolina as John Branch, had studied at the same college, and had long known the navy secretary. He had urged Jackson to appoint him to the cabinet. When Jackson had decided to offer a post to John M. Berrien, whom Eaton had also long known, the president had sent him with the offer. The Georgian had gladly accepted. In short, when the cabinet was formed, these men and all others who formed it were on the friendliest terms of "harmony" and "unity" with him. He now realized, Eaton said, that Ingham, Branch, and Berrien had quickly begun to conspire to drive him away. They had said as much in their recent publications. But he knew nothing about their activities then. "Had Mr. Berrien frankly informed me, that he and his associates considered my appointment 'an insuperable bar' to their acceptance [of cabinet posts]" Eaton said, he would have told the president to let him or them go, and the matter would have been solved right at the start.

Eaton admitted that the issue the public was hearing about most since the cabinet dissolution—visiting and leaving cards and attending large or small parties—sounded "ridiculous" and "trifling." "But even these have been rendered of some importance . . . [in demonstrating] the motives of men, and accounting for events of higher importance." So he had to discuss this matter further "and beg[ged] to be pardoned for doing so."

Eaton told how upon returning from their two-week honeymoon, he and Margaret had found waiting at their home numerous cards, indicating that individuals had called on them in their absence. Among these cards were those of Mr. and Mrs. John C. Calhoun. Consequently, Eaton said, he and his wife had followed etiquette and called on the Calhouns; Mrs. Calhoun greeted them in the parlor "with much politeness."

Later, Eaton said, he had promised to hire one of Calhoun's friends as his chief clerk, but had to change his mind because of unforeseen circumstances. He had explained this matter fully to the office seeker but had never discussed it with Calhoun. When the vice president learned about it, "he broke off all intercourse with me, official as well as private."

Soon after the formation of Jackson's administration, it became clear, Eaton said, that, among certain members of the cabinet, "there was a settled design to put a ban on my family. . . . Old slanders were revived, and new ones circulated. Families coming to the city, were beset on the way, and on their arrival." He never complained, Eaton said, because "it is the right of every man, and of every woman, to visit whom they please." He always had people at his parties "quite as respectable, and equally as agreeable" as Ingham, Branch, and Berrien, so their absence was of little consequence. It was therefore ridiculous for Berrien or anyone else to insist that Jackson threatened to fire them if they refused to visit Margaret Eaton.

There was more to the problem then visitations. In the fall of 1829, whisperings had begun that Eaton had conspired with Margaret's first husband, John Timberlake "to defraud the government of large sums of money." This charge was simply ridiculous, Eaton said, but it was part of the plot. "If I could have been driven from all respectable society, or had fixed upon me collusion and fraud, in obtaining the funds of the Government, then would the Cabinet have been relieved of my presence."

When Congress came into session in December of 1829, "a war of exclusion" began, Eaton said. The president discussed the matter with

Richard M. Johnson, who volunteered to visit the three cabinet members as a friend. "Through him the President made no requisition, and no threat. For myself," Eaton continued, "I knew nothing of it." Besides, if the three secretaries really believed that Jackson had threatened dismissal for their not meeting socially with the wife of one of their cabinet colleagues and felt such "indignity and insult," why did they keep silent for thirteen months? "I must conclude," Eaton said, "that the President had not insulted them by any dishonorable and improper requisition, or else that they loved their offices better than their honor, and that their present violence is caused *only* by the loss of . . . [these offices]." Branch had even met with Eaton soon after meeting with Johnson, and they shook hands on their common agreement that no one should be forced to visit someone he or she did not want to see. All the recent letters and newspaper articles to the contrary, the three secretaries' insistence about being forced to socialize with Margaret Eaton was simply not accurate. They were "vainly attempt[ing] to attribute the dissolution of the Cabinet to a false ground."

What then was behind the "relentless persecution" against him? Eaton asked. "Could it be that my wife was indeed the cause? Was it merely to exclude a female from their 'good society'? Was one woman so dangerous to public morals, and so formidable in influence and power" that cabinet members, congressmen, and a "confederacy of fashionable ladies" had to battle against her? "The idea is truly ridiculous! She was lone and powerless. Those who liked her society, sought it; and those who did not, kept away. . . . The *motive,* therefore, was not to exclude us from society. It is a matter *too small* to account for the acts and the untiring zeal of so many *great* men."

Perhaps, then, the motive was to force him out of the cabinet, Eaton said. Was he that "dangerous to the interest of the country, or to its institutions?" Or was he incompetent or unfaithful to the president? "Nothing of this sort entered into the minds of my traducers," Eaton concluded. *"Major Eaton is not the friend of Mr. Calhoun,'"* a supporter of the vice president had said one day in 1829, and this was the reason for all the attempts at exclusion: Eaton was not in Calhoun's camp. "Let it be borne in mind," Eaton said, "that the principals— those who have been actively employed against me, are the friends of Mr. Calhoun—his devoted, active partizans [*sic*]."

Eaton then launched into a long attack on Duff Green, the "chief manager" of the "instrument of Mr. Calhoun," the *United States Telegraph*. He related all he had done for Green, producing detailed information about loans he had provided that had allowed the editor to begin the newspaper. During the first years of the administration, Green, his wife, and his daughters had attended parties at the Eaton house, and the Eatons had attended gatherings at theirs. Then things changed, and Green began to draw away. Why? "Because bad men are apt to dislike those from whom they have received favors. But that he should descend so far as to become the traducer of a female, because she is the wife of one to whom he is under obligations, never to be repaid, is indeed strange! . . . This man is a fit associate of Messrs. Ingham, Branch and Berrien."

He went on, "Thus through this chosen organ of Mr. Calhoun, we are possessed of the true motive which actuated my kind assailants. Their plan was that General Jackson should be president but for four years, and that Mr. Calhoun should succeed him." Martin Van Buren's appointment as secretary of state was a threat to this plan. The Calhoun conspirators wanted as many of their supporters around Jackson as possible. Therefore, Eaton had to be removed, sent to Europe, and replaced by a Calhoun man. Eaton was not qualified to be secretary of war, his attackers kept saying, but somehow he could be sent overseas as the nation's representative. "He and his family were not fit and good society for the families of such pure honorables as Ingham, Branch and Berrien, but they were quite 'good society' enough," Eaton sarcastically said, "for one of the first and most powerful monarchs of Europe." It was all a conspiracy to eliminate Jackson, Van Buren, and Eaton, so that John C. Calhoun might become president of the United States, he insisted. "All the visiting cards that were ever printed and circulated in this city, were as nothing, compared to this grand— this important design."

Eaton continued, "The situation of the President was now easily to be perceived. With a Cabinet politically divided; and personally, as may be presumed, not very friendly, it was impossible for him to move along in the arduous duties of his station, with satisfaction to himself, or advantage to the country." To help Jackson and the nation, Eaton therefore resigned, and Van Buren decided to follow suit. It was believed that "the others would appreciate the motives which had occasioned . . . [the resignations] and place their offices again at the disposition of the President, that he might organize a new Cabinet of homogeneous material." But Ingham, Branch, and Berrien could see no reason to quit. "Having gone into the Cabinet to produce *discord,* they could perceive no reason why they should retire from it, to restore *harmony.*" Having successfully achieved their plot of getting rid of Eaton and Van Buren, why should they want to leave?

Not having the decency simply to resign, the three men engaged in a war of print, aided by Duff Green. As a gentleman, Eaton said, he had no choice; he had to act. The public was aware of what followed, especially with Ingham. "He is suffering merited punishment," Eaton said, "in the contempt of the brave, the abhorrence of the honorable, and the detestation of the community." Eaton had similarly challenged Berrien. The former attorney general was a "traducer of a woman" and more than willing to destroy a family which had never done a thing to him. Yet he was too cowardly to respond to a challenge. "It must be ever so. Base men are not brave!" he concluded. As for Branch, whom Eaton called "the dupe of his own littleness of mind, and the victim of his more wily associates," he felt but "pity and contempt."

Eaton also had contempt for the "restless, troubled spirit, that, through such secret agencies, moved and controlled all this intrigue and management." He said of John C. Calhoun: "The time will come when the victims of his policy shall rise before him, like the shades which appalled the insidious and heartless usurper Richard, to disturb his slumbers, and to drive peace from him. . . . Detraction has struck at everything around me," Eaton concluded. Critics insisted that "the persecution against me originated in great regard and delicacy for public feeling and morals, yet what are the proofs to authorize *the rumors,* about which Mr. Ingham and Mr. Berrien *would not trouble themselves to enquire,* but which, notwithstanding, they could slyly and secretly whisper into circulation? They have produced none!" Margaret Eaton was a good woman, unfairly wronged by insidious innuendo.

Reaction to Eaton's *Appeal,* as his publication came to be called, was swift and wide ranging. Washington's newspapers all reprinted it, as did editors all over the nation. Andrew Jackson, who certainly played a role in its composition, as clearly indicated by the nature of the prose, saw the statement as "an able document," and everyone who read it believed that it was "condemnation to the conspirators, Calhoun, Ingham, Branch, Berrien, Duff Green and Co."[18]

Numerous pro-Jackson newspapers praised the *Appeal*. The *Washington Globe* published excerpts from a host of newspapers supporting Eaton's position, and a New York newspaper said Eaton's commentary "bore the impress of truth and honesty." "It is written with pathos, energy, and judgment," a Nashville newspaper believed, "and it is well calculated to soften the opposition of foes and to strengthen the attachment of friends." A Connecticut editor was much more direct. "The Major completely nullifies their foolish fanfarronade about the extra respectability of their families—shows that Johnny Calhoun was at the bottom of the whole plot—that Duff Green is an ungrateful hypocrite, and John Branch a ninny."[19]

Opponents were equally sharp in their criticism. Several editors believed that someone else wrote at least a part of Eaton's *Appeal;* and a Providence newspaper, which agreed, also characterized it as "fourteen columns of 'remarks of his wife,' which nobody will read, giving an official account of the petticoat administration." The *Telegraph* did not publish the *Appeal* until September 28 and did not complete its presentation until October 6. Two days later, almost a month after it came out in the *Globe,* the *Telegraph* sharply criticized it, contending "that Mr. Eaton's opposition to Mr. Calhoun grew out of the refusal of Mrs. Calhoun to recognize Mrs. Eaton," and for that same reason Eaton attacked Ingham, Branch, and Berrien. Ten days later, Duff Green weighed in himself, insisting he had been out of town when the *Appeal* first appeared. He vociferously denied Eaton's account of loans to the *Telegraph* and told of alleged efforts on the part of the Jackson administration to destroy the newspaper simply because Green refused to go along with "the gratification of Major Eaton's private malice, and Mr. Van Buren's thirst for office."[20]

Individual responses were equally varied. In Tennessee, Governor William Carroll found the *Appeal* ably written and certain to make "a favorable impression on the mind of every unprejudiced reader." Congressional candidate Robert M. Burton thought the *Appeal* came out at just the right time "when the people were sickened and insulted at the continual assaults upon an injured female." People were now talking about Eaton as a successor to Felix Grundy in the Senate because Grundy was considered a Calhoun man. A relative of Andrew Donelson, who was a member of the legislature, said that Eaton's publication "made considerable impression on the members and in fact on all who had read it." Andrew was not as impressed. He pointed out that Jackson's friends, like Emily and himself, were opposed to Margaret Eaton, so Eaton's argument about a grand conspiracy in favor of Calhoun made no sense.[21]

Secretary of the Treasury Louis McLane raved about the publication. Only "a few *pretended* Jackson men" refused to praise it, he said. "This exposé has completely annihilated the Calhoun faction," McLane insisted, and has tremendously helped Van Buren and the president. Van Buren called it "the ablest paper of the sort that I have ever read." He wished Eaton had not had to participate in such a "disgusting contest," but he knew his friend had only been doing his duty.[22]

John M. Berrien could not have disagreed more. He was so angered at what he read in Eaton's *Appeal* that he published a long rejoinder. Unfortunately, even his supporters wished he had not done so. One newspaper, while praising him, said, "The American people have heard enough to make them blush for the honor and dignity of their country." Another newspaper, indicating that it thought "the public are uninterested in further details of the well-known transactions at Washington," printed only a brief synopsis. Eaton himself had had enough. He left Washington for Tennessee, a great sigh of relief emanating even from his friends. Artist Ralph E. Earle told John Overton to "*keep Mrs. Eaton in Tennessee if possible until Congress rises*—everything is going on smoothly, but if she should return before adjournment of Congress God knows what would be the consequences." Eaton, according to this resident portrait painter in Jackson's house, was happy with his reception in Tennessee, and there was "nothing to fear if Mrs. Eaton will conduct herself with prudence," that is, if she kept quiet and out of the limelight. Eaton asked the *Globe's* Francis Blair to fight any further battles for him in Washington and told Amos Kendall that it was up to all his Washington friends to take any necessary further action.[23]

Public interest in this dispute was clearly dying out, but John C. Calhoun had yet to be heard from. The vice president had been busy with the Seminole Affair controversy, and on August 3, 1831, he had published his Fort Hill address, a justification of nullification, his first public support of the doctrine. This publication proved controversial because it publicly split the president and the vice president. Calhoun was in enough difficulty already without taking on Eaton. He was away more than he was present in Washington, generally following the schedule of Congress and returning to South Carolina when the legislative body was not in session. Thus, he was never in the middle of all the controversy sweeping around Margaret Eaton, even though increasingly he was labeled as the major villain. The cabinet dissolution appalled him, and he placed all the blame on Martin Van Buren, ridiculing Andrew Jackson's willingness to go along with such a transparent charade meant only to cover for Van Buren's and Eaton's departure. It convinced him, he said, that Jackson was "unworthy of his station and that to continue him six years longer would utterly ruin his reputation and destroy the party, that supported him, and embarrass the country." Clearly the new cabinet was going to be built around those expressing "subserviency to Mrs. Eaton." It was "our time as patriots & Republicans," he told Ingham, "to save the country from embarrassment & the party from ruin."[24]

Despite this attitude and the increasingly harsh press debates, Calhoun remained silent in South Carolina. His stock in Washington continued to fall, however, as Andrew Jackson became convinced that he was planning to run for president in 1832, something Jackson believed he had been conspiring to do since 1828. When a friend provided extracts of Calhoun's letters, which were critical of Jackson's ability and character, and also accused Calhoun of calling Margaret Eaton the real president of the United States, these written and uncorroborated oral comments enraged the president even more. The vice president, however, was as firm as Jackson in maintaining his position, "I am determined to keep my temper," he said, but he was equally determined "not to yield the hundredth part of an inch."[25]

Yet when Calhoun read Eaton's *Appeal*, he lost his temper and wrote an extended response, publishing it in the *Pendleton (SC) Messenger* on October 19, 1831. It appeared in the Washington papers on October 31 and November 1, 1831, and caused the dying embers of the cabinet controversy to flare up once again.[26]

Calhoun defended his statement, saying that Eaton had "gratuitously dragged my name into his controversy" with those of Ingham, Branch, and Berrien. "The main drift" of his *Appeal,* indeed, was "to hold me up as the real author of all the discord," Calhoun said, "which, he would have the public believe, originated in a low and miserable squabble on my part, in relation to the succession to the Presidential chair." In order for the public to consider the validity of this overall theme, Calhoun believed he had to correct what he insisted were serious errors of fact.

Calhoun remonstrated that his wife had never visited Margaret Eaton, she had never left her card, and he had never left one for her. If Eaton simply remembered the etiquette of Washington, he would know his story was false. Senators and their families made the first call on the vice president and his family; therefore Eaton would have had to make the first call, which Calhoun said he then would have been obligated to return. Before his marriage, Eaton had indeed called on Calhoun, and the vice president, not finding him at home at a later time, had left his card. That was the only connection the Calhouns had ever had with the Eatons. Floride Calhoun had never visited Margaret Eaton on her own.

Calhoun said that what actually happened was that the Eatons had paid a visit on the Calhouns at a time when he was not home, but his wife was. She received them courteously, he said; "she could not with propriety do otherwise." When Calhoun came home that evening, his wife told him of the visit, and they had a brief discussion of Margaret Eaton's standing in Washington society. The next morning Floride Calhoun indicated her determination not to return the Eaton visit. Calhoun said that he "approved of her decision, though I foresaw the difficulties in which it would probably involve me; but that I viewed the question involved, as paramount to all political considerations, & was prepared to meet the consequences." Social norms came before political benefit, Calhoun believed.

He did not have any political motives in this social matter, Calhoun insisted. If he had, he would have been "base enough" to socialize with the Eatons because everyone knew that was the way to get on Jackson's good side. Instead, he and his wife took "a high and sacred regard to duty. . . . It was not, in fact, a question of the exclusion of one already admitted into society, but the admission of one already excluded." Even before her marriage to John Timberlake, Margaret Eaton had not been accepted into society, "and the real question was, whether her marriage with Maj. Eaton, should open the door already closed on her; or, in other words, whether official rank & patronage should, or should not, prove paramount to that censorship, which the [female] sex exercises over itself; and, on which, all must acknowledge, the purity and dignity of the female character must depend." In the case of Margaret Eaton, Calhoun said, "the great victory, that has been achieved, in favor of the morals of the country, by the high minded independence and virtue of the ladies of Washington, . . . [must not] be lost by perverted and false representations of the real question at issue." The Eaton Affair was a social, not a political matter.

Calhoun also denied the accuracy of Eaton's rendition of what had happened to Calhoun's office-seeking friend. The whole matter had occurred several months after Floride Calhoun had decided not to visit Margaret Eaton, so there was no connection between the two issues. Besides this, Calhoun had become upset not because his nominee had been rejected, but because Eaton gave it to someone else after he had specifically promised it to Calhoun's man and had never even had the courtesy to tell Calhoun why.

Then, Calhoun argued, Eaton had placed the blame for the dissolution of the cabinet on him because a Calhoun supporter supposedly had said that Eaton was not a friend. Just who was this individual? Eaton should have named him. Eaton was also mistaken about Ingham, Branch, Berrien, and Green. They were all faithful Jacksonians. Besides, "Gen. Green's course has been of his own choosing, without an attempt on my part to influence him." In truth, Andrew Jackson "had no friend more zealous & honest in his cause." There was no conspiracy, Calhoun said.

Having corrected, he believed, the factual errors in Eaton's *Appeal*, Calhoun now turned to the "general charges and insinuations." He had never tried to determine selections for the cabinet, and he had never done anything to hurt the administration. He certainly had nothing to do with the dissolution of the cabinet "unless indeed . . . the refusal of Mrs. Calhoun to visit Mrs. Eaton on grounds exclusively connected with the dignity and purity of her sex" or his determination to protect his good name in the Seminole Affair "should be considered sufficient reasons to render me responsible." In the Seminole Affair, he had never said anything about Margaret Eaton, though had he done so, he believed it would have strengthened his argument. Writing to a friend in private, at the same time, Calhoun asserted that "Jackson's attempt to regulate the intercourse of female society" had done "incalculable injury to his character & influence, as well as discredit to the country."[27]

When Calhoun's published statement reached Washington, Duff Green became so excited he stopped the presses to get it into the *Telegraph* immediately. The *Globe* ridiculed Calhoun's arguments of self-sacrifice, insisting that the public knew very well that all of Calhoun's "political efforts are exclusively intended for his own advancement." The *Telegraph* responded that its rival had "been guilty of more than its usual share of vituperation and perversion" and then attacked Eaton and the *Globe* with equal gusto.[28]

In Franklin, Tennessee, John and Margaret Eaton saw John Calhoun's rebuttal, which they must have discussed in great detail. They did not respond, however, letting the matter rest. Andrew Jackson and his new cabinet also seemed to feel that silence was the best response. There was a war to be fought against the president's perceived new conspiracy against the people, the Bank of the United States. There was no time to continue battling the plot against Margaret Eaton, particularly since she was not even in Washington anymore. The Indians still had to be moved across the Mississippi River, and Nat Turner's Slave Rebellion, which had occurred in Virginia that fall, was also a troublesome worry. So, too, was the earlier publication of the first issue of William Lloyd Garrison's abolitionist newspaper, *The Liberator*. The imminent future would see civil war threatened over nullification. It was finished, this battle over Margaret Eaton, and the nation moved on to other matters that the Eaton Affair had previously overshadowed.

There was no epitaph to mark the end of this long-fought controversy, but a long article in the *United States Telegraph* came close to providing one. Once she married John Eaton, Duff Green said, Margaret Eaton "resolved on forcing herself on society. The love of conquest never burned with greater violence in any other bosom. . . . Practiced in the *arts* of her *caste*," she flattered Jackson and pressured her husband into defending her. At the very time that Eaton was chasing Ingham around the offices of the Treasury Department, Green said, "his Bellona" was bragging in public that her husband would punish her assailants. "Almost any other woman would have fled into her closet; yet she, at the time when public scrutiny was investigating her character, instead of retreating from the public gaze, was parading in the most frequented streets, and showing herself in the most public places." It was all unwomanly.

Green ridiculed John Eaton's call for "deep sympathy for female character." He had "as high a reverence for the sex as any other man," the editor said, "but there are those who have unsexed themselves, and it is upon the vices and against the machinations of such, and in defence of these virtues which elevate woman, lovely woman, beyond the reach of party conflicts, that . . . [he] entered the lists."[29] Clearly, Green argued, Margaret Eaton was no true woman, and thus she did not deserve the protection that Andrew Jackson and John Henry Eaton tried so hard to provide her, and that she tried to ensure. These were the core issues of the Eaton Affair. Margaret Eaton was impure, and she did not know her proper place as a woman, so she rightfully suffered the consequences. It was too bad that she took so many others down with her.

A friend of Jackson's was even more pointed. "It would have been better for the president," Walter Overton said, "to have left Mrs. E to stand or fall on her own merits & not to have made her the test by which he tries his friends."[30] If only Andrew Jackson had ignored Margaret Eaton's plight, she would have remained a curiosity in Washington and played no role in his administration. As it was, he made her an important figure and allowed her to dominate social and political life as few women in American history ever had or would.

Even Martin Van Buren paid the price, temporarily, for his friendship with her. When his name came up in January 1832 for Senate confirmation to the post of United States minister to Great Britain, John C. Calhoun, as vice president, cast the tie-breaking vote rejecting him. He gloated after the victory: "It will kill him, sir, kill him dead." Of course, it did not. Van Buren simply gained Jackson's further support and found new public sympathy. He became vice president of the United States in 1832 and president in 1836. Calhoun, meanwhile, resigned the vice presidency to reenter the Senate and become the open champion of states' rights. During the debate in 1833 over the Force Bill against South Carolina nullification, Calhoun returned to Margaret Eaton. He included in the text of his anti-Jackson remarks his disgust with "circumstances too disreputable to be mentioned here." Similarly, in 1836, he blamed the bad state of American monetary currency on, among other things, Jackson's obsession with "regulating social intercourse, declaring who they [cabinet] should visit, and who they should not visit." In Calhoun's mind, Margaret Eaton remained an important villain. She had, after all, been instrumental in the loss of his best chance to be president. It might not have been fair or even logical, but Andrew Jackson's split with John C. Calhoun was the result of the convoluted debates over a woman's morality, a debate that Calhoun missed—except at the very end—but paid the price for, anyway.[31]

9

"An Influential Personage Now"

John C. Calhoun, Martin Van Buren, and John Henry Eaton were now no longer part of the Jackson administration. Calhoun resigned the vice presidency to return to the United States Senate, Van Buren was biding his time before his election as Jackson's vice president in the 1832 election, and Eaton was thinking of replacing Hugh L. White as senator from Tennessee. Andrew Jackson still felt a strong sense of loyalty to his former secretary of war. After all, Eaton had voluntarily given up his cabinet post, and he remained a political supporter and staunch friend. As Jackson had already shown in his battle for Margaret Eaton's honor, he never gave up on his friends.

Politics, however, was also influential in Jackson's thinking about Eaton's future. Though he had sprung into the presidency out of Tennessee, where he remained a popular figure, Jackson had confusing political problems on his home turf. The Andrew Erwin faction that had opposed him during his early political days continued its opposition now. His own supporters had splintered into two wings and later coalesced into further factions. At first, Eaton, William B. Lewis, and John Overton headed one faction, but they faced stern opposition from a new pro-Jackson group, one that opposed their dominance in state and national politics. Such powerful figures as the state's two senators, Hugh L. White and Felix Grundy, future president James K. Polk, and Jackson's nephew, Andrew Jackson Donelson, made up the second faction. Tennessee was experiencing "vague no-party politics," as one later historian phrased it, and Jackson was not always the beneficiary.[1]

As the 1830s progressed, the political situation in Tennessee grew more chaotic. The Erwin and the Overton factions came to see a common cause in supporting the Bank of the United States that Jackson attacked with such a passion. At the same time, the 1833 and 1835 battles between James Polk and John Bell over the office of Speaker of the House of Representatives and Hugh White's 1836 leadership in opposing Jackson's support of Martin Van Buren for the presidency split the Tennessee Democratic party into ever more confusing factions. The result of this political turmoil was the birth and ascendancy of the Whig party in Andrew Jackson's state and the obvious weakening of the ever-splintering Democrats.[2]

This disturbing situation was evident in the presidential elections of 1828 and 1832. Jackson carried the state almost unanimously, but in 1828 only 50 percent of the eligible voters had cast their ballots, and in 1832, this percentage had dropped to less than 30 percent. Clearly Jackson had not sparked an outpouring of support in his home state, and the factional battles and the controversy over Margaret Eaton in Washington had only added to the fissures and lack of enthusiasm in Tennessee. Duff Green even predicted that if Henry Clay could be convinced to sit out the 1832 election and Jackson's opponents could unite behind one candidate, "I am convinced that he [Jackson] might be driven back to the Hermitage without a single electoral vote out of Tennessee."[3]

When Andrew Jackson considered Eaton's future, therefore, he had to do it within the context of the political discord both at home and in Washington. Jackson wanted to keep Eaton close to him. He hoped his other old friend, Hugh White, who in 1831 was still in Jackson's camp, would accept the War Department so that Eaton might once again enter the United States Senate. Naively, Jackson ignored the fact that Eaton and White belonged to different political factions in Tennessee and that White was worried about Martin Van Buren's increasing influence in Washington. Jackson was sure White would take the secretaryship, out of the obligations of friendship.[4]

Jackson wrote to White on April 9, 1831, eleven days before the official announcement of Van Buren's and Eaton's resignations, asking him to become secretary of war and thus "not only render important services to your country, but [also] render an act of great friendship to me." He commiserated over the many recent deaths in White's family, offering him a room in the White House and sincere consolation. Since 1825, White had lost his wife, eight children, and a daughter-in-law, his wife having only recently died on March 25, 1831. Jackson wanted White to set his grief aside, or at least come to the White House where they could share their mutual sorrows. This bond of the loss of loved ones only made Jackson feel more certain of White's cooperation.[5]

White's negative reaction, therefore, shocked Jackson. The Tennessee senator feigned unhappiness and sorrow over Eaton's departure from the cabinet but warned Jackson that if the former secretary of war returned to Tennessee he would "have difficulties to encounter, with some of our friends." He gently refused Jackson's offer of office, citing his unsuitability, and argued that as Jackson's "*personal* and *political friend*," he could not accept a post from him.[6]

The death of White's wife and all his other recent family losses were valid reasons for White's refusal, but he really did not wish to become part of Jackson's cabinet under any circumstances. He remained in the Senate, much to Jackson's dismay, and when he ran against Martin Van Buren in the 1836 presidential contest, he split from his old friend Jackson, publicly and finally.[7]

The president eventually chose Michigan's Lewis Cass to be secretary of war, but the problem of Eaton's future remained unresolved. Jackson still wanted him close by in the Senate, so he now looked toward the seat of Tennessee's other senator, Felix Grundy, up for reelection in 1833. Though Grundy had been faithful to Jackson in the Senate, he, too, was part of the anti-Overton-Eaton-Lewis faction and unhappy over the direction of national and state politics. Jackson had begun to suspect his loyalty because of his leanings toward John C. Calhoun, as evidenced by his murky role in the publication of Calhoun's Seminole War dispute pamphlet. When White refused the cabinet post, Jackson decided that Eaton should go after Grundy's seat, insisting that Eaton's victory would "nail the conspirators to the counter." Still, he did not issue any public statement of support.[8]

John Eaton's chances for election to the Senate revolved around state and national political battles and, of course, his wife's infamous reputation. The signals were mixed. A Nashvillean friendly to the presidential hopes of Supreme Court Justice John McLean said that people in Tennessee's capital city blamed Margaret Eaton for breaking up Jackson's cabinet, while another Tennessean blamed John Eaton and William B. Lewis for all the president's problems. A pro-Eaton Jacksonian worried about Nashville snubbing Margaret but promised that he and his family would try to ensure a proper welcome. Jackson was so confused about all he was hearing from home that he pleaded with his old friend John Overton to tell him exactly where the state stood.[9]

The Eatons left Washington on September 19, 1831, after John's *Appeal* appeared in print. He hoped the change of scenery would result in fewer problems, but after arriving in Baltimore Margaret became so ill that almost a week later she was still "too weak & feeble to leave her bed." The couple could proceed no farther until October 2. Meanwhile, back in Washington, Andrew Jackson also took to his bed for an extended period. The stress was taking its toll on the president and the woman he had defended. It was most discouraging.[10]

Matters looked better when the Eatons arrived in Tennessee in late October. Supporters in Nashville and Franklin immediately held gatherings in their honor. Almost every one of the members of the state legislature and other political and civic leaders, some two hundred people, subscribed to a Nashville dinner. John Branch happened to reach the city at this time on his travel south and attended the dinner, but when he was ignored he quietly left. Mayor William Armstrong welcomed Eaton home, insisting that the city's "affection [had been] increased and confidence strengthened from the conviction that he had undergone the ordeal of public scrutiny, and . . . come forth unscathed and unhurt." During the long series of toasts, one testimonial received the heartiest assent. To enthusiastic applause, the toast rang out: "Woman—where woman is the theme, palsied be the hand and blistered the tongue that would be raised but to defend her, or speak but to praise her."[11]

More than a hundred men attended the banquet in Franklin on

November 11, 1831, and reacted enthusiastically to all the toasts of praise for Eaton. Once more, the testament that received the loudest applause defended Margaret's honor: "The Law of the Jewish Talmud—He that slandereth his neighbor, or those of his neighbor's household, shall be taken without the gates of the city and beaten with stripes, and all the people shall say, *Amen.*"[12]

To make the Eatons' welcome complete, numbers of Nashville society women visited Margaret. They extended invitations to the theater, and when one leading society woman gave a large party, "all the fashionables of our little Town attended," a Jacksonian said. "I go in support of the old chief," this individual added, "and so far as the reception of Eaton may be considered as a support of the Genl, he has been thus far well supported here." Governor William Carroll went so far as to say that "Major Eaton never stood as well in Tennessee as he does now; and if his friends urge him for the Senate a year hence the probability is in favor of his election." Viewing all this activity from the perspective of the nation's capital, the *Washington Globe* ridiculed John C. Calhoun's recently published claim of having achieved a *"great moral victory"* over Margaret Eaton. "Is it nullified?" the *Globe* gloated. John Henry Eaton seemed to be riding high; the Washington scandal had apparently not hurt his chances of returning to the United States Senate, and even the Democratic factionalism in Tennessee seemed to provide no serious stumbling block.[13]

A great deal still depended on Felix Grundy, a man who had once lived at Margaret Eaton's father's boardinghouse. In the late spring of 1831, Richard M. Johnson had explained Eaton's situation to Grundy, though at that time he was still hopeful that Eaton would take Hugh White's Senate seat. If White refused the cabinet office, Johnson said, he hoped Grundy would take it. Whatever he did, Johnson advised Grundy "as a friend to take a decided stand to gratify Eaton & his friends." That same day, however, Grundy was still upbraiding Eaton for his role in the Calhoun Seminole War pamphlet controversy. Meanwhile, Eaton's supporters considered Grundy's role in that publication as proof that he was a friend of the former vice president. They used this argument in touting Eaton for Grundy's Senate seat. Eaton's candidacy increasingly came to be seen as a continuation of the cabinet battles in Washington, the rivalry between Van Buren and Calhoun. "I have no doubt," one contemporary said, [that Eaton's election] "would please our good President and be a sore stab to Mr. Calhoun etc."[14]

Eaton remained mum in his Franklin home as Washington and Tennessee politicians pondered his fate. He seemed happy to be away from the nation's capital, "relieved of the weight of mountains that were upon him." Unfortunately, Margaret became sick again, apparently never having recovered from the illness she had contracted on her way to Baltimore in the fall of 1831. Throughout 1832, she took to her bed at regular intervals, the stress of the controversy that had swirled around her in Washington evidently continuing to take its toll. When she and John traveled back East in 1832 for him to play a minor role in the Democratic national convention in Baltimore, Margaret became so sick in New York City that she believed herself "at the point of death." To try to cure her, doctors shaved and blistered her head. After she felt better, John became "quite ill with Cholera symptoms." Physicians used the same techniques on him but only made matters worse. The two ailing people made it back to Washington, and John "was most violently attacked with complaint in the Bowels . . . [which] terminated in a very severe bilious," Margaret reported to a friend. He recovered, however, but then Margaret became ill again and seemed to be "declining every day. I dread to anticipate," John worried, "but fear greatly the result." When Margaret did not get better after eight months of illness, John Eaton, who was concerned over her increasing feebleness, took her to a specialist in Philadelphia, and she began to improve.[15]

No doubt because of all these health problems, rumors began to circulate that John Eaton would not run for the Senate. In the fall of 1832, with his and Margaret's health better and Andrew Jackson meeting in Nashville with supporters and allegedly ready to give recalcitrant legislators "a *drilling*," Eaton formally threw his hat into the ring. Jackson, however, was still unwilling to state his support publicly, and this hesitancy allowed Grundy and his followers to insist that the president had "*no political* preference for Eaton, that it is merely a personal friendship, entertained for him," and that "*politically* . . . [Jackson] prefer[ed] Mr. Grundy." Jackson told several friends that he was amazed at such an erroneous interpretation of his position, but in a public letter he was not that forthright. While he praised Eaton's loyalty and steadfastness and condemned those who had tried to destroy the administration through him, he did not demand Eaton's election. "Mr. Grundy, our present Senator," Jackson wrote members of the legislature, "has so far as I know ably supported the administration but it is for you to say whether the public interest will be best promoted by the election of Major Eaton in preference to Mr. Grundy. It is not for me to judge of this . . . All I can say is that should the Legislature elect Either it is believed the State will be ably served." This was hardly a ringing endorsement of Eaton. Jackson could still not bring himself to oppose publicly an old friend like Felix Grundy for another old friend, John Henry Eaton. In reality, Eaton had drifted away from Jackson on issues like the Bank, while Francis Preston Blair and family had replaced him and his wife as social intimates. Jackson simply was not as close to Eaton as he had once been and did not feel any personal or political need for him as he once had.[16]

There were, in fact, three candidates for the Senate seat, all open supporters of Andrew Jackson and all three a part of the fractious Nashville political establishment: Felix Grundy, John Henry Eaton, and Ephraim Foster. In 1817–1818, the three men, along with Andrew Jackson, had together been part of the founding of the Nashville theater, so they knew each other well. Eaton had earlier been a U.S. senator, Grundy now held that post, and Foster would gain it in 1839. Of the three, only Foster, who, like Eaton, had served under Jackson in the military, did not claim Jackson's support.[17]

Early in the election year of 1833, Eaton's candidacy suffered a severe setback, which had to make him wonder about his chances. The Tennessee legislature worked on naming the state's new counties, and "Eaton" was one of the names suggested. Shockingly, only seven out of the sixty-five legislators who cast their ballots on the matter supported the suggestion. The legislature honored Andrew Jackson, choosing to name five of the ten new counties after him, so its refusal to vote for Eaton County was no slap at the president. It was aimed at Eaton himself, at a time when his campaign for the Senate seat should have prevented such an embarrassing affront in the very body that would be choosing the new officer.[18]

October 1833 arrived and the legislature began its vote. After seventeen ballots, the count remained deadlocked: Grundy, 23; Foster, 20;

and Eaton, 17. Another week of polling showed Grundy holding firm at 23 votes but Eaton gaining at Foster's expense. Now Eaton had 20 votes to Foster's 17. "I think you can calculate on seeing Eaton in the Senate," a confident supporter wrote Francis P. Blair of the *Globe.* This prediction proved erroneous. On the fifty-fifth ballot, Foster withdrew and Eaton, seeing that his candidacy was lost, unsuccessfully tried to withdraw, too. Grundy won reelection, gathering 33 votes to Eaton's 18 and Foster's 9. Tennessee Jacksonians were split more than ever before, and in 1835 and 1836, they were crushingly defeated at the state level by a newly organized Whig party. In Andrew Jackson's home state, his political party was in difficult straits, and John and Margaret Eaton were central figures in the collapse.[19]

John Eaton was "mortified by his defeat," but he remained outwardly calm. Not so Margaret. When a Virginia visitor met her in the early days after the election, he found her openly upset over her husband's defeat. "The madame talked of nothing else," he said, and "seemed much disappointed and dissatisfied." John Henry Eaton was not going to return to the Senate, and this failure meant that he and Margaret still had to decide their futures. Would they remain in Franklin where Eaton might lawyer and politic, or should they accept defeat and return to Washington to begin again? Behind it all remained the question of Margaret's role in the loss. Did John Eaton lose the election because of the obvious split in Tennessee Jacksonianism or, more directly, because Margaret Eaton was his wife? If the latter was the case, would this stigma shadow him no matter where he went? At least one onlooker seemed to think so. "Eaton is a man of some cleverness," this observer wrote, "but he has prostrated himself by his marriage. No man could ever get along decently in public life, with such a fool of a wife." "Our friend John Eaton is harassed to death by a very sick hypochondriac wife," another critical observer noted. Even Margaret's recent serious illnesses (apparently tuberculosis) were grist for the mills of criticism. The former war secretary was worried, said William B. Lewis, that his wife had "fallen victim to the cruel and relentless persecutions of monsters in the shape of Human beings."[20]

Despite John Eaton's disappointing defeat in the Senate race, Jackson continued his support. A simple gesture, no doubt inspired by Margaret, helped maintain Jackson's devotion. The Eatons paid a visit to the Hermitage in the spring of 1832 and walked to Rachel's tomb in the garden behind the house. Then they informed Jackson what they had done. He was clearly touched, remarking that Rachel was "their sincere friend," and so was he.[21]

Jackson took care of friends like these, but even before he could act, Eaton briefly became president of the Ohio and Chesapeake Canal Company, much to Martin Van Buren's disgust. The vice president did not believe Eaton had the business acumen to handle the job. Eaton did not last long, and once more Jackson came to his rescue. On March 28, 1834, he nominated Eaton to a three-year term as governor of the Florida Territory, the nomination sailing through the Senate on April 24, the date Eaton received his formal commission. Unfortunately, Eaton was then sabotaged. Hugh L. White wrote a letter to a friend in Florida, taking credit for Eaton's appointment. In the letter, White defended Jackson, insisting that if Eaton did not work out, he, Hugh White, not Jackson, should be held responsible. Eaton was "mortified." Why would White so blatantly hint that he was incompetent? He was, after all, popular in Florida because of his successful negotiation of Indian treaties while secretary of war.[22]

Whether because of this letter, or because he saw little potential for political or monetary success in Florida, or because Margaret did not want to go there, John Eaton showed little enthusiasm for his appointment to govern the 40,000-person territory. He let it be known that he preferred the governorship of the Michigan Territory to a post in Florida. William B. Lewis and Francis P. Blair urged Jackson not to give in. Others, more politically acceptable to the people in Michigan, were available for that post, they said, and, besides, Florida held real promise for Eaton. Bubbling to the surface yet again, however, was the suspicion that Margaret was behind Eaton's uncertainty. "Maj. E. is not the man I once thought him," Postmaster General William Barry's army officer son said. "He was a good man but his wife has ruined him. How much happier would this man have been, had he married a plain, prudent, unpretending woman!" Andrew Jackson agreed that Eaton was no longer the man he once was, though he did not blame Margaret. When John Coffee's son inquired of the president whether he should invite Eaton to write his deceased father's biography, Jackson believed the work would "be faithfully done" because Eaton was "always the sincere friend of your father and reveres his memory." But, Jackson worried, Eaton was "becoming fond of ease. . . . He will not finish, if he commences it."[23]

John Eaton remained loyal to Jackson, and Margaret agreed to go to Florida. It was not his first acquaintance with the territory, having joined with several other Tennesseeans to invest in land there in 1818. The Eatons did not rush south after his April appointment, however, perhaps indicating that John Eaton no longer had significant property interests there. They did not arrive in Tallahassee, the territorial capital, until December 11, 1834, conveniently long after the end of the hot and humid summer season.

It was not an impressive place, this territorial capital, only a little over ten years old, its first capitol building, a log cabin, having only recently been replaced by a larger though hardly imposing two-story brick building. The town's population was minuscule, less than fifteen hundred people. Its only redeeming quality seemed to be a market with a wide selection of fish, meat, and vegetables. "I have seen a noisy senseless crowd, a legislative council with little wisdom, [and] a fashionable circle with little taste," a future governor said disdainfully of the tiny capital city. Ralph Waldo Emerson was even briefer, pronouncing the town "a grotesque place." The territory's economy was based on cotton and lumber, but the most significant activity remained the battle to eliminate the Seminole Indians from within its borders.[24]

The expected arrival of the Eatons became the main topic of conversation in a Tallahassee tavern just before their appearance. Cracking almonds with their teeth, Florida politicians, who were suspicious of any appointees from Washington, discussed their new governor and especially his famous wife. "She will cut a dash with us new country people certainly," one predicted, "but she is the new overseer's wife, and must be received." "Well enough for you to say," another rejoined, "you who have no wife." "I shall call on the lady, if my wife will let me," another joked, and then the conversation drifted off to what kind of a job Eaton would do as governor. Although it was not out of the realm of possibility in this drinking crowd, there is no indication, in the course of this talk about Margaret Eaton, that anyone brought up the gruesome example of early Florida Indian treatment of women suspected of adultery. Such a woman was stripped of her clothing, her hair shorn, and then she was sent to her parents to be hidden in shame.[25]

The Eatons received a warm welcome when they arrived in Tallahassee on December 11, 1834. Only future governor Robert Reid, who had earlier expressed such a low opinion of the capital city, indicated a similarly negative evaluation of the Eatons. After the briefest observation, he concluded that "Gov. E. is a rowdy—his wife drunk or crazy." Other citizens of the city did not agree. They decided that their new governor and his wife deserved a proper reception, so they went to the old fort and pulled out an ancient gun for a proper salute. The cannon barely functioned, and it took all night to fire off the requisite rounds to honor the new governor properly. "The intervals between the discharges were so long," Margaret remembered, "that we forgot about it, until suddenly would come a little short surly boom! and we knew that the citizens were tugging away at that old gun." Floridians also gave a public banquet on December 13 to honor their new first couple, much to the Eatons' delight. A local Indian chief provided his own welcome. The first day John was on the job, this man came to the governor's office, stood studying him, then departed in silence, apparently satisfied with the cut of the new official's figure.[26]

The welcome from one of the territory's leaders was not so enthusiastic. Richard K. Call, the man who had made the improper advance on Margaret Eaton in her father's boardinghouse in the 1820s and then never forgave her for that rebuff, was a large plantation owner near Tallahassee, the huge luxurious garden in front of his home clearly displaying his prosperity to all who passed. At the time of the boardinghouse assault on Margaret, he had been the territorial delegate to Congress (1823–1825), and he had continued to be one of Florida's leading businessmen and politicians. Between 1832 and 1834, for example, he built one of the nation's first railroads, the Tallahassee–St. Marks Road, and he would later command troops in the Second Seminole War and become Florida's territorial governor. His personality had changed little from those early days in the Franklin House. He exuded energy and aggressiveness. In him remained, as a later historian described it, "the same deadly sin of pride, to the point of arrogance." He maintained his personal dislike for Margaret, and he saw John's appointment as a political affront to him and his political faction. No doubt John Branch, Eaton's former cabinet foe, who had recently established himself at Live Oak Plantation just outside Tallahassee, was similarly displeased at Eaton's arrival, although there is no record of their meeting.[27]

Eaton and Call never set aside their disdain for one another, but Margaret and Call's wife, Mary, got along well, the earlier unfortunate incident apparently never coming up in conversation between the two women. They actually spent little time together, however, because Margaret did not stay in Tallahassee much. The governor was expected to reside part of the time in Pensacola, and Margaret much preferred that city to the territorial capital. Pensacola's population was slightly larger than Tallahassee's, it had a longer history going back to 1696, and its location on the Gulf of Mexico made it a more pleasant and interesting place than the inland city. Eaton wanted to be with his wife and family, so he usually traveled with them and soon developed the reputation of being the absent governor. He ignored the anti-abolitionist fervor that developed during his tenure, and he similarly took no action on a statehood referendum. He did, however, sell bonds to help keep the territory solvent, and, concerning a much less significant issue, he battled Washington over its refusal to provide him with a janitor.[28]

Margaret made the most of her time and, not surprisingly, according to the tales told about her, acted in her usual unorthodox fashion. She and her daughters swam in the lake near the governor's mansion, and she allowed the sun to tan her skin despite the contemporary fashion that women should be pale. She wore Spanish-style dresses, her tan causing her to be mistaken for a Spaniard. At the racetrack she allegedly bet like a man, although in a green velvet dress, topped by a bonnet decorated with white ostrich feathers caressing her shoulder, she looked very much the woman. It was all fun, unconventional but enjoyable, and the men seemed to agree. They surrounded her everywhere she appeared, but the territory's women were shocked. Margaret Eaton continued to flout society's norms and maintained her reputation for unorthodoxy.[29]

Other than horse racing, there was little amusement to divert Margaret in Tallahassee. "Patgoes" was an exception. A slave carried a wooden bird on a pole, and women attached a ribbon in the color of their choice to this carving, quickly giving the drab bird "an abundant and gaudy plumage." At a set time and place, the women and their escorts—the latter carrying firearms—assembled. The man who shot the bird was proclaimed king and his lady the queen of a subsequent ball. Whether John Eaton ever became the successful marksman, and Margaret Eaton the queen of a ball, is unfortunately unknown.[30]

During their short stay in Florida, Margaret even took a trip back to Washington, and while there she caused new controversy. She approached Amos Kendall, now the postmaster general, on behalf of a mail-contractor company Kendall believed had received unfair financial advantage during William Barry's term in office. Later, Kendall accused Margaret of offering him a bribe on behalf of the contractors, saying she offered his wife a carriage with a pair of horses in exchange for his support of the specious claim. Eaton also became involved, but Jackson stepped in and told Kendall to ignore the Florida governor.[31]

According to Margaret, John Eaton spent most of his time in Florida issuing divorces. Soon after the arrival of the Eatons in Tallahassee, a very attractive woman latched on to the first lady. Clearly, Margaret realized, this woman wanted something from the new governor and was trying to get it through her. She was correct. The woman asked Margaret to go with her to see Eaton to get a divorce; Margaret refused. "I had already been accused of trying to control my husband's official position," she said, and she did not intend to give anyone any further ammunition on that count. As in Washington before, Margaret's outspokenness gained her the reputation of being the power behind the throne—no matter the lack of proof.[32]

The woman seeking a divorce went to see the governor on her own, and Eaton gladly acceded to her request. "Certainly, madam, if you want it I will give it to you. . . . I simply give you the divorce because you are a mighty pretty woman." When Margaret protested against such a lenient attitude toward marriage, Eaton just laughed and said, "I am going to give them as fast as they ask for them. If they cannot live together in peace I am not going to keep them together." He gave as many as seven divorces a day, Margaret remembered in horror, and he jokingly told her that he would divorce her if she did not stop criticizing him. She stopped nagging, but she never approved, calling Eaton "a little too good-hearted" on this account. There was nothing she could do. In granting the divorces, Eaton was not, however, vicariously severing his own connection with Margaret. There is no evidence that their marriage continued anything but happy.[33]

The Seminole Indians were a much more serious problem for Eaton. He tried to implement the expulsion policy Jackson had begun with his excursion into Florida during the First Seminole War. In order to force the United States Senate to take quick action, Eaton expressed the opinion that earlier treaties of removal became invalid if not ratified within a year. Receiving the rebuff from Andrew Jackson he must have expected, Eaton kept calling for immediate action, insisting that regular forces, not militia, be given the task. In early January 1836, he wrote to Lewis Cass, his successor in the War Department, calling for "prompt action and a good force" against the Indians who were adamantly refusing to be moved off their lands. When the administration prepared to send in Winfield Scott, one of the nation's premier military men, Eaton was unimpressed in the face of martial greatness. He sent Scott a host of suggestions for waging this Second Seminole War, and when the general did not follow his advice exactly, he felt no compunction about pointing it out to him.[34]

Eaton maintained a determined interest in the Indian war, but he was not to see its completion. On March 16, 1836, he received a commission as minister to Spain, and on April 19, he left Florida. Indicating that he and Richard Call had not overcome their mutual animosity, he warned Andrew Jackson about two of Call's suggestions for territorial office. He labeled them both "nullifiers, & *anties*," eliciting a sharp response from Call. He also felt touchy about Call's being named his replacement as governor before his own appointment as minister to Spain had been confirmed. It really did not matter, he decided, because he never "intended, under any state of things again to return to Florida." He was happy to be leaving. Floridians, other than the Call faction, felt friendlier toward him than he felt toward their territory. Since Eaton was president of the local racing club, the editor of the Tallahassee newspaper said he hoped Eaton would return to fulfill his duties there.[35]

The Eatons traveled to Washington to prepare for the ocean crossing to Europe that summer of 1836. The Spanish minister to the United States paid a courtesy visit, as did the daughter of Cornelius P. Van

Ness, the current American minister to Spain. Both showed Margaret special attention. The Senate, meanwhile, routinely confirmed John's appointment, all this social and political activity indicating that the recent scandals were no longer at issue, or, to be cynical, that no one wanted to stand in the way of Margaret Eaton leaving the country and removing herself from the Washington social scene. At the same time, the nation prepared to elect Martin Van Buren president and Richard M. Johnson vice president of the United States that November.[36]

The Eatons played no role in the 1836 election. In midsummer, they boarded a sailing ship, the *Independent,* in New York harbor for the ocean crossing, six people in their party: Margaret and John, Margaret's two daughters, seventeen-year-old Mary Virginia and eleven-year-old Margaret Rosa, and two servants, one of whom was a black male. On board ship was Richard Rush, the famed diplomat, who was going to England to bring back the money willed to the United States for the establishment of the Smithsonian Institution. He, his family, and the Eatons got along well, Margaret remembering Rush as being "as devotedly kind to me as if I had been his sister," and Rush reporting to Andrew Jackson that the Eatons "added much to the pleasantness of a good passage." Margaret and her daughters proved to be "the life of the cabin, rendering many an hour that would have been tedious, cheerful and sprightly," Rush said.[37]

Once the ship arrived in Liverpool on August, 31, 1836, the Eatons found that they had to wait for transportation to Spain. They took advantage of the layover to tour London and renew acquaintances with Sir Charles Vaughan, the former British minister to the United States. The American minister to England, Andrew Stevenson, opened his home to them, and everywhere they went, they received a friendly reception. The British were interested in meeting the infamous Margaret Eaton, although they displayed the usual British restraint and reserve. The couple made such a good impression on the proprietor of Long's Hotel in London that, though noted for being tight with his money, he later sent them some special punch and a goose. They even traveled to Paris, where Margaret ran up some large bills, shopping in the famous women's stores.[38]

In early October, the Eatons boarded the *Iberia* and set sail for Spain, stopping in Lisbon to do some more sightseeing. Sailing on to

Cadiz, they encountered a terrible storm causing damage to the ship and seasickness to most of the passengers. This frightening experience did not prevent Margaret from playing a practical joke on the English physician who attended her for her queasiness. The doctor gave her some opium and told her to eat a little piece of it intermittently to settle her stomach. In conspiracy with her husband, Margaret pretended to eat all the opium at one time and convinced the doctor that she was in a severe coma. She kept up the ruse until the ship's captain ran up with a bucket of water prepared to douse her out of her stupor. Then she admitted the joke, once more demonstrating a forwardness unusual for women of that time.[39]

There was, however, a serious side to Margaret, too. When the ship limped into Cadiz, and a smaller boat was sent out to bring the Eaton family in, Margaret tied herself with handkerchiefs to her husband and the two children. "If one goes down, let all go down together," she said. John broke down in tears. "Yes, Margaret; we have clung together in life, and we will cling together in death." And, as if to make their peace with their past, one of the first things they did after arrival in the region was to visit the grave of John Timberlake at Port Mahon.[40]

The Eatons found themselves in a country torn with discord, having never recovered from the Napoleonic Wars of the early nineteenth century. Ferdinand VII had become king of Spain in 1808, but his reign had been a constant struggle between liberal elements trying to follow the lead of the French Revolution and his own absolutism, which attempted to maintain the status quo. In 1823, for example, the Holy Alliance had to use force to prop up his monarchy. When his queen died in 1829, the choice of her successor was particularly important because rival political groups and rival family members hoped to gain advantage. Since Ferdinand seemed willing to let others make the choice for him, the intrigue was intense.

The winner was his niece, Maria Cristina de Bourbon of Naples. It was said that when the forty-five-year-old sickly Ferdinand saw a miniature of the twenty-three-year-old "tall, fair, and blue eyed" Cristina, he quickly made up his mind to marry her. Her eyes, as a contemporary put it, "thirsted for pleasure." The American writer Washington Irving said, "her whole face [was] radiant with sweetness," and another American noted that even her ears were beautiful. Clearly

Ferdinand had good reason to be smitten, and he eagerly awaited her arrival in his court.[41]

The young woman was an immediate hit with the expectant Spanish people. "Elegantly dressed in sky blue" when she entered Madrid, she was as beautiful as they had heard, and her kindness to the soldiers who guarded her and her openness to all the people she encountered as she moved through Spain to meet her husband-to-be in Madrid endeared her to the populace. "Without exaggeration," a contemporary remarked, "one may say that Cristina awoke the enthusiasm of all that saw her." When the king met her on December 11, 1829, he was satisfied that he had made a good choice. The wedding the next day was a splendid and joyful affair.[42]

Ten months later, on October 10, 1830, Cristina gave birth to a child, Isabella; and fifteen months after that, on January 30, 1832, another child, Luisa Fernanda, arrived. Unfortunately, both babies were girls. Many years previously, in 1713, Philip V had turned tradition on its ear and promulgated the so-called Salic law forbidding a woman from ruling Spain. In 1789, Charles IV had issued the pragmatic sanction, which decreed that a female could not have precedence to the throne over her brothers, but she did have precedence over her uncles. Don Carlos, brother of Ferdinand, insisted that this pronouncement had been made after his birth, so it did not apply to him. He maintained his precedence to the throne, under Salic law, over Ferdinand's daughters.

What made the debate so crucial was the reigning monarch's poor health. He and those around him, including Cristina, worried that he might die any day, and then the disagreement would provoke internal conflict. To make sure that his daughter would succeed him and that Cristina would be the regent, Ferdinand officially proclaimed the pragmatic sanction in force and specifically declared that Carlos had no claim to the throne. On June 20, 1833, Ferdinand summoned the Cortez to pledge their allegiance to Isabella. This grand ceremony, which was meant to settle matters once and for all, only caused Don Carlos and his followers to intensify their intrigue.

Ferdinand died on September 29, 1833, and the controversy burst into open conflict, as he had earlier predicted it would. "Spain is a bottle of beer and I am the cork. Without me it would all go off in the froth," he had frequently said. England and France immediately recognized Isabella, but Russia, Prussia, Austria, and the Vatican refused. Don Carlos was still living in Portugal, where he had gone to avoid Ferdinand's ceremonies of fealty to Isabella, but he now returned to Spain, and the nation erupted into civil war. Cristina ruled the nation as regent for her tiny daughter, a task that would have tried the most clever monarch. Unfortunately, Cristina had little experience; and, besides, she had an inconvenient secret. She was having an affair with Ferdinand Muñoz, a corporal of her guard and the son of a tobacco shopkeeper. As she tried to battle the Carlists, she secretly married her lover on December 27, 1833, and on November 17, 1834, she just as secretly delivered his child. She had a second daughter on November 8, 1835, a son in 1838, and another daughter in 1840. Meanwhile, the Carlist War raged on over succession to the Spanish throne. Though the private liaison between Cristina and Muñoz remained an open secret and a problem throughout the nation, the supporters of the baby queen and her regent emerged victorious, in 1839, in the bitter civil war.[43]

It was to this fractious land with its scandalous regent, a place that Longfellow described as "an exhausted country marked with all the signs of death and desolation," that Margaret Eaton and her husband, the new minister to Spain, arrived in 1836. After a leisurely four weeks in Cadiz, which so angered the State Department that it docked Eaton a month's pay, they made the extremely dangerous trip to Madrid. At one point partisans of the civil war nearly kidnapped the party. Then Margaret almost caused a diplomatic stir on her first day in the city. Cristina was driving by in her grand carriage, followed by the baby queen in a second vehicle. A Spanish woman the Eatons had befriended on the trip told Margaret that she was to rise when the Regent and Queen drove by. "Madam, I will never rise and stand before any human being but Andrew Jackson," Margaret replied. When Cristina drew near, however, Margaret made the proper show of respect, which Cristina acknowledged with a nod of noblesse oblige.[44]

Unfortunately, neither Margaret nor Cristina ever recorded their thoughts on this occasion. The scandalous regent of Spain and the notorious "Pompadour Peg" of the United States had much in common. Margaret had been the butt of unproven rumor about alleged immoral behavior, while Cristina was the subject of whispering about her secret marriage and births. Here were two soul sisters, born a continent and classes apart, yet both the victims of personal and political suffering because of affections of their heart. Even more, they were the principal actresses in the political drama that swirled around them, and both played their roles forthrightly.

It would make for a good story to say that the two maligned women became friends, but there is no evidence to support such a claim.[45] Margaret is never shy in her memoirs, but these pages contain no indication of any special friendship with Cristina. There was no mutual soul-baring behind closed doors, no secret rendezvous to discuss present problems or explain past controversies. The two women saw each other numerous times, and the regent seemed taken with the Eatons, but no close or lasting relationship ever developed.

Margaret was not very diplomatic or respectful of monarchy during her stay in Spain. She created several potentially embarrassing stirs with her blunt style. When Eaton received his official notice of acceptance, which contained the words that the monarch had "condescended" to see him, Margaret took offense and urged him not to go. Even when he explained that this term was part of normal diplomatic language, she remained unconvinced. Later, when she was invited to an audience at the palace, she insisted on trying to walk up a flight of stairs reserved for royalty, and a guard had to stop her. When she reached the unheated audience room, she grew so cold that she threatened to leave if the queen did not arrive at the appointed time. The embassy official accompanying her paled at the suggestion. "Good heavens! Mrs. Eaton, that would ruin us all. We would be packed off to the United States in an hour. For mercy's sake do not ruin us." Margaret remained stubborn and said she "would not die of the pneumonia for any Queen of Spain." In desperation, the worried American diplomat somehow got word to Cristina's lady-in-waiting. This grand dame apologized for the delay, but then told Margaret that she could not take her daughter Virginia into the audience. Margaret said she did not want to violate any court regulations, but she would not leave her daughter alone in a strange building. The lady-in-waiting departed and soon returned to report that Virginia was welcome, after all.[46]

Cristina finally made her grand entrance, complimented the teenaged Virginia on her striking beauty, and hoped the Eatons would enjoy their stay in Madrid. She said she would be pleased to see Margaret again soon. Margaret, for once remembering proper protocol, determined not to turn her back on the monarch as she left the room. Hesitatingly she walked backward, worried all along that she would trip over the train of her dress. She made it out, however, and when the door closed behind her, she happily blurted out to a surprised attending official, "Through much tribulation have I got out of that room."[47]

The regent was always considerate to Margaret whenever they saw each other. On one occasion, she asked Virginia to kiss the little Queen Isabella's cheek, but the seven-year-old refused to accept the kiss and Cristina reprimanded her on the spot. Throughout their time in Spain, the Eatons maintained a good relationship with Cristina, whose "sweet amiability" Margaret came to appreciate. Her repeated attention to Virginia, even at the expense of her own daughter, the queen, was particularly appealing to Margaret, the proud mother. As for the increasingly plump Isabella, Margaret considered her "as hateful a little wretch as ever I laid my eyes on—disfigured with scrofula, bad tempered, ill natured, cross grained, and insufferably proud."[48]

Unfortunately for Margaret's reputation and that of her husband, several Americans were sending negative reports back to the United States. Frank Hillery, a former slave of Louis McLane's, secretary of treasury and state under Andrew Jackson and twice U.S. minister to England, had accompanied the Eatons on their trip to Europe and had developed a hostility toward Margaret and a sympathy for John. "I am very sorry to tell you," he wrote his former mistress, Mrs. Louis McLane, "that, I am not at all Pleased with Mrs Eaton. She is the most complete Peaice of deception that ever god made, and as a mistress: it would be Cruelty to put a dumb brute, under her Command." Eaton, on the other hand, was "all gentlem[an], and, in my opinion," said Hillery, 'deserves a more amiable Companion, then he has. I know[,] madam[,] he wishes himself back in Tennessee."[49]

Even more persistently negative and damning of the Eatons was Cornelius P. Van Ness, the man Eaton was replacing in Spain. Despite his daughter's solicitous concern for the Eatons before their departure from Washington, Van Ness was angry about being replaced by Eaton. He remained in the country and wrote damning letters from Madrid to President Martin Van Buren, his longtime friend from Kinderhook, New York. He told the president that the highest echelons of Spanish government believed John Eaton "entirely destitute of talent and . . . the most stupid man they have ever seen placed in a similar station." Worse still, they recognized "*who* and *what* is the real minister," an obvious reference to Margaret Eaton. Although he was not at the ministry when the Eatons arrived in Madrid, Van Ness castigated John as "not only incapable of putting together two common ideas but of comprehending a single one." Even worse, he was "a man of indolent habits who wants to do nothing but sit by his fireside and chew tobacco." Then Van Ness retracted his comment about tobacco chewing and the fireside. Instead, he said that "he and *she,* together, regularly dispose of two bottles of rum (of the strongest kind in the spirit) every three days; that is, 4 glasses each and every day, besides wine; and while they are taking it, and he chewing, she smokes her cigars." To raise Van Buren's anger to a total boiling point, Van Ness also said that Margaret was telling people that Van Buren, the president of the United States, had been chasing after her daughter Virginia "and pressed his suit in the presence of General Jackson, but that she utterly refused him much to his chagrin and mortification."[50]

That John Eaton, like most men in the nineteenth century, chewed tobacco is no surprise. Spittoons were a regular part of the furnishings of that day. On February 7, 1840, he wrote the commander of the United States Squadron, then off Spain, to send him six pounds of "Virginia Cavendish chewing tobacco." No one else had ever mentioned that Margaret smoked cigars, however, so this accusation seems improbable. The Eatons may well have done a good bit of drinking, but Van Ness's apparent anger at being replaced puts the vigor of his accusations into question.[51]

While Van Ness displayed such antagonism toward the Eatons in a flood of letters to the president, John Eaton did not send a single report to the State Department until late April, 1837, more than six months after his departure from the United States. The first letter itself was primarily a complaint that the house of the United States minister in Spain was almost completely empty of furniture, and that next year's finances to run the office were down to $800 due to Van Ness's earlier spendthrift ways. Worse still, Eaton asked permission to take a vacation on the continent and also insisted that he be able to return to the United States any time he wished, after giving three months' notice. When Secretary of State John Forsyth requested more detailed information on Eaton's conversations with Spanish officials, Eaton incredibly responded: "To detail to you officially the conversations of people without their consent and offer speculative theories about men and things which may or may not be correct do not appear to me to be within the line of my official duty [as a diplomat]." This neglect to communicate with Washington even had Andrew Jackson shaking his head. He had told Eaton before his departure about the unacceptable silence of some other diplomats, and Eaton had promised he would be different. Were he still president, Jackson hinted to Van Buren, he would fire Eaton. "My rule was where my friend failed to his duty faithfully I removed him sooner than an enemy." Andrew Jackson wanted no more of John Eaton if he did not do his job. Friendship extended to defense of wronged women, not bungling diplomats.[52]

What was even more exasperating to the State Department was Eaton's excessively pro-Spanish behavior, even at the expense of American citizens. He defended Spain's inability to pay its American creditors and urged that Congress simply authorize payments from its own funds. He defended Spain's right to tax American citizens in Spain, and when an American turned up missing in the country raging with civil war, Eaton expressed little interest in searching for him. "He must have died," he nonchalantly declared.[53]

In Eaton's letters to his superior and in the secretary of state's responses, there was—to use the words of a later historian—"an underlying tone of antagonism." Eaton felt that Secretary Forsyth was not answering his questions, and Forsyth insisted that Eaton was simply refusing to acknowledge reality. Eaton was particularly angered when the State Department told the bankers Rothschild not to extend him any further credit, thus intimating, he said, that he was a swindler. He also insisted that Forsyth had never responded to his desire to leave Spain on short notice. This last matter was apparently the final straw. In April 1840, Martin Van Buren finally took Andrew Jackson's advice and recalled John Eaton.[54]

At first, the deposed diplomat reacted happily. He came bounding into the house while Margaret was preparing a dinner party and said,

"Margaret, I reckon you might as well put up your gold and silver, for I have heard from the United States and we have got marching orders." Margaret was upset at the news. "I should have liked to have spent my life in Madrid," she later recalled. The dinner party went on anyway, and it was a sad affair for her and for the other ministers in attendance. The Eatons were a popular couple, and Virginia had cut a particularly wide swath in the diplomatic community. A British diplomat wanted to marry her, but so did a number of other suitors. For the time being, however, she remained single and prepared to return with her resigned parents to the United States.[55]

Once reality sank in, both Eatons became angry over the turn of events. John "felt very much provoked at the suddenness of the recall," particularly considering his and Margaret's long friendship with President Van Buren. Margaret was "chagrined and humiliated," but knew there was nothing to do but pack. Despite the end of the Carlist War, the countryside remained dangerous, so John departed alone, while Margaret, the daughters, and a servant left together at a later time. Fortunately, the only problem Margaret faced on her trip was a dissolute married nobleman trying to seduce Virginia. John had, by that time, rejoined his family, so he tracked the individual down, grabbed him "by the collar," Margaret recalled, and "shook him till the man was well nigh breathless."[56]

John Eaton was certainly angry at the aristocrat for his indecent proposal to his stepdaughter, but he was also venting his anger at Martin Van Buren and the State Department. In April 1840, the month of his departure from Europe, Eaton wrote Van Buren expressing his friendly feelings for the president. He also wrote to Andrew Jackson, expressing his unhappiness that he "has been dismissed." Jackson quickly realized that Eaton was coming "home not in good humor." Arriving in Washington, Eaton wrote the English minister in London that the American political scene in 1840 made 1828 and 1832 seem tame, and added that "many of the heretofore & present supporters of the administration are despondent & distressful." John Eaton was clearly in a bad mood.[57]

It was not long after this letter that Eaton made a fateful decision. Despite a meeting in which the president insisted that it was only Eaton's repeated demands to be relieved that prompted the recall,

Eaton publicly supported William Henry Harrison for the presidency over Martin Van Buren, much to Andrew Jackson's shock and disgust. "How I regret, for his account, the apostasy of Eaton," Jackson said. "He comes out against all the political principles he ever professed, and against those on which he was supported and elected senator—'O tempora! O Mores!'" Jackson was so angry that he, who had defended Margaret Eaton so vociferously, now cut off all communication with the Eatons over this political disloyalty. In the Hermitage drawing room, he turned Eaton's portrait to the wall. When he told Andrew J. Donelson of his disgust, what thoughts must have run through the mind of the nephew who, ten years previously, had experienced his uncle's wrath over the apostate and his wife.[58]

Harrison defeated Van Buren for the presidency, but if there was any suspicion that Eaton had supported him in the hope of gaining a patronage post, it quickly vanished. John received no political office, and he and the family moved in with Margaret's mother to a house on I street, once part of the Franklin Hotel complex. Margaret's father had died on January 4, 1837, at the age of eighty-six, while she was in Spain, leaving his property, mostly real estate, to his wife Rhoda.[59]

Eaton now undertook a legal career, arguing cases before the Supreme Court. He was at one point even elected president of the Washington Bar Association. Margaret was extremely pleased at the warm welcome they received from their friends on their return from Europe. As she phrased it: "The storms that had been raised for political reasons, so far as we were personally concerned, had lulled." Still, the Eatons were not entirely free of innuendo. Their old friend and former brother-in-law, William B. Lewis, thought John was suffering from some sort of mental illness. "I have thought ever since he returned from Spain," Lewis said, "that he would kill himself drinking or perhaps blow his brains out."[60]

But Eaton did not. He did drink, having a wine cellar of 100 bottles, but he also read, his library consisting of 260 books. He maintained his successful legal career and lived a comfortable life. He persistently pressed his case for full payment of the salary he insisted he had earned that first month in Cadiz and finally received his money during the James K. Polk administration in the mid-1840s. He also battled with his old nemesis, Andrew Jackson Donelson, over some money he insisted Donelson owed him. Later, however, he successfully represented Donelson's financial interests against the U.S. Treasury Department. Before the Supreme Court, he successfully represented Stockton and Stokes, the carriage makers Margaret had allegedly tried to bribe Amos Kendall for. John now pressed the company's suit against Amos Kendall's actions while he was postmaster general. He won a judgment of $12,000 against Kendall, so angering his former Jacksonian colleague that Kendall had to leave the courtroom during Eaton's summation for fear that he would be "guilty of some outrage" if he stayed and listened. Clearly, John Eaton had totally separated himself from the Jacksonians.[61]

During these years, John and Margaret Eaton lived a satisfying life, residing during the winter months in Washington and then traveling to Franklin for the summers. After mid-1841, Margaret's health improved, and she did not suffer the debilitating illnesses that had earlier crippled her. Her mother continued to live near them, maintaining an active role in their lives. Margaret's social life was no longer controversial, and she was now an accepted member of Washington society, attending events at the Executive Mansion and hosting well-attended parties of her own. One congressman disdainfully noted that Margaret was "an influential personage here now," President John Tyler's son spending "one half of his evenings with her Ladyship." She also worked among the less fortunate of the city, Supreme Court Justice James M. Wayne, calling her "Alma Mater." At the same time, she made sure that all Washington knew that she was living a prosperous life. A Washingtonian later remembered seeing her during those days "in a carriage with four horses and liveried servants. . . . There was nothing in Washington to compare with her equipage, not even the president's own. . . . I have never seen anyone so beautiful," he concluded. As always, Margaret Eaton made sure that everyone noticed her, whether they wanted to or not.[62]

Eaton continued to support the Whig party, but he was not afraid to write to Democratic president James K. Polk in support of a government officeholder. Margaret visited the White House on a few occasions "as an act of courtesy to the Chief magistrate of the Republic." It bothered John, however, that his support of the Whigs kept him separated from Andrew Jackson. He decided to try to mend fences with his old friend, Margaret no doubt encouraging him to do so. In the summer of 1844, less than a year before Jackson's death, Eaton discovered some correspondence in his Franklin home that he thought Jackson might want to have. He wrote the former president and accepted an invitation to visit the Hermitage. Jackson's anger melted when he saw his old friends, and it was perhaps at this time that he showed a small part of the fervor that had stimulated his defense of Margaret Eaton in the first place. During dinner at the Hermitage one night, the wife of a court judge was bragging about her social importance, although she actually came from humble background and her brother, a former tailor, was sitting next to her at the table—a living refutation of her pretensions. Andrew Jackson put up with her as long as he could stand it and then, with all the innocence he could muster, turned to her brother and said: "You know I really never have had a comfortable coat on my back since you quit tailoring."[63]

It was fortunate that the Eatons restored their friendship with Andrew Jackson when they did in 1844, because he died the following year. He was buried in the garden on the grounds of the Hermitage, next to his beloved Rachel. He attained that peace, finally, that he had sought all his life. He and Rachel were together again, this time forever.[64]

Margaret's life in the late 1840s and 1850s centered not on Nashville and the Hermitage but on Washington and her children, Mary Virginia and Margaret Rosa Timberlake. While in Spain, she heard about the passage of a March 3, 1837, law changing the regulations concerning navy pensions. In August 1828, soon after the death of John Timberlake, she had written the Navy Department asking for a pension under the then applicable law. Her claim at that time was denied. Hearing that the law had been changed, she had her brother-in-law, the Reverend French S. Evans, inquire about obtaining John Timberlake's pension for herself and her children. Armed with a sworn statement from Rhoda O'Neale giving Margaret's wedding date to Timberlake and Virginia's and Margaret's birth dates, Evans made inquiry of the secretary of the navy on March 27, 1837. Within ten days, the attorney general ruled that since she had remarried, Margaret Eaton had no claims on a pension, but that her two children "by a liberal construction" of the law, were entitled to half pay from their father's death in 1828 until they reached the age of twenty-one. On April 15, 1837, Virginia (eighteen years old) and Margaret (twelve years old) were each granted the sum of $20 a month.[65]

John Eaton viewed his stepdaughters as his own, and he readily used his substantial wealth in their support. His law practice was profitable, and he still owned property in Tennessee and perhaps in Florida. In 1843, his mother willed him a part of her estate, in North Carolina, though precisely what, if anything, he actually obtained is unclear. While he provided for his stepchildren generously, he left their upbringing to Margaret, reflecting the attitude of the times that children were the mother's primary responsibility. When he prepared his last will and testament in 1848, he left everything he owned to Margaret and the children.[66]

Both daughters proved challenging, though in radically different ways. As had been the case in Europe, Virginia (Ginger) was extremely popular with men in America as well. A constant parade of suitors appeared at the Eaton front door, most of whom Margaret and her mother viewed critically and then sent away. Margaret Rosa was a much quieter person, and her social life was, therefore, much more staid.

Ginger's most flamboyant suitor was Philip Barton Key, the son of Francis Scott Key. Margaret believed the young Key drank too much and was too outrageous in his behavior to be a worthy husband for her daughter. One time, according to Margaret's later remembrances, Key rode his horse through the front door and up the stairs in the Eaton residence searching for Ginger, whom he had learned was lying ill in her room. Ginger did not marry Key, although the attraction was strong. Instead, in May 1843, she became the wife of the Duke de Sampayo, the secretary of the French legation in Washington. Soon after, the couple moved overseas when Sampayo was transferred home to France. Ginger never returned to the United States. In the late 1850s, an irate husband, the later famous Civil War general Daniel Sickles, shot and killed Key in the middle of a Washington street; Key's liaison with Sickles's young wife had motivated the desperate act. Margaret's refusal to allow her daughter to marry Key was apparently correct.[67]

In 1844, the much quieter Margaret Rosa married Navy Lieutenant John B. Randolph. The marriage was a happy one. Randolph was frequently at sea, but he was home enough to father four children: John

Chapman, John H. Eaton, Mary, and Emily. Then tragedy struck. Randolph contracted a fever while on a cruise in Asia and died in Washington on July 20, 1854. Just eight months later, on March 24, 1855, Margaret Rosa also died, cholera the assigned cause. The Eatons became the full-time guardians of four young children, John very much enjoying his stepgrandchildren, no doubt especially thrilled that one carried his name.[68]

Unfortunately, he did not enjoy the children long. In September 1856, his heart gave out and he died.[69] Margaret took his departure hard, the fact that he left her a rich widow hardly mitigating her grief. She still had her aged but vibrant mother, and she still had the Randolph children. She successfully fought off a legal inquiry into her administration of Eaton's estate and prepared to proceed with the rest of her life.[70] She had been married to John Eaton for over twenty-six turbulent years and, without him, she must have looked forward to a quiet future life. She was, after all, almost fifty-seven years of age. How could she ever surpass what she had already lived through?

10

"They Are Now Her Neighbors"

The death of her husband in 1856 had restored Margaret Eaton to widowhood, a condition she had previously known for only a brief period at the death of John B. Timberlake in 1828. At that time, as now, she had children to care for; and though her father had died many years previously, she still had her mother's support. She grieved John Eaton's passing, but her grief could not divert her obligation to care for the children of her deceased daughter and son-in-law. The four Randolph children had become her wards, and she dedicated her life to raising them, continuing to live on I Street near Twentieth in the house she and John Eaton had shared from the early days of their marriage, on the site of her father's boardinghouse.

No doubt because of her own love of music and dancing and the remembrance of the dance prize she had received from Dolley Madison during her teenage years, Margaret enrolled her grandchildren in Marini's Dancing Academy, not far from their home. The children quickly became attached to one of the school's teachers, a young Italian immigrant named Antonio Buchignani. They begged their grandmother to invite him home for dinner, and, impressed with his manners and bearing, she agreed. He became a frequent visitor to the dinner table in 1859, each time enhancing the good impression he had made initially on Margaret and her mother. Then, one day, one of the children asked Margaret why the teacher could not move in with them. They had the room, he was alone in a new country, and they all liked him so much. Margaret hesitated, but seemed convinced when he showed her some letters from Italy purporting to prove that he was of noble ancestry and the fiancé of a countess.

Antonio moved in and continued to impress Margaret and her mother with his character, personality, and manners. One day, Margaret was preparing to take the children to their parent's graves and that of John Eaton in Oak Hill Cemetery along Rock Creek, when Antonio asked if he could come along. She welcomed his interest, and they traveled to the cemetery together. Upon arrival, Margaret went after a watering can and on her return found Antonio already at her daughter's grave, hunched in silent prayer. She was touched. Another time, when they were walking somewhere, they passed some cows, and Margaret mentioned how frightened she was of the animals. Antonio immediately responded: "Fear nothing while with me; I will guard you as my life."[1]

It was soon after that Antonio asked Margaret to marry him, promising to take care of the Randolph children and manage her finances carefully. Her mother urged her to accept the proposal because she liked Antonio and thought he would be good for her daughter and the children. Margaret agreed. On June 7, 1859, the fifty-nine-year-old Margaret O'Neale Timberlake Eaton married her grandchildren's nineteen-year-old Italian dancing teacher, Antonio Buchignani. Family members and the public were shocked and appalled. How could an elderly woman raising her grandchildren ever marry someone so young? It was disgraceful. Once again, Margaret became a pariah in Washington society, the story circulating that an Episcopal priest had refused "to perform what he considered a sacrilegious ceremony." The Randolphs were particularly upset, and Margaret wrote one of them a scathing letter. She said that she much preferred to have married Antonio "a Gentleman of Birth and Ancestry," than to have joined the "illustrious" Randolphs. She could be sure, Margaret told this relative, that "your Illustrious Family has not been Tarnished by any communication with my most excellent" husband. It was unfortunate this woman did not read Italian, Margaret patronizingly continued, because some letters written in that language proved Antonio's high status. The Randolphs remained unimpressed, but the public animosity did not last long. Antonio charmed others as he had charmed his wife; society relented and accepted the *fait accompli* of Mr. and Mrs. Antonio Buchignani.[2]

In thinking about this union later in her life, Margaret insisted that she "did not love this third husband. My heart was in the grave with John H. Eaton. . . . I did respect him" though, "and he loved me." She had some obvious doubts about it all, however. She made Antonio sign a prenuptial agreement the day of their marriage, placing all her money and property, some $90,000, in the hands of a trustee. She would allow Antonio to marry her, but she would not allow him to marry her money. He agreed to the conditions, the wedding went forward, and the early years of marriage went well. Sadly, however, Rhoda O'Neale died in April 1860, significantly in the arms of her new son-in-law. The recent bride lost a valued adviser.[3]

Antonio no longer plied his trade as dancing instructor. Through Margaret's influence, the Lincoln administration offered him a job as secretary to the American consul in Naples, but he refused that offer as well as a captaincy in the army. Instead, he became an assistant librarian for the House of Representatives. Throughout the difficult Civil War years, the Buchignanis did not feel the conflict's influence significantly. There is no evidence, for example, of any contacts with people in Tennessee. The husband and wife enjoyed their marriage, and the Randolph children matured, pleased with their domestic condition. Margaret continued to reach out to those around her. An old man later remembered her coming to his house to swab his throat with silver nitrate when he, a young boy, had diphtheria and had refused to accept the treatment from his parents. "With firm hand and violent speech she undertook to handle me," he recalled, and, for her effort, she had her dress ruined from his "resistance and consequent ejections." Margaret long felt the loss of her mother, Rhoda O'Neale, but overall, her life was pleasant. As a newspaper reporter later described it, Antonio "played cards with other young men, had a good berth of it, and a grandmother in the berth." Margaret was so happy, she found an artist to paint their portraits together and decided to hand over ownership of the $14,000 house to her husband. To accomplish this, she had to find a new trustee, since her original one was a southerner and presently living in an area at war with the nation.[4]

In addition to her own finances, Margaret had the children's money to manage. As their guardian, she was due funds from their father's estate, but there was some difficulty in receiving the money. Several months before her June 1859 marriage, she had to wait for the expected payment until she sent a certificate proving her guardianship. Several months after the wedding, the trustee supervising these funds refused to stay on in that position because of unspecified "harassment and disturbance" he had experienced from Margaret and her lawyer. Then he decided that since she had remarried, Margaret could no longer be a guardian. The matter would have to be settled in court. What eventually happened is unknown, but clearly Margaret's finances were in turmoil.[5]

This matter seemed not to affect Margaret, Antonio, or the children. Their lives continued happy as the Civil War wound down and the Union persevered. One day in 1865, however, the calm was shattered when two policemen appeared at their door, inquiring from Margaret whether any of her silver setting was missing. No, she responded, she did not think so, but she would look. When she investigated, she discovered that a substantial amount of silver was indeed missing, later valued at $700. As she walked back toward the door to alert the police, Antonio stopped her along the way and told her to tell the lawmen nothing. Once he and Margaret were alone, he confessed to the theft. She then accompanied him to the police station and told the authorities that she had forgotten telling her husband to sell the silverware. It was all a misunderstanding.[6]

In future days, Margaret noticed objects regularly disappearing from the house, obviously sold by Antonio, despite his well-paying job and her inherited wealth. Unwilling to face the reality that Antonio was a common thief, a kleptomaniac, or for some reason squandering money, she tried to ignore the problem. Then he confronted her with his wish to leave Washington and move to New York City, telling her that a friend had assured him that an investment in a business there would yield a huge $20,000-a-year income. It was a difficult decision. She had lived in Washington most of her life, and it would be difficult for her to leave. Besides, there was the matter of the repeated disappearances of her belongings. She mulled it over, no doubt wishing her mother was still alive to advise her. Finally she agreed to move. Antonio sold the house and they moved to Gramercy Park in New York, where she gave him $20,000 to begin his business, apparently a cigar store.[7]

The move to the big city turned out to be disastrous. Antonio kept demanding ever more money from Margaret for his business, and he grew increasingly upset when she did not provide it in sufficient quantity or speed to suit his purposes. Finally, in the fall of 1866, he demanded that she sign everything she owned over to him or he would return to Europe. She thought he was bluffing, but when she received a letter allegedly written on an Atlantic Ocean steamship, she panicked and promised him half her wealth if he stayed. He agreed but then reiterated his demand for all her money. She and Antonio's business partner rushed to Washington, where she signed over everything, one later estimate being "the princely sum of nineteen houses and six square blocks of real estate," with a value of $73,000. She did it, of course, to guarantee Antonio's return to their home.[8]

Meanwhile, Emily, the youngest granddaughter, seventeen years of age, seemed ill with consumption, the disease Margaret had once suffered herself. The teenager became increasingly morose, but Margaret brushed it off. She could not see what was happening—or refused to believe it. Antonio had gone to Washington to sell all the property Margaret had deeded to him, while Emily said she was going to New Jersey to see a cousin. In fact, the two, Antonio and Emily, step grandfather and step granddaughter, boarded a ship in New York harbor and steamed off to Europe, leaving behind a shocked and penniless wife and grandmother. They left her a letter of praise and remorse and a $100 bill, otherwise stripping her of everything: her wealth, her affections, her reputation. She now had to depend for support on one of the Randolph grandsons, John, who had a job at the customs house in New York. That same fall of 1866, she was also taken to court in a dispute over a property sale her deceased mother had made in 1850. The Randolph side of the family was "inexpressibly mortified and indignant. . . . Nothing can exceed," a relative said, "the degradation [*sic*] of being connected with such a character as Mrs. E."[9]

Antonio and Emily lived together without benefit of clergy in Lucca, Italy, quickly going through Margaret's money and finding themselves in financial trouble. Taking their baby and the little money they still had left, they migrated to Montreal, where he opened a store (perhaps a restaurant), but it was unsuccessful. Desperate for money, he want to New York in September 1868 to collect some funds unaccountably owed him from his earlier activities there. Margaret learned of his return and immediately took out a warrant for his arrest, citing the abduction of Emily, who was only seventeen years old in 1865. She charged Antonio with taking Emily to Italy "where she lived in open prostitution with him." The judge immediately issued the warrant, and a policeman quickly found Antonio in a hotel. He was brought before a judge, where Margaret confronted him. She demanded that he provide her with financial support of $8 a week, which the judge promptly raised to $10.

Antonio refused, saying he was broke, and he was remanded to custody. He showed no remorse for what he had done to Margaret financially and personally, and, without emotion, was led out of the courtroom. On September 10, 1868, however, a lawyer posted a bond of $500 guaranteeing that Margaret would receive the support the court had ordered. Antonio was released, but he quickly jumped bail and returned to Canada. Margaret never received any financial support from him. The following year, she obtained a divorce, clearing the way for him to marry Emily. Since the couple now had two children, a marriage did seem appropriate. Eventually, there were a total of three such great-grandchildren who lived in New York, but Emily's disposition is unknown. A Washington newspaper reporter later recorded, according to what he called reliable information, that in late 1872, Antonio Buchignani "was shot by a horny-handed granger in a bar-room at Memphis."[10]

Margaret was now alone, except for her loyal grandson and some other sympathetic relatives. "In the silence of my loneliness," she later said, "I sometimes hear[d] the voice of that dead, darling husband [John H. Eaton] like a strain of music in a hushed midnight." A woman who talked to her during this time was shocked at her appearance. The once vibrant beautiful female was "now, an old, feeble and jaded woman, deserted by friends—forgotten by the world . . . [eking out] a bare existence in a retired boardinghouse which overlooks Washington Square." Political leader Thurlow Weed interceded for her with the mayor of New York, and the result was a job for her grandson. This helped a bit.

Margaret and her grandson lived a spartan life together in New York City from 1870 to 1873. Daughter Virginia remained married to the Duke de Sampayo in Europe, and their only child was married to a Rothschild. Virginia completely turned her back on the United States and obviously on her mother to the point that she refused to allow her husband to take a diplomatic post here, preferring to remain in Paris. In 1873, Margaret and her grandson returned to Washington and took up residence at 388 Pennsylvania Avenue, hardly one of the better neighborhoods in the city at that time. John Randolph worked in the War Department, rising through the hierarchy to become an undersecretary in the twentieth century. He remained loyal to his grandmother all his life.[11]

Margaret now became a relic from Washington's past. The people who had known her during her problem days in the Jackson presidency were dying away, and she herself was now a white-haired old woman in her seventies. She lived in comparative obscurity, most Sundays "clad in shabby-genteel garments" sitting in a side aisle of the Metropolitan Methodist Church "listen[ing] attentively to the sermon," but "quietly withdraw[ing] at its close." Newspaper reporters discovering her existence and anxious to interview her for what they no doubt hoped would be a sensational article occasionally relieved the tedium. She talked freely to numerous reporters about her childhood, her marriages, and her lifetime of adventure at home and abroad. She particularly enjoyed praising Andrew Jackson and castigating the society women who had snubbed her during her youth.

Reporters were universally taken with her, most commenting on the beauty they saw still shining through the aged and wrinkled body. "Her form, of medium height, straight and delicate, and of perfect proportions, has never bent to time nor sickness, nor curved itself to the weight of misfortunes. . . . Her dark violet eyes shine with the wit and spirit which still characterize her conversation; and the perfect nose of almost Grecian proportions, and finely curved mouth, with the firm, round chin, complete a profile of faultless outline." They all echoed the fact that though she was now old, "when at all excited, her beautiful, fiery eyes gleam and sparkle with original fire." In her "maturer years," another reporter noted, "she [still] held that powerful influence over men that requires a master mind no less than a lovely face."[12]

Clearly Margaret had not lost her power over males nor had she shed her willingness to speak her mind to reporters or anyone else who would listen. One day a Washington resident saw her on the sidewalk in front of his house "engaged in a furious altercation [with another woman] over the merits and demerits of General Jackson." When in 1873 she read contemporary historian James Parton's account of her role in the Jackson presidency, she sat down with her minister in New York City, the Reverend Charles F. Deems of the Church of the Strangers, and dictated her memoirs to set the record straight, to make her "contribution to the truth of history." She regularly visited the cemetery where her husband and children were buried, sitting on a bench and talking to the superintendent about her life in old Washington or exchanging stories about Franklin with a woman from that Tennessee city whom she chanced to meet among the graves.[13]

Despite her strong will, her body slowly began breaking down, and her resoluteness turned to uncertainty. In the spring of 1879, when she went to the Oak Hill Cemetery to tend to her relatives' graves, she became confused and lost her way. Finding the plots, finally, she tenderly placed flowers on them and talked to her buried relatives as though they were still alive. She knew she would join them soon, she told an onlooker. "It is the last time," she said. "I shall never come here again till I come to stay. It is a beautiful place to rest in at last."[14]

That fall, she grew fatally ill, her condition complicated by her financial inability, for two years, to afford the medication she needed. The sun shone into her room at the Lochiel House, a home for destitute women at 512 Ninth Street, N.W., as she lay on her deathbed. She wished she could go out into the yard to enjoy the brightness. One of the relatives or friends around the bed said she could do that another day, but she disagreed. "No, not tomorrow. Tomorrow I shall be here only a little while." That night she could not sleep, yearning for the dawn. On November 9, 1879, at noon, with the sun shining brightly into her room, she expired. "I am not afraid to die," she said, "but this is such a beautiful world to leave."[15]

Her funeral was, according to the press, well attended. Mrs. Rutherford B. Hayes, wife of the president, sent flowers, as did George W. McCrary, the secretary of war. The president "regretted his inability to be present at the funeral, and tendered his deepest sympathy." After the service, with the pastor of the Metropolitan Methodist Church presiding and her brother-in-law, the Reverend French S. Evans, assisting, Margaret's remains were taken to the Oak Hill Cemetery and placed next to John Henry Eaton and near her daughter and son-in-law. The monument over her grave gives details about John, but says nothing about her. To this day, one of the most famous women in American history—about whom a contemporary newspaper editorialized that "so long as the history of American politics is written and studied, her name must be remembered"—has no granite notation of her passing, not even her name and dates. Were she alive, however, she would certainly enjoy the ultimate irony. "Doubtless among the dead populating the terraces [of the cemetery] are some of her assailants [from the cabinet days] and cordially as they may have hated her, they are now her neighbors." In the end, Margaret Eaton was included among the leaders of Washington society, and she must have enjoyed that final victory. She could only hope that Andrew Jackson knew it, too.[16]

Conclusion

Andrew Jackson and "Peggy" Eaton—their names are linked in the historical image of the nineteenth century. Both lived their lives to the fullest and made no apologies about it. Yet society judged them differently. Americans admired Old Hickory for his stubborn unwillingness to bend before anyone or anything, but they criticized Peggy for that same character trait. Jackson was a male and could act the way he did; Eaton was a female, and society saw her behavior as totally inappropriate for a woman. Jackson always considered criticism as conspiratorially motivated; she considered it the result of the small-minded jealousy of other women. Society matrons, who stubbornly confronted the two determined individuals, believed their campaign against Margaret Eaton was a clear-cut protection of the community's morality, nothing more, nothing less.

The controversy, therefore, was a combination of social, political, and personal forces. Margaret Eaton lived a public life that society considered inappropriate for any proper female. Even if she had remained an innkeeper's daughter, her behavior would still have been considered scandalous; but, at least, it would not have been unexpected for someone of her station. Instead of keeping her place, however, she attempted to become part of gentility, to redeem her allegedly wayward impure past behavior by marrying a major politician and currying the support of the nation's president. This simply would not do. She must not enter the established circle of middle-class women whose overarching duty it was to protect society from those immoral values that Margaret Eaton represented. Allow this woman into society, women believed, and society itself was in danger of dissolution.

The massive change in America seen in the ascendancy of the masses with the election of Andrew Jackson made the possibility of such a cataclysm that much more believable. Women had to protect society from such disruption; they had to exclude Margaret Eaton. It was their husband's, father's, brother's, and son's duty to accept this decision. Women ruled the moral world, and men had no option but to follow their lead.

To Andrew Jackson, Margaret Eaton was just another of many wronged females who over his lifetime he had known and defended. His mother had died suddenly because of the hated British, and his wife, Rachel, had been judged a violator of contemporary mores in marrying him, for which she then paid the ultimate price. She had become the focus of society's wrath, for political, not social purposes, as Jackson saw it, and that had killed her. He believed that every woman he had defended in his life had been the victim of such ulterior motives, including Margaret Eaton. The social justifications for the animosity toward her were only a subterfuge. The real reasons were political and personal—to get him. Margaret Eaton was pilloried so that political enemies could bring down her husband and, through him, destroy the president himself.

It was perfectly clear to Andrew Jackson: the world was full of conspirators out to get vulnerable defenseless women and eventually to get him. Throughout his life he demanded absolute personal loyalty, to make up for the mother and later the wife that enemies had taken away from him. The world was a dangerous place; conspiracies were everywhere. Even friends and relatives could not be trusted if they disagreed with him. So it was with Margaret Eaton's plight. She was, in his eyes, a wronged woman, and anyone who thought otherwise was part of a conspiracy, a conspiracy in which she was only the penultimate victim. The final victim, the real object of the conspiracy, was none other than Andrew Jackson himself. It was as obvious to him as reality could be. He had seen it all many times before, he stubbornly insisted.

Jackson was wrong; this was no political conspiracy against Margaret Eaton or against him. It was, indeed, a matter of societal norms, but he made it into the political crisis that so enveloped him. At first he blamed Henry Clay, but this accusation quickly proved inaccurate, so he settled on John C. Calhoun, the vice president he never really trusted. Calhoun saw the debate over Margaret Eaton for what it was, a purely social event. Women, including his wife, took the stand they did because of prevailing social mores and attitudes. He was mystified, therefore, to watch the dispute develop into the political imbroglio that inexorably destroyed his relationship with Jackson and his presidential hopes. Cabinet secretaries and their wives and daughters saw the snubbing of Margaret Eaton in the same way. They did not comprehend Jackson's insistence that the attacks on her were attacks on him. Protection of proper womanhood and thus society as a whole, not destruction of their own administration, was at the heart of it all, they believed. Jackson's relatives, the Donelsons, saw it that way, too. Jackson could not. It was more sinister than that; for him it was deeply personal.

There were, of course, real political differences among the members of Jackson's official family, and the fact that they were apparent in the major social issue of the day is not surprising. Both Calhoun and Martin Van Buren had their eyes set on the Executive Mansion, and there were deep disagreements over the very nature of the Union—whether individual states were sovereign or the national government supreme. Politicians also disagreed over tariffs and a host of other such immediate issues. The Jacksonian coalition was in the process of becoming, and its growing pains were real and evident. Personal ambitions and prejudices were also present. Margaret Eaton, as has so often happened in American history, provided the convenient single vehicle for debating these myriad differences. It was easier to castigate Margaret Eaton than it was to battle the complex of frightening changes abroad in contemporary society and the political conflict inherent in the new party system.

Without question, Martin Van Buren realized better than anyone else that Jackson had made the social matter of the ladies into a litmus test of political loyalty. Van Buren took advantage of the situation presented him, but he hardly initiated it. That was Andrew Jackson's work. It was he who made the social issue into the dire conspiracy he envisioned trying to destroy him. Before he took that step, the politicians around him were simply following the tenets of society and acceding to their females' decision to ostracize a woman they considered unfit for inclusion in their proper circle.

Women, therefore, brought on the Eaton Affair; but so, too, did Andrew Jackson and Margaret Eaton. The proper place for a woman, whose reputation was built on scandalous rumors of immorality, outspokenness, aggressiveness, and general unwomanly behavior, was certainly not in the circle of cabinet wives, not even in society at all. Margaret Eaton dared live her life in a way that contemporaries found improper for a woman. She was no saint and she was no crusader; but she was not the sinner rumor made her out to be, either. Using modern lexicon, she was "brazen," "uncouth," "pushy," and "uppity," the opposite of what a woman was supposed to be. Such unwomanly behavior, not impurity, was her major sin. She just did not know her proper place or her proper role, and she thus represented a threat to those who thought they did.

Andrew Jackson moved on from battling the conspiracy he saw in the attacks on Margaret Eaton and found new conspiracies to battle in the Bank of the United States and other such perceived threats. Even after she had faded from the public eye, Margaret Eaton continued to live her life in violation of society's mores far into old age. The affair of the president and the innkeeper's daughter remains important because it informs us about the politics and personalities of an important era. Even more, however, it illuminates the debate over woman's proper role in American society—then and ever since.

Notes

ABBREVIATIONS

AJ	Andrew Jackson, Andrew Jackson Papers
AJD	Andrew Jackson Donelson, Andrew Jackson Donelson Papers
AK	Amos Kendall, Amos Kendall Papers
ASP	*American State Papers, Naval Affairs.* 6 vols. (1861)
B-L	Blair-Lee Family Papers
DAB	*Dictionary of American Biography*
DG	Duff Green, Duff Green Papers
DU	Duke University, Special Collections Department, William R. Perkins Library
DW	Daniel Webster
EACB	Eaton Affair Copy Book
ED	Emily Donelson, Emily Donelson Papers
ESE	Ezra Stiles Ely
FPB	Francis P. Blair
FG	Felix Grundy, Felix Grundy Papers
HC	Henry Clay, Henry Clay Papers
HLW	Hugh Lawson White
HSP	Historical Society of Pennsylvania, Philadelphia
HSW	Historical Society of Washington, D.C.
JB	John Branch, John Branch Papers
JBT	John B. Timberlake
JC	John Coffee, John Coffee Papers
JCC	John C. Calhoun, John C. Calhoun Papers
JCMcL	John C. McLemore
JHE	John Henry Eaton
JMB	John MacPherson Berrien, John MacPherson Berrien Papers
JNC	John N. Campbell
JO	John Overton, John Overton Papers
JQA	John Quincy Adams, *Memoirs of John Quincy Adams.* 12 vols., Charles Francis Adams, ed. (1874–1877)
JSB	John Spencer Bassett, ed., *Correspondence of Andrew Jackson.* 7 vols. (1926–1935)

LC   Library of Congress
MBS   Margaret Bayard Smith, Margaret Bayard Smith Papers, *The First Forty Years of Washington Portrayed by the Family Letters of Mrs. Samuel Harrison Smith,* Gaillard Hunt, ed. (1906)
ME   Margaret Eaton, *The Autobiography of Peggy Eaton* (1932)
MaHS   Massachusetts Historical Society, Boston
MVB   Martin Van Buren, Martin Van Buren Papers
NARS   National Archives and Records Service
NR   *Niles' Register*
NYHS   New-York Historical Society
NYPL   New York Public Library, Astor, Lenox, and Tilden Foundations, Rare Books and Manuscripts Division
NYT   *New York Times*
PHC   Mary W. M. Hargreaves and James F. Hopkins, eds., 8 vols to date. *The Papers of Henry Clay* (1959–)
PJC   E. Edwin Hemphill, Robert L. Merriwether, and Clyde Wilson, eds., 22 vols to date. *The Papers of John C. Calhoun* (1959–)
PU   Princeton University Library, Department of Rare Books and Special Collections
RCHS   *Records of the Columbia Historical Society*
RG   Record Group
RJ   Rachel Donelson Jackson
RKC   Richard K. Call
RMJ   Richard Mentor Johnson
SDI   Samuel D. Ingham, Samuel D. Ingham Papers
SHC   Southern Historical Collection, University of North Carolina
SR   Scholarly Resources
THQ   *Tennessee Historical Quarterly*
THS   Tennessee Historical Society
TSLA   Tennessee State Library and Archives, Nashville
UNC   University of North Carolina
UP   University of Pennsylvania, Special Collections Department, Van Pelt Library
USG   *United States Gazette,* Philadelphia
UST   *United States Telegraph,* Washington, D.C.
UVA   University of Virginia, Special Collections Department, Alderman Library
VHS   Virginia Historical Society
WBL   William B. Lewis
WG   *Washington Globe*
WNI   *Washington National Intelligencer*
WON   William O'Neale
WP   *Washington Post*
WTB   William T. Barry

PROLOGUE

1. Stephen Vincent Benet and John Farrar, *The Heart of Peggy O'Neill: A Play in Seven Scenes* (1924); Edgar Lee Masters, *Andrew Jackson and Peggy Eaton,* in *Dramatic Duo-*

logues: Four Short Plays in Verse (1934); author unknown, *Mrs. Peggy O'Neal Eaton: A Play in Five Acts* (1903), Copyright Deposits, 1901–1944, LC; Charles E. Miner, Jr., and Irving J. Fleet, *An American Affair: A New Musical Play* (1993); Samuel Hopkins Adams, *The Gorgeous Hussy* (1934); Margaret Botsford, *The Reign of Reform or, Yankee Doodle Court by a Lady* (Baltimore, 1830); Mary C. Dillon, *The Patience of John Morland* (New York, 1909); Daniel Dourbridge, *Men and Things, or Reflections in Rhyme: A Posthumous Poem,* John H. Quarts, ed. (Boston, 1834); Major Jack Downing, *The Life of Andrew Jackson, President of the United States* (Philadelphia, 1834), 200–209, 220–24; Charles Keats, *Petticoat Wars in the White House: A Novelized Biography of Peggy O'Neill* (Fort Lauderdale, 1973); Alfred Henry Lewis, *Peggy O'Neal* (Philadelphia, 1903).

2. Queena Pollack, *Peggy Eaton: Democracy's Mistress* (New York, 1932).
3. James Parton, *The Life of Andrew Jackson.* 3 vols. (New York, 1861), 3:287.
4. Salmon P. Chase Diary, February 5(?), 1830, Salmon P. Chase Papers, LC.
5. Mary C. Francis, *A Son of Destiny: The Story of Andrew Jackson* (New York, 1902), 241.

CHAPTER 1: "GREAT GOD! DO YOU MENTION *HER* SACRED NAME?"

1. Reda C. Goff, "A Physical Profile of Andrew Jackson," *THQ* 28 (Fall 1969): 297–309.
2. Ellen Call Long, *Florida Breezes; or Florida, New and Old* (Gainesville, 1962), 94.
3. Thomas A. Bailey, *Presidential Saints and Sinners* (New York, 1981), 46; Samuel Lorenzo Knapp to A. Ward, 1830, Letter IX, in Samuel Lorenzo Knapp, *Sketches of Public Characters* (New York, 1830), 79–80.
4. There are many biographies of AJ and even more books on various aspects of his life. In writing this chapter on AJ's early life, I have leaned extensively on the three books that I find the most insightful: Robert V. Remini, *Andrew Jackson and the Course of American Empire, 1767–1821* (New York, 1977); *Andrew Jackson and the Course of American Freedom, 1822–1832* (New York, 1981); and James C. Curtis, *Andrew Jackson and the Search for Vindication* (Boston, 1976). The most thorough guide to material on Andrew Jackson is Robert V. Remini and Robert O. Rupp, eds., *Andrew Jackson: A Bibliography* (Westport, CT, 1991).
5. For a broader interpretation of the meaning of death in Andrew Jackson's life, see Curtis, 10–12.
6. Albert Somit, "Andrew Jackson, Legend and Reality," *THQ* 7 (December 1948): 298.
7. James Parton, *The Life of Andrew Jackson.* 3 vols. (New York, 1861), 1:104.
8. This account of the Andrew Jackson-Rachel Donelson romance and marriage is based on Harriet Chappell Owsley, "The Marriage of Rachel Donelson," *THQ* 36 (Winter 1977): 479–92; Paul F. Boller, Jr., *Presidential Wives* (New York, 1988), 65–70; Sol Barzman, *The First Ladies* (New York, 1970), 58–63; Margaret Bassett, *Profile and Portraits of American Presidents and Their Wives* (Freeport, ME, 1969), 74–76; Remini, *Course of American Empire,* 57–69.
9. Anne H. Wharton, *Social Life in the Early Republic* (Philadelphia, 1902), 248.
10. Remini, *Course of American Empire,* 64.
11. Ibid., 121.
12. Owsley, 490–91, and Barzman, 62, accept the Parton version I follow here. Remini, *Course of American Empire,* 121–23, tells a different but equally ludicrous version.

13. Remini, *Course of American Empire,* 173.

14. For a detailed account of this incident with the child as told by Andrew Jackson to a contemporary, see Elijah H. Mills, *Selections From the Letters of the Honorable E. H. Mills* (Cambridge MA, 1881), January 22, 1824, 31–32.

15. For a detailed account of AJ's physical problems during his presidency, see Francis Tomlinson Gardner, "The Gentleman from Tennessee," *Surgery, Gynocology and Obstetrics* 80 (1949): 405–11. A detailed discussion of AJ's health and his death is Robert V. Remini, "The Final Days and Hours in the Life of General Andrew Jackson," *THQ* 39 (Summer 1980): 167–77. A thorough analysis of Tennessee politics is Paul H. Bergeron, *Antebellum Politics in Tennessee* (Lexington, KY, 1982). See also Richard P. McCormick, *The Second American Party System: Party Formation in the Jacksonian Era* (Chapel Hill, 1966), 222–28.

16. There is no biography of JHE. The most complete brief sketch of his life, including a bibliography, is Thomas A. McMullen and David Walker, *Biographical Directory of American Territorial Governors* (Westport, CT, 1984), 98–99; AJ to John P. Todd, January 12, 1817, AJ, NYHS.

17. See Robert P. Hay, "The Case for Andrew Jackson in 1824: Eaton's *Wyoming Letters,*" *THQ* 29 (Summer 1970): 139–51.

18. AJ to WBL, February 14, 1825, JSB, 3:276.

19. The most complete analysis of this election is Robert V. Remini, *The Election of Andrew Jackson* (Philadelphia, 1962).

20. John Niven, *John C. Calhoun and the Price of Union: A Biography* (Baton Rouge, 1988), 131.

21. M. J. Heale, *The Presidential Quest: Candidates and Images in American Political Culture, 1787–1852* (London, 1982), 195; Boller, 65; Robert V. Remini, *Henry Clay: Statesman for the Union* (New York, 1991), 326; AJ to DG, August 13, 1827, AJ, LC.

22. JHE to RJ, December 18, 1823, February 8, 1824, JHE to JO, March 2, 1824, JSB, 3:217, 225–26, 235n–36n; HC to Charles Hammond, December 23, 1826, *PHC,* 5:1023–24; AJ to RJ, March 2, 1824, April 8, 1824, JSB, 3:232–33, 245. JHE and HC also had an extended debate over whether JHE actually composed a letter critical of HC. See JHE to HC, March 28, 1825, HC to JHE, March 30, 1825, JHE to HC, March 31, 1825, HC to JHE, April 1, 1825, JHE to HC, April 2, 1825, *PHC,* 4:191–208.

23. James Campbell to David Campbell, December 19, 1826, Campbell Family Papers, DU; JHE to De Witt Clinton, June 25, 1824, July 23, 1824, De Witt Clinton Papers, Columbia University; JHE to JC, September 25, 1826, JSB, 3:314–15; JHE to Chandler Price, March 14, 1824, AJ to JCC, July 18, 1826, *PJC,* 8:579–80, 10:158–60; JHE to AJ, February 8, 1827, January 21, 1828, JSB, 3:341–42, 389–90. Later in 1828 JHE once more urged silence on Jackson. JHE to AJ, August 21, 1828, JSB, 3:428–29.

24. Henry A. Wise, *Seven Decades of the Union* (Philadelphia, 1881), 113, cited in Remini, *Course of American Freedom,* 149; Barzman, 64; Bassett, 77.

25. Wise, 116, cited in Remini *Course of American Freedom,* 154.

26. Remini, *Course of American Freedom,* 155, 416n.

CHAPTER 2: "MY LORD! WHAT A PRETTY GIRL THAT IS!"

1. JHE to Colonel Campbell, Campbell Family Papers, DU; JHE to RJ, December 7,

1823, JSB, 3:215–16; AJ to RJ, February 6, 1824, in Avery O. Craven, ed., "Letters of Andrew Jackson," *Huntington Library Bulletin* 3 (February 1933):126.

2. ME, 67; AJ to RJ, December 21, 1823, JSB, 3:217–18; AJ to RJ, December 28, 1823, in Mary French Caldwell, *General Jackson's Lady: A Story of the Life and Times of Rachel Donelson Jackson* (Nashville, 1936), 387–88; AJ to RJ, February 6, 1823, Craven, 125–26; AJ to RJ, March 19, 27, 1824, April 5, 1825, JSB, 3:238–41, 244.

3. Pauline Wilcox Burke, *Emily Donelson of Tennessee.* 2 vols. (Richmond, 1941), 1:121–23. In later years, AJ frequently insisted on the depth of his wife's affection for ME.

4. Herbert J. Doherty, Jr., *Richard Keith Call, Southern Unionist* (Gainesville, 1961), 30–33. This account is staunchly pro-Richard Call, thus very negative toward ME.

5. ME, in her memoirs, insists that she "never was called Peggy in all my life." Certainly there are instances of derogatory use of that name in reference to her, but she is here speaking of regular personal use. ME, 21.

6. Queena Pollack, "An Irish Innkeeper and His Internationally Known 'Innkeeper's Daughter,'" *American Irish Historical Society Journal* 28 (1930): 94; Queena Pollack, *Peggy Eaton: Democracy's Mistress* (New York, 1932), 3; John Alexander Carroll and Mary Wells Ashworth, *George Washington,* vol. 7, *First in Peace* (New York, 1957), 7:628–30.

7. Allen C. Clark, "Margaret Eaton (Peggy O'Neal)" *RCHS* 44–45 (1942–1943): 4, 5; ME, 2; Pollack, "Innkeeper," 93; *Washington Gazette,* June 29, July 2, November 9, 1796, December 23, 1797. Because ME's death before publication prevented her from correcting an editor's error, O'Neale is spelled "O'Neil" throughout ME. Such discrepancies abound throughout the literature, because even contemporaries frequently misspelled the name due to its many variations.

8. J. Franklin Jameson, "Diary of Edward Hooker, 1805–1808," *Annual Report of the American Historical Association for the Year 1896.* 2 vols. (Washington, DC, 1897), 1:927.

9. ME, 1; W. B. Bryan, *A History of the National Capital.* 2 vols. (New York, 1914, 1916), 1:292; Jameson, 927; Richard Howell's father, Ebenezer, did not mention Rhoda in his 1787 will, located at 928F, B.29, p. 177 in the Division of Archives and Records Management, New Jersey Department of State, Trenton. None of Richard Howell's biographical sketches found in reference books located in the New Jersey Historical Society, Newark, mentioned that Richard Howell had a sister.

10. *WP,* November 10, 1879.

11. Allen C. Clark Papers, HSW; W. B. Bryan, "Hotels of Washington Prior to 1814," *RCHS* 7 (1904): 104–5; Clark, 5; Pollack, 21; Leon Phillips, *That Eaton Woman* (Barre, MA, 1974), 5; *WNI,* December 2, 1805, November 28, 1806, November 4, 1817, December 2, 1813, May 7, 1816;

12. ME, 2; Bryan, *History,* 1:380; Bryan, "Hotels," 104–6; Virginia Tatnall Peacock, *Famous American Belles of the Nineteenth Century* (Philadelphia, 1901), 70; Jameson, 920.

13. R. Sunderland, *A Sketch of the Life of William Gunton* (Washington, DC, 1878), 14–15; John W. Reps, *Washington on View: The Nation's Capital Since 1790* (Chapel Hill, 1991), 54–55; Stilson Hutchins and Joseph West Moore, *The National Capital, Past and Present* (Washington, DC, 1885), 41; Jameson, 927; Mrs. John A. Logan, *Thirty Years in Washington . . .* (Hartford, 1901), 57.

14. The Reverend French S. Evans provided this genealogical information in 1885. It is preserved in the Allen C. Clark Papers, HSW; Judith Sibley, United States Military Academy Archives, to author, November 13, 1995; Robert O'Neale to George Gorham, November 9, 1817, WON (father) to George Gorham, November 19, 1817, in U.S. Military Academy Application Papers, 1805–1866, NARS, Microfilm Publication 688.

15. Elbridge Gerry, Jr. *The Diary of Elbridge Gerry, Jr.* Preface and Notes by Claude Bowers (New York, 1927), xx; WTB to wife, February 24, 1815, in WTB, "Letters of William T. Barry," *William and Mary College Quarterly Historical Magazine* 13 (1904–1905): 238; transcript of this letter is in WTB, UVA; ME, 5–6.

16. Jameson, 921, 923, 928, 929; Bryan, *History,* 1:381.

17. Maria Clinton to Pierre Van Cortlandt, April 6, 1812, Pierre Van Cortlandt Papers, NYPL; Martha J. Lamb and Mrs. Burton Harrison, *History of New York.* 3 vols. (New York, 1896), 3:595–96; John P. Kaminski, *George Clinton, Yeoman Politician of the New Republic* (Madison, 1993), 290–91; estate of George Clinton, Pierre Van Cortlandt Papers, NYPL.

18. Ann King Gregorie, *Thomas Sumter* (Columbia, SC, 1931), 260; John Milledge to William Robertson, April 18, 1808, in Sally Harriet Milledge, ed., *Correspondence of John Milledge, Governor of Georgia, 1802–1806* (Columbia, SC, 1949), 149.

19. Information on boarders who lived in the O'Neale establishment is found in the *Congressional Directories* of the period; Clark, 6; Jameson, 926.

20. Jameson, 926–28.

21. Pollack, "Innkeeper," 93; Clark, 5.

22. This incident is described in Lyon's sketch in the *DAB.*

23. Jameson, 926.

24. Unless otherwise indicated, information for this sketch of ME's early life is based on ME and on Pollack. Both these sources must be handled with care, but each provides important data not available anywhere else.

25. ME spells the dance master's name as Genera. In *WNI,* March 10, 1812, a Mr. Generes announces a concluding ball for his dancing school at Mr. Crawford's New Assembly Room.

26. *WNI,* March 19, 1812; Clark, 9; Mary Caroline Crawford, *Romantic Days of the Early Republic* (Boston, 1912), 186. For James Monroe's major role during the British invasion of the capital, see Harry Ammon, *James Monroe; The Quest for National Identity* (New York, 1971), 328–44; *WP,* November 10, 1879; George Robert Glieg, *A Narration of the Campaign of the British Army at Washington . . .* (London, 1836), 129.

27. Maud B. Morris, "An Old Washington Mansion (2017 I Street Northwest)," *RCHS* 21 (1918): 127.

28. WTB to ?, March 2, 1815, WTB, "Letters," 238–39.

29. James Gallatin to Albert R. Gallatin, February 28, 1829, Albert Gallatin Papers, NYHS.

30. *New York City Directory, 1814.*

31. *DAB; National Cyclopedia of American Biography;* Edward A. Fitzpatrick, *The Educational Views and Influence of De Witt Clinton* (New York, 1969), 52.

32. *DAB;* James Renwick, *Life of De Witt Clinton* (New York, 1840), 37, 47.

33. In the Old Testament, Malachi 3:19, the verse appears: "And the day that is coming will set them on fire, leaving them neither root nor branch, says the Lord of hosts." *WP,* November 10, 1879.

34. In the manuscript of ME's book in LC, there is included a paragraph that does not appear in the printed version. In the section on page 21 of the handwritten manuscript, ME says that a man offered Timberlake $50,000 to marry his daughter, and she later threw herself at Timberlake. He refused the father's money and the daughter's sexual favors out of loyalty to ME. ME, Misc. Collections, LC.

35. For a detailed description of this house, see Appendix 23 in "Explanation of the Accounts and Vouchers of John B. Timberlake and of Lieutenant Robert B. Randolph. . . ," May 27, 1830, *ASP,* 3:675.

36. Ibid., 1:674–75.

37. John Timberlake File, Navy Widow 1186, Old War Pensions, RG 15, NARS.

38. *WNI,* May 7, 1816; WON to Abraham Bradley, III, May 27, 1820, Abraham Bradley III Papers, HSW.; WON to James Buchanan, November 12, 1823, James Buchanan Papers, HSP.

39. AJ's later Secretary of the Treasury Louis McLane introduced JBT's petition in the House of Representatives. John A. Munroe, *Louis McLane* (New Brunswick, NJ, 1973), 126.

40. *ASP,* 1:674–75.

41. JQA said that JHE had approached the secretary of the navy and "had been exceedingly urgent that Timberlake should be sent to sea," JQA, 8:202.

42. Carl B. Swisher, *Roger Brooke Taney* (New York, 1936), 135, in Felix A. Nigro, "The Van Buren Confirmation Before the Senate," *Western Political Quarterly* 14 (March 1961): 150. In 1824, Edward Coate Pinkney wrote the poem "A Health," which begins, "I fill this cup to one made of loveliness"; it was long believed to have been inspired by ME. Pinkney's biographers call that frequently repeated tale "a very improbable story." They asert that Pinkney's wife was the inspiration for this poem. Thomas Oliver Mabbott and Frank Lester Pleadwell, *The Life and Works of Edward Coate Pinkney* (New York, 1926), 43n, 120.

43. Power of Attorney, enclosed in AJ to ESE, April 10, 1829, EACB, AJ, LC; extract of a letter of WON to JBT, November 20, 1826, Branch Family Papers, SHC, UNC; ME, 46, 39.

44. Josephine Seaton, *William Winston Seaton of the "National Intelligencer"* (Boston, 1871), 166–71; Phillips, 46–47; H. P. Caemmerer, *Washington, the National Capital,* Senate Document no. 332, 71st Cong., 3rd sess., 47; Morris, 127; Traveller, *Sketches of History, Life, and Manners in the United States* (New Haven, 1826), 177.

45. *ASP,* 3:654; JHE to AK, February 22, 1830, in *WNI,* June 28, 1830; Wilhemina B. Bryant, *A History of the National Capital.* 2 vols. (New York, 1916), 2:60–61; Phillips, 47; ME, 37.

46. St. Elia Vallette to ME, April 18, 1829, Misc. Manuscripts (Eaton, Mrs. Margaret [O'Neal]), NYHS; E. A. F. Hollock to ME, April 18, 1829, EACB, AJ, LC.

47. David R. Barbee, "Andrew Jackson and Peggy O'Neale," *THQ* 15 (March 1956): 43n; Journal of the U.S. *Constitution,* April 2, 3, 1828, in Daniel Todd Patterson Papers, Naval Historical Foundation Collection, LC.

48. Barbee, 43n; ME, 40–41; Thomas Norman to ME, April 1829, Misc. Manuscripts (Eaton, Mrs. Margaret [O'Neal]), NYHS; Amasa Paine to AJ, August 20, 1829 [*sic*], enclosed in AJ to ESE, April 10, 1829, EACB, AJ, LC.

CHAPTER 3: "THERE ARE GREAT OBJECTIONS MADE TO HIS WIFE"

1. AJ to JC, January 17, 1829, JSB, 4:1–2; John Chambers to John J. Crittenden, January 28, 1829, John J. Crittenden Papers, LC.
2. JHE to AJ, December 7, 1828, AJ, SR.
3. Madame Celnart, *The Gentleman's and Lady's Book of Politeness and Propriety . . .* (Boston, 1833), 210–12; Karen Halttunen, *Confidence Men and Painted Women: A Study of Middle-Class Culture in America, 1830–1870* (New Haven, 1982), 135–38.
4. Robert Desha to Editor, *UST,* November 24, 1831.
5. David Lindsey, *Andrew Jackson and John C. Calhoun.* (Woodbury, NY, 1973), 117–18; John T. Moore, *Tennessee, The Volunteer State.* 4 vols. (Chicago, 1923), 2:199; Anne Royall, *The Black Book, or a Continuation of Travels.* 3 vols. (Washington, DC, 1829), 1:126.
6. JHE to E. G. W. Butler, December 28, 1828, Butler Family Papers, Historic New Orleans Collection, printed in *Historic New Orleans Collection Newsletter* 2 (September 1984): 6; Thomas P. Govan, "John M. Berrien and the Administration of Andrew Jackson," *Journal of Southern History* 5 (February 1939): 457; *WNI,* January 5, 1829; *New York Spectator,* n.d., in Esther Singleton, *The Story of the White House.* 2 vols. ((New York, 1907), 1:202–3.
7. Charles Hammond to David Chambers, January 21, 1829, Charles Hammond Papers, Ohio Historical Society; Louis McLane to ?, February 12, 13, 1829, James Bayard Papers, University of Delaware, quoted in Chase C. Mooney, *William H. Crawford, 1772–1834* (Lexington, KY, 1974), 315n.
8. *DAB;* MBS to Mrs. Kirkpatrick, January 1, 1829, MBS, 352–53.
9. C. C. Camberleng to MVB, January 1, 1829, MVB, LC; E. Bates to Julia Bates, December [January] 4, 1829, E. Bates Papers, VHS.
10. E. Bates to Julia Bates, December [January] 4, 1829, E. Bates Papers, VHS; Catherine Macomb Mason to John Mason, February 22, 1829, John Mason Papers, Burton Historical Collection, Detroit Public Library.
11. ME, 51–52.
12. *UST,* January 16, 1829, in Kenneth Lawrence Smith, "Duff Green and the *United States Telegraph, 1826–1837,* Ph.D. diss., College of William and Mary, 1981, 144; ME, 52–53; Allen C. Clark, "Margaret Eaton (Peggy O'Neale)," *RCHS,* 44–45 (1942–43):12.
13. ME, 53–54.
14. Robert B. Satterfield "A. J. Donelson: A Moderate Nationalist Jacksonian," Ph.D. diss., Johns Hopkins University, 1962, 19.
15. ED to "My Dearest Mother," January 29, 1829, quoted in Edna Colman, *Seventy-Five Years of White House Gossip* (Garden City, NY, 1926), 156; Frances M. Trollope, *Domestic Manners of the Americans,* 125, quoted in Marquis James, *The Life of Andrew Jackson* (Indianapolis, 1938), 488.
16. Alfred Mordecai to Ellen Mordecai, February 11, 1829, in Sarah Agnes Wallace, ed.,

"Opening Days of Jackson's Presidency as Seen in Private Letters," *THQ* 9 (December 1950): 368–69; *Washington National Journal,* April 7, 1829.

17. John Campbell to David Campbell, March 26, 1829, Campbell Family Papers, DU; DW to Mrs. Ezekiel Webster, February 19, 1829, DW, *The Writings and Speeches of Daniel Webster,* nat. ed. 18 vols. (Boston, 1903), 17:470; William Smith to James Barbour, March 17, 1829, James Barbour Papers, NYPL.

18. The status of women in nineteenth-century America has received close scrutiny since the publication of the groundbreaking essay by Barbara Welter, "The Cult of True Womanhood, 1820–1860," *American Quarterly* 18 (Summer 1966): 151–74. For an extended discussion of the impact of gender roles and attitudes on the Jacksonian period, see John F. Marszalek, "The Eaton Affair: Society and Politics," *THQ* 55 (Spring 1996): 6–19.

19. JCC, "Reply to John H. Eaton's Address," *PJC,* 11:474–75; Charles M. Wiltse, *John C. Calhoun, Nullifier* (New York, 1949), 28–29; ME's brother-in-law, the Reverend French S. Evans, later insisted that Floride Calhoun had indeed left a card, his wife receiving it for ME. The issue was debated without resolution. *WG,* November 7, 1831.

20. Mrs. Edward Everett to Mrs. Nathan Hale, March 1, 1829, Everett-Hopkins Papers, MaHS.

21. ME, 54–55.

22. Ibid., 55–57.

23. Hasia Diner, *Erin's Daughters in America: Irish Immigrant Women in the Nineteenth Century* (Baltimore, 1983), 112.

24. Ben Perley Poore, *Reminiscences of Sixty Years.* 2 vols. (Chicago, 1890), 2:122.

25. John Chambers to John J. Crittenden, December 29, 1828, John J. Crittenden Papers, LC; William C. Rives to Thomas Gilmer, February 17, 1829, William C. Rives Papers, LC; AK to FPB, February 14, 1829, B-L, PU; Virginia L. Glenn, "James Hamilton, Jr., A Biography," Ph.D. diss., University of North Carolina, 1964, 125–27; Robert Y. Hayne to MVB, February 14, 1829, MVB, LC.

26. Gideon Welles to John M. Niles, February 9, 1829, Gideon Welles Papers, LC.

27. Donald Chidsey, *Andrew Jackson, Hero* (Nashville, 1976), 89; DW to Ezekiel Webster, February 23, 1829, *Writings and Speeches,* 16:188; MBS to Mrs. Kirkpatrick, January 12, 1829, in MBS, 258.

28. AJ to MVB, February 14, 1829, JSB, 4:4–5; William Allen Butler, *Martin Van Buren: Lawyer, Statesman and Man* (New York, 1862), 24–25.

29. Henry B. Stanton, *Random Recollections* (New York, 1886), 22–23; David Crockett, *Life of Martin Van Buren,* in James E. Pollard, *The Presidents and the Press* (New York, 1947), 187; Robert V. Remini, *Martin Van Buren and the Making of the Democratic Party* (New York, 1959), 13.

30. MVB to AJ, February 20, 1829, JSB, 4:9–10; James A. Hamilton to MVB, February 21, 23, 1829, MVB, LC.

31. *DAB;* William Armstrong Ingham, *Samuel Dulucenna Ingham* (Philadelphia, 1919), 15; Philip S. Klein, *Pennsylvania Politics, 1817–1832: A Game Without Rules* (Philadelphia, 1940), 314–16; HC to Charles Hammond, May 2, 1825, *PHC,* 4:328.

32. C. Jay Smith, "John MacPherson Berrien," in Horace Montgomery, ed., *Georgians in Profile: Historical Essays in Honor of Ellis Merton Coulter* (Athens, GA, 1958), 168–74; Henry S. Foote, *Casket of Reminiscences* (Washington, DC, 1874), 14–15; Royce C.

McCray, Jr., "John MacPherson Berrien of Georgia (1781–1856)," Ph.D. diss., University of Georgia, 1971, 413.

33. *DAB;* Anne Royall, *Black Book, or a Continuation of Travels.* 3 vols. (Washington, DC, 1829), 3:117; Satterfield, 22; AK to FPB, March 7, 1829, B-L, PU.

34. *DAB;* Julius Franz Kany, "The Career of William Taylor Barry," master's thesis, Western Kentucky State Teachers College, 1934; WTB to wife, February 24, 1815, "Letters of William T. Barry," *William and Mary College Quarterly Historical Magazine* 13 (1904–1905): 238.

35. AJ to FPB, March 7, 1829, B-L, PU; For a discussion of the twists and turns in this process, see L. Paul Gresham, "The Public Career of Hugh Lawson White," Ph.D. diss., Vanderbilt University, 1944, 254–58.

36. JHE to HLW, February 23, 1829, Sally N. Scott, ed., *A Memoir of Hugh Lawson White* (Philadelphia, 1856), 266; L. Paul Gresham, "The Public Career of H. L. White," *THQ* 3 (December 1944), 308.

37. Edward Everett to Alexander H. Everett, February 15, 1829, Edward Everett Papers, MaHS; DW to Ezekiel Webster, February 23, 1829, *Writings and Speeches,* 16:187–88.

38. Louis McLane to MVB, February 19, 1829, E. K. Kane to MVB, February 19, 1829, James Hamilton, Jr., to MVB, February 19, 1829, MVB, LC.

39. *UST,* February 26, 1829; DW to Ezekiel Webster, March 2, 1829, *Writings and Speeches,* 16:189; Levi Woodbury to SDI, March 2, 1829, SDI, UP; William Cullen Bryant to Gulian C. Veerplanck, February 27, 1829, William Cullen Bryant II and Thomas G. Voss, eds., *The Letters of William Cullen Bryant.* 6 vols. (New York, 1975), 1:277.

40. C. C. Cambreleng to MVB, March 1, 1829, MVB, LC; RMJ to AJ, March 9, 1829, AJ, LC.

41. Edward Everett to Alexander H. Everett, February 15, 1829, Edward Everett Papers, MaHS; James Gallatin to Albert R. Gallatin, February 28, 1829, Albert Gallatin Papers, NYHS; AK to FPB, March 7, 1829, B-L, PU; Edward Everett to Alexander H. Everett, March 18, 1829, Edward Everett Papers, MaHS.

42. ME, 77–83.

43. "Narrative by Major William B. Lewis," October 25, 1859, in James Parton, *The Life of Andrew Jackson.* 3 vols. (New York, 1861), 3:160–61; AJ, "Memorandum on Cabinet Formation and the Eaton Affair," *c.* January, 1830, AJ, LC.

44. AJ to FPB, March 7, 1829, B-L, PU; AJ to R. E. W. Earle, March 16, 1829, AJ, SR; AJ to John Coffee, March 22, 1829, JSB, 4:4—15; James A. Hamilton to MVB, February 23, 1829, MVB, LC.

45. AJ to JCMcL, April 1829, AJ, NYHS, quoted in Remini, *Andrew Jackson and the Course of American Freedom,* 165; Robert V. Remini, "Election of 1832," in Arthur M. Schlesinger, Jr., *History of American Presidential Elections.* 4 vols. (New York, 1971), 1:495; MBS to J. Bayard Smith, February 25, 1829, MBS, 281–82; MBS to Maria Boyd, March 15, 1829, MBS, LC; Chidsey, 90. A young Salmon P. Chase thought the term "millenium of minnows" was appropriate. "It is so truly," he said. Salmon P. Chase to Thomas Sparhawk, April 20, 1829, Salmon P. Chase Papers, microfilm, University Publications of America.

46. Frederick Jackson Turner, *The United States, 1830–1850* (New York, 1935), 14–18.

47. Mrs. Basil Hall to "My Dearest Jane," December 29, 1827, January 7, 1828, Una Pope-

Hennessy, ed., *The Aristocratic Journey: Letters of Mrs. Basil Hall* (New York, 1931), 165, 175; Smith, 2; Arthur M. Schlesinger, Jr., *The Age of Jackson* (Boston, 1945), 4.

48. Unless otherwise indicated, the following account of the AJ inauguration and celebrations is based on MBS to Mrs. Kirkpatrick, March 11, 1829, in MBS, 290–98 and Edwin A. Miles, "The First People's Inaugural—1829," *THQ* 37 (Fall 1978): 293–307.

49. Josephine Seaton, *William Winston Seaton of the National Intelligencer* (Boston, 1871), 210.

50. Salmon P. Chase Diary, March 4, 1829, Salmon P. Chase Papers, LC.

51. Wiltse, 13.

52. MVB to James A. Hamilton, February 21, 1829, *Reminiscences of James A. Hamilton* (New York, 1869), 94.

53. Salmon P. Chase Diary, March 4, 1829, Salmon P. Chase Papers, LC; James A. Hamilton to MVB, March 5, 1829, MVB, LC.

54. Richard W. Thompson. *Recollections of Sixteen Presidents.* 2 vols. (Indianapolis, 1874), 1:146.

55. MBS to Mrs. Kirkpatrick, January 1, 1829, MBS, 253.

56. AK to FPB, March 5, 1829, in Elbert Smith, *Francis Preston Blair* (New York, 1980), 36.

57. William Seale, *The President's House.* 2 vols. (Washington, DC, 1986), 1:177–79; MBS to Mrs. Kirkpatrick, March 11, 1829, MBS, 290–96.

58. MBS to Mrs. Kirkpatrick, March 11, 1829, MBS, 296; Miles, 293–307; Wiltse, 307; *WNI,* March 6, 1829.

59. MBS to Mrs. Boyd, Spring 1829, MBS 288–89.

CHAPTER 4: "SHE IS AS CHASTE AS A VIRGIN"

1. *UST,* March 18, 1829; MBS to Mrs. Boyd, Spring 1829, MBS to J. Bayard H. Smith, March 12, 1829, MBS, 290, 298–99.

2. *New York Enquirer,* March 13, 1829; AK to FPB, March 7, 1829, B-L, PU.

3. AJ to R. E. W. Earle, March 16, 1829, AJ, SR; Edward Everett to Alexander H. Everett, March 18, 1829, Edward Everett Papers, MaHS; ME, 75–77; Wilhemina B. Bryant, *A History of the National Capital* (New York, 1916), 87n.

4. James H. Smylie, "American Presbyterians and Transforming American Culture," *American Presbyterians* 67 (Fall 1989): 191–92; Curtis Dahl, "The Clergyman, the Hussy, and Old Hickory: Ezra Stiles Ely and the Peggy Eaton Affair," *Journal of Presbyterian History* 52 (Summer 1974): 137–55; Tom Bentley Throckmorton, "Ezra Stiles Ely—Benefactor of Jefferson Medical College," *Journal of the Iowa State Medical Society* 29 (March 1939): 135–40; Jean Matthews, *Toward a New Society; American Thought and Culture, 1800–1830* (Boston, 1991), 44–45; James R. Rohret, "Sunday Mails and the Church-State Theme in Jacksonian America," *Journal of the Early Republic* 7 (Spring 1987): 72; James G. Smoot, "A Presbyterian Minister Calls on Presidential Candidate Andrew Jackson," *THQ* (September 1962): 288; ESE to AJ, December 10, 1828, AJ, LC; AJ to ESE, December 16, 1828, AJ, LC.

5. ESE to AJ, January 28, 1829, JSB, 4: 3–4; ESE to AJ, March 4, 1829, AJ, SR; Herbert J. Doherty, Jr., *Richard Keith Call, Southern Unionist* (Gainesville, 1961), 53; ESE to AJ, March 18, 1829, AJ, SR.

6. ESE to AJ, March 18, 1829, EACB, AJ, LC.

7. AJ to RKC, July 5, 1829, JSB, 4:50; AJ to ESE, March 23, 1829, in James Parton, *The Life of Andrew Jackson*. 3 vols. (New York, 1861), 3:186–91.

8. ESE to AJ, April 4, 1829, EACB, AJ, LC.

9. AJ to ESE, April 10, 1829, Parton 3:192–95.

10. ESE to AJ, May 2, 30, 1829, EACB, AJ, LC; AJ later learned that ESE's friend, Philadelphia publisher Samuel Bradford, found that "the only impropriety" he could find against ME and JHE was their traveling together on a steamboat from New York to Albany and back again, "leaving [behind] Mr. T. who was indisposed; but who insisted on his wife's taking the trip." AJ to RKC, July 5, 1829, JSB, 4:52.

11. For a collection of letters that Andrew Jackson obviously recruited, with WBL's and JHE's help, see EACB, AJ, LC.

12. ME, 78–87.

13. Mr. Colman to James A. Hamilton, March 18, 1829, James A. Hamilton, *Reminiscences* (New York, 1869), 126–27; James A. Hamilton to MVB, July 16, 1829, MVB, LC.

14. R. E. W. Earle to AJ, April 3, 1829, AJ, SR; JQA, 8:128; Mrs. Nevins to David H. Nevins, April 5, 1829, Griswold Family Papers, UVA; Virgil Maxcy to JCC, April 6, 1829, *PJC*, 11:17.

15. Harriet Chappell Owsley, "Andrew Jackson and His Ward, Andrew Jackson Donelson," *THQ* 41 (Summer 1982): 124–39; Laura C. Holloway, *The Ladies of the White House, or, in the House of the Presidents* (Philadelphia, 1881), 334–35. Pauline Wilcox Burke, *Emily Donelson of Tennessee*. 2 vols. (Richmond, 1941), 2:205. The Burke biography is the most thorough, although often an uncritical, account of ED's life.

16. Part of a draft of AJD to AJ, [*c.* October 30, 1830], AJD, LC, and AJ, SR; John Donelson to JC, April 20, 1829, JC, THS in TSLA.

17. John C. Fitzpatrick, ed., "The Autobiography of Martin Van Buren," *American Historical Association, Annual Report for 1918*, (Washington, DC, 1920), 344–45.

18. JHE to ED, April 8, 9, 1829, JSB, 4:29–30; ED to ME, April 10, 1829, AJD to JHE, April 10, 1829, AJD to JC, April 15, 1829, AJD, LC.

19. *WNI*, July 9, 1829; Burke, 1:202–3; AJD to AJ, October 25, 1830, JSB, 4:189–90.

20. David Campbell to his brother, August 19, 1829, Campbell Family Papers, DU; *USG*, June 16, 1829, clipping in John Agg Papers, DU.

21. AJ to JCMcL, April 26, 1829, JSB, 4:20; Joseph C. Johnston to HC, July 8, 1829, *PJC*, 8:74.

22. AJ to RKC, July 5, 1829, JSB, 4:52–53; William T. Brent to HC, September 19, 1829, *PHC*, 8:104; WTB to "My Dear Daughter," May 16, 1829, in I. J. Cox, contr. "Letters of William T. Barry, 1806–1810, 1829–1831," *American Historical Review* 16 (January 1911): 331–32.

23. WTB to "My Dear Susan," June 25, 1829, in Cox, 334; John Waller Barry to "My Dear Sister," June 26, 1829, in Cheryl Conover, ed., "The Kentuckian in 'King Andrew's Court,'" *Register of the Kentucky Historical Society* 81 (Spring 1983): 209.

24. David Campbell to Mary Campbell, May 24, 1829, Campbell Family Papers, DU.

25. Ibid., May 27, 1829.

26. Ibid., June 3, 1829.

27. Ibid., May 24, 1829; AJ to JCMcL, May 3, 1829, JSB 4:31.

28. Charles J. Love to AJ, April 15, 1829, JSB, 4:23; AK to FPB, April 21, 1829, B-L, PU; AJ to JC, May 30, 1829, AJ to JCMcL, May 3, 1829, JSB, 4:438–39, 31; AJ to Judith Walker Rives, June 26, 1829, AJ, SR.

29. AJ to WON, April 13, 1829, AJ, LC; ME, 95; David Campbell to his brother, August 19, 1829, Campbell Family Papers, DU; ME, 93–94.

30. ME, 96–104.

31. ESE to JNC, August 27, 1829, Stauffer Collection, HSP; Memorandum by AJD, September 3, 1829, JSB, 4:68–70.

32. MBS to Mrs. Kirkpatrick, January 1, 1829, MBS to Mrs. Boyd, February 16, 1829, MBS, 250, 280; Salmon P. Chase Diary, January 1, 1829, Salmon P. Chase Papers, LC; JQA, 8:129.

33. "Narrative by General Jackson, [September 3, 1829]," Parton, 3:197–201.

34. Louis R. Harlan, "Public Career of William Berkeley Lewis," *THQ* 7 (March, June 1948): 3–37, 118–51.

35. "Narrative by General Jackson," Parton, 3:197–201.

36. ME, 105–10; Statement of ESE to JNC and Nathan Towson, September 11, 1829, Gratz Collection, HSP.

37. Parton, 3:201; AJ to AJD, September 3, 1829 [addendum to September 3, 1829, narrative], AJ, SR; Memorandum of AJD, September 3, 1829, AJ to ESE, September 3, 1829, JSB, 4:70–72, 67–68.

38. Salmon P. Chase Diary, September 5, 1829, Salmon P. Chase Papers, LC; W. Simonton to WBL, November 19, 1829, EACB, AJ, LC; Edward I. Chase to Salmon P. Chase, September 9, 1829, Salmon P. Chase Papers, LC; William Wirt to Salmon P. Chase, December 21, 1829, William Wirt Papers, Maryland Historical Society.

39. ME, 111–14; Statement of O. B. Brown, September 3, 1829, EACB, Edward Wyer to AJ, September 15, 1829, AJ, LC; T. Fillebrown to JHE, September 16, 1829, Peter Brady to WBL, September 16, 1829, EACB, AJ, LC.

40. William Ryland to AJ, September 28, 1829, P. G. Randolph's statement of the interview between JHE and Mr. Beale [October 7, 1829], James L. Edwards to JHE, October 9, 1829, Judge J. Anderson to AJ, October 15, 1829, Francis B. Ogden to John E. Hyde, November 22, 1829, Hyde to Ogden, November 26, 1829, Ogden to JHE, November 30, 1829, EACB, AJ, LC.

41. General C. Parker to WBL, September 22, 1829, EACB, AJ, LC.

42. W. Bradford to AJ, October 10, 1829, EACB, AJ, LC.

43. T. Fillebrown to JHE, September 22, 1829, EACB, AJ, LC.

44. Frances Tomlinson Gardner, "The Gentleman from Tennessee," *Surgery, Gynecology and Obstetrics* 80 (1949): 405–11.

45. Information on the cabinet meeting is derived from Parton, 3:203–6; MVB to James A. Hamilton, September 24, 1829, James A. Hamilton, *Reminiscenses,* 146–48; Salmon P. Chase Diary, September 5, 1829, Salmon P. Chase Papers, LC; JQA, March 25, 1830, 8:206–7; Curtis Dahl, "The Clergyman, the Hussy, and Old Hickory: Ezra Stiles Ely and the Peggy Eaton Affair," *Journal of Presbyterian History* 52 (Summer 1974): 141.

46. JHE to JNC, September 12, 1829, EACB, AJ, LC; Salmon P. Chase Diary, September 5, 1829, Salmon P. Chase Papers, LC; AJ to ESE, September 3, 1829, JSB, 4:67–68;

JNC to JHE, September 12, 15, 1829, JHE to JNC, September 16, 1829, EACB, AJ, LC and Gratz Collection, HSP; JNC to JHE, September 17, 1829, Gratz Collection, HSP.

47. "Mr. Houston's statement of an interview between Major Eaton and Rev. Mr. Campbell in his presence," October 14, 1829, EACB, AJ, LC.

48. DG to JNC, October 19, 1829, EACB, AJ, LC.

49. JNC to DG, October 19, 1829, EACB, AJ, LC; JNC to AJ, October 19, 1829, AJ, SR; AJD to JNC, October 20, 23, 1829, Presidential Candidates Collection, HSP.; AJ to JCMcL, November 24, 1829, JSB, 4:88; JC to AJD, November 3, 1829, JC, TSLA; M. T. Simpson to John McLean, September 22, 1829, John McLean Papers, LC; AJ to JC, September 20, 1829, AJ, SR; MBS to Mrs. Kirkpatrick, January 26, 1830, MBS, 311–12; *New York World,* March 28, 1864, in William B. Sprague, *Memorial of the Rev. John N. Campbell . . .* (Albany, 1864), 62–63; *UST,* October 22, 1829.

50. AJ to JCMcL, *c.* September 15, 1829, AJ, SR; AJD to JC, September 20, 1829, AJD, LC; Major Norris to James Barbour, November 15, 1829, James Barbour Papers, NYPL.

CHAPTER 5: "ET TU BRUTE"

1. Josiah S. Johnston to HC, November 14, 1829, Robert P. Letcher to HC, December 21, 1829, John Vance to HC, December 28, 1829, *PHC,* 8:127–28, 159–60, 164–65.

2. MVB, *Autobiography,* 347; Edward Everett to Alexander H. Everett, November 28, 1829, Edward Everett Papers, MaHS.

3. *WNI,* July 7, 1829; Esther Singleton, *The Story of the White House.* 2 vols. (New York, 1907), 201; Alfred A. Mordecai to his sisters, March 4, 1830, Alfred Mordecai Papers, LC; Thomas Hamilton, *Men and Manners in America.* 2 vols. (Edinburgh, 1834), 2:137–38; Madeleine Vinton Dahlgren, *Etiquette of Social Life in Washington* (Washington, DC, 1873), 4–5.

4. M. A. De Wolfe Howe, ed., *The Life and Letters of George Bancroft.* 2 vols. (New York, 1908), 1:196.

5. MVB, *Autobiography,* 347; Helen Nicolay, *Andrew Jackson, the Fighting President* (New York, 1929), 284.

6. Anne H. Wharton, *Social Life in the Early Republic* (Philadelphia, 1902), 216–17, 227; Clement R. Martzolff, "Caleb Atwater," reprinted from the *Ohio Archaeological and Historical Quarterly* (Columbus, 1905), 266; FG to Mr. McGovock, July 28, 1829, FG, SHC, UNC; MVB, *Autobiography,* 348; Bess Furman, *White House Profile: A Social History of the White House, Its Occupants and Its Festivities* (New York, 1951), 113; WTB to "My dear Daughter," November 27, 1829, WTB, "Letters of William T. Barry," *William and Mary College Quarterly Historical Magazine,* 13 (1904–1905):243.

7. MVB, *Autobiography,* 348–50.

8. Ibid., 351–52.

9. Ibid., 342; Josiah S. Johnston to HC, December 12, 1829, *PHC,* 8:136.

10. James Parton, *The World's Famous Women . . .* (New York, 1888), 134–35; MVB, *Autobiography,* 352; E. F. Chambers to SDI, December 21, 1829, SDI, UP; JQA, January 3, 7, 1830, 8:162, 166; Mrs. Basil Hall to her daughter, January 21, 1828, Una Pope-Hennessy, ed., *The Aristocratic Journey: Letters of Mrs. Basil Hall* (New York, 1931), 188.

The following year, Mrs. Huygens insisted that she left the party only because her husband felt "indisposed in consequence of exposure on that evening," and that two days later Jackson visited their home. *Washington National Journal,* August 2, 1831. Despite his friendship toward the Eatons, Vaughan wrote to his home office about Andrew Jackson's "Quixotic" friendship with ME and worried: "The President is . . . likely to get himself in trouble over it." Harold Eberlein and Cartlandt Van Dyke Hubbard, *Historic Homes of George-Town & Washington City* (Richmond, 1958), 339. When he was leaving the country, Krudener told HC of "my hope of seeing the Presidential Chair and the Federal government restored by you to their former dignity." Paul de Krudener to HC, August 16, 1830, *PHC,* 8:251

11. MVB, *Autobiography,* 353–54; AJ to MVB, January 24, 1829, JSB, 4:122; [AJ Memorandum on the Eaton Affair], January 24, 1830, AJ, LC; DW to Mr. Dutton, January 15, 1830, DW, *The Writings and Speeches of Daniel Webster,* nat. ed. 18 vols. (Boston, 1903), 17:483; AJ to JCMcL, November 24, 1829, JSB, 4:89.

12. JHE to Nicholas Biddle, November 20, 1829, Nicholas Biddle Papers, LC; John Belohlavek, *George Mifflin Dallas, Jacksonian Patrician* (University Park, PA, 1977), 31; Thomas Patterson to HC, December 13, 1829, *PHC,* 8:138.

13. A.B.C.O.Z. [*sic*] to Susan Decatur, December 12, 1829, Decatur to AJ, December 31, 1829, AJ to Decatur, January 2, 1830, AJ, LC; AJ to Francis Preston, March 5, 9, 1830, AJ, SR; Charles G. Sellers, *James K. Polk, Jacksonian 1795–1843.* 2 vols. (Princeton, NJ, 1957), 1:143; John Campbell to his brother, December 27, 1830, Campbell Family Papers, DU; Eliza Johnston to HC, December 12, 1829, *PHC,* 8:135.

14. John Campbell to David Campbell, January 6, 13, 1830, Campbell Family Papers, DU.

15. Ibid., December 27, 1829; JHE to JB, January 19, 1830, Branch Family Papers, SHC, UNC; AJ to JB, January 26, 1830, JB to AJ, January 27, 1830, JHE to JB, January 27, 18, 1830, AJ, SR; James Parton, *The Life of Andrew Jackson.* 3 vols. (New York, 1861), 3:309.

16. Furman, 108.

17. JQA, February 6, 1830, 8:184–86.

18. *Kentucky Reporter,* July 20, 1831, in *Baltimore Patriot and Mercantile Advertiser,* July 27, 1831. See Thomas Brown, "The Miscegenation of Richard Mentor Johnson as an Issue in the National Election Campaign of 1835–1836," *Civil War History* 39 (March 1993): 5–30.

19. This account of Johnson's meeting with the three secretaries is based primarily on SDI's statement, most readily available in Parton, *Andrew Jackson,* 3:303–7. A corroborating statement is JMB to RMJ, July 7, 1831, *NR,* July 30, 1831. RMJ critiqued the SDI account in RMJ to SDI, July 31, 1831, *WNI,* August 12, 1831. In another letter, RMJ similarly insisted that AJ "disclaimed on all occasions, any right, or desire, or intention to regulate the private or social intercourse of his cabinet." But RMJ indicated in this and other letters that he made such comments on his own. RMJ to SDI and JMB, June 30, July 20, 1831, *NR,* July 30, August 20, 1831, and RMJ to John McLean, July 14, 1831, John McLean Papers, LC.

20. Memorandum in Jackson's Handwriting, [January 29, 1830], JSB, 4:123–24; see also AJ to AJD, August 5, 1829, JSB, 4:323–26.

21. WTB to Mrs. Taylor, February 25, 1830, I. J Cox, contr. "Letters of William T. Barry,

1806–1810, 1829–1831," *American Historical Review* 16 (January 1911): 334; JQA, March 3, 1830, 8:197; FPB to AK, February 11, 1829, B-L, PU.

22. WTB to Mrs. Taylor, February 25, 1830, in Cox, 334–35; JQA, March 18, 1830, 8:203; Henry R. Storrs to Peter B. Porter, March 18, 1830, Peter B. Porter Papers, Buffalo and Erie County Historical Society.

23. JQA, January 7, 1830, 8:165–67; JHE to AK, February 22, 1830, *WNI,* June 28, 1830.

24. *DAB;* AK to FPB, Novenber 22, 1829, B-L, PU; Powrie Vaux Doctor, "Amos Kendall: Propagandist of Jacksonian Democracy, 1828–1836," Ph.D. diss., Georgetown University, 1939, 104; Terry L. Shoptaugh, "Amos Kendall: A Political Biography," Ph.D. diss., University of New Hampshire, 1984, 1.

25. JB to U.S. Senate, February 27, 1830, with enclosure of AK to JB, February 24, 1830, *PJC,* 11:128–36; Francis Preston to AJ, March 16, 1830, AJ, LC.

26. JB to U.S. Senate, February 27, 1830, *PJC,* 11:128–36; "Explanation of the Accounts and Vouchers of John B. Timberlake and of Lieutenant Robert B. Randolph, as Purser and Acting Purser of the Frigate Constitution," May 27, 1830, *ASP,* 3:654–84; "Proceedings of a Court of Inquiry in the Case of Lieutenant Robert B. Randolph of the Navy," February 27, 1833, *ASP,* 4:301–49. The most complete account of the assault on AJ is John M. Belohlavek, "Assault on the President: The Jackson-Randolph Affair of 1833," *Presidential Studies Quarterly* 12 (Summer 1982): 361–68; AJ to Robert M. Burton, May 29, 1830, AJ, SR.

27. Robert V. Remini, *Andrew Jackson and the Course of American Freedom* (New York, 1981), 101–2.

28. Charles M. Wiltse, *The New Nation, 1800–1845* (New York, 1961), 106; JQA, February 6, 1830, 8:185.

29. George W. Bungay, *Off-Hand Takings; or Crayon Sketchings of the Notable Men of Our Age* (New York, 1854), 86; Gaillard Hunt, *John C. Calhoun* (Philadelphia, 1907), 222, 228; Mary Bates, *The Private Life of John C. Calhoun* (Charleston, 1852), 8; Irving Bartlett, *John C. Calhoun: A Biography* (New York, 1993), 163; Margaret Coit, *John C. Calhoun: An American Portrait* (Boston, 1950), 193; JQA, February 28, 1830, 8:195.

30. E. F. Chambers to SDI, December 21, 1829, SDI, UP; John Vance to HC, December 28, 1829, *PHC,* 8:164–65; JQA, December 30, 1829, 8:159; J. Vance to Charles Hammond, January 29, 1831, Charles Hammond Papers, Ohio Historical Society.

31. William W. Freehling, *Prelude to Civil War: The Nullification Controversy in South Carolina* (New York, 1966), 189–92; Richard Latner, *The Presidency of Andrew Jackson: White House Politics, 1829–1837* (Athens, GA, 1979), 68–70; AJ to JO, December 31, 1829, JSB, 4:108; AK to FPB, January 28, 1830, B-L, PU; JQA, March 27, 1830, 8:209; FPB to AK, February 11, 1830, B-L, PU; WTB to Mrs Taylor, February 25, 1830, Cox, 335.

32. Samuel L. Bradford to WBL, February 28, 1832, AJ, LC. Bradford said that both he and Barry had received this information from "General Overton." Since JO was AJ's closest friend, why he would work through intermediaries rather than with AJ directly is unclear. For more information on this alleged meeting, see Charles A. Wickliffe to HLW et al., December 24, 1831, Herbert Weaver and Paul H. Bergeron, eds., *Correspondence of James K. Polk* (Nashville, 1969), 1:430–33; JQA, February 21, 1821, 8:477.

33. "William B. Lewis to L. C. Stanbaugh, March 11, 1830, Another Note by Major Lewis," Parton, 3:297–99; Pennsylvania Legislature to AJ, March 20, 1830, L. C. Stan-

baugh to WBL, March 31, 1830, Parton, 3:299–301; H. Petrikin to AJ, April 2, 1830, JSB, 4:131–32; C. C. Cambreleng to A. C. Flagg, April 5, 1830, Azariah C. Flagg Papers, NYPL; AK to FPB, March 18, 1830, B-L, PU; Josiah S. Johnston to HC, Early April, 1830, *PHC,* 8:187–88.

34. *NR,* April 24, 1830; George Keyser to WON, April 23, 1830, AJ, LC; Robert V. Remini, *The Life of Andrew Jackson* (New York, 1988), 195–97.

35. Littleton W. Tazewell to John Tazewell, January 8, 1830, Tazewell Family Papers, Virginia State Library and Archives; Donald B. Cole, *The Presidency of Andrew Jackson* (Lawrence, 1993), 80.

36. WBL to James Parton, October 25, 1859, in Parton, 3:322–25; John Forsyth to William H. Crawford, April 10, 1830, William Henry Crawford Papers, LC; AJ to JC, April 10, 1830, JSB, 4:135.

37. AJ to JCC, May 13, 1830, JSB, 4;136; JCC to AJ, May 13, 1830, AJ, LC.

38. AJ to James A. Hamilton, May 18, 1830, JCC to AJ, May 29, 1830, AJ, LC; AJ to JCC, May 30, 1830, JSB, 4:137, 140–41.

39. AK to FPB, October 2, 1830, B-L, PU.; Oliver Dyer, *Great Senators . . . Forty Years Ago . . . Recollections* (New York, 1889), 180–81.

40. AJ to JC, June 14, 1830, JSB, 4:146; Stephen S. Lawrence, "A Franklin Treaty of 1830," *Williamson County Historical Society* (Franklin, TN, 1970), 1:99.

41. AJD to JC, June 17, 21, 1830, AJD, LC.

42. *WNI,* June 17, 1830; John Campbell to David Campbell, June 10, 1830, Campbell Family Papers, DU; *Albany Argus,* June 21, 1830; AJD to JC, June 17, 1830, AJD, LC.

43. *WNI,* July 5, 1830; HC, Jr., to HC, July 12, 1830, *PHC,* 8:234; Battalion Orders No. 5, June 24, 1830, United States Military Academy Archives; James A. Hamilton to AJ, June 27, 1830, AJ, LC; Sylvanus Thayer to Charles Gratiot, June 27, 1830, enclosing June 23, 1830, order.

44. *Albany Argus,* June 28, 30, 1830.

45. Harriet Butler to Benjamin Butler, June 15, 16, 1830, Benjamin F. Butler Papers, New York State Library; AJ to JC, July 9, 1830, JSB, 4:160; JHE to David Campbell, June 10, 1830, Campbell Family Papers, DU; H. Steele to A. C. Flagg, July 5, 1830, Azariah C. Flagg Papers, NYPL; *Nashville National Banner and Nashville Whig,* July 19, 1830; AJ to WBL, June 26, 28, 1830, AJ to JC, July 9, 1830, JSB, 4:156, 157, 160; Stanley F. Horn, *The Hermitage: Home of Old Hickory* (Richmond, 1938), 113.

46. ME to AJ, June 9, June 9, 1830, with appended note by AJD, June 10, 1830, JSB, 4:145–46.

47. AJ to MVB, July 12, 1830, JSB, 4:161; JCMcL to JC, July 16, 21, 1830, JC, TSLA.

48. AJ to JHE, July 19, 1830, AJ to JC, July 20, 1830, JSB, 4:163–65.

49. AJ to WBL, July 21, 28, 1830; JQA, March 3, 1830, 8:197; Anonymous to AJ, August 18, 1830, AJ, SR.

50. AJ to JHE, August 3, 1830, JSB, 4:165–69.

51. Horn, 149–50; ME, 72–73.

52. AJ to WBL, August 15, 1830, AJ, SR; AJ to WBL, August 17, 31, 1830, JSB, 4:173–74, 178–79; ME, 150–53;

53. Henry McRaven, *Nashville, "Athens of the South"* (Chapel Hill, 1949), 43–44; David Grimsted, *Melodrama Unveiled: American Theater and Culture, 1800–1850* (Chicago, 1968), 228–29.

54. Kay Shelburne Trickey, "Small Town Boy Makes Good," *Williamson County Historical Society* (Franklin, TN, 1981), 12:39; *WNI,* August 31, 1830; *Nashville Banner and State Gazette,* August 14, 1830.

55. ME, 163—69. ME also states that the Indians left her a boy to raise, whom she and JHE took care of for three years. In a condescending manner, she describes the young boy's characteristics and how he ran away in Tennessee. This is the only mention of the child here or in any other source.

56. AJ to WBL, August 25, 1830, JSB, 4:176–78; AJ to WBL, August 15, 1830, AJ, SR; AJ to WBL, August 17, 1830, JSB, 4:173–74.

57. AJ to WBL, August 7, 1830, JSB, 4:170; DG to James Hamilton, Jr., August 22, 1830, PJC, 11:219–220.

58. *WNI,* November 1, 1830; *Nashville Banner and State Gazette,* October 6, 1830; DG to James Hamilton, Jr., September 29, 1830, DG, SHC, UNC; AJD to ED, September 7, October 20, 1830, AJD, LC.

59. AJ to Mary Eastin, October 24, 1830, JSB, 4:186–88.

60. DG to Edward Bell (?), October 8, 1830, DG, SHC, UNC; MVB to AJ, July 25, 1830, MVB, LC.

CHAPTER 6: "ONE OF THE MOST BASE AND WICKED CONSPIRACIES"

1. John Campbell to David Campbell, November 6, 1830, Campbell Family Papers, DU; B. W. Richard to John McLean, December 1, 1830, John McLean Papers, LC.

2. Alfred Balch to Nicholas P. Trist, July 30, 1830, Nicholas P. Trist Papers, LC.

3. William C. Carr to Dorcas Carr, December 17, 1830, William C. Carr Papers, Missouri Historical Society.

4. *UST,* December 28, October 27, November 3, 1830; Commissions for Thomas Carberry, James Dunlap, and WON, March 2, 1831, AJ, SR; Charles H. Ambler, ed., *The Life and Diary of John Floyd, Governor of Virginia* (Richmond, 1918), 148.

5. AJD to ED, September 8, 1830, AJ, SR.

6. AJD to AJ, October 25, 1830, JSB, 4:89–91.

7. Ibid.

8. AJ to AJD, October 26(?), 27(?), 1830, AJD to AJ, October 27, 1830, AJ to AJD, October 27(?), 1830, JSB, 4:191–92.

9. Part of a draft of a letter from AJD to AJ, *c.* October 1830, AJ, SR; AJD to AJ, October 30, 1830, JSB, 4:195–96.

10. AJ to AJD, October 30, 1830, AJD to AJ, October 30, 1830, JSB, 4:196–97.

11. Statement of AJD, November 10, 13, 17, 21, 1830, JSB, 4:200–205.

12. AJD to ED, November 20, 1830, JSB, 4:207; ED to AJD, November 30, 1830, AJD, LC.

13. JCMcL to AJD, November 10, 1830, JSB, 4:197.

14. Mary Eastin to AJ, December 5, 1830, AJ, SR; AJ to ED, November 28, 1830, JSB, 4:207–9.

15. AJ to JCMcL, December 25, 1830, AJ to Mary Eastin, January 1, 1831, AJ, SR.

16. Mrs. SDI to ED, November 28, 1830, AJD to ED, December 2, 1830, AJD, LC; JCMcL to AJD, December 24, 1831 [1830], AJD, LC.

17. AJD to ED, January 9, 1831, AJD, LC; AJD to ED, January 15, 1831, AJ to ED, Janu-

ary 20, 1831, JSB, 4:226–27; JC to AJD, February 6, 1831, AJD to ED, February 8, 1831, JC to AJD, February 6, 1831, AJD, LC.

18. AJD to JC, February 21, 1831, AJ to ED, March 10, 1831, AJD, LC.

19. AJ to AJD, March 10, 1831, JSB, 4:248–49.

20. AJ to AJD, March 24, 1831, JSB, 4:251–54; AJD to JB, April 1, 1831, AJD, LC.

21. Robert M. Burton to AJ, October 16, 1830, AJ, LC.

22. AJ to Robert M. Burton, November 6, 1830, AJ, SR.

23. AJ to JC, December 6, 1830, AJ to AJD, November 28, 1830, JSB, 4:211–12, 207–9; James Guinn to AJ, December 18, 1830, AJ, LC.

24. AJD to ED, March 3, 1831, AJD, LC; AJ to AJD, March 24, 1831, JSB, 4:251–54.

25. WTB to Susan, January 2, 1831, typescript, WTB, UVA.

26. Gideon Welles to MVB, December 27, 1831, MVB, LC; AJ to John Rhea, January 4, 1831, Richard R. Stenberg, "A Note on the Jackson-Calhoun Breach of 1830–31," *Tyler's Quarterly Historical and Genealogical Magazine* 21 (October 1939): 65–66; JCC to Samuel Southard, January 28, 1831, JCC, LC; JQA, January 30, 14, 15, 1831, 8:304–6, 274–75, 177.

27. WBL to JO, January 13, 1831, JO, TSLA; *WNI,* January 18, 1831; JQA to Joseph Blunt, January 21, 1831, Andre de Coppet Collection, PU; FG to [?] Washington, January 24, 1831, FG, PU; George M. Dallas to SDI, January 20, 1831, George M. Dallas Papers, HSP.

28. Donald A. Ritchie, *Press Gallery, Congress and the Washington Correspondents* (Cambridge, MA, 1991), 19–20.

29. *DAB;* see also Kenneth L. Smith, "Duff Green and *The United States Telegraph,* 1826–1837," Ph.D. diss., College of William and Mary, 1981.

30. Smith, 47–54, 63–66.

31. AJ to WBL, June 26, 1830, JSB, 4:256; AK to FPB, April 30, 1830, B-L, PU; DG to AJD, July 15, 1830, copy volume, DG, SHC, UNC.

32. AK to FPB, August 22, 1830, B-L, PU; FPB to AJ, August 17, 1830, JSB, 4:174.

33. William E. Smith, "Francis P. Blair, Pen-Executive of Andrew Jackson," *Mississippi Valley Historical Review* 17 (March 1931): 545–47; see also Michael W. Singletary, "The New Editorial Voice for Andrew Jackson: Happenstance or Plan?" *Journalism Quarterly* 53 (Winter 1976): 672–78.

34. Robert V. Remini, *The Life of Andrew Jackson* (New York, 1988), 200.

35. AK to FPB, October 2, 1830, B-L, PU; DG to JCC, November 19, 1830, *PJC,* 11:261–62; AK to Virgil Maxcy, November 12, 1830, AK Misc. Papers, NYPL.

36. *UST,* February 17, 1831; JCC to James H. Hammond, February 16, 1831, in Thomas E. Watson, *The Life and Times of Andrew Jackson* (Thomason, GA, 1912), 338; James A. Hamilton to AJ, February 24, 1831, in James A. Hamilton, *Reminiscences* (New York, 1869), 196.

37. For a sampling of newspaper reaction, see *NR,* March 26, 1831; *UST,* February 17, 1831; *WG,* February 19, 1831.

38. "Jackson's Case Against Calhoun, February, 1831," AJ to AJD, March 24, 1831, JSB, 4:228–36, 251–53. Thomas A. Clay argued that because Calhoun wanted a supporter of his to be secretary of war, he "began to undermine Eaton" early in the administration. "Calhoun's friends immediately avowed their determination not to associate with Eaton's family." Thomas M. Clay, "Two Years with Old Hickory," February 23,

1831," *Atlantic Monthly* 60 (1887): 191. JQA also implicated JHE, charging him with having the conversation with Ringgold during the Monroe-Jackson dinner and then passing along the information to AJ. He said nothing about WBL. JQA, February 18, 1831, 8:320.

39. FG to ? January 24, 1831, FG, SHC, UNC; Joseph H. Parks, *Felix Grundy, Champion of Democracy* (Baton Rouge, 1940), 178–81; JHE to Editor, n.d., *UST,* March 28, 1831; DG to JHE, February 16, 1831, copy volume, DG, SHC, UNC; AJ to AJD, March 24, 1831, JSB, 4: 251–53; Philip Hone, *The Diary of Philip Hone, 1828–1851* (New York, 1936), 36.

40. *NR,* March 26, 1830; J. Watson Webb to MVB, April 3, 1831, MVB, LC; DG to Alexander Hamilton, March 7, 1831, copy volume, DGSHC, UNC; AJ to Charles J. Love, March 7, 1831, JSB, 4:245–46; George Plitt to James Buchanan, March 10, 1831, James Buchanan Papers, LC.

41. DG to Governor Wolfe of Pennsylvania, April 4, 1831, DG, SHC, UNC; see also DG to William Ingalls, April 4, 1831, DG, SHC, UNC and DG to Littleton W. Tazewell, April 4, 1831, Tazewell Family Papers, Virginia State Library and Archives; MVB, *Autobiography,* 395.

CHAPTER 7: "A WANT OF HARMONY"

1. A leading scholar of Jacksonian America emphasizes the fact that MVB and AJ were hardly "political soulmates," in James C. Curtis, "In the Shadow of Old Hickory: The Political Travail of Martin Van Buren," *Journal of the Early Republic* 1 (Fall 1981): 250–53.

2. MVB, *Autobiography,* 402–6.

3. John Waller Barry to Susan Taylor, April 19, 1831, Cheryl Conover, ed., "The Kentuckian in 'King Andrew's Court': The Letters of John Waller Barry," *Register of the Kentucky Historical Society,* 81 (Spring 1983): 173; MVB, *Autobiography,* 407–8; Queena Pollack, *Peggy Eaton* (New York, 1932), 150.

4. JHE to AJ, April 7, 1831, AJ to JHE, April 8, 1831, JSB, 4:257–58.

5. *WNI,* April 7, 11, 1831; *NR,* April 9, 1831; *UST,* April 13, 14, 15, 1831; *WG,* April 9, 1831.

6. MVB to AJ, April 11, 1831, JSB, 4:260–62.

7. AJ to MVB, April 12, 1831, JSB, 4:262–63.

8. SDI to AJ, April 18, 1831, Memorandum in Jackson's Handwriting, April 18, 1831; JMB to AJ, AJ to JMB, JMB to AJ, April 19, 1831, SDI to AJ, April 19, 1831, JSB, 4:263–64, 266, 264–65; SDI to JMB, April 19, 1831, in Richard C. McCrary, Jr., "'The Long Agony is Nearly Over,' Samuel D. Ingham Reports on the Dissolution of Andrew Jackson's First Cabinet," *Pennsylvania Magazine of History and Biography* 100 (April 1976): 235–37.

9. SDI to JMB, April 20, 1831, JMB, SHC, UNC; JMB to SDI, April 27, 1831, SDI, UP.

10. *WG,* April 20, 1831; *UST,* April 20, 1831.

11. John Waller Barry to Susan Taylor, April 19, 1831, in Conover, 172; Charles Vaughan to Lord Palmerston, April 21, 1831, in Pollack, 129–30; *UST,* April 22, 1831; *USG,* April 26, 1831; Robert V. Remini, *Andrew Jackson and the Course of American Freedom* (New York, 1981), 316.

12. *Washington National Journal,* July 26, 1831; *Albany Evening Journal,* April 23, 1831; *New*

York Courier and Enquirer, in *UST,* April 30, 1831; *Rhode Island American and Gazette,* April 23, 1831; *Boston Advertiser,* April 28, 1831.

13. *New Hampshire Journal,* May 2, 1831; *NR* in *WNI,* May 3, 1831; *Rhode Island American and Gazette,* April 27, 1831; *Middlesex Gazette,* n.d., in John R. Irelan, *A History of the Life, Administration and Times of Martin Van Buren, Eighth President of the United States* (Chicago, 1887), 151.

14. Research notes of James A. Newton, Lincoln-Sudbury Regional High School, Sudbury, MA, in author's possession; James Barber, *Andrew Jackson: A Portrait Study* (Washington, DC, 1991), 155–56; JQA, 8:359–60; *Baltimore Patriot and Mercantile Advertiser,* April 25, 1831.

15. AJ to JC, April 24, 1831, JSB, 4:268–69; AJ to Samuel Jackson Hays, April 23, 1831, AJ to Hardy M. Cryer, April 25, 1831, AJ, SR.

16. HC to Francis Brooke, May 1, 1831, Calvin Colton, ed., *Private Correspondence of Henry Clay* (Cincinnati, 1856), 299–301; HC to Peter B. Porter, May 14, 1831, Peter B. Porter Papers, Buffalo and Erie County Historical Society; Clement Eaton, *Henry Clay and the Art of American Politcs* (Boston, 1957), 167.

17. Charles H. Ambler, *The Life and Diary of John Floyd, Governor of Virginia* (Richmond, 1908), 148; George Watterston, "Notes on United States History 1825–1849," George Watterston Papers, LC.

18. John Waller Barry to Susan Taylor, April 19, 1831, in Conover, 173.

19. JMB to SDI, May 20, 1831, SDI, UP; *WNI,* May 18, 1831; SDI, to JMB, May 7, 1831, JMB, SHC UNC.

20. *NR,* June 11, 1831; Francis Scott Key to Roger B. Taney, June 14, 1831, "Letters of Francis Scott Key . . ." *Maryland Historical Magazine* 5 (March 1910): 24–25; JMB to AJ, June 15, 1831, in James Parton, *The Life of Andrew Jackson.* 3 vols. (New York, 1861), 3:356–57.

21. JB to AJD, May 8, 1831, JSB, 4:279–80; Joseph White et al. to JB, May 10, 1831, Branch Family Papers, SHC, UNC.

22. *Raleigh Star,* May 11, 1831; JB to AJ, May 12, 1831, JSB, 4:279; SDI to JMB, May 7, 1831, in McCrary, 241; *American Statesman* (Salem, NJ), n.d. in *WG,* May 15, 1831; JMB to SDI, May 20, 1831, SDI, UP; AJD to JB, May 21, 1831, AJD, LC; AJ to ED, May 25, 1831, AJ, SR; AJ to JC, May 26, 1831, JSB, 4:285.

23. *WG,* June 4, 1831; JB to AJD, June 10, 1831, AJD to JB, June 15, 1831, AJD, LC; AJD to JB, June 18, 27, 1831, AJD, LC.

24. DG to Littleton W. Tazewell, April 4, 1831, Tazewell Family Papers, Virginia State Library and Archives; AJ to SDI, April 22, 1831, AJ, LC; SDI to JMB, May 4, 1831 in McCrary, 239; SDI to Editor, May 6, 1831, *NR,* May 28, 1831.

25. *New York Journal of Commerce,* June 3, 4, 1831, in *Boston Advertiser,* June 11, 1831, and *USG,* June 10, 1831; *WG,* June 13, 1831; *UST,* June 14, 1831.

26. *Washington National Journal,* June 17, 1831; AK to Gideon Welles, June 20, 1831, Gideon Welles Papers, LC; JHE to JMB, June 17, 1831, JMB, Georgia Historical Society; JHE to SDI, June 17, 1831, in Parton, 3:364–65.

27. AJD to JB, June 27, 1831, AJD, LC; JMB to JHE, June 18, 1831, JHE to JMB, June 22, 1831, JMB to JHE, June 23, 1831, *NR,* July 30, 1831; JMB to SDI, June 25, 1831, SDI, UP.

28. SDI to JHE, JHE to SDI, June 18, 1831, in Parton, 3:365.

29. SDI to JHE, JHE to SDI, June 20, 1831, in Parton, 3:366; SDI to AJ, June 20, 1831, AJ, SR. Randolph said the encounter was completely civil. P. G. Randolph to Editor of *Globe*, June 23, 1831, in *WG*, June 24, 1831.

30. ME, 156–59; SDI to AJ, June 21, 1831, JSB, 4:300–301; DG to John Floyd, June 21, 1831, copy volume, DG, SHC, UNC; M. W. Richards to John McLean, June 24, 1831, John McLean Papers, LC; *UST*, June 21, 1831; *WG*, June 22, 1831.

31. JQA, June 27, 1831, 8:372; AJ to JCMcL, June 27, 1831, JSB, 4:305; AJ to R. G. Dunlop, July 18, 1831, AJ, SR; AJ to JC, Thomas L. Smith, Philip G. Randolph, and WLB, June 22, 1831, JSB, 4:300–301; JC to AJ, WLB to AJ, Randolph to AJ, T. L. Smith to AJ, June 22, 1831, *NR*, June 25, 1831; JHE to FPB, June 23, 1831 in *WG*, June 24, 1831.

32. AJ to SDI, AJ to MVB, AJ to AJD, June 23, 1831, JSB, 4:301–3; AK to Editor of *WG*, July 16, 1831, in *WNI*, July, 21, 1831; Nicholas P. Trist to SDI, July 7, 1831, SDI, PU; SDI to AJ, June 30, 1831, AJ, LC; *Baltimore Patriot and Mercantile Advertiser*, August 3, 1831.

33. *Doylestown Democrat*, n.d., in *NR*, July 9, 1831. Alexis de Tocqueville writes that Ingham "claimed" that AJ "was in love" with ME, Alexis de Tocqueville, *Journey to America* (New York, 1971), 199.

34. Philip S. Klein, *Pennsylvania Politics, 1817–1837; a Game Without Rules* (Philadelphia, 1940), 320; *UST*, June 24, 25, 1831; *USG*, June 24, 1831; *Rhode Island American and Gazette*, June 25, 1831; John Sargent to HC, June 27, 1831, *PHC* 8:368; ESE to SDI, June 27, 1831, SDI, UP; WBL to AJ, June 27, 1831, AJ, SR.

35. AK to Isaac Hill, July 15, 1831, Isaac Hill Papers, New Hampshire Historical Society; Alfred Balch to AJ, May 7, 1831, AJ, LC; *Baltimore Patriot and Mercantile Advertiser*, May 21, 1831; *Richmond Enquirer*, n.d., in *Vermont Patriot and State Gazette*, June 13, 1831; D. Bradley to John McLean, June 7, 1831, John McLean Papers, LC; *WG*, June 13, 1831.

36. George Watterston, "Notes on United States History 1825–1849," George Watterston Papers, LC; *Washington National Journal*, June 21, 1831.

37. AJ to R. G. Dunlap, July 18, 1831, AJ, SR; *Richmond Enquirer*, n.d. in *NR*, May 7, 1831; AJD to JC, May 20, 1831, AJD, LC; SDI to JMB, April 19, 1831, May 7, 1831, in McCrary, 236, 241; FPB to John J. Crittenden, June 10, 1831, John J. Crittenden Papers, LC.

38. AJ to AJD, April 19, 1831, JSB, 4:265–66; AJ to AJD, April 20, 1831, AJ, SR; JC to AJ, April 28, 1831, JSB, 4:270–71; JCMcL to AJD, May 1, 1831, AJD to ED, May 4, 1831, AJD, LC.

39. AJ to AJD, May 5, 1831, JSB, 4:273–78; AJ to Mary Eastin, May 10, 1831, AJ to Hardy M. Cryer, May 10, 1831, AJ, SR.

40. AJD to ED, May 17, 1831, AJD to JC, May 20, 1831, AJD, LC.

41. AJD to ED, May 21, 1831, AJD, LC; AJ to Hardy M. Cryer, May 20, 1831, Misc. Files, THS, TSLA; AJ to ED, May 25, 1831, AJD, LC; AJD to ED, May 25, 1831, AJD, LC; AJ to JC, May 26, 1831, JSB, 4:285.

42. AJD to JB, May 21, 29, June 15, 1831, AJD, LC.

43. AJD to ED, June 16, 1831, AJD to AJ, June 18, 1831, JSB, 4:296–97; AJD to JB, June 16, 18, 1831, AJD, LC.

44. A good brief synopsis of this long and detailed argument appears in JQA, July 26,

1831, 8:387–88; *WG,* July 19, 1831, is a good example of the back-and-forth argument between the *WG* and the *UST;* Young Hickory to Editor, n.d. in *WG,* July 23, 1831; JHE to JMB, July 28, 1831, JMB to JHE, July 29, 1831, JMB, Georgia Historical Society; *UST,* August 2, 1831.

CHAPTER 8: "THEY SHALL NOT DRIVE ME FROM MY GROUND"

1. AJ to Mary Eastin, July 8, 1831, AJ, SR.
2. DG to SDI, July 4, 1831, SDI, UP; *Baltimore Patriot and Mercantile Advertiser,* July 16, 1831; *Harrisburg Reporter,* n.d., in *WG* July 26, 1831; JHE to JC, July 27, 1831, JC, TSLA.
3. JHE to FPB, July 5, 1831, B-L, PU; Arthur Campbell to David Campbell, September 2, 1831, Campbell Family Papers, DU; AJ to Robert Livingston, July 8, 1831, JSB, 4:309; JHE to William A. Davis et al., July 12, 1831, *WG,* July 22, 1831.
4. *Baltimore Patriot and Mercantile Advertiser,* August 2, 1831; *Rhode Island American and Gazette,* August 9, 1831; Willie Blount to AJ, September [?], 1831, AJ, LC.
5. *WG,* August 20, 1831.
6. MBS to Jane Bayard Kirkpatrick, August 29, 1831, MBS, LC;
7. MBS to Mrs. Samuel Boyd, August 29, 1831, MBS, 319–21.
8. Queena Pollack, *Peggy Eaton* (New York, 1932), 167; Edward Channing, *A History of the United States.* 6 vols. (New York, 1912–1925), 5:388; Alfred Balch to AJ, July 21, 1831, JSB, 4:314–16.
9. AJ to Mary Eastin, July 8, 1831, AJ, SR; AJ to AJD, July 10, 1831, JSB, 4:310–11
10. AJ to AJD, July 11, 1831, JSB, 4:311–12.
11. JCMcL to JC, July 29, 1831, JC, TSLA; JCMcL and John Bell to AJ, July 29, 1831, JSB, 4:323; JC to AJD, August 8, 1831, JC, TSLA; Alfred Balch to Nicholas P. Trist, August 13, 1831, Nicholas P. Trist Papers, LC.
12. AJ to MVB, September 5, 1831, AJ, LC; Alfred Balch to AJ, September 14, 1831, AJ, LC.
13. AJD to ?, October 20, 1831; AJD to JC, October 4, 1831, AJD, LC.
14. AK to Gideon Welles, August 1, 1831, Gideon Welles Papers, LC; Louis McLane to MVB, September 6, 1831, MVB, LC; AJ to MVB, September 5, 1831, JSB, 4:346.
15. JHE to JC, September 5, 1831, JC, TSLA.
16. *Rhode Island American and Gazette,* September 9, 1831; AK to Gideon Welles, September 12, 1831, Gideon Welles Papers, LC; AJ to JO, September 13, 1831, John Samuel Claybrook Papers, TSLA..
17. *WG,* September 15, 1831. A copy of the pamphlet is available in TSLA and the Buffalo and Erie County Historical Society, with the added words: "in reply to Messrs. Ingham, Berrien, Branch, on the dissolution of the cabinet."
18. AJ to MVB, September 18, 1831, JSB, 4:350.
19. *New York Standard,* n.d. in *WG,* September 23, 1831; *Nashville Whig,* n.d., in *WG,* October 13, 1831; *People's Advocate (CT),* n.d. *WG,* October 6, 1831.
20. *Baltimore Patriot and Mercantile Advertiser,* September 16, 1831; *Connecticut Journal,* September 23, 1831; *Rhode Island American and Gazette,* September 23, 20, 1831; *UST,*

September 28 to October 6, 8, 18, 1831; verification that JHE endorsed a loan of $3,000 for DG on May 20, 1826, JSB, 3:301–2.

21. William Carroll to AJ, September 27, 1831, JSB, 6:509; Robert M. Burton to AJ, October 5, 1831, AJ, LC; Stockley Donelson to AJD, September 28, 1831, Kenneth Thomas Collection, TSLA; AJD to Sir, September 17, 1831, AJD, LC.

22. Louis McLane to MVB, September 17, 1831, MVB, LC; MVB to AJ, October 11, 1831, JSB, 4:354–59.

23. *WNI*, September 24, 1831; *Rhode Island American and Gazette*, September 30, 1831; R. E. W. Earle to JO, December 25, 1831, quoted in Frances Clifton, "John Overton as Andrew Jackson's Friend," *THQ* 11 (March 1952): 35; *Boston Advertiser*, September 30, 1831; JHE to FPB, September 24, 1831, JHE to AK, September 20, 1831, B-L, PU.

24. JCC to SDI, May 4, 1831, *PJC*, 11:377–79.

25. AJ to JC, May 29, 1831, JSB, 4:286; Alfred Balch to AJ, *c.* June 25, 1831, AJ, SR; AJ to AJD, July 10, 1831, JSB, 4:311; JCC to Virgil Maxcy, August 1, 1831, Galloway, Maxcy, Markoe Papers, LC.

26. JCC, "Reply to John H. Eaton's Address," *Pendleton (SC) Messenger*, October 19, 1831, *PJC*, 11:474–81.

27. JCC to Bolling White, October 19, 1831, *PJC*, 11:474–83.

28. *UST*, October 28, 1831; *WG*, November 1, 1831; *UST*, November 4, 1831. According to one of his biographers, JCC published his statement as "a matter of honor." "He responded rhetorically, at the risk of political death," since a duel was an impossibility. Irving Bartlett, *John C. Calhoun: A Biography* (New York, 1993), 174–75.

29. *UST*, October 7, 1831.

30. Walter H. Overton to JO, December 21, 1831, quoted in Clifton, 34.

31. Felix A. Nigro, "The Van Buren Confirmation Before the Senate," *Western Political Quarterly* 14 (March 1961): 148–59; JCC, "Speech on the Force Bill [in Senate]" February 15, 1833, *PJC*, 12:60; JCC, "Remarks on the State of the Currency [in Senate]," *PJC*, 13:141.

Chapter 9: "An Influential Personage Now"

1. Paul H. Bergeron, "Tennessee's Response to the Nullification Process," *Journal of Southern History* 39 (February 1973): 24–25; Richard P. McCormick, *The Second American Party System: Party Formation in the Jacksonian Era* (Chapel Hill, 1966), 227.

2. Eugene I. McCormac, *James K. Polk: A Political Biography* (Berkeley, 1922), 62–91.

3. McCormick, 227; Charles G. Sellers, *James K. Polk, Jacksonian*. 2 vols. (Princeton, 1957), 1:137–41; DG to John D. Logan, October 12, 1831, copy volume, DG, SHC, UNC.

4. Thomas P. Abernethy, "The Origin of the Whig Party in Tennessee," *Mississippi Valley Historical Review* 12 (March 1926): 507–8.

5. AJ to HLW, April 9, 1831, JSB, 4:258–60, 296n.

6. HLW to AJ, April 20, 1831, JSB, 4:267–68.

7. John Spencer Bassett, *The Life of Andrew Jackson* (New York, 1931), 537.

8. D. Bradley to John McLean, June 7, 1831, John McLean Papers, LC; Bassett, 538; Richard E. Ellis, *The Union at Risk; Jacksonian Democracy, States' Rights, and the Nullification Crisis* (New York, 1987), 69; AJ to Hardy M. Cryer, April 25, 1831, AJ, SR; J.

Gwin to FG, May 25, 1831, FG, SHC, UNC; AJ to Robert M. Burton, October 19, 1831, AJ, SR.

9. Mr. Hill to John McLean, May 7, 1831, John McLean Papers, LC; R. G. Dunlop to AJ, June 30, 1831, AJ, SR; Alfred Balch to AJ, May 7, 1831, AJ, LC; Alfred Balch to AJ, July 21, 1831, JSB, 4:314–16; AJ to JO, September 16, 1831, AJ, SR.

10. AJ to MVB, September 18, 1831, JSB, 4:350–51; JHE to AK, September 20, 24, 1831, B-L, PU; AJ to JC, October 3, 1831, JSB, 4:353; AJD to ED, September 27, 1831, AJD, LC.

11. JCMcL to AJD, November 9, 1831, AJD, LC; JSB, 4:374n; Bassett, 530–31; *WG*, November 15, 1831.

12. *Western Weekly Review* [Franklin, TN], November 18, 1831.

13. AJ to MVB, November 14, 1831, JSB, 4:374–75; JCMcL to AJD, November 9, 1831, JSB, 4:374n; William Carroll to AJ, November 13, 1831, JSB, 4:372–73; *WG*, November 15, 1831.

14. RMJ to FG, May 12, 1831, Correspondence by Author Collection, TSLA; FG to JHE, May 12, 1831, FG, SHC, UNC; Robert M. Burton to AJ, October 5, 1831, AJ, LC; WBL to David Campbell, November 3, 1831, Campbell Family Papers, DU.

15. AJ to JC, November 21, 1831, JSB, 4:377; JHE to AJ March 13, 1832, JSB, 4:418; *Proceedings of a Convention of Republican Delegates . . .* (Baltimore, 1832); PE to JO, July 23, 1832, John Samuel Claybrooke and JO Papers, TSLA; JHE to J. Johnston, December 29, 1832, Misc. Manuscripts, LC; JHE to Hardy M. Cryer, April 10, 1833, THS Misc. Files, TSLA.

16. George Childress to Dixon Allen, August 4, 1832, Campbell Family Papers, DU; William Richard Caswell to George Gillespie, September 5, 1832, William Richard Caswell Papers, SHC, UNC; Lunsford P. Yandell to Susan Yandell, September 17, 1832, Yandell Family Papers, Filson Club Historical Society; JCMcL to AJ, September 25, 1832, AJ to JCMcL, September 28, 1832, AJ to David Burford, September 10, 1831, AJ "To a Committee," September (?) 1832, JSB, 4:473–79.

17. Henry McRaven, *Nashville, "Athens of the South"* (Chapel Hill, 1949), 64; Arda S. Walker, "John Henry Eaton, Apostate," *East Tennessee Historical Society Publications* 24 (1952): 35.

18. D. Hubbard to "Dear Sir," May 9, 1833, Brown-Ewell Papers, Filson Club Historical Society.

19. W. A. Wade to William B. Campbell, October 2, 1833, Campbell Family Papers, DU; John P. Harrison to FPB, October 8, 1833, Correspondence by Author Collection, TSLA; Walker, 35; Stanley J. Folmsbee, Robert E. Corles, and Enoch L. Mitchell, *History of Tennessee.* 4 vols. (New York, 1960), 1:313–15, 341.

20. William B. Campbell to David Campbell, November 15, 1833, John Campbell to William B. Campbell, November 22, 1833, Campbell Family Papers, DU; E. K. Kane to MVB, January 2, 1833, MVB, LC, in Walker, 36; WBL to JO, December 2, 1832, JO, THS, TSLA.

21. AJ to Sarah [*sic*], April 30, 1832, AJ, LC.

22. MVB, *Autobiography,* 364; United States Department of State, *The Territorial Papers of the United States,* vol. 25, *The Territory of Florida,* Clarence E. Carter, ed. (Washington, DC, 1960), 3(?); John Waller Barry to his sister, June 4, 1834, Cheryl Conover,

ed., "'To Please Papa.' The Letters of John Waller Barry, West Point Cadet, 1826–1830," *Register of the Kentucky Historical Society* 80 (1982): 180.

23. WBL to AJ, July 25, 1834, JSB, 5:276; FPB to AJ, August 18, 1834, JSB, 5:284; Conover, 186; AJ to John D. Coffee, December 24, 1834, JSB, 5:314–15.

24. There is no adequate study of JHE's Florida governorship or ME's life there. A superficial treatment is Gene Burnett, "Peg Eaton, Florida's Femme Fatale," *Florida Trend* (February 1977): 71–73; See also William Warren Rogers, "Peggy O'Neil, Tallahassee's Most Notorious Woman," *Springtime Tallahassee Official Program* (1982): 35; John Lee Williams, *The Territory of Florida* (New York, 1837), 121–22; Rowland H. Rerick, *Memoirs of Florida.* 2 vols. F. P. Fleming, ed. (Atlanta, 1902), 1:133n.

25. Ellen Call Long, *Florida Breezes; or, Florida, New and Old,* (Gainesville, 1962), 76; John Lee Williams, *A View of West Florida* (Gainesville, 1976), 71; J. E. Dovell, "The Gorgeous Hussy of Tallahassee," Vertical File, State Library of Florida. According to this typewritten manuscript, "despite the chitchat that preceded her, precious little is known about Peggy Eaton's short reign as the hostess in the governor's mansion in Tallahassee."

26. "Diary of Robert Raymond Reid 1833–1835," 2 vols. Transcript by Historical Records Survey, WPA, 1939, 1:1 quoted in Herbert J. Doherty, Jr., *Richard Keith Call, Southern Unionist* (Gainesville, 1961), 83; Charlton W. Tebeau, Jr., *A History of Florida* (Coral Gables, 1971), 122, 148, 145; Caroline Mays Brevard, *A History of Florida.* 2 vols. James Alexander Robertson, ed. (Deland, FL, 1925), 1:121.

27. Thomas A McMullen and David Walker, *Biographical Directory of American Territorial Governors* (Westport, CT, 1984), 99–101; Doherty, 82; Margaret Lowrie Chapman, Introduction to Long, xiii; Dorothy Clifford, "The Controversial 'Gorgeous Hussy,'" *Tallahassee Democrat,* March 31, 1974, Vertical File, State Library of Florida.

28. Williams, *Territory,* 122–23; Dovell, 272–73; Frederick W. Dau, *Florida, Old and New* (New York, 1934), 196; Long, 105; Rogers, 33, 35; Rerick, 1:178.

29. Gene M. Burnett, *Florida's Past, People and Events That Shaped the State* (Englewood, FL, 1986), 124; Rogers, 35; Brevard, 1:120.

30. Williams, *View,* 78–79; Brevard, 1:121.

31. Queena Pollack, *Peggy Eaton* (New York, 1932) 193, 194–95; AK, *The Autobiography of Amos Kendall* (Boston, 1872), 351–57; AJ to AK, July 19, 1835, JSB, 5: 356–57, 356n; Doherty, 83.

32. ME, 172.

33. Ibid., 172–73.

34. John K. Mahon, *History of the Second Seminole War, 1835–1842* (Gainesville, 1967), 89, 94, 122; JHE to Lewis Cass, January 9, 1836, JHE to Winfield Scott, February 3, 1836, JHE to MVB, February 24, 1836, in *American State Papers, Military Affairs* (Washington, DC, 1861), 7:219, 229, 252.

35. JHE to AJ, April 10, 12, 1836, U.S. Department of State, *The Territory of Florida* 25:269, 272–73; Mahon, 154; Rogers, 35.

36. ME, 174.

37. Ibid., 174–75; Richard Rush to AJ, September 26, 1836, AJ, SR.

38. Francis F. Wayland, *Andrew Stevenson, Democrat and Diplomat, 1785–1857* (Philadelphia, 1949), 170; ME, 175–76.

39. ME, 176–81.

40. Ibid., 181–82; Pollack, 201.

41. Edgar Holt, *The Carlist War in Spain* (London, 1967), 27; Robert Sencourt, *The Spanish Crown 1808–1931; An Intimate Chronicle of a Hundred Years* (New York, 1932), 130–31.

42. Sencourt, 132; Holt, 28.

43. Holt, 35; Frances Gribble, *The Tragedy of Isabella II* (Boston, 1913), 30; Sencourt, 151–81.

44. ME, 186–87.

45. An intimate friendship is imaginatively sketched in Leon Phillips, *That Eaton Woman: In Defense of Peggy O'Neale Eaton* (Barre, MA, 1974), 145–50.

46. ME, 188–91.

47. Ibid., 191–92.

48. Ibid., 192–94. Actually, Isabella suffered from a skin disease that one author has called ichthyosis, which caused her to have dry, scaly skin. Holt, 198.

49. Francis Hillery to Mrs. Louis McLane, October 29, 1836, John A Munroe, ed., "Mrs. (Louis) McLane's Colored Boy and Peggy O'Neale," *Delaware History* 10 (1963): 365–66.

50. C. P. Van Ness to MVB, February 10, 1837, and March 2, 1837, postscript, MVB, LC.

51. JHE to Isaac Hull, February 7, 1840, JHE, Misc. Documents, LC.

52. JHE to John Forsyth, May 6, April 27, 1837, Correspondence of American Secretaries of State, John Forsyth Papers, NARS, in Walker, 37–38; AJ to MVB, June 6, 1837, JSB, 5:489.

53. JHE to John Forsyth, August 10, 1837, November 2, 1839, Correspondence of American Secretaries of State, John Forsyth Papers, NARS, in Walker, 38–39.

54. JHE to John Forsyth, May 12, December 27, 1838, March 21, 1840, John Forsyth to JHE, August 4, 1837, October 12, 1839, Diplomatic Instructions of the Department of State, NARS, in Walker, 39–40.

55. ME, 195–96.

56. Ibid., 196–200.

57. JHE to MVB, April 18, 1840, MVB, LC; AJ to AK, April 16, 1840, JSB, 6:159; JHE to Andrew Stevenson, July 31, 1840, Stevenson Family Papers, LC.

58. ME, 201–2; AJ to AK, May 15, 1841, AJ to Andrew J. Hutchings, September 7, 1840, JSB, 6:113, 74–75; MVB, *Autobiography,* 365; AJ to AJD, October 8, 1840, JSB, 6:80.

59. *Washington Star,* June 23, 1935; WON's Last Will and Testament [1837], Records of the U.S. District Court, D.C., RG 21, NARS.

60. ME, 202–3; WBL to his daughter, April 2, 1846, WBL Manuscripts, NYPL, in Walker, 43.

61. Inventory of Personal Estate of JHE, and "Additional Inventory," JHE, Case No. 3784, R.G. 21, NARS; Walker, 42; JHE to AJD, May 13, 1847, November 10, 1850, December 25, 1853, AJD, LC; AK, *Autobiography,* 350–57, in Walker, 42.

62. JHE to E. H. Foster, June 27, 1841, Mary Ludwig Suydon Collection, HSP; Invitation, January 9, 1843, Willie Magnum Papers, DU; Arthur Campbell to David Campbell, October 11, 1842, Campbell Family Papers, DU; ME, 202–3; *WP,* November 10, 1879.

63. JHE to James K. Polk, March 12, 1845, James K. Polk Papers, LC; ME, 63–64; *WP,* November 10, 1879.

64. The best description of AJ's death may be found in Robert V. Remini, "The Final Days and Hours in the Life of General Andrew Jackson," *THQ* 39 (Summer 1980): 167–77, and in chap. 33, "We Will All Meet in Heaven," in Remini's *Andrew Jackson and the Course of American Democracy, 1833–1845* (New York, 1984).

65. John Timberlake File, Navy Widow 1186, Old War Pensions, RG 15, NARS.

66. Copy of Williamson County, Tennessee, Will Book 1842–1847, p. 110, in AJ, TSLA; Transcript of Wills Probated 1801–1888, 7:402, Records of the U.S. District Court, District of Columbia, RG 21, NARS.

67. Pollack, 219–20; Tom A. Dozier, "She Met Real Peggy Eaton," *Nashville Banner*, September 27, 1936, AJ, TSLA; W. A. Swanberg, *Sickles the Incredible* (New York, 1956), 40–56.

68. Pollack, 224–25.

69. In her memoirs, ME wrote that JHE died in 1859, 204.

70. *NYT*, September 18, 1856; Estate of JHE, Case No. 3784, Records of the U.S. District Court, District of Columbia, RG 21, NARS.

Chapter 10: "They Are Now Her Neighbors"

1. *NYT*, September 12, 1868; *Washington National Republican*, November 10, 1879.

2. *NYT*, September 12, 1868; ME, 206; F. A. Dickins to H. P. Randolph, June 9, 1859, F. A. Dickins Papers, SHC, UNC. Buchignani's age is variously given, but he clearly was in his early twenties. *Louisville Courier-Journal*, n.d., in Toner Collection, No. 1, Rarebook Room, LC; Margaret Buchignani to Margaret Randolph Dickins, August 27, 1859, F. A. Dickins Papers, SHC, UNC.

3. ME, 206; Queena Pollack, *Peggy Eaton* (New York, 1932) 240–41, 243.

4. Pollack, 246; *NYT*, September 12, 1868; Albion K. Parris, "Recollections of Our Neighbors in the First Ward in the Early Sixties," *RCHS* 29/30 (1928): 275; *New York World*, September 20, 1868.

5. ME to F. A. Dickins, undated but received March 19, 1859, copy, Randolph and Nicholas Papers, UVA; Louis E. Harvie to Margaret Randolph Dickins, September 2, 10, 1859, F. A. Dickins Papers, SHC, UNC.

6. *NYT*, September 12, 1868.

7. Ibid.

8. Unnamed, undated newspaper clipping, in Toner Collection; *NYT*, September 12, 1858.

9. *NYT*, September 12, 1858; Pollack, 258; ME, 207; *Columbus Alexander v. Margaret Buchignani* et al., No. 801, Equity Docket, Filed on October 23, 1866, Records of the U.S. District Court, District of Columbia, RG 21, NARS; Gabriella (Chaan) de Potestad to Margaret Randolph Dickins, July 27, 1869, F. A. Dickins Papers, SHC, UNC.

10. *New York Herald*, September 11, 16, 1868; *NYT*, September 12, 1868; Pollack, 259–61; *Philadelphia Press*, November 10, 1879; Allen E. Clark, "Margaret Eaton (Peggy O'Neale)," *RCHS*, 44–45 (1942–1943): 25; *Washington Sunday Capital*, March 29, 1874.

11. ME, 204; Harriet A. Weed and Thurlow Weed Barnes, *The Life of Thurlow Weed.* 2 vols. (Boston, 1883), 1:364; *Atlanta Constitution*, n.d., in Toner Collection. Virginia de

Sampayo was still a resident of Paris in 1886; her daughter was separated from a Prince Caracciolo, whom she had married ten to twelve years previously. Jules Boufue to John B. Randolph, May 18, 1886, Allen C. Clark Papers, HSW.

12. Mary S. Lockwood, *Historic Houses in Washington, Its Noted Men and Women* (New York, 1889), 79; Augustus Buell, *History of Andrew Jackson.* 2 vols. (New York, 1904), 2:253n; *WP,* in *Nashville Daily American,* February 9, 1878, Vertical File, State Library of Florida; *Washington National Republican,* n.d., in Toner Collection; *Washington Sunday Capital,* March 29, 1874.

13. Byron Sunderland, "Washington as I First Knew It," *RCHS* 5 (1902): 203; ME, 211; *Washington Star,* September 18, 1921; Tom A. Dozier, "She Met Real Peggy Eaton," *Nashville Banner,* September 27, 1936. In the Special Collections Department, Mitchell Memorial Library, Mississippi State University, there is a book by DG, personally inscribed to the Reverend Deems; their relationship is unknown. DG, *Facts & Suggestions, Biographical, Historical, Financial, and Political . . .* (New York, 1866).

14. Pollack, 277.

15. *Boston Herald,* n.d., in Toner Collection; Pollack, 277–78; Washington *Sunday Star,* June 23, 1935.

16. *NYT,* November 12, 1879; *Washington Star,* June 23, 1935; Clark, 29; H. D. Appleby to James B. Whitfield, February 8, 1946, Peggy Eaton Vertical File, State Library of Florida; *WP,* November 10, 1879; *Washington Star,* May 4, 1901.

Bibliography

MANUSCRIPTS

Buffalo and Erie County Historical Society: Porter, Peter B.
Columbia University, Rare Books and Manuscripts, Library: Clinton, De Witt.
Detroit Public Library, Burton Historical Collection: Mason, John.
Duke University, Special Collections Department, William R. Perkins Library: Agg, John;
    Campbell Family; Eaton, John Henry; Ingham, Samuel D.; Troup, George Michael.
Filson Club Historical Society, Louisville: Brown-Ewell; Yandell Family.
Florida, State Library of, Tallahassee: Vertical File.
Georgia Historical Society, Savannah: Berrien, John M.
Historical Society of Pennsylvania, Philadelphia: Buchanan, James; Chase, Salmon P.;
    Dallas, George M.; Gratz; Presidential Candidates; Suydon, Mary Ludwig.
Historical Society of Washington, D.C.: Bradley, Abraham III; Clark, Allen C.; Dudley,
    Blandina.
Library of Congress: Berrien, John M.; Biddle, Nicholas; Blair Family; Calhoun, John C.;
    Chase, Salmon P.; Crawford, William H.; Crittenden, John J.; Donelson, Andrew
    Jackson; Eaton, John Henry; Eaton, Margaret O'Neale; Galloway-Maxcy-Markoe;
    Jackson, Andrew; McLean, John; Mordecai, Alfred; Patterson, Daniel T. (Naval His-
    torical Foundation); Polk, James K; Shriner, Michael; Smith, Margaret Bayard;
    Stevenson Family; Toner; Trist, Nicholas P.; Van Buren, Martin; Watterston, George;
    Webster, Daniel; Welles, Gideon.
Maryland Historical Society, Baltimore: Wirt, William.
Massachusetts Historical Society, Boston: Everett, Edward; Everett-Hopkins.
Missouri Historical Society, St. Louis: Carr, William C.
National Archives and Record Center, Washington, D.C.: Record Groups 15, 21; Micro-
    film 688.
New Hampshire Historical Society, Concord: Hill, Isaac.
New Jersey Department of State, Division of Archives and Record Management, Trenton:
    Will and Probate Records.
New York Historical Society: Eaton, Margaret; Gallatin, Albert; Jackson, Andrew.
New York Public Library, Astor, Lenox, Tilden Foundations, Rare Books and Manuscripts
    Division: Bailey, Theodorus; Jackson-Lewis (Ford); Van Cortlandt, Pierre.
New York State Library, Albany: Butler, Benjamin F.; Clinton, George.

Ohio Historical Society, Columbus: Hammond, Charles.
Pennsylvania, University of, Library: Ingham, Samuel D.
Princeton University Library: Blair-Lee; de Coppet, Andre.
Scholarly Resources (microfilm): Jackson, Andrew.
Southern Historical Collection, University of North Carolina, Chapel Hill: Berrien, John
    M.; Branch Family; Caruthers, Robert L.; Caswell, William Richard; Dickens, Fran-
    cis Asbury; Green, Duff; Grundy, Felix; Hamilton, James, Jr.; Polk, Lucius J.
Tennessee State Library and Archives, Nashville: By Author; Campbell, David; Clay-
    brooke, John Samuel-Overton; John; Coffee, John-Dyas; Hurja, Emil; Horn, Stanley
    F; Jackson, Andrew; Johnson, Richard M.; Overton, John (Murdock); Tennessee
    Historical Society, Miscellaneous Files; Thomas, Kenneth.
United States Military Academy Archives: O'Neale and Eaton material.
University Publications of America (microfilm): Chase, Salmon P.
Virginia Historical Society, Richmond: Bates, Edward; Sergeant, John.
Virginia State Library and Archives, Richmond: Tazewell Family
Virginia, University of, Special Collections Department, Alderman Library: Barry,
    William T.; Griswold Family; Randolph and Nicholas.

NEWSPAPERS

Albany Argus, 1828–1832.
Albany Evening Journal, 1830–1832.
Arkansas Gazette [Little Rock], 1831.
Baltimore Patriot and Mercantile Advertiser, 1828–1832.
Berkshire Journal [Lenox, MA], 1829–1831.
Boston Advertiser, 1831.
Connecticut Journal [Hartford], 1831.
Eastern Argus [Portland, ME], 1831.
Forney's Sunday Morning Chronicle [Washington, DC], November 9, 16, 1879.
Nashville Banner, September 27, 1936.
Nashville Banner and State Gazette, 1830.
Nashville National Banner and Nashville Whig, 1829–1831.
New York Enquirer, 1829.
New York Herald, September 11, 16, 1868.
New York Journal of Commerce, 1831.
New York Times, September 12, 1868.
New York World, September 20, 1868.
Niles' Weekly Register [Baltimore], 1828–1832.
Philadelphia Press, November 10–13, 1879.
Rhode Island American and Gazette [Providence], 1829–1831.
United States Gazette [Philadelphia], 1831.
United States Telegraph [Washington, DC], 1828–1832.
Washington Daily Journal, 1829–1831.
Washington Gazette, 1796, 1797.
Washington Globe, 1831.
Washington National Intelligencer, 1801–1832.

Washington National Journal, 1831.
Washington National Republican, November 10, 1879.
Washington Post, April 23, 1922, November 4, 1935.
Washington Star, November 8, 1879, May 4, 1901, April 29, 1917, September 18, 1921, June 23, 1935.
Washington Sunday Capital, March 29, 1874.
Western Weekly Review [Franklin, TN], 1829–1831.

CORRESPONDENCE, MEMOIRS, AND REMINISCENCES

Books

Adams, Charles Francis, ed. *Memoirs of John Quincy Adams.* 12 vols. (1874–1877).
Alcott, William A. *The Young Wife; or Duties of Woman in the Marriage Relation* (1972, originally published in 1837).
Ambler, Charles H., ed. *The Life and Diary of John Floyd, Governor of Virginia* (1918).
American State Papers, Military Affairs (1861).
American State Papers, Naval Affairs (1861).
Ames, Mary Clemmer. *Ten Years in Washington . . .* (1873).
Bassett, John S., ed. *Correspondence of Andrew Jackson.* 7 vols. (1926–1935).
Bates, Mary. *The Private Life of John C. Calhoun* (1852).
Benton, Thomas Hart. *Thirty Years' View, 1820–1850.* 2 vols. (1854).
Binns, John. *Recollections of the Life of John Binns* (1854).
Bohn's Manual of Etiquette in Washington and Other Cities in the Union (1857).
Bryant, William Cullen II, and Thomas G. Voss, eds. *The Letters of William Cullen Bryant.* 6 vols. (1975).
Bungay, George W. *Off-Hand Takings; or Crayon Sketches of the Notable Men of Our Age* (1854).
Butler, William A. *Martin Van Buren: Lawyer, Statesman and Man* (1862).
———. *A Retrospect of Forty Years, 1825–1865* (1911).
Carroll, John Alexander and Mary Wells Ashworth, ed. *George Washington Vol. 7, First in Peace* (1957).
Celnart, Madame. *The Gentleman's and Lady's Book of Politeness and Propriety . . .* (1833).
Chevalier, Michel. *Society, Manners and Politics in the United States* (1839).
Colman, Edna. *Seventy-Five Years of White House Gossip* (1926).
Colton, Calvin, ed., *The Private Correspondence of Henry Clay* (1856).
Cooley, Eli Field. *A Description of the Etiquette at Washington City* (1829).
Crockett, David. *The Life of Martin Van Buren, Heir-Apparent . . .* (1835).
———. *A Narrative of the Life of David Crockett* (1834).
Dahlgren, Madelaine Vinton. *Etiquette of Social Life in Washington* (1873).
Democratic Party National Convention *Proceedings* (1832–1952).
Derby, John Barton. *Political Reminiscences* (1835).
Dewey, Orville. *On the Duties of Consolation and the Rites and Customs Appropriate to Mourning* (1825).
Eaton, John Henry. *Candid Appeal to the American Public . . .* (1831).

————. *The Life of Andrew Jackson . . .* (1824).

Eaton, Margaret. *The Autobiography of Margaret Eaton* (1932).

Ellet, Elizabeth F. *The Court Circles of the Republic . . .* (1869).

Elliot, Jonathan. *Historical Sketches of the Ten Miles Square Forming the District of Columbia* (1830).

Elliot, William. *The Washington Guide* (1837).

Ely, Ezra Stiles. *The Duty of Christian Freemen to Elect Christian Rulers . . .* (1828).

Etiquette for Ladies: A Manual of the Most Approved Rules of Conduct in Polished Society . . . (1843).

Fitzpatrick, John C., ed. *The Autobiography of Martin Van Buren* (1920).

Foote, Henry S. *Casket of Reminiscences* (1874).

Forney, John W. *Anecdotes of Public Men* (1873).

Gerry, Elbridge. *The Diary of Elbridge Gerry* (1927).

Glieg, George Robert. *A Narrative of the Campaigns of the British Army at Washington and New Orleans . . .* (1836).

Gobright, L. A. *Recollections of Men and Things at Washington during the Third of a Century* (1869).

Green, Duff. *Facts & Suggestions; Biographical, Historical, Financial, and Political . . .* (1866).

Grund, Francis J. *Aristocracy in America.* 2 vols. (1839).

Hall, Basil. *Travels in North America in the Years 1827–1828.* 3 vols. (1829).

Hamilton, James A. *Reminiscences of James A. Hamilton* (1869).

Hamilton, Thomas. *Men and Manners in America.* 2 vols. (1834).

Hargreaves, Mary W. M., and James F. Hopkins, eds. *The Papers of Henry Clay.* 8 vols. (1959–).

Hellman, George S., ed. *[Washington Irving] Letters to Henry Breevort* (1915).

Hemphill, W. Edwin, Robert L. Merriwether, and Clyde Wilson, eds. *The Papers of John C. Calhoun.* 22 vols. (1959–).

Hone, Philip. *The Diary of Philip Hone, 1828–1851* (1936).

Howe, M. A. de Wolfe, ed. *The Life and Letters of George Bancroft.* 2 vols. (1908).

Hunt, Gaillard, ed., *The First Forty Years of Washington Society Portrayed by the Family Letters of Mrs. Samuel Harrison Smith* (1906).

Irving, Pierre M. *Life and Letters of Washington Irving.* 4 vols. (1864), vol. 2.

Knapp, Samuel Lorenzo. *Memoirs of General Lafayette, with an Account of His Tour Through the United States* (1825).

————. *Sketches of Public Characters by Ignatius Loyola Robertson* (1830).

Logan, Mrs. John A. *Thirty Years in Washington . . .* (1901).

Long, Ellen Call. *Florida Breezes; or Florida, New and Old* (1962, originally published in 1883).

Martineau, Harriet. *Retrospect of Western Travel.* 2 vols. (1838), vol. 1.

————. *Society in America.* 3 vols. (1837).

Martzolff, Clement R. *Caleb Atwater* (1905).

McIntyre, J. W., ed. *The Writings and Speeches of Daniel Webster,* nat. ed. 18 vols. (1903).

Milledge, Salley Harriet, ed. *Correspondence of John Milledge, Governor of Georgia, 1802–1806* (1949).

Mills, Elijah H. *Selections From the Letters of the Honorable E. H. Mills* (1881).

Moser, Harold D., ed. *The Papers of Andrew Jackson: Guide and Index to the Microfilm Edition* (1987).

New York City Directory, 1814.

Ossoli, Margaret Fuller. *Woman in the Nineteenth Century . . .* (1855).

Parton, James. *The Life of Andrew Jackson.* 3 vols. (1861).

Poore, Ben Perley. *Reminiscences of Sixty Years.* 3 vols. (1890).

Pope-Hennessy, Una, ed. *The Aristocratic Journey: Letters of Mrs. Basil Hall, 1827–1828* (1931).

Royall, Anne. *The Black Book.* 3 vols. (1829).

Sargent, Nathan. *Public Men and Events . . .* 2 vols. (1875).

Scott, Nancy N., ed. *A Memoir of Hugh Lawson White* (1856).

Seaton, Josephine. *William Winston Seaton of the "National Intelligencer"* (1871).

Seward, Frederick W. *Reminiscences of a War-Time Statesman and Diplomat, 1830–1915* (1916).

Smith, Margaret Bayard. *What Is Gentility? A Moral Tale* (1828).

Sprague, William B. *Memorial of the Rev. John N. Campbell . . .* (1864).

Stanton, Henry B. *Random Recollections* (1886).

Stickney, William, ed. *The Autobiography of Amos Kendall* (1872).

Tocqueville, Alexis de. *Democracy in America.* 2 vols. (1945).

———. *Journey to America* (1971).

Traveller [Anne Royall]. *Sketches of History, Life, and Manners in the United States* (1970, originally published in 1826).

Trollope, Frances. *Domestic Manners of the Americans* (1932).

United States Department of State. *The Territorial Papers of the United States,* vol. 25, *The Territory of Florida,* Clarence E, Carter, ed. (1960).

Weaver, Herbert, and Paul H. Bergeron, eds. *The Correspondence of James K. Polk,* vol. 1, *1817–1832* (1969).

Webster, Fletcher, ed. *The Private Correspondence of Daniel Webster.* 2 vols. (1956).

West, Elizabeth Howard. *Calendar of the Papers of Martin Van Buren* (1910).

West, Lucy Fisher, ed. *The Papers of Martin Van Buren: Guide and Index to General Correspondence and Miscellaneous Documents* (1989).

Williams, John Lee. *The Territory of Florida* (1837).

———. *A View of West Florida* (1976, originally published in 1827).

Wise, Henry A. *Seven Decades of the Union* (1881).

Articles

Barry, William T. "Letters of William T. Barry," *William and Mary College Quarterly Historical Magazine* 13 (1904–1905): 236–44; 14 (1905–1906): 19–23, 230–41.

Clay, Thomas M., ed. "Two Years with Old Hickory," *Atlantic Monthly* 60 (1887): 187–99.

Conover, Cheryl, ed. "The Kentuckian in 'King Andrew's Court': The Letters of John Waller Barry, West Point Cadet, 1826–1830," *Register of the Kentucky Historical Society* 81 (1983): 168–98.

———. "'To Please Papa': The Letters of John Waller Barry, West Point Cadet, 1826–1830," *Register of the Kentucky Historical Society* 80 (1982): 183–212.

Cox, I. J., contr. "Letters of William T. Barry, 1806–1810, 1829–1831," *American Historical Review* 16 (1911): 327–36.

Craven, Avery O., ed. "Letters of Andrew Jackson," *Huntington Library Bulletin* 3 (1933): 109–34.

"Focus," *Historic New Orleans Collection Newsletter* 2 (September 1984): 6–7.

Horn, Stanley F., ed. "Some Jackson-Overton Correspondence," *Tennessee Historical Quarterly* 6 (1947): 161–75.

Jackson, Andrew. "Calendar of the Jackson-Lewis Letters, 1806–1864," *Bulletin of the New York Public Library* 4 (1900): 292–320.

———. "Letter to Richard K. Call," *Gulf State Historical Magazine* 1 (1903): 438–39.

Jameson, J. Franklin, ed. "Diary of Edward Hooker, 1805–1808," *Annual Report of the American Historical Association for the Year 1896*. 2 vols. (1897).

Kendall, Amos. *The Autobiography of Amos Kendall* (1872).

"Letters of Chief Justice Marshall," *Proceedings of the Massachusetts Historical Society* 2nd sec., 14 (1900): 321–60.

Munroe, John A., ed. "Mrs. (Louis) McLane's Colored Boy and Peggy O'Neale," *Delaware History* 10 (1963): 361–66.

Owsley, Harriet C. "Jackson Manuscripts in the Tennessee Historical Society and the Manuscript Division of the Tennessee State Library and Archives: A Bibliographic Note," *Tennessee Historical Quarterly* 26 (1967): 97–100.

Padgett, James A., ed. "The Letters of Colonel Richard M. Johnson of Kentucky," *Register of the Kentucky Historical Society* 38 (1940): 186–210; 39 (1941): 22–46, 172–88, 260–77, 358–67; 40 (1942): 69–91.

Parris, Albion K. "Recollections of Our Neighbors in the First Ward in the Early Sixties," *Records of the Columbia Historical Society* 29/30 (1928): 269–89.

Ratcliffe, Donald J., ed. "My Dinner with Andrew," *Timeline* 4 (1987): 50–54.

Sunderland, Byron. "Washington as I First Knew It," *Records of the Columbia Historical Society* 5 (1902): 195–211.

Wallace, Sarah Agnes, ed. "Opening Days of Jackson's Presidency as Seen in Private Letters," *Tennessee Historical Quarterly* 9 (1950): 367–71.

SECONDARY MATERIALS

Books

Abernethy, Thomas P. *From Frontier to Plantation in Tennessee: A Study in Frontier Democracy* (1932).

Adams, Henry. *A History of the United States, 1801–1817*. 9 vols. (1921), vols. 1, 4, 8.

Alexander, Holmes. *The American Telleyrand . . .* (1935).

Ames, William E. *A History of the National Intelligencer* (1972).

Ammon, Harry. *James Monroe; The Quest for National Identity* (1971).

Anthony, Katherine. *Dolley Madison: Her Life and Times* (1949).

Aresty, Esther B. *The Best Behavior: The Course of Good Manners . . . as Seen Through Courtesy and Etiquette Books* (1970).

Bailey, Thomas. *The Pugnacious Presidents, White House Warriors on Parade* (1980).

———. *Presidential Saints and Sinners* (1981).

Banner, Lois W. *American Beauty . . .* (1983).

Barber, James G. *Andrew Jackson: A Portrait Study* (1991).

———. *Old Hickory: A life Sketch of Andrew Jackson* (1990).

Barker-Benfield, G. J. *The Horrors of the Half-Known Life: Male Attitude toward Women and Sexuality in Nineteenth-Century America* (1976).

Bartlett, Irving H. *Daniel Webster* (1978).

———. *John C. Calhoun: A Biography* (1983).

Barzman, Sol. *The First Ladies* (1970).

Bassett, John S. *The Life of Andrew Jackson* (1931).

Bassett, Margaret. *Profile and Portraits of American Presidents and Their Wives* (1969).

Baxter, Maurice G. *One and Inseparable: Daniel Webster and the Union* (1984).

———. *Henry Clay and the American System* (1995).

Baym, Nina. *Woman's Fiction: A Guide to Novels by and about Women in America, 1820–1870* (1978).

Belohlavek, John M. *George Mifflin Dallas: Jacksonian Politician* (1977).

———. *"Let the Eagle Soar!" The Foreign Policy of Andrew Jackson* (1985).

Berg, Barbara J. *The Remembered Gates: Origins of American Feminism: The Woman and the City, 1800–1860* (1978).

Bergeron, Paul H. *Antebellum Politics in Tennessee* (1982).

Blue, Frederick J. *Salmon P. Chase; A Life in Politics* (1987).

Boller, Paul F., Jr. *Presidential Wives* (1988).

Booth, Edward T. *Country Life in America as Lived by Ten Presidents of the United States* (1947).

Boyer, Paul. *Urban Masses and Moral Order in America, 1820–1920* (1978).

Brady, Cyrus T. *The True Andrew Jackson* (1906).

Brevard, Caroline Mays. *A History of Florida,* James Alexander, ed. 2 vols. (1925).

Brown, Herbert Ross. *The Sentimental Novel in America, 1789–1860* (1940).

Brown, Richard D. *Modernization: The Transformation of American Life, 1600–1865* (1976).

Bryan, Wilhelmina B. *A History of the National Capital.* 2 vols. (1916).

Buell, Augustus. *A History of Andrew Jackson.* 2 vols. (1904).

Burke, Pauline Wilcox. *Emily Donelson of Tennessee.* 2 vols. (1941).

Burnett, Gene M. *Florida's Past, People and Events That Shaped the State* (1986).

Busey, Samuel C. *Pictures of the City of Washington in the Past* (1898).

Caemmerer, H. P. *Washington, the National Capital.* Senate Document No. 332, 71st Cong., 3rd sess., 45–49.

Caldwell, Mary French. *General Jackson's Lady: A Story of the Life and Times of Rachel Donelson Jackson* (1936).

Channing, Edward. *A History of the United States.* 6 vols. (1912–1925).

Chapman, Charles E. *A History of Spain* (1918).

Chidsey, Daniel Barr. *Andrew Jackson, Hero* (1976).

Clayton, W. W. *History of Davidson County, Tennessee* (1880).

Coit, Margaret. *John C. Calhoun: An American Portrait* (1950).

Cole, Donald B. *Martin Van Buren and the American Political System* (1984).

———. *The Presidency of Andrew Jackson* (1993).

Conrad, Susan P. *Perish the Thought: Intellectual Women in Romantic America, 1830–1860* (1976).

Cott, Nancy E. *The Bonds of Womanhood . . .* (1977).

Crawford, Mary A. C. *Romantic Days of the Early Republic* (1912).

Curtis, James C. *Andrew Jackson and the Search for Vindication* (1976).

———. *The Fox at Bay: Martin Van Buren and the Presidency, 1837–1841* (1970).

Cutler, H. G. *History of Florida.* 3 vols. (1923).

Dau, Frederick W. *Florida, Old and New* (1934).

Degler, Carl N. *At Odds: Women and the Family in America . . .* (1980).

Dictionary of American Biography (1928–1958).

Diner, Hasia. *Erin's Daughters in America . . .* (1983).

Doherty, Herbert J., Jr., *Richard Keith Call, Southern Unionist* (1961).

Douglas, Ann. *The Feminization of American Culture* (1977).

Dyer, Oliver. *General Andrew Jackson* (1891).

———. *Great Senators . . . Forty Years Ago . . . Recollections* (1889).

Eaton, Clement. *Henry Clay and the Art of American Politics* (1957).

Eberlein, Harold, and Cartlandt Van Dyke Hubbard. *Historic Homes of George-Town & Washington City* (1958).

Ellis, Richard E. *The Union at Risk: Jacksonian Democracy, States' Rights, and the Nullification Crisis* (1987).

Evans, Sara M. *Born for Liberty: A History of Women in America* (1989).

Fitzpatrick, Edward A. *The Educational Views and Influence of De Witt Clinton* (1969).

Folmsbee, Stanley J., Robert E., Corlew, and Enoch L. Mitchell. *History of Tennessee.* 4 vols. (1960).

Francis, Mary C. *A Son of Destiny: The Story of Andrew Jackson* (1902).

Freehling, William H. *Prelude to Civil War: The Nullification Controversy in South Carolina* (1966).

Fryer, Judith. *The Faces of Women: Women in the Nineteenth-Century American Novel* (1976).

Furman, Bess. *White House Profile: A Social History . . .* (1951).

Gorer, Geoffrey. *Death, Grief, and Mourning.* (1977).

Green, Constance M. *Village and Capital, 1800–1878* (1962).

Gregorie, Anne King. *Thomas Sumter* (1931).

Gribble, Francis. *The Tragedy of Isabella II* (1913).

Grimsted, David. *Melodrama Unveiled: American Theater and Culture 1800–1850* (1968).

Hale, Will T., and Dixon L. Merritt. *A History of Tennessee and Tennesseeans.* 8 vols. (1913).

Halttunen, Karen. *Confidence Men and Painted Women: A Study of Middle-Class Culture in America 1830–1870* (1982).

Harris, Susan K. *Nineteenth-Century American Women's Novels: Interpretive Strategies* (1990).

Haywood, Marshall de Lancey. *John Branch, 1782–1863* (1915).

Heale, M. J. *The Presidential Quest: Candidates and Images in American Political Culture, 1787–1852* (1982).

Hinsdale, Mary L. *A History of the President's Cabinet* (1911).

Holloway, Laura C. *The Ladies of the White House or, in the Home of the Presidents* (1881).

Holt, Edgar. *The Carlist Wars in Spain* (1967).

Horn, Stanley F. *The Hermitage: Home of Old Hickory* (1938).

Hudson, Frederic. *Journalism in the United States, 1690–1872* (1873).

Hunt, Gaillard. *John C. Calhoun* (1907).

Hurd, Charles. *The White House . . .* (1940).

Hutchins, Stilson, and Joseph West Moore. *The National Capital, Past and Present* (1885).

Ingham, William A. *Samuel Delucenna Ingham* (1919).

Irelan, John R. *A History of the Life, Administration and Times of Martin Van Buren, Eight President of the United States* (1887).

James, Marquis. *The Life of Andrew Jackson* (1938).

———. *The Raven, Sam Houston* (1929).

Johnson, Gerald W. *Andrew Jackson: An Epic in Homespun* (1927).

Johnson, Paul. *The Birth of the Modern World Society, 1815–1830* (1991).

Kaminski, John P. *George Clinton, Yeoman Politician of the New Republic* (1993).

Kasson, John F. *Rudeness and Civility: Manners in Nineteenth-Century Urban America* (1990).

Klapthor, Margaret B. *The First Ladies,* 2nd ed. (1979).

Klein, Philip S. *Pennsylvania Politics, 1817–1837; A Game Without Rules* (1940).

Knobel, David. *Paddy and the Republic: Ethnicity and Nationality in Antebellum America* (1986).

Lamb, Martha J., and Mrs. Burton Harrison. *History of New York.* 3 vols. (1896).

Larkin, Jack. *The Reshaping of Everyday Life, 1790–1840* (1988).

Latner, Richard B. *The Presidency of Andrew Jackson: White House Politics, 1829–1837.* (1979).

Lindsey, David. *Andrew Jackson and John C. Calhoun* (1973).

Lockwood, Mary. *Historic Houses in Washington, Its Noted Men and Women* (1889).

———. *Yesterdays in Washington.* 2 vols. (1915).

Lystra, Karen. *Searching the Heart: Women, Men, and Romantic Love in Nineteenth-Century America* (1989).

Mabbott, Thomas Oliver, and Frank Lester Pleadwell. *The Life and Works of Edward Coate Pinkney* (1926).

Mahon, John K. *History of the Second Seminole War, 1835–1842* (1967).

Matthews, Jean. *Toward a New Society; American Thought and Culture, 1800–1830* (1991).

McCormac, Eugene I. *James K. Polk: A Political Biography* (1922).

McCormick, Richard P. *The Second American Party System; Party Formation in the Jacksonian Era* (1966).

McMullen, Thomas A. and David Walker, *Biographical Directory of American Territorial Governors* (1984).

McRaven, Henry. *Nashville, "Athens of the South"* (1949).

Meserve, Walter J. *Heralds of Promise: The Drama of the American People During the Age of Jackson, 1829–1849* (1986).

Meyer, Leland W. *The Life and Times of Colonel Richard M. Johnson of Kentucky* (1932).

Miller, Douglas T. *The Birth of Modern America, 1820–1850* (1970).

Minnigerode, Meade. *Some American Ladies: Seven Informal Biographies* (1926).

Mooney, Chase C. *William H. Crawford, 1772–1834* (1974).

Moore, John T. *Tennessee, the Volunteer State.* 4 vols. (1923).

Munroe, John A. *Louis McLane* (1973).

National Cyclopedia of American Biography (1898–1984).

Nicolay, Helen. *Andrew Jackson, The Fighting President* (1929).

Niven, John. *Gideon Welles: Lincoln's Secretary of the Navy* (1983).

———. *John C. Calhoun and the Price of Union* (1988).

———. *Martin Van Buren: The Romantic Age of American Politics* (1983).

———. *Salmon P. Chase: A Biography* (1995).

Parks, Joseph H. *Felix Grundy, Champion of Democracy* (1940).

――――. *John Bell of Tennessee* (1950).

Parton, James. *The World's Famous Women . . .* (1888).

Peacock, Virginia T. *Famous American Belles of the Nineteenth Century* (1901).

Perry, Lewis. *Boats against the Current: American Culture between Revolution and Modernity, 1820–1860* (1993).

――――. *Intellectual Life in America* (1984).

Pessen, Edward. *Jacksonian America* (1978).

Peterson, Merrill D. *The Great Triumverate: Webster, Clay and Calhoun* (1987).

Phillips, Leon. *That Eaton Woman: In Defense of Peggy O'Neale Eaton* (1974).

Pollack, Queena. *Peggy Eaton: Democracy's Mistress* (1932).

Pollard, James E. *The Presidents and the Press* (1947).

Puckle, Bertram S. *Funeral Customs: Their Origins and Development* (1968).

Pugh, David G. *Sons of Liberty: The Masculine Mind in Nineteenth Century America* (1983).

Remini, Robert V. *Andrew Jackson and the Bank War* (1967).

――――. *Andrew Jackson and the Course of American Democracy, 1833–1845* (1984).

――――. *Andrew Jackson and the Course of American Empire, 1767–1821* (1977).

――――. *Andrew Jackson and the Course of American Freedom, 1822–1832* (1981).

――――. *The Election of Andrew Jackson* (1963).

――――. *Henry Clay: Statesman for the Union* (1991).

――――. *The Legacy of Andrew Jackson: Essays on Democracy, Indian Removal and Slavery.* (1988).

――――. *The Life of Andrew Jackson* (1988).

――――. *Martin Van Buren and the Making of the Democratic Party* (1959).

――――. *The Revolutionary Age of Andrew Jackson* (1976).

Remini, Robert V., and Robert O. Rupp, eds. *Andrew Jackson: A Bibliography* (1991).

Renwick, James. *The Life of De Witt Clinton* (1840).

Reps, John W. *Washington on View: The Nation's Capital Since 1790* (1991).

Rerick, Rowland H. *Memoirs of Florida.* 2 vols. F. P. Fleming, ed. (1902).

Rice, Kym S. *Early American Taverns . . .* (1983).

Riegel, Robert E. *Young America, 1830–1840* (1940).

Ritchie, Donald A. *Press Gallery: Congress and the Washington Correspondents* (1991).

Rogin, Michael. *Fathers and Children: Andrew Jackson and the Subjugation of the American Indian* (1975).

Ryan, Mary P. *The Empire of the Mother: American Writing about Domesticity, 1830–1860* (1982).

――――. *Women in Public: Between Banners and Ballots* (1990).

Saum, Lewis O. *The Popular Mood of Pre-Civil War America* (1980).

Schlesinger, Arthur M., Jr. *Learning How to Behave: A Historical Study of American Etiquette Books* (1946).

Schlesinger, Arthur M., Jr. *The Age of Jackson* (1945).

Seale, William. *The President's House.* 2 vols. (1986).

Sellers, Charles G. *James K. Polk, Jacksonian, 1795–1843* (1957).

――――. *The Market Revolution: Jacksonian America, 1815–1846* (1991).

Sencourt, Robert. *The Spanish Crown 1808–1931: An Intimate Chronicle of a Hundred Years* (1932).

Singleton, Esther. *The Story of the White House.* 2 vols. (1907).

Smith, Culver. *The Press, Politics, and Patronage: The American Government's Use of Newspapers, 1789–1875* (1977).

Smith, Elbert B. *Francis Preston Blair* (1980).

———. *Magnificent Missourian: The Life of Thomas Hart Benton* (1958).

Smith, William E. *The Francis Preston Blair Family in Politics.* 2 vols. (1933).

Stephenson, John S. *Death, Grief and Mourning* (1985).

Sumner, William Graham. *Andrew Jackson* (1899).

Sunderland, R. *A Sketch of the Life of William Gunton* (1878).

Swanberg, W. A. *Sickles the Incredible* (1956).

Swisher, Carl B. *Roger B. Taney* (1936).

Tebbel, John, and Sarah M. Watts. *The Press and the Presidency from George Washington to Ronald Reagan* (1985).

Tebeau, Charlton W. *A History of Florida* (1971).

Turner, Frederick Jackson. *The United States, 1830–1850* (1935).

Von Holst, Hermann E. *The Constitutional and Political History of the United States, 1828–1846.* 8 vols. (1889–1892).

Wasserstrom, William. *Heiress of All the Ages: Sex and Sentiment in the Genteel Tradition* (1959).

Watson, Harry L. *Liberty and Power: The Politics of Jacksonian America* (1990).

Watson, Thomas E. *The Life and Times of Andrew Jackson* (1912).

Wayland, Francis F. *Andrew Stevenson, Democrat and Diplomat, 1785–1857* (1949).

Wechter, Dixon. *The Hero in American History: A Chronicle of Hero Worship* (1941).

Weed, Harriet, and Thurlow Weed Barnes, eds. *The Life of Thurlow Weed.* 2 vols. (1884).

Welter, Barbara. *Dimity's Convictions: The American Woman in the Nineteenth Century* (1976).

Wharton, Anne H. *Social Life in the Early Republic* (1902).

Wiltse, Charles M. *John C. Calhoun, Nullifier, 1829–1839* (1949).

———. *The New Nation, 1800–1845* (1961).

Young, James Sterling. *The Washington Community, 1800–1828* (1966).

Articles

Abernethy, Thomas P. "The Origin of the Whig Party in Tennessee," *Mississippi Valley Historical Review* 12 (1926): 504–22.

Barbee, David Rankin. "Andrew Jackson and Peggy O'Neale," *Tennessee Historical Quarterly* 15 (1956): 37–52.

Basch, Norma. "Equilty vs. Equality: Emerging Concepts of Women's Political Status in the Age of Jackson," *Journal of the Early Republic* 3 (1983): 297–318.

Belohlavek, John M. "Assault on the President: The Jackson-Randolph Affair of 1833," *Presidential Studies Quarterly* 12 (1982): 361–68.

Bergeron, Paul H. "Tennessee's Response to the Nullification Process," *Journal of Southern History* 39 (1973): 23–44.

Brown, Thomas. "The Miscegenation of Richard Mentor Johnson as an Issue in the National Election Campaign of 1835–1836," *Civil War History* 39 (1993): 5–30.

Bryan, Charles Faulkner, Jr. "The Prodigal Nephew: Andrew Jackson Donelson and the Eaton Affair," *East Tennessee Historical Society Publications* 50 (1978): 92–112.

Bryan, W. B. "Hotels of Washington Prior to 1814," *Records of the Columbia Historical Society* 7 (1904): 71–106.

Burnett, Gene. "Peg Eaton, Florida's Femme Fatale," *Florida Trend* (1977): 71–73.

Chappell, Gordon T. "The Life and Activities of General John Coffee," *Tennessee Historical Quarterly* 1 (1942): 125–46.

Clark, Allen C. "Margaret Eaton (Peggy O'Neale)," *Records of the Columbia Historical Society* 44–45 (1942–1943): 1–33.

Clifton, Frances. "John Overton as Andrew Jackson's Friend," *Tennessee Historical Quarterly* 11 (1952): 23–40.

Croffert, W. A. "Peggy O'Neale and General Jackson: A Washington Belle Who Caused a Cabinet to Fall," *Putnam's* 4 (1908): 719–25.

Cullen, Joseph P. "The Madame Pompadour of America," *American History Illustrated* 1 (1966): 20–29.

Curtis, James C. "In the Shadow of Old Hickory: The Political Travail of Martin Van Buren," *Journal of the Early Republic* 1 (1981): 249–68.

Dahl, Curtis. "The Clergyman, the Hussy, and Old Hickory: Ezra Stiles Ely and Peggy Eaton," *Journal of Presbyterian History* 52 (1974): 137–55.

Davis, Madison. "The Navy Yard Section," *Records of the Columbia Historical Society* 4 (1901): 199–221.

Evans, Sara. "Visions of a Women-Centered History," *Social Policy* 12 (1982): 46–49.

Farrell, Brian. "Bellona and the General: Andrew Jackson and the Affair of Mrs. Eaton," *History Today* 8 (1958): 474–84.

Feller, Daniel, "Politics and Society: Toward a Jacksonian Synthesis," *Journal of the Early Republic* 10 (1990): 135–61.

Galloway, Linda Bennett. "Andrew Jackson, Jr.," *Tennessee Historical Quarterly* 9 (1950): 195–216, 306–43.

Gardner, Francis Tomlinson. "The Gentleman from Tennessee," *Surgery, Gynocology and Obstetrics* 80 (1949): 405–11.

Goff, Reda C. "A Physical Profile of Andrew Jackson," *Tennessee Historical Quarterly* 28 (1969): 297–309.

Govan, Thomas P. "John M. Berrien and the Administration of Andrew Jackson," *Journal of Southern History* 5 (1939): 447–67.

Green, Fletcher M. "Duff Green, Militant Journalist of the Old School," *American Historical Review* 52 (1946–47): 247–64.

Gresham, L. Paul. "The Public Career of Hugh Lawson White," *Tennessee Historical Quarterly* 3 (1944): 291–318.

Harlan, Louis R. "Public Career of William Berkeley Lewis," *Tennessee Historical Quarterly* 7 (1948): 3–38, 118–52.

Hay, Robert P. "The Case for Andrew Jackson in 1824: Eaton's *Wyoming Letters*," *Tennessee Historical Quarterly* 29 (1970): 139–51.

Hoffman, William S. "John Branch and the Origins of the Whig Party in North Carolina," *North Carolina Historical Review* 35 (1958): 299–315.

Hogeland, Ronald W. "The Female Appendage: Feminine Life-Styles in America, 1820–1860," *Civil War History* 17 (1971); 101–14.

Hutchins, Stilson. "Margaret O'Neill Eaton," *International Review* 8 (1880): 126–33.

Jackson, Charles O. "American Attitudes to Death," *Journal of American Studies* 11 (1977): 297–312.

Kelley, Robert. "Prebyterianism, Jacksonianism, and Grover Cleveland," *American Quarterly* 18 (1966): 613–36.

Kerber, Linda K. "Separate Spheres, Female Worlds, Woman's Place: The Rhetoric of Women's History," *Journal of American History* 75 (1988): 19–39.

Latner, Richard B. "The Eaton Affair Reconsidered," *Tennessee Historical Quarterly* 36 (1977): 330–51.

———. "A New Look at Jacksonian Politics," *Journal of American History* 61 (1975): 943–69.

Lawrence, Stephen S. "A Franklin Treaty of 1830," *Williamson County Historical Society.* (1970), 1:99.

Lerner, Gerda. "The Lady and the Mill Girl: Changes in the Status of Women in the Age of Jackson," *Midcontinent American Studies Journal* 10 (1969): 5–15.

Lowe, Gabriel Jr. "John H. Eaton, Jackson's Campaign Manager," *Tennessee Historical Quarterly* 11 (1952): 99–147.

MacDonald, W. "Belle of Jackson's Day," *Saturday Review of Literature* 9 (August 6, 1932): 29.

Marszalek, John F. "The Eaton Affair: Society and Politics," *Tennessee Historical Quarterly* 55 (1996): 6–19.

McCrary, Richard C., Jr. "'The Long Agony Is Nearly Over': Samuel D. Ingham Reports on the Dissolution of Andrew Jackson's First Cabinet," *Pennsylvania Magazine of History and Biography* 100 (1976): 231–42.

Miles, Edwin A. "The First People's Inaugural—1829," *Tennessee Historical Quarterly* 37 (1978): 293–307.

Morris, Maude B. "An Old Washington Mansion (2017 I Street Northwest)," *Records of the Columbia Historical Society* 21 (1918): 114–28.

Nigro, Felix A. "The Van Buren Confirmation before the Senate," *Western Political Quarterly* 14 (1961): 148–59.

Owsley, Harriet Chappell. "The Marriage of Rachel Donelson," *Tennessee Historical Quarterly* 36 (1977): 479–92.

———. "Andrew Jackson and His Ward, Andrew Jackson Donelson," *Tennessee Historical Quarterly* 41 (1982): 124–39.

"Peggy O'Neale, or Doom of the Republic," *The Southern Review* 26 (1873): 213–31, 281–97.

Perrinne, William. "The Inn Keeper's Daughter Who Dissolved a President's Cabinet," *Ladies Home Journal* 18 (1900): 5–6, 42.

Pessen, Edward. "Society and Politics in the Jacksonian Era," *Register of the Kentucky Historical Society* 82 (1984): 1–27.

Pollack, Queena. "An Irish Innkeeper and His Internationally Known 'Innkeeper's Daughter'," *American Irish Historical Society Journal* 28 (1930): 93–95.

Remini, Robert V. "The Election of 1832," in Arthur M. Schlesinger, Jr., ed. *The History of American Presidential Elections.* 4 vols. (1971), 1: 495–516.

———. "The Final Days and Hours in the Life of General Andrew Jackson," *Tennessee Historical Quarterly* 39 (1980): 167–77.

Rogers, William Warren. "Peggy O'Neil, Tallahassee's Most Notorious Woman," *Springtime Tallahassee Official Program* (1982): 32–33, 35.

Rohret, James R. "Sunday Mails and the Church-State Theme in Jacksonian America," *Journal of the Early Republic* 7 (1987); 53–74.

Seidel, Katheryn L. "The Southern Belle as an Antebellum Ideal," *Southern Quarterly* 15 (1977): 387–401.

Singletary, Michael W. "The New Editorial Voice for Andrew Jackson: Happenstance or Plan?" *Journalism Quarterly* 53 (1976): 672–78.

Smith, C. Jay, Jr. "John MacPherson Berrien, Secretary of the Navy in the Cabinet of President Jackson," in Horace Montgomery, ed. *Georgians in Profile: Historical Essays in Honor of Ellis Merton Coulter* (1958): 168–91.

Smith, William E. "Francis P. Blair, Pen-Executive of Andrew Jackson," *Mississippi Valley Historical Review* 17 (1931): 543–56.

Smoot, James G. "A Presbyterian Minister Calls on Presidential Candidate Andrew Jackson," *Tennessee Historical Quarterly* 21 (1962): 287–90.

Smylie, James H. "American Presbyterians and Transforming American Culture," *American Presbyterians* 67 (1989): 189–97.

Somit, Albert. "Andrew Jackson, Legend and Reality," *Tennessee Historical Quarterly* 7 (1948): 291–313.

Stenberg, Richard R. "Jackson's Quarrel with the Alleged 'Calhounite' Cabinet Members in 1830–31," *Tyler's Historical and Geneological Register* 22 (1941): 208–28.

———. "The Jefferson Birthday Dinner, 1830," *Journal of Southern History* 4 (1938): 334–45.

———. "A Note on the Jackson-Calhoun Breach of 1830–31," *Quarterly Historical and Genealogical Magazine* 21 (1939): 65–69.

Throckmorton, Tom B. "Ezra Stiles Ely: Benefactor of Jefferson Medical College," *Iowa State Medical Society Journal* 29 (1939): 135–40.

Trickey, Kay Shelburne. "Small Town Boy Makes Good," *Williamson County Historical Society* (1981), 12:39.

Vallendingham, Edward N. "Andrew Jackson and John C. Calhoun: Their Famous Quarrel, Peggy Eaton's Share in the Affair," *Pearson's Magazine* 9 (1903): 418–27.

Walker, Aida S. "John Henry Eaton, Apostate," *East Tennessee Historical Society Publications* 24 (1952): 26–43.

Watson, Harry L. "The Age of Jackson: Old Hickory's Democracy," *Wilson Quarterly* 9 (1985): 101–35.

Welter, Barbara. "The Cult of True Womanhood: 1820–1860," *American Quarterly* 18 (1966): 151–74.

Wharton, A. H. "Petticoat Politics," *Lippincott* 68 (1901): 494–99.

Dissertations, Theses, Papers

Allgore, Catherine. "Sex and Scandal in Washington City: A Consideration of the Life of Margaret 'Peggy' Eaton." Unpublished seminar paper, Yale University, 1993.

Capowski, Vincent Julian. "The Making of a Jacksonian Democrat: Levi Woodbury, 1789–1831." Ph.D. diss., Fordham University, 1966.

Doctor, Powrie Vaus. "Amos Kendall: Propagandist of Jacksonian Democracy, 1828–1836." Ph.D. diss., Georgetown University, 1939.

Driscoll, William Dennis. "Benjamin F. Butler: Lawyer and Regency Politician." Ph.D. diss., Fordham University, 1966.

Glenn, Virginia L. "James Hamilton, Jr., of South Carolina: A Biography." Ph.D. diss., University of North Carolina, 1964.

Gresham, L. Paul. "The Public Career of Hugh Lawson White." Ph.D. diss., Vanderbilt University, 1944.

Kany, Julius Franz. "The Career of William Taylor Barry." Master's thesis, Western Kentucky State Teachers College, 1934.

Kinard, James F. "William T. Barry: A Study in Political Failure." Master's thesis, University of Virginia, 1949.

Marshall, Lynn L. "The Early Career of Amos Kendall: The Making of a Jacksonian." Ph.D. diss., University of California, Berkeley, 1962.

McCrary, Royce Coggins Jr. "John MacPherson Berrien of Georgia (1781–1856): A Political Biography." Ph.D. diss., University of Georgia, 1971.

Satterfield, Robert B. "Andrew Jackson Donelson: A Moderate Nationalist Jacksonian." Ph.D. diss., Johns Hopkins University, 1962.

Shoptaugh, Terry L. "Amos Kendall: A Political Biography." Ph.D. diss., University of New Hampshire, 1984.

Smith, Kenneth L. "Duff Green and *The United States Telegraph,* 1826–1837." Ph.D. diss., College of William and Mary, 1981.

FICTION

Books:

Adams, Samuel Hopkins. *The Gorgeous Hussy* (1934).

Botsford, Margaret. *The Reign of Reform or, Yankee Doodle Court by a Lady* (1830).

Dillon, Mary C. *The Patience of John Morland* (1909).

Dourbridge, Daniel. *Men and Things, or Reflections in Rhyme: A Posthumous Poem,* John H. Quarts, ed. (1934).

Downing, Major Jack. *The Life of Andrew Jackson, President of the United States* (1834).

Keats, Charles. *Petticoat Wars in the White House: A Novelized Biography of Peggy O'Neill* (1973).

Lewis, Alfred Henry. *Peggy O'Neal* (1903).

Plays

Author unknown. *Mrs Peggy O'Neal Eaton: A Play in Five Acts* (1903), Copyright Deposits, 1901–1944, Library of Congress.

Benet, Stephen Vincent and John Farrar. *The Heart of Peggy O'Neill: A Play in Seven Scenes* (1924).

Masters, Edgar Lee. *Andrew Jackson and Peggy Eaton* in *Dramatic Duologues: Four Short Plays in Verse* (1934).

Miner, Charles E. Jr. and Irving J. Fleet. *An American Affair: A New Musical Play* (1993).

Acknowledgments

The idea for this book originated many years ago when I wrote a paper on the Eaton Affair in the senior seminar of the late Dr. David J. Gorman at Canisius College in Buffalo, New York. Ever since, I have frequently thought about this topic, but because of other projects, it is just now, over thirty-five years later, that I have been able to return to it.

As I wrote this book, my thoughts repeatedly returned to David Gorman, and I remembered yet again all I owed to him. Not only did he introduce me to this topic—and many others besides—but he also encouraged me to pursue graduate school. Later he became a close friend. Dedicating this book to him is hardly repayment for all his advice, encouragement, and friendship, but somehow I think he is pleased to know that he continues to influence my life so many years after he first taught me at Canisius.

I am also thankful to colleagues at Mississippi State University. I was the recipient of research grants from the Criss Fund, the Humanities and Arts Program, and the Department of History. For this support, I especially want to thank History Department Head Charles D. Lowery, College of Arts and Sciences Associate Dean Donald J. Mabry, the late Vice President for Research Ralph E. Powe, Provost Derek J. Hodgson, and President Donald W. Zacharias. Michael B. Ballard, Charles D. Lowery, and William E. Parrish read through every page of an earlier draft of this manuscript and, as always, offered invaluable criticism and encouragement. Peggy Bonner, Lonna Reinecke, Torri Gandy, Andrea Miller, and Lana Simpson provided excellent word-processing skills and helped me with a variety of other tasks as well. Fred Faulk provided his usual high quality photographic support. Students in several graduate seminars researched and discussed the topic with me.

Numerous librarians and archivists were extremely helpful. They included Joyce Ann Tracy at the American Antiquarian Society; Bernard R. Crystal of Columbia University; William R. Erwin, Jr., Patricia Webb, and Janie Morris of Duke University; Connie Cartledge, Jeff Flannery, Mary Wolfskill, Ernest Emrich, Ron Cogin, Katie McDonough, and Michael Klein at the Library of Congress; Jessica M. Pigza, Debra Gousha, and Jennifer Bryan of the Maryland Historical Society; Virginia H. Smith of the Massachusetts Historical Society; Philip Abbot of the New Hampshire Historical Society; David J. Franz and Rosalind Libbey of the New Jersey Historical Society; Megan Hahn and Richard Fraser of the New-York Historical Society; James Corsaro of the New York State Library; Richard A. Shrader of the University of North Carolina; Tob Gearhart, Laura Russell, and Linda Stanley of the Historical Society of Pennsylvania; Lynn Farrington and Nancy M. Shawcross of the University of Pennsylvania; Lori Gilbert and Robert Parks of the Pierpont Morgan Library; Margaret (Peggy) Sherry, Marcela Fitzpatrick, Charles Greene, and Alice V. Clark at Princeton University; Mary Dessypris of the Library of Virginia; Ervin Jordan of the University of Virginia; Graham Dozier and Jon Bigler of the Virginia Historical Society; and Bonnie Hedges and Gail R. Redmann of the Historical Society of Washington, D.C.

Other librarians and archivists, too numerous to mention, responded to my inquiries through the mail. Particularly helpful were Richard Y. Wang of the Alabama Department of Archives and History; Noel VanGorden of the Detroit Public Library; James J. Holmberg and James T. Kirkwood of the Filson Club; Cynthia Wise of the State Library of Florida; Pamela Williams of the University of Florida; Dennis Northcott of the Missouri Historical Society; Michael P. Musick and David A. Pfeiffer of the National Archives and Records Service; and Judith Sibley of the United States Military Academy.

I was fortunate to receive good advice from a number of other historians, including Catherine A. Allgore of Yale University; Richard Latner of Tulane University; Louise G. Lynch of College Grove, Tennessee; John McDonough of the Library of Congress; Harold D. Moser of the Papers of Andrew Jackson, University of Tennessee;

James A. Newton of the Lincoln-Sudbury (Massachusetts) Regional High School; Robert V. Remini, University of Notre Dame; James F. Sefcik of the Louisiana State Museum; and William W. Rogers of Florida State University. Professors Latner and Remini read the entire manuscript and offered thoughtful critiques.

Joyce Seltzer was my original editor, but she joined another publisher while I was still doing research. Bruce Nichols took over the task and guided me through the publication process. Both Joyce and Bruce are outstanding professionals and warm individuals, and I am fortunate to have worked with each of them. I also appreciate the excellent editorial work of Norah Vincent.

Family and friends provided all kinds of support from noticing mistakes in the text, as Rowan Williams did, to listening to me talk about my work, as my mother, Regina K. Marszalek, my mother-in-law Martha Kozmer, and my sons and their partners (John, Chris, Jamie, Michael, Teresa, and Shannon) did. Cumpy and Allie, two dogs extraordinaire, woke me in the middle of the night for an entire week to remind me to keep writing.

My wife, Jeanne Kozmer Marszalek, as always, was my research associate and inspiration throughout the process. She planned all the research trips and kept us going both inside and outside the libraries. She even enlisted two of her former classmates from St. Mary's College: Kathy Seggerson of Atlanta and Kay Janiszewski of Pasadena, Maryland, to help search catalogs and to photocopy in libraries we visited close to their homes. This book, whatever its merits, is the better for Jeanne's devotion and hard work. I know I am the better for her love and companionship for the last thirty years.

Index

Adams, John, 29
Adams, John Quincy, 93, 95, 103, 122–24,
    148–49, 164
    Eaton (John Henry), attack on reputation
      of, 85
    Jackson opposed by, 14–15, 18–19, 52,
      60, 69, 77, 115–16, 121, 126
    presidential administration of, 15, 16, 18,
      19, 49, 52, 53, 61, 66, 69–72, 75, 78,
      91, 120, 121
    presidential election of 1824 and, 14–15,
      19, 121
    presidential election of 1828 and, 18–20,
      77
    as secretary of state (Monroe administra-
      tion), 13, 126, 127, 149
Adams, Mrs. John Quincy, 149
American Revolution, 12, 28, 29, 41, 69
    Jackson and, 2–3, 11, 13
Armstrong, John, 31
Armstrong, William, 203

Balch, Alfred, 184
Baldwin, Henry, 59
Bancroft, George, 108
Bankhead, Minnie, 64
Barry, Leonard, 89
Barry, John Waller, 166
Barry, Mrs. William, 89, 91, 92, 109, 110,
    114
Barry, William T., 208
    described, 61
    Eaton Affair and, 27, 89, 106–7, 114,
      115, 119, 166
    as postmaster general (Jackson adminis-
      tration), 61, 106–7, 109, 111, 114,
      115, 119, 124, 159–60, 162, 166, 212
    War of 1812 and, 32
Bell, John, 184, 201

Belton, Francis Smith, 33, 35
Benton, Jesse, 11, 14
Benton, Thomas Hart, 11, 16–17, 175
Berrien, John MacPherson, 48
    as attorney general (Jackson administra-
      tion), 60, 109, 113–14, 116–19,
      187–91
    described, 60
    Eaton Affair and, 103, 113–14, 116–19,
      162–70, 174–82, 185–93, 195, 196
    resigns his cabinet post, 162–70,
      174–82
Berrien, Mrs. John, 113–14, 170
Biddle, Nicholas, 114
Binns, John, 15–16
Blair, Francis Preston, 124, 163, 176, 206–8
    described, 151
    Eaton Affair and, 76, 119, 151–54, 168,
      169, 178, 181, 185, 193
    Jackson supported by, 17, 151, 206
Blount, William, 4
Blunt, Willie, 181
Bradford, Samuel, 92–93
Branch, John, 203, 211
    described, 60–61
    Eaton Affair and, 103, 107, 110, 113–19,
      138, 162–70, 175–79, 185–92, 195,
      196
    resigns his cabinet post, 162–70, 175–82
    as secretary of the navy (Jackson adminis-
      tration), 60–61, 103, 107, 110,
      113–20, 138, 187–91
    Timberlake investigation and, 120
Branch, Mrs. John, 109, 110, 113–14, 170,
    183
Brown, O. B., 99
Bryant, William Cullen, 63
Buchanan, James, 38, 156
Buchignani, Antonio, 228–33

Buchignani, Margaret O'Neale Timberlake
    Eaton. *See* Eaton, Margaret O'Neale
    Timberlake
Burr, Aaron, 10
Burton, Robert M., 146, 192
Butler, Benjamin, 130
Butler, Harriet, 130

Calhoun, Floride, 70, 75, 109, 110, 134,
    196, 197, 239
    described, 54
    Eaton (Margaret) and, 52–55, 73, 122,
    123, 153, 183–84, 188, 192, 195, 239
Calhoun, John C.
    Appeal, his reply to Eaton's, 193–97
    described, 123–24
    Eaton Affair and, 52–54, 66, 106–7, 110,
    121–24, 132, 136, 143, 147, 148,
    154–55, 157, 165–67, 169, 179, 183,
    184, 188–99, 204–5, 238–39
    Jefferson Day dinner clash with Jackson,
    125–26
    presidential ambitions of, 19–20, 59, 63,
    66, 106–7, 121–26, 148–50, 152–53,
    155–56, 158, 165, 190, 195, 197, 199,
    204–5, 239
    presidential election of 1828 and, 17,
    19–20, 66, 121
    resigns vice presidency, 198–200
    as secretary of war (Monroe administra-
    tion), 13, 126–27, 152–53
    Seminole Affair and, 126–28, 138,
    144–46, 148, 152–54, 157, 158, 194,
    197, 202
    as U.S. senator, 198–99
    as vice president (John Quincy Adams ad-
    ministration), 16, 19, 53, 57
    as vice president (Jackson administra-
    tion), 52–55, 59, 63, 66, 69, 73, 75,
    85, 102, 106–11, 121–28, 132, 136,
    138, 143–50, 152–61, 165–67, 169,
    176, 179, 183, 184, 188–98, 238–39
Call, Mary, 211
Call, Richard K., 22, 210–11, 213
    Eaton Affair and, 23–24, 78, 83
Cambreleng, Churchill C., 49, 63
Campbell, David, 89–90
Campbell, John (U.S. treasurer), 172–73
Campbell, John N. (Rev.), 93–99, 101–6,
    182
Campbell, Mrs. John N., 93–95
Carroll, William, 192, 204
Cass, Lewis, 181, 202, 213
Charles IV, king of Spain, 216
Chase, Salmon P., 69, 95, 99, 103

Civil War, Eaton (Margaret) and, 230, 231
Clay, Edward Williams, 164–65
Clay, Henry, 60, 88, 114, 120, 129, 148,
    155, 174, 201
    Eaton Affair and, 49, 66, 73, 80, 106–7,
    121, 123, 151, 157, 165–67, 238
    Jackson opposed by, 13–17, 19, 61, 66,
    73, 80, 106–7, 111, 121, 123, 157,
    158, 165–67, 238
    presidential election of 1824 and, 14–15,
    66, 121
    presidential election of 1828 and, 17, 19
    as secretary of state (John Quincy Adams
    administration), 15, 49
    as Speaker of the House, 13
Clay, Mrs. Henry, 80
Clinton, De Witt, 17, 33–35
Clinton, George, 28, 31, 34
Clinton, Maria (daughter of George), 28
Clinton, Mrs. De Witt, 34
Coffee, John, 4, 17, 127, 165, 176, 208–9
    Eaton Affair and, 129, 132, 133, 144–46,
    184
    Indian negotiations and, 129, 134
Craven, Elijah, 93–96, 98, 99
Craven, Mrs. Elijah, 98, 99
Crawford, William H., 126–28, 152
    presidential election of 1824 and, 14, 58
Crockett, Davy, 59

Davis, Varina Howell, 25
Decatur, Stephen, 37, 114
Decatur, Susan, 114
Deems, Charles F., 235
Desha, Mrs. Robert, 147
Desha, Robert, 47, 146–48, 177
Dickinson, Charles, 9, 12, 15
Dinsmore, Silas, 10–11
Don Carlos, brother of Ferdinand VII of
    Spain, 216–17
Donelson, Andrew Jackson (nephew of An-
    drew Jackson), 23, 60, 166, 173,
    223–24
    described, 85–86, 139–40
    Eaton (Margaret) and, 85–88, 94, 95, 97,
    98, 101–2, 105, 129, 131, 132,
    135–36, 138–48, 150, 151, 154,
    157–60, 168–70, 176–78, 183–85,
    193, 239
    at Jackson's presidential inauguration, 51
    Tennessee politics and, 201
Donelson, Daniel (nephew of Andrew Jack-
    son), 60
Donelson, Emily (niece of Andrew Jackson),
    23, 129, 166

described, 86
Eaton (Margaret) and, 73, 79, 82, 85–88,
  105, 107, 109, 115–16, 119, 131, 132,
  135–36, 138–48, 157–60, 176–78,
  183–85, 193, 239
at Jackson's presidential inauguration, 51
Donelson, John (father of Rachel), 5
Donelson, Mrs. John (mother of Rachel),
  5–6
Donelson, Rachel. *See* Jackson, Rachel
  Donelson Robards
Donelson, Samuel (brother of Rachel), 5, 85
Donelson, Stokely (nephew of Andrew Jack-
  son), 147, 148
Dudley, Charles E., 130
Dudley, Mrs. Charles, 130

Earle, Ralph E., 193
Eastin, Mary (niece of Andrew Jackson), 79,
  82, 87, 136, 142–43, 176, 184
Eaton, John Henry
  Appeal (published reply to his and Mar-
    garet's attackers), 185–97, 203
  background of, 14
  death of, 227–30, 233, 235, 236
  duels threatened by, 103–4, 168–75, 179,
    182, 191
  as governor of Florida Territory, 208–13
  Indian negotiations and, 129, 134–35,
    138–39, 167, 208
  Jackson, biography of, 12, 14
  Jackson, personal relationship with, 17,
    21, 44, 46, 47, 50, 66, 76–77, 81, 91,
    92, 96, 98, 175, 200–202, 205–9, 213,
    221–25
  as lawyer, 223–26
  Margaret, early relationship with, 23, 38,
    40–41, 44, 46–47, 49, 55, 64, 79–83,
    99–102
  Margaret, married life with, 12, 21,
    47–55, 62–67, 70–73, 76–94, 97–121,
    124, 126, 128–48, 150, 153–56,
    159–215, 217–27, 237
  as minister to Spain, 213–15, 217–22
  at O'Neale boardinghouse, 22, 23, 25,
    38, 40–41, 47, 49, 64, 79–83, 99–102
  presidential election of 1824 and, 14, 17
  presidential election of 1828 and, 17–18,
    20, 96
  recalled from Spain, 221–23
  resigns his cabinet post, 160–86, 190–91,
    194, 200, 202
  as secretary of war (Jackson administra-
    tion), 62–67, 70–73, 76–94, 97–121,

    124–26, 128–48, 150, 153–56, 159,
    187–90, 197–98, 208
  Timberlake investigation and, 119–21
  U.S. Senate, unsuccessful attempt to re-
    turn to, 201–7
  as U.S. senator, 14, 17, 22, 53, 58, 76,
    126, 150
Eaton, Margaret O'Neale Timberlake. *See
  also* Jackson, Andrew: Eaton (Margaret)
  and
  birth of, 24
  Buchignani (Antonio), relationship with,
    228–33
  Campbell's attacks against reputation of,
    93–99, 101–6, 182
  children born to, 38
  Civil War and, 230, 231
  death of, 235–36
  dinner party hosted by, 138
  early romantic involvements, 32–35
  Eaton (John), death of, 227–30, 233,
    235, 236
  Eaton, early relationship with, 23, 38,
    40–41, 44, 46–47, 49, 55, 64, 79–83,
    99–102
  Eaton, married life with, 12, 21, 47–55,
    62–67, 70–73, 76–94, 97–121, 124,
    126, 128–48, 150, 153–56, 159–215,
    217–27, 237
  Eaton's resignation from cabinet, her reac-
    tion to, 160–61
  Eaton's U.S. Senate defeat, her reaction
    to, 207
  Ely's attacks against reputation of, 78–83,
    92–94, 97–99, 101–6, 174, 182
  health of, 203, 205, 207, 224, 233–35
  Indian negotiations and, 134–35
  Jackson (Rachel), relationship with, 23,
    79–81, 86, 133, 208
  at O'Neale boardinghouse, 22–24,
    27–31, 34–36, 39–41, 44, 46, 49, 56,
    79–83, 99–102, 134
  in Spain, 214–15, 217–22, 225
  Timberlake (John Bowie), death of,
    42–48, 55, 81, 187, 215, 225–26,
    228
  Timberlake, early relationship with,
    35–36
  Timberlake, married life with, 36–42,
    79–83, 95–101, 188, 196
  at Vaughan parties, 54–55, 112, 119
  War of 1812 and, 31–32
Eaton, Myra Lewis, 14
Ely, Ezra Stiles
  described, 77–78

Ely, Ezra Stiles, *cont'd.*
    Eaton (Margaret), attacks against reputa-
        tion of, 78–83, 92–94, 97–99, 101–6,
        174, 182
    Eaton, confrontation with, 92–94, 97
Ely, Mrs. Ezra, 80, 93
Emerson, Ralph Waldo, 209
Eppes, John Wayles, 28
Erwin, Andrew, 200, 201
Evans, French S., 27, 175, 225, 236
Everett, Edward, 62, 64
Ferdinand VII, king of Spain, 215–17
Floyd, John, 139, 166
Forsyth, John, 127, 152, 221
Foster, Ephraim, 206–7

Gadsby, John, 41–42
Gallatin, Albert, 33, 64
Gallatin, James, 64
Garrison, William Lloyd, 197
Generes, Mr. (dance master), 30–31
Gerry, Elbridge, 27
Gerry, Elbridge, Jr., 27
Giusta, Antoine, 72
Graham, George, 88
Green, Duff, 152, 177, 185
    Campbell's charges and, 104
    described, 149–50
    Eaton (Margaret), newspaper attacks on,
        85, 135–36, 150, 167, 169–71, 174,
        178, 181, 190–92, 196–98
    Jackson, split with, 150–51, 154–56,
        161, 165, 201
    Jackson supported by, 16, 150
Green, Mrs. Duff, 190
Grundy, Felix, 149, 154, 193, 201–7

Hall, William, 146, 147
Hamilton, Alexander, 59
Hamilton, James A., 59, 85, 127
Hamilton, James, Jr., 63, 70
Hammond, Charles, 16, 48
Harrison, William Henry, 149, 223
Hayes, Mrs. Rutherford B., 236
Hayes, Rutherford B., 236
Hayne, Robert Y., 57, 125, 126
Hayward, Mrs. (schoolmistress), 30
Henshaw, J. H., 100
Hermitage, the, 45, 46, 131, 132, 141, 147,
    201, 223, 225
    construction of, 13
    Jackson (Andrew) grave, 225
    Jackson (Rachel) grave, 21, 128, 133,
        144, 180, 208, 225
Hill, Isaac, 17

Hillery, Frank, 219
Houston, Sam, 91
Howell, Richard, 24–25
Huygens, Chevalier A. de Bangeman,
    112–13
Huygens, Madam, 112–13, 118, 132
Hyde, John E., 100

Ingham, Mrs. Samuel, 75, 177
    Eaton (Margaret) and, 109–10, 114,
        116–17, 137–38, 143, 153, 169–71,
        173, 174, 183–84
Ingham, Samuel D.
    described, 59–60
    Eaton Affair and, 103, 114, 116–19, 144,
        156, 161–79, 185–92, 194–96, 198
    resigns his cabinet post, 161–82
    as secretary of the treasury (Jackson admin-
        istration), 59–60, 109, 114, 116–19,
        125, 144, 154, 156, 187–91, 198
Irving, Washington, 215
Isabella II, queen of Spain, 216–17, 219
Jackson, Andrew. *See also* Jackson, Andrew:
    O'Neale (Margaret) and; Jackson, An-
    drew: Rachel (wife) and
    American Revolution and, 2–3, 11, 13
    Bank of the United States and, 114, 123,
        137, 150, 197, 201, 206, 240
    Battle of New Orleans and, 1, 12, 14, 32,
        69, 96
    biography of (by John Henry Eaton), 12,
        14
    British and, 1–3, 10–15, 32, 69, 96, 238
    cabinet appointments, 57–67, 187
    childhood of, 2
    death of, 225
    described, 1–6, 57–58
    duels and, 2, 6, 8–12, 14–16, 81, 124,
        175
    Eaton (John Henry), personal relation-
        ship with, 17, 21, 44, 46, 47, 50, 66,
        76–77, 81, 91, 92, 96, 98, 175,
        200–202, 205–9, 213, 221–25
    Freemasons and, 4
    government bureaucrats removed by, 84
    as governor of Florida Territory, 13
    health of, 3–4, 9, 11, 13, 81, 102, 104,
        109, 121, 125, 175, 203
    the Hermitage, 13, 21, 45, 46, 128,
        131–33, 141, 144, 147, 180, 201, 208,
        223, 225
    Indians and, 1–2, 4, 10–13, 60, 126–29,
        134–35, 137, 138, 144–46, 148–49,
        152–54, 157, 158, 167, 194, 197, 202,
        213

Jackson, Andrew, *cont'd.*
  Jefferson Day dinner clash with Calhoun, 125–26
  as judge, 4
  as lawyer, 4, 7
  as "Old Hero," 1–2, 12, 18, 71, 109, 129
  as "Old Hickory," 11, 14, 61, 65–66, 84, 90, 111, 130, 237
  at O'Neale boardinghouse, 22–25, 81, 134
  presidential election of 1824 and, 13–15, 17, 19, 121, 150
  presidential election of 1828 and, 15–20, 22, 44, 52, 58, 61, 77–78, 96, 120, 121, 201, 238
  presidential election of 1832 and, 124–25, 150, 200, 201
  presidential election of 1836 and, 201
  presidential inauguration of, 1, 20, 51–52, 54, 67–75, 80, 82
  Seminole Affair and, 13, 126–28, 138, 144–46, 148, 152–54, 157, 158, 194, 197, 202
  as slaveholder, 10
  Spanish and, 10, 13, 126–28, 148–49
  Tennessee militia and, 4, 11
  as U.S. congressman, 4
  as U.S. senator, 4, 22, 58
  War of 1812 and, 1, 11–14, 32, 69, 96
  women, gallantry toward, 6–12, 15, 16, 21, 24, 77, 82, 184, 238
Jackson, Andrew: Eaton (Margaret) and, 52, 57, 217, 220, 234–37
  cabinet dinner party at White House, 107–9
  cabinet meeting concerning Campbell-Ely attacks, 101–5
  cabinet resignations, 158–86, 190–91, 194
  cabinet showdown involving Branch, Berrien, and Ingham, 116–19, 178, 189
  death of John Timberlake and, 44–47
  defending her honor, 21, 24, 44, 48, 49, 64–66, 73–74, 76–124, 126, 128–48, 150, 151, 153–208, 223, 225, 238–40
  early relationship, 22–24
  presidential inauguration and, 70–73, 76, 82
Jackson, Andrew: Rachel (wife) and, 5, 10, 22
  death of Rachel, 20–22, 44, 45, 48–49, 51, 69, 73, 75, 86, 91, 107, 109, 128, 133, 144, 180, 208, 225, 238
  defending her honor, 6, 8–9, 15, 16, 20–21, 44, 46, 49, 64, 77–81, 96, 121, 184, 238

  first meeting, 6–7
  Lyncoya (adopted son), 11, 18
  presidential election of 1828 and, 17, 18, 20, 44, 52, 96
  wedding, 8
Jackson, Andrew, Jr. (adopted son of Andrew), 51
Jackson, Andrew, Sr. (father of Andrew), 2, 3, 24
Jackson, Elizabeth (mother of Andrew), 103
  death of, 3, 5, 12, 238
  described, 2
  political attacks against, 16
Jackson, Lyncoya (adopted son of Andrew and Rachel), 11, 18
Jackson, Rachel Donelson Robards (wife of Andrew Jackson), 51, 58, 140–42, 150. *See also* Jackson, Andrew: Rachel (wife) and
  described, 5, 18
  Eaton (Margaret), relationship with, 23, 79–81, 86, 133, 208
  health of, 18, 20
  Robards (Lewis) (first husband) and, 5–8
Jackson, Robert (brother of Andrew), 3
Jefferson, Thomas, 18, 28, 33, 64, 70, 110
Jesus Christ, 2, 69, 82
Johnson, Richard M., 154, 170, 181–82, 185, 189, 204
  Jackson cabinet appointments, comments on, 63–64
  Jackson's emissary in cabinet showdown involving Branch, Berrien, and Ingham, 116–17, 178, 189
  as vice president (Van Buren administration), 214
Johnston, David Claypoole, 165
Johnston, Eliza, 114
Jones, William, 32
Joseph, Saint, 83

Kendall, Amos, 66, 125, 150–52, 161, 173
  described, 120
  Eaton Affair and, 64, 76, 124, 185, 186, 193
  Jackson supported by, 17, 120
  as postmaster general (Jackson administration), 212, 224
Kendall, Mrs. Amos, 173, 212
Key, Francis Scott, 71, 98, 167, 226
Key, Philip Barton, 226
Kirke, Mr. (schoolmaster), 31
Krudener, Paul de, 112
Lafayette, Marquis de, 23, 41
Lewis, Myra. *See* Eaton, Myra Lewis

Lewis, Mrs. William B., 51
Lewis, William B., 17, 62, 64, 82, 85, 127, 143, 156, 159–61, 168, 176, 208, 223
  cabinet meeting concerning Campbell-Ely attacks, 101–2
  described, 96
  Eaton cabinet resignation and, 171–74
  at Jackson's presidential inauguration, 51
  presidential election of 1832 and, 124–25
  Tennessee politics and, 200–203, 207
  Timberlake investigation conducted by, 96, 99
Lincoln, Abraham, 148, 230
Longfellow, Henry Wadsworth, 217
Louis XV, king of France, 163
Luisa Fernanda, daughter of Ferdinand VI and Maria Cristina of Spain, 216
Lyon, Matthew, 29–30

McCrary, George W., 236
McLane, Louis, 88
  Eaton (Margaret), attacks against reputation of, 48, 219
  Jackson cabinet appointments, comments on, 63
  as secretary of state (Jackson administration), 219
  as secretary of the treasury (Jackson administration), 182, 185–86, 193, 219
McLane, Mrs. Louis, 88, 182, 219
McLean, John, 61, 203
McLemore, John C., 129, 131, 142–45, 184, 185
Macomb, Alexander, 33, 110
Macomb, Mrs. Alexander, 110, 111
Madison, Dolley, 31, 36, 228
Madison, James, 18, 28, 31
Maria Cristina, queen of Spain, 215–19
Marshall, John, 70
Maxcy, Virgil, 85, 152
Milledge, John, 28, 30
Monroe, James, 17, 18
  presidential administration of, 13, 61, 70, 126, 127, 148–49, 152–53
  as secretary of state (Madison administration), 31
Múñoz, Ferdinand, 217

Nau, Madame (schoolmistress), 33
New Orleans, Battle of, 1, 12, 14, 32, 69, 96

O'Neale, Georgiana (sister of Margaret), 27
O'Neale, John (brother of Margaret), 27

O'Neale, Margaret. *See* Eaton, Margaret O'Neale Timberlake
O'Neale, Mary (sister of Margaret), 27
O'Neale, Rhoda Howell (mother of Margaret), 23, 36, 38, 43, 44, 46, 47, 55, 80, 81, 99–101, 223, 225, 228, 229
  boardinghouse and bar, described, 25–30, 35
  death of, 230, 232
  described, 22, 24–25
  family, described, 26–27
  Margaret's birth, 24
  War of 1812 and, 31–32
O'Neale, Robert (brother of Margaret), 26–27
O'Neale, William (father of Margaret), 23, 33–34, 36, 37, 39, 40, 43, 46, 47, 55, 56, 61, 64, 76, 80, 81, 89, 92, 97, 99–101, 119, 126, 204, 210, 237, 240
  boardinghouse and bar, described, 25–30, 35
  death of, 223, 228
  described, 22, 24–25, 139
  family, described, 26–27
  financial difficulties, 38, 41–42, 44
  as penitentiary inspector, 77, 139
  War of 1812 and, 31–32
O'Neale, William, Jr. (brother of Margaret), 26–27
Overton, John, 4
  Eaton (Margaret) and, 129, 131, 133, 186, 193
  Jackson (Rachel) and, 5–6, 8, 9, 51
  Tennessee politics and, 200–203
Overton, Mrs. John, 133–34
Overton, Walter, 198

Palmerston, Lord, 163
Parker, Daniel, 31–33
Parton, James, 235
Perry, Matthew C., 39
Philip V, king of Spain, 216
Pleasanton, Mrs. (Washington socialite), 138
Pleasants, James, 39
Polk, James K., 114, 201, 223, 224
Polk, Sarah, 114
Porter, Letitia, 66
Porter, Peter B., 66

Randolph, Emily, 227–33
Randolph, John, 232–34
Randolph, John B., 226–29, 231, 236
Randolph, John Chapman, 226–31
Randolph, John H. Eaton, 227–31

Randolph, Margaret Rosa Timberlake. *See* Timberlake, Margaret Rosa
Randolph, Martha Jefferson, 110
Randolph, Mary, 227–31
Randolph, Mrs. Phillip G., 181
Randolph, Phillip G., 27, 173, 181
  as second in Eaton (John) duel threats, 103, 115, 171, 172
Randolph, Robert B., 120–21
Reid, Robert, 210
Rhea, John, 148
Ringgold, Tench, 71, 127
Ritchie, Thomas, 17
Rives, Mrs. William, 88
Rives, William C., 57, 88
Robards, Lewis, 5–8
Robards, Rachel. *See* Jackson, Rachel Donelson Robards
Root, Richard R., 33–35
Royall, Anne, 48
Rush, Mrs. Richard, 88–89
Rush, Richard, 89, 214
Ryland, William, 47, 100
Sampayo, Duke de, 226, 234
Scott, Winfield, 33, 213
Seminole Affair, 13, 126–27, 138, 144–46, 148, 152–54, 157, 158, 194, 197, 202
Sevier, John, 8–9, 12
Sickles, Daniel, 226
Simms, Dr. (family physician), 42
Smith, Margaret Bayard, 53, 93, 134
  Eaton (Margaret), attacks against reputation of, 48–49, 66, 182
  Jackson (Rachel), attacks against reputation of, 49, 58
  Jackson's presidential inauguration, comments on, 71–73
Smith, Samuel Harrison, 48
Smith, Thomas L., 172–73
Southard, Samuel L., 36, 43, 148
Stark, Robert, 6–7
Stevenson, Andrew, 214
Sumter, Thomas, 28
Swift, Jonathan, 49

Taney, Roger B., 167
Tecumseh (Shawnee Indian), 116
Thayer, Sylvanus, 129
Timberlake, John Bowie, 49, 119–21, 124
  death of, 42–48, 55, 81, 187, 215, 225–26, 228
  Margaret, early relationship with, 35–36
  Margaret, married life with, 36–42, 79–83, 95–101, 188, 196

  Navy Department investigation of, 119–21
  War of 1812 and, 37–39, 96
Timberlake, Margaret. *See* Eaton, Margaret O'Neale Timberlake
Timberlake, Margaret Rosa (daughter of John and Margaret), 44, 46, 47, 50, 55, 187, 211, 228, 236
  birth of, 38
  death of, 227
  Navy pension from father, 225–26
  in Spain, 214, 222
  as wife of John B. Randolph, 226–27
Timberlake, Mary Virginia (Ginger) (daughter of John and Margaret), 44, 46, 47, 50, 55, 187, 211, 220, 228
  birth of, 38
  Navy pension from father, 225–26
  in Spain, 214, 218–19, 222
  as wife of Duke de Sampayo, 226, 234
Timberlake, Mrs. (mother of John), 36, 38
Timberlake, William (son of John and Margaret), 38
Towson, Mrs. Nathan, 115
Towson, Nathan, 71, 88
  Eaton Affair and, 64–66, 72, 97–98, 104, 115, 117, 172, 174
Trist, Nicholas P., 176, 184
Turner, Nat, 197
Tyler, John, 224

Van Buren, Martin, 57, 173, 175
  cabinet dinner party hosted by, 109–12
  described, 58–59
  Eaton (John) recalled from Spain by, 221–23
  Eaton (Margaret) and, 86–87, 106–13, 115, 118, 119, 122–24, 136, 193, 194, 222
  as governor of New York, 49, 58, 59
  minister to Britain (Jackson administration), unsucessful nomination as, 162, 185, 198
  as New York political boss, 16, 58, 130
  as president, 116, 198, 201, 214, 220–23
  presidential ambitions of, 63, 66, 106–7, 111, 119, 122–25, 148–49, 152–53, 155, 156, 158, 161, 165, 190, 192, 204, 239
  presidential election of 1824 and, 58
  presidential election of 1828 and, 58–59
  presidential election of 1832 and, 200
  presidential election of 1836 and, 201, 202, 214
  presidential election of 1840 and, 223

Van Buren, Martin, *cont'd.*
  resigns his cabinet post, 158–66, 169,
    190–91, 194, 200, 202
  as secretary of state (Jackson administra-
    tion), 58–59, 63, 70, 86–87, 106–13,
    115, 118, 119, 121–25, 130, 136, 144,
    148–50, 152–53, 155, 156, 190, 192,
    239
  as U.S. senator, 58, 130
  as vice president (Jackson administra-
    tion), 198, 200, 208
Van Ness, Cornelius P., 213–14, 219–20
Vaughan, Charles, 88, 110, 115, 163, 214
  Eaton (Margaret) at parties hosted by,
    54–55, 112, 119

War of 1812, 18, 64, 116
  Jackson and, 1, 11–14, 32, 69, 96

O'Neale family and, 31–32
Timberlake (John Bowie) and, 37–39, 96
Washington, George, 24, 29
Watkins, Tobias, 91
Watterston, George, 166
Wayne, James M., 224
Webb, James Watson, 155
Webster, Daniel, 114, 125, 126
  Jackson opposed by, 52, 58, 62–63
Weed, Thurlow, 234
Welles, Gideon, 148
White, Hugh Lawson, 47, 62, 76, 114, 187,
    208
  cabinet post offered by Jackson, 201–3
White, Mrs. Hugh Lawson, 202
Wirt, William, 99, 148
Woodbury, Levi, 63